# A STRANGER IN
# SPAIN

# A STRANGER IN
# SPAIN

*by*

## H. V. MORTON

DODD, MEAD & COMPANY, INC.

NEW YORK

For
MARY

Cover picture of Toledo: Tony Stone
Photolibrary, London


First published 1955
Paperback edition first published 1986
in the United States of America by
Dodd, Mead & Company, Inc.
Copyright © 1955 Dodd, Mead & Company, Inc.

ISBN 0–396–08797–3

Printed in Great Britain

# Contents

# Illustrations

# Acknowledgements

My thanks are due for much practical help to His Excellency Mariano de Urzaiz y Silva, Duke of Luna, Director General of the Spanish Tourist Office, and to the Secretary General, the Hons Gabriel García-Loygorri. I should also like to thank Don Aurelio Vall. and Don Manuel de Barandica y Uhagón, of the Foreign Office, Madrid; the Rev. Monsignor Edwin Henson, of the English College, Valladolid; Don Evaristo Ron Vilas, Spanish Consul in Cape Town; Mr Douglas Young of Somerset West, Cape Province, formerly British Consul at Malaga.

My thanks are also due to the following for kind permission to make quotations from copyright works: to the Executors of the late A. F. Tschiffely and Messrs Hodder & Stoughton, Ltd, for a passage from *Round and About Spain*; to Mr V. S. Pritchett and Messrs Chatto & Windus for a passage from *The Spanish Temper*; to Miss Kate O'Brien and Messrs William Heinemann, Ltd, for a passage from *Farewell Spain*; to Mr Roy Campbell and the Harvill Press for a quotation from *Poems of St. John of the Cross*; and to Mr R. Brinsley Ford for information about his great-grandfather and for permission to use certain pictures in his possession.

H. V. M.

Madrid,
   September, 1954

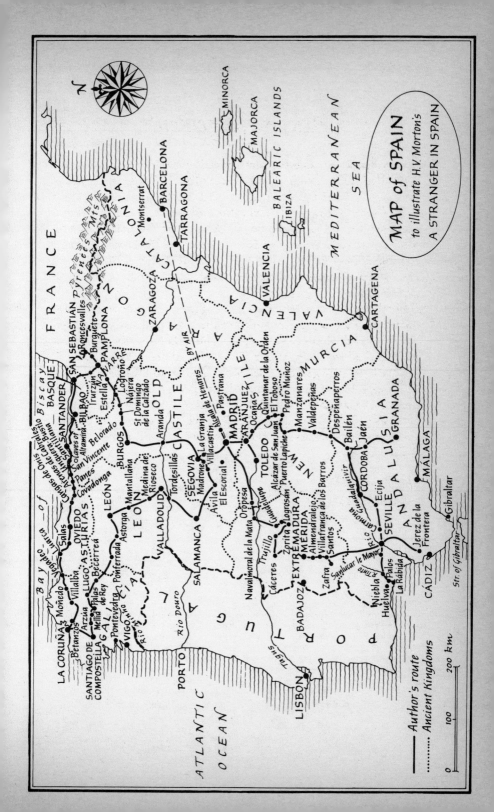

MAP of SPAIN
to illustrate H.V. Morton's
A STRANGER IN SPAIN

Author's route
Ancient Kingdoms

In A.D. 409 the Roman Province of Spain was overrun by the Vandals, the Alani and the Suevi, barbarians from the North, and the country was eventually dominated by the Visigothic kings. Spain recovered some of its former prosperity and became once more Christian, but the line of the Visigoths ended with Roderick who, in 711, was routed in battle with the invading Arabs. The Moslems, under the leadership of Mûsâ and Tarik, flooded Spain, pushing the Christians before them to the mountains of the North where developed the kingdoms, led (739–1035) by Léon-Asturias and Navarre, which salvaged the remnants of the old civilization at the height of the Moslem occupation. In the South the emirate founded by 'Abd-ar-Rahmân I (758–790) and strengthened by

## CASTILE AND LEÓN

| | |
|---|---|
| 1035 | Ferdinand I, the Great, who died in |
| 1065 | and whose kingdoms were divided among his sons; Sancho II, Castile; Alfonso, León and Asturias; Garcias, Galicia. The kingdoms were reunited by Alfonso |
| 1072 | Alfonso VI |
| 1109 | Urraca, wife of Alfonso I of Aragon; the marriage was declared void, but their son Alfonso, ruling Galicia, succeeded her |
| 1126 | Alfonso VII, succeeded by his sons |
| 1157 | Sancho III, Castile; Ferdinand II, León (1157–1188) |
| 1158 | Alfonso VIII in Castile |
| 1188 | Alfonso IX in León |
| 1214 | Henry I, son of Alfonso VIII, in Castile |
| 1217 | Berengaria, daughter of Alfonso VIII, wife of Alfonso IX, abdicated in favour of her son Ferdinand, intending the union of Castile and León |
| 1217 | Ferdinand III (St. Ferdinand) who finally united Castile and León |
| 1252 | Alfonso X, the Wise |
| 1284 | Sancho IV |
| 1312 | Alfonso XI |
| 1350 | Pedro the Cruel, deposed by his illegitimate brother |
| 1369 | Henry II (of Trastamara) |
| 1379 | John I |
| 1390 | Henry III |
| 1406 | John II |
| 1454 | Henry IV, the Impotent, succeeded by his sister |
| 1474 | Isabel the Catholic, who had married Ferdinand of Aragon in 1469, was succeeded by their daughter |
| 1504 | Joan the Mad and Philip I, her husband, who died in 1506. After his death she became insane and her father, Ferdinand, acted as regent, continuing the union of Castile and Aragon |

## ARAGON

| | |
|---|---|
| 1035 | Ramiro I |
| 1065 | Sancho Ramirez, who, in 1076, also became king of Navarre |
| 1094 | Pedro, also king of Navarre |
| 1104 | Alfonso I, the Battler, also king of Navarre, whose marriage with Urraca of Castile was declared void. He was succeeded in Aragon by his brother |
| 1134 | Ramiro II, the Monk, married his daughter Petronilla to Raymond Berenger, Count of Barcelona, thus uniting Aragon and Catalonia |
| 1137 | Petronilla and Raymond |
| 1163 | Alfonso II |
| 1196 | Pedro II |
| 1213 | James I, the Conqueror |
| 1276 | Pedro III |
| 1285 | Alfonso III |
| 1291 | James II |
| 1327 | Alfonso IV |
| 1336 | Pedro IV |
| 1387 | John I |
| 1395 | Martin I, who died without children |
| 1410 | Interregnum. The cortes chose as their king, Ferdinand of Antequera, son of John I of Castile and his wife Eleanor, daughter of Pedro IV of Aragon |
| 1412 | Ferdinand I (of Antequera) |
| 1416 | Alfonso V, the Magnanimous, who spent most of his time in Italy. Aragon was administered by his brother John, who succeeded him |
| 1458 | John II, who gained the throne of Navarre through his wife, Blanche, but left it to his daughter. He was succeeded In Aragon by his son |
| 1479 | Ferdinand II of Aragon and, by his marriage with Isabel of Castile, Ferdinand V of Castile and León. He annexed the southern part of Navarre from his half-sister |

In 1492 the discovery by Columbus of the New World opened new fields for Spanish conquest and colonization his grandson Hakam I (796–822) flowered into the mighty tenth-century Caliphate of Córdoba. This was at the peak of its magnificence under the rule of 'Abd-ar-Rahmān III (912–961), but later division and dissension caused its ruin. By spasmodic but often hard and heroic fighting, the Christian states Castile and Aragon reconquered the peninsula from the Moslems until, as a result of the campaigns of Ferdinand III of Castile and James I of Aragon, the Arabs held only Granada and the coast as far as Cádiz. In 1492 Granada fell to Ferdinand V of Aragon, whose marriage with Isabel of Castile and his conquest of the southern part of Navarre in 1512 united Spain.

## SPAIN

1506    Ferdinand V, regent after the death of Philip I and the incapacity of Joan the Mad. On Ferdinand's death the regency went to Charles, third son of Philip and Joan

1516    Charles I of Spain, also Charles V of the Holy Roman Empire. He abdicated, leaving his Hapsburg inheritance and the Empire to his brother Ferdinand and Spain and the Netherlands to his son

1556    Philip II, who married: 1543 María of Portugal, 1554 Mary Tudor of England, 1559 Elizabeth of Valois, and 1570 Anne of Austria. He incorporated Portugal into his dominions

1598    Philip III

1621    Philip IV, whose second wife was his niece, Mariana of Austria; succeeded by his epileptic son

1665    Charles II, who married: 1679 Marie Louise of Orleans, and 1689 Mariana of Neuberg. By will he left his kingdom to Philip, Duke of Anjou, grandson of Louis XIV and María Teresa, daughter of Philip IV. This disputed will led to the War of the Spanish Succession and the loss to Spain of the Netherlands

1700    Philip V, the first Bourbon king of Spain, who married: 1702 María Louisa of Savoy, and 1714 Elizabeth Farnese of Parma. He abdicated in favour of his son

1724    Louis I, who reigned only a few months

1724    Philip V again, succeeded by the son of his first marriage

1746    Ferdinand VI, who had married María Magdalena Barbara of Portugal in 1729; succeeded by his half-brother

1759    Charles III, who married Maria Amelia of Saxony

1788    Charles IV, whose wife was María Luisa of Parma. Her lover, Godoy, became virtual ruler of Spain. During Napoleon's attack on Spain Charles abdicated in favour of his son

1808    Ferdinand VII, imprisoned by Napoleon

1808    Joseph Bonaparte, brother of Napoleon

1814    Ferdinand VII, restored. Revolution removed him from power 1820–1823. His fourth wife, María Christina of Naples, bore him two daughters, the elder, by the ancient law of Castile and León, succeeding him

1833    Isabel II, her mother María Christina acting as regent until 1841. She married in 1846 her cousin Francisco d'Assisi, and was deposed by revolution in 1868, abdicating in favour of her son Alfonso. The new *cortes*, however, elected to the throne Prince Amadeo of Savoy, son of Victor Emmanuel II of Italy

1870    Amadeo I, purely a nominal king, abdicated

1873    Republic declared, but the country in a state of anarchy

1874    Alfonso XII, son of Isabel II, proclaimed king. He married: 1878, Mercedes, daughter of the Duke of Montpensier; and 1879 María Christina of Austria. Six months after his death a posthumous son, Alfonso XIII, was born

1885    María Christina, mother of Alfonso XIII, as Queen Regent

1902    Alfonso XIII formally enthroned. He married: 1906 Victoria Eugénie of Battenberg, and left Spain in 1931

1931    Republic, ended by Civil War

1936    Civil War, concluded by the victory of General Franco and the *Falange*

1939    General Franco assumed the tide of *Caudillo*, and reinstituted the *cortes* in 1942

1947    As a result of a referendum Spain was declared a monarchy, though without a king until the death of General Franco. The present heir to the throne is Don Juan Carlos, grandson of Alfonso XIII

# Chapter I

*Arriving in Madrid—Spanish decorum and beauty—the Victorianism of Spain—a visit to the Royal Palace—Knights of the Royal Armoury—the Plaza Mayor—the Spanish Marriage fiasco—a Prince of Wales in Madrid—he attends a bull-fight and climbs a garden wall*

§ 1

THE aircraft descended upon a landscape that was just as I had expected it to be. The trees had vanished centuries ago, much of the top soil had gone, and the bones of the land lay stark and bare in various shades of brown. There was a lonely dignity about it as there is about most wide, uncluttered landscapes, and blue and purple hills rose far off on the edge of the sky. Three or four small feathers of cloud, which I was to learn are characteristic of Castile, hung in the sky as if puffed there by a locomotive; but perhaps that is too earthy a metaphor, for they also suggested the wing feathers of cherubim and seraphim. Against the undulations of the plain the Madrid air-port wore the gay and impertinent look of a pleasure steamer upon a sombre lake.

A glass partition and a door guarded by two armed men in sage green uniforms, wearing hats of black patent leather and of a shape that recalled Napoleon, separated the travellers from a café which overflowed to a strip of lawn and white railings. Here Spaniards were sipping drinks and pointing to the sky as the aluminium shells came gliding down from Lisbon, Paris and Rome. The Customs House smelt like a night club. A South American 'plane had just come in, and many a shrill and costly-looking female was unlocking her neat air luggage, watched by the two Civil Guards, who had the eyes of melancholy stags.

I was impressed by the white cotton gloves which the Customs officers drew on before they probed into the luggage. I was soon to learn that white gloves are a symbol of the Spanish sense of fitness. A glove is an aristocratic symbol, and was once worn only by kings and bishops. As the world becomes more democratic one sees fewer gloves, and the clenched fist, of course, is always bare.

There were Mexicans, Peruvians, and other South Americans in the queue at the passport window, *conquistadores* in reverse, returning to visit the old country, and I watched them, thinking that Spain is one of the few places where America does not mean the United States. All the *Americanos* were, of course, tourists, and so was I. The word *turista* is to modern Spain much as *peregrino* was in the Middle Ages. It is entirely comprehensible.

'Why have you come to Spain?'

'*Turista!*'

The stamp descends immediately upon the passport, a pair of dark eyes pass sadly over you, loaded with the vast melancholy of those who have to deal with the public; and you are free to step into Spain.

§ 2

My rooms were featureless and might have been in London, Paris or Rome, indeed the only touch of a Spanish hand was a picture of the Crucifixion above the bed. The afternoon sun shot in and took possession when, after a struggle with one of those webbing bands unknown in less sunny climes, I lifted the wooden shutters a yard or two and revealed what lay beyond. I saw a low huddle of roofs beautifully covered with mulberry-coloured tiles, long and semi-circular in shape, of the kind seen on Byzantine churches all over Greece. Beyond was a hideous concrete block of flats, every window shuttered and no doubt in every room a slumbering Spaniard. To the left was evidently a large seminary, where a solitary priest was slowly pacing a corridor, breviary in hand. He was the only sign of life in Madrid's *siesta*, or rather in that portion of it visible from my window. He was young and sallow and his lips were moving. His soutane was new and well-cut, perhaps the best soutane one could buy. He had evidently been recently ordained and was the pride of his family, who had all gathered to hear him say his first Mass. As the black figure paced up and down he became for me symbolic of Spain: this tireless spirit of Orthodoxy scorning repose on a hot, sunny afternoon. So might he have paced beside the heretic, and so did Philip II pace the corridors of the Escorial.

More than once I stretched my hand to the telephone, then, remembering where I was, withdrew it. What a fearful solecism it would be to shatter a friend's *siesta*! It would be at least an hour before I could ring up anyone. What should I do? Should I go out and walk along the shady side of the street, past the shuttered shops? No; the lethargy which is Spain's first gift to the stranger was already taking control, and

I thought the best thing was to smoke a cigarette and wait until Madrid became perpendicular again.

I have sometimes wondered whether other nations are as ignorant of our history as we are of theirs. The story of Spain, so unlike that of any other nation in Europe, is little known in England except to the student, and even those who have absorbed a lot of Spain, who have read Cervantes and have heard the music of Manuel de Falla, who have seen the paintings of Velázquez and El Greco, perhaps even Goya in reproduction, would be hard put to it to tell you anything of the history of Spain except at one or two points where it touched ours: when Henry VIII married Catherine of Aragon and when Philip II tried to conquer Elizabethan England with the Spanish Armada. It is surprising to realize that the great St. Ferdinand of Castile, who warred against the Moors so stoutly, had an English grandmother; or that Edward II, the first Prince of Wales, had a Spanish mother; that the Black Prince brought from Spain the huge ruby now set in front of the Imperial State Crown of England; that John of Gaunt used to call himself 'Monseigneur d'Espagne' and fancied himself the King of Castile; or that Spanish blood ran in the veins of Richard III, Edward IV, Elizabeth of York, and, thin no doubt by that time, of Henry VIII and Elizabeth. . . .

The telephone rang. The *siesta* was over. The traffic policemen's whistles would be blowing again, and the crowded tramcars and antique taxis circulating once more; the steel shutters would be coming down from the shop windows.

'Hello,' said the voice of a friend. 'Welcome to Spain! Will you have dinner with me tonight? Good! Then I'll call for you round about ten.'

'About *ten*?'

'Yes, or is that a bit too early?'

'No, I'll expect you then.'

And I, who regard it as one of life's greatest pleasures to be in bed at ten, groaned inwardly.

§ 3

I went out into the warm streets. All strange cities seem enormous until you have become acquainted with them, and Madrid is no exception. I thought the Calle de Alcalá one of the finest avenues in Europe. The hub of Madrid's wheel is the Puerta del Sol—the Gate of the Sun, of Moorish Madrid—at first a confusion and then, when you have become more familiar with the city, a fascination. It is a magnet. Somehow you always find yourself there; if you are lost, you go there and recover your bearings.

It was delightful to move with the crowds as this summer day was ending, and to glance into the good-looking shop windows—especially admirable shoe shops—and to hear all round the rattle and volley of Castilian. How different a language seems when you hear it spoken rapidly, loudly, confidently and colloquially in its native land. I took a chair on the pavement outside a café and ordered a *café con leche*. The people who passed and re-passed were well dressed. There was a high proportion of sun-glasses among the men, and I noticed with interest the Spanish habit of wearing the jacket hung from the shoulders with the arms swinging loosely, a relic I suppose of the Spanish cloak. The women were hatless and their hair was beautifully tended. All these people had made an effort. They were not dressed up or flamboyant, neither had they that rich look one used to notice in Bond Street, but they were living up to a certain standard of fitness. As I looked at them I remembered the white cotton gloves in the Customs House.

When I had finished my coffee I walked slowly along the Avenida de José Antonio, where the crowds were thicker, the shops continuous, and the smell of petrol and oil from the oldest motors in use in the world more penetrating. José Antonio! In the days to come I was to be haunted by that name. There are hundreds of streets called after him. You see his name in huge letters above war memorials outside churches. It is everywhere. No one can be in Spain for even a few days without becoming familiar with it. There must come a moment in every stranger's visit to Spain when, unable to bear it any longer, he goes up to the first Spaniard he sees and asks, 'Who was José Antonio?' And the answer is perfectly simple. He is the yet uncanonized saint of Nationalist Spain. He was the son of General Primo de Rivera. He founded the Falangist movement and was shot by Communists eighteen years ago during the Civil War.

As I strolled on, glancing into the shop windows, wondering who could possibly want a little model of a *banderillero* in the act of sticking darts into a bull, a young man attached himself to me and walked beside me whispering. Imagining him to be a tout, I told him sharply to go away in what I believed to be good Castilian, and was consequently humiliated when he replied in English, asking me to buy a fountain pen, which he furtively withdrew from his breast pocket. These whispering pen vendors haunt the streets of Madrid. The

4

pens they offer appear identical with the American original, but are made in Barcelona. The pen men are never rude and are easily shaken off. They just replace the pen in a breast pocket and with a philosophic sigh, as if they had been doing it as a wager, fade into the crowds. But you soon get to know them and they soon get to recognize you.

Such people, also taxi-drivers and hotel porters, are a stranger's first contacts in a foreign capital. And I must not forget the dear old black-market cigarette women of Madrid, highly respectable little old women in black dresses and aprons who have a regular beat on the pavements and carry trays full of American cigarettes. There is nothing at all furtive about them. They will sell you their technically forbidden goods under the eye of a policeman.

When darkness fell Madrid began to take seats as if for a nocturnal pageant or procession. Every pavement chair was occupied. Offices and shops had let down their shutters and the day's work was over. Then into the main avenues thousands of men and women came from a hundred tributaries, by underground, bus and on foot, to stroll about and walk up and down, and down and up. This was the nightly *paseo*, that queer relic of the seventeenth century when the aristocracy took the air in the evening along the Paseo del Prado. The same thing used to happen in St. James's Park in the eighteenth century, when the whole of London society could have been seen strolling up and down, dressed for dinner. I tried six or seven cafés before I was able to pounce on a vacated seat from which I could watch this parade. The crowds were different from the hungry, hunting crowds which shamble along Piccadilly towards Leicester Square at night: they were a more decorous crowd, a crowd dressed neatly for the occasion, and they reminded me of an old-fashioned church parade.

It was extraordinary to see a large proportion of the population of a modern city circulating in this way and I thought it a pleasant sight. There was nothing vulgar about it, no cat-calls or whistles, or obvious casual encounters; on the other hand no women would have put on those neat little frocks, black patent leather shoes, and have made sure that their hair was looking right, had they not expected to be noticed and admired. No doubt they were, but they did not seem conscious of it. If they heard a compliment they did not turn round and smile: they passed on in the lamplight, often three or four together, heads well up, backs straight, dignified and serious.

It took me a week to get used to the fantastic hours of eating. In the 'twenties Primo de Rivera tried to make Spain eat at European times, but even a dictator could not do this. When the habit began I do not know, but it is not an ancient one. In 1786 when Dr. Townsend, rector of Pewsey, in Wiltshire, visited Spain, the king and members of the royal family dined about midday, the old-fashioned courtiers dined at one-thirty, and the more modern at two o'clock. A German named Fischer, who toured Spain about ten years later and had a keen eye for such things, does not mention unusual mealtimes, and neither does Richard Ford, who never missed a Spanish peculiarity. It is impossible to imagine these late hours in any city before the arrival of street lighting, and I suppose Spain's habit of dining at ten is perhaps no older than the gas lamp.

By the time my friend arrived at the hotel I was tired and would much rather have had a sandwich and have gone to bed. For him the evening was just beginning, and in his cheerful company I revived and we went out together.

## § 4

We dined at a small restaurant in surroundings which reminded me vaguely of the old Café Royal. It belonged to the red plush and gilt cupid era of restaurant décor. There were massive sideboards, gilt mirrors, silver candelabra, and some of the waiters had perhaps been selected to match this atmosphere. I was shown a little Chinese room at the back which is pointed out as one in which the scandalous Isabel II sometimes came by a back stair to meet her latest lover.

We ordered *langostinos*, which are Dublin Bay prawns, cold in mayonnaise, *tournedos* with mushrooms and port wine sauce, and *fraises du bois* flavoured with orange juice. We drank a pale dry sherry and a red wine of La Rioja.

'I haven't seen such well-dressed crowds in any European capital since the last war,' I said.

'Ah, but you must remember,' replied my friend, 'that every Spaniard is at heart a grandee, and his last economy would be in outward show. Thousands of the well-dressed men you've noticed tonight, wearing well-cut suits and shoes made by hand in Majorca, have only one suit and they go back to a bed-sittingroom. You may be as poor as a church mouse in Spain, but you must put up a show. It's the same with the girls. They are not expensively dressed, but they are very neat. Salaries are desperately low, so low that Spaniards who can't

6

get into some racket or other, or pull down a sinecure job, have to take on extra work, like teaching languages, in their spare time. I know a man who has six different jobs! It's said the Spaniard is lazy. You ought to see the way some of them work! When Spaniards are never to be found at their offices the foreigner jumps to the conclusion that they're still in bed, but the truth is that they're probably trying to earn an honest peseta somewhere else.'

'Shall I see the awful poverty which English people are told exists here?'

'No, not this year. You see, we've had two good harvests. The trouble with Spain is that she has no fat stored away. She lives from harvest to harvest. A bad harvest and the country is on the bread line. The poverty stories that everyone has read were written two years ago after a run of bad harvests. Also the European press loves to exaggerate Spanish difficulties. You will never convince the average Spaniard that the foreign editors of some of the best known English newspapers are not secret Communists.'

'Is Franco popular?'

'No one is ever popular in Spain. It's an old Spanish custom! Franco is respected for having ended the Civil War and for having got Spain to work again, and in my opinion his feat in steering the country through post-war Europe is a miracle. I think it would be right to say that the average man admires Franco—as much as any Spaniard can admire any other Spaniard—as an honest man, but as always in Spain, the people round him, who began by doing good, have done well. All Governments in this country feather their own nests and everybody knows it.'

'What is Franco like?'

'He's a soldier, and a God-fearing one like Cromwell. The sword in one hand and a holy relic in the other. Actually he would have been perfectly happy in a garrison town. He has no dynastic ambitions. He has no son. His only daughter is married and he lives a quiet domestic life with his wife in the old palace of the Pardo, about sixteen miles out of Madrid. He isn't a dictator in the European sense at all. He's just a soldier who has put down a rebellion and proclaimed military law and intends to see the law kept.'

'What do you think of the future?'

'Can anyone in the world think of the future? The future of Spain is anyone's guess. People in England and America don't realize that the late Don Alfonso XIII never abdicated. He just cleared out and went into exile. Spain is really a monarchy without a king. Franco is the Head of the State and he is pledged to bring back a king someday. Should anything happen to Franco, and providing the whole country didn't blow up, he would be succeeded by a Regency Council pledged to the same purpose. This was decided by a referendum held in 1947, when the vote in favour of a return of the monarchy was something like fourteen millions to one.'

'And who is to be the new King of Spain?'

'Well, nobody knows for certain. Don Alfonso left a son, Don Juan, now a middle-aged man, who lives in Portugal. He has a son, a boy of sixteen, Don Juan Carlos, who is being educated by the Jesuits, and most people believe that he will be chosen king someday.'

'And then?'

He lifted his arms like a Spaniard and let them fall limply and despairingly.

'Who can say? There are some who believe that Spain is naturally a monarchist country, and others who think that the return of the king —of any king—will start another civil war. But who knows?'

We discussed American Aid and Spain's need of agricultural machinery and other things. He told me that some Spaniards were opposed to American Aid. They feared that Spain, having avoided the two world wars, might be drawn into the third.

We changed the subject. We talked about Spanish women. I told him that the thousands of *señoritas* I had seen that night wandering about freely in the streets did not tally with the still accepted idea that women in Spain were closely guarded.

'All that began to go during the Republic,' he said, 'and the Civil War ended it. At one time during the War, when Franco's troops were besieging Madrid, they were opposed by a battalion of women who opened fire on them with rifles and machine guns.'

'What happened to the old Spanish gallantry?'

'Well, as a matter of fact,' he replied, 'I don't think the girls were fired on when they were running away! Why I mentioned this is to show you that a country can't go through what Spain has experienced and still keep its women in purdah. Women were given the vote and they still have it. The Republic allowed divorce, but the Church has, of course, now put a stop to that. The *duenna* is a more or less spiritual inhibition, a kind of ghostly presence. I'd say that women in Spain today are very much as they were in Victorian England. There was a time in England when it was not done to dine alone with a man or to

8

travel alone in a hansom with him. It's like that here. Girls are well behaved. They know that if they weren't, no man would ever marry them! And marriage and a large family is the dream of every normal Spanish female. Having married, she then disappears from life and begins to rule her family. The only people in Spain more powerful than the mothers are the grandmothers.'

'Do tell me,' I said, 'why old brown palm leaves are tied to so many balconies in Madrid.'

'That's easy,' he replied. 'They come from the date palms at Elche, in the south-east near Alicante. Every Easter they are tied into bundles which are blessed by the priests and sold all over Spain as a protection against lightning.'

My friend rushed off to attend some party. It was just after midnight. I walked back through the Puerta del Sol, which was as crowded as ever. The police whistles shrilled in the night. Hundreds of old cars were changing gear and backfiring. How anyone sleeps in this part of Madrid I cannot imagine. I noticed the number of small children, dressed up as if for a party and in the last stages of exhaustion, who were being dragged along by their parents. This was the first time I noticed the Spanish passion for *los niños*, those pale-faced little creatures droop-ing on shoulders, or trying to keep up, who should have been in bed five hours ago. I noticed a father carrying a little boy who had fallen asleep. A look of adoration crossed the man's face and he kissed the child awake. Its eyes focused him with difficulty, its face struggled into a smile, then down went the head again upon his shoulder. In Spain children seem to be treated either as dolls or adults.

As I neared my hotel I became conscious of a whispering shadow beside me and there before me, moving with me, was another of those horrid pens.

§ 5

One morning I went to the Royal Palace of Madrid, which stands upon ground that drops steeply to the valley of the Manzanares. From the back windows of their palace the kings of Spain looked across a bare and uninviting plateau to the mountains of the Sierra de Guadarrama, which on this particular morning were the colour of grape hyacinths. The palace is vast and creamy white in colour and its hundreds of windows gaze blindly down across a large square to a pretty garden planted with box hedges and flower beds, where, above a central fountain, Philip IV rides the Great Horse, baton in hand.

This is the king we know so well from the portraits by Velázquez, pale, haunted, inbred, with those wonderful upturned moustaches whose structure he is said to have preserved at night in little scented leather cases called *bigoteras*; and you would never think, to see him so proudly riding, how unhappy he really was, how haunted by failure and death, how he used to pray and weep at his own tomb and how he confided his troubles and his thoughts to an obscure nun.

The English visitor, seeing the Royal Palace at Madrid for the first time, compares it with Buckingham Palace and says that it must be ten times as large, which is true. But he should remember that Buckingham Palace is an overgrown private house, while the palace of the kings of Spain was built not only as a residence for the royal family, but also to house the departments of state. It is not old. It was begun in 1738, and finished twenty-six years later, to replace a wonderful old palace which had been adapted, rebuilt and reconstructed by all the kings of Spain from the eleventh century onwards. It was an incredible collection of old buildings with wooden stairways and galleried court-yards and it went up in flames on Christmas night in 1734.

Its history was the history of Madrid. When the Arabs invaded Spain in 711, they settled in the rich and sunny south, in Andalusia, leaving the Christians to seek refuge in the mountains of the north, where they planned a resistance movement. Madrid was one of the strong points which the Arabs established in No Man's Land, and just as an old castle was the origin of many an English town, so the *kasr*, or fort, called an *Alcázar* by the Spaniards, was the centre of these Arab strongholds. The *Alcázar* of Majrît, as Madrid was first called, was built on the shelf of rock looking north, into unoccupied Spain, and it was one of those which fell when the Christians were strong enough to go over to the offensive in the eleventh century. It was never recaptured by the Arabs. As you look at this bleak scene today, it is strange to know that the countryside was once heavily wooded and that the forests were full of wild boars and bears. The early kings of Castile turned the *Alcázar* into a hunting-lodge, and added to it from time to time. It was rebuilt in the fifteenth century and when Philip II made Madrid the capital of Spain in 1561, it became the seat of the most powerful court and government in the world. All the Hapsburg kings of Spain held court there, hedged about with the most rigid etiquette in Europe.

## The departure of Alfonso XIII

The modern palace is a monument of Bourbon Spain, and one imagines that young Philip V, the first Spanish Bourbon, may not perhaps have grieved when he saw the ramshackle old Hapsburg palace go up in flames. I walked across to an enormous courtyard where in the old days the changing of the guard took place, with a band and a regiment of horse artillery on parade. It must have been the great sight of a Madrid morning. The supreme moment came when the guns came rumbling along and the band broke into the Royal March, a grenadier march which tradition says was sent by Frederick the Great to Ferdinand VI of Spain, with the suggestion that it should be played upon six silver flutes. Both these kings were amateur performers, Frederick upon the flute and Ferdinand upon the violin.

I sat in a vaulted hall facing a grand staircase, in company with a batch of the day's tourists, and while we waited for a guide to appear I watched the palace servants with interest. They still wear what is evidently the old royal livery of blue tailcoats caught back with brass buttons like Marlborough's infantry. Most of them were of an age which would have made them in the twenties or thirties when Alfonso XIII left his country twenty-three years ago, and no doubt some of them were on duty upon that day in April when the crowds could be heard in the palace, shouting for a republic. As the demonstrators grew bolder, the king, it is said, decided to leave the country rather than order his guards to fire upon them. A group of weeping servants and retainers saw him step from a french window on the terrace and take a seat in his car, which he drove himself to Cartagena, where a cruiser was waiting with steam up. He was landed without ceremony at Marseilles and took with him as his shroud—such a Spanish thought—the cruiser's flag, in which presumably he lies wrapped in his coffin in Rome. I looked at the dignified flunkeys, as grave as priests as they moved about the empty palace with little to do now but to wind up the hundreds of clocks and sweep the rugs and carpets. Do they ever dream of getting the royal bedchamber in order and putting an extra polish to the throne-room?

We ascended the marble stairs behind a guide and beheld a melancholy vista of great rooms upon whose ceilings cupids and goddesses frolicked above gilt chairs and couches, and the heavy crystal chandeliers in long perspective grew smaller in the distance. Some of the rooms were almost unbelievably ugly, designed as they were to strike the spectator with awe, and sometimes we emerged from a debauch of chinoiserie into a vast hall, or audience chamber, where the chandeliers were even larger and the artists, as if in a frenzy, had splashed on the gold and filled the ceiling with a turmoil of mythology. Sometimes a king or a queen gazed gravely from a gold frame, and here I met for the first time María Luisa, the amorous queen of Charles IV, as painted by Goya; and I marvelled that any court painter could have been allowed to give such a literal glimpse of this royal virago. Royal portraits are painted not for kindly friends and relatives who will forgive much, but for posterity, and this picture of a queen seemed to me to break all the conventions.

We entered the throne-room where the Bourbon kings gave audience and held those receptions known as *besamanos*—to kiss hands—and where they lay in state at death. In this room Richard Ford saw the body of Ferdinand VII 'dead and dressed in full uniform, with a cocked hat on his head, and his stick in his hand, his face, hideous in life, now purple like a ripe fig'. In the throne-room of the earlier Hapsburg palace another English observer, Lady Fanshawe, had seen the lying-in-state of Philip IV, 'his head on the pillow, upon it a white beaver hat, his head combed, his beard trimmed, his face and hands painted'. Such was the last glimpse of a face that still lives in the pictures of Velázquez.

One cannot look unmoved at the great gold throne of all the Spains. It stands upon a dais in that enormous hall of mirrors and beneath a baroque canopy guarded by four life-sized lions which stand gazing outward with one foot upon a globe. The guide said that the throne-room is now used only when Franco receives a foreign ambassador. Someone in the crowd asked if Franco occupied the throne on these occasions.

'No, never!' was the reply. 'The *Caudillo* has *never* done so! It would not be proper.'

I was expecting someone to ask if the throne would be occupied again, but no one did so. It stood there empty, rather pathetic, but at the same time I think we were all conscious of its dignity. I thought with sympathy of the boy who is being educated by the Jesuits. The throne of Spain is more than life-size and it does not look very comfortable. No doubt the extraordinary organization which once surrounded it could be revived: the *mayordomos*, the *alabarderos*, the *gentiles hombres de casa y boca*, the Monteros, the halberdiers, the lackeys and the others who for centuries observed the Byzantine formality of the Spanish court. I think of all the functionaries the Monteros de Espinosa were the most interesting. In remote times a huntsman of

Espinosa, which is a small village in the north of Spain, saved the life of the king and as a reward the men of the village had the privilege of guarding him through the night. Unlike our own Yeomen of the Guard, who made the king's bed in Tudor times, the Monteros were merely sentries who paced up and down outside the royal bedchamber. In the old days members of the corps had to be born in Espinosa and the wives of members were careful to go to this village to have their children, but I believe in later years the Monteros were recruited from officers on the retired list. At eleven o'clock every night in monarchist Spain a procession passed down the grand staircase of the palace, every door was locked by an official in antique costume and a tricorne hat who held an enormous bunch of keys, and from that moment the palace was in charge of the Monteros de Espinosa. Two members of the corps took up their position outside the king's bedroom door. They never spoke or sat down, but paced quietly up and down until daylight relieved them.

The politician may well speculate upon the problems of a monarchist revival in Spain, and not less interesting perhaps is it to wonder, should such an event occur, how much of the elaborate court etiquette would be revived. Unlike all other kings, no King of Spain ever signed his name. His letters and state documents were signed simply *Yo, el Rey* —'I, the King.' Certain grandees had the right to retain their hats in the king's presence, others could put them on as they were talking to him, still others after they had finished. Before the time of the motor-car, at the beginning of the century, six hundred and thirty-seven people were employed in the royal stables and coach houses, and upon state occasions the king drove out in a coach drawn by eight horses wearing ostrich plumes of red and yellow and housed with embroidered cloths that fell to the ground. The only pageantry in Franco's Spain is seen when an ambassador presents his credentials to the *Caudillo*. Then the crowds witness, with who knows what ancestral memories, a splendid squadron of Moors go riding past upon horses with gilded hoofs.

§ 6

More interesting than the dead and lonely palace was the Royal Armoury in a corner of the palace yard. I think the Spaniards know better than we do how to show off armour. We just hang up a suit as if it were an empty tin, but the Spaniards like to fill the armour with a human shape, to clothe the dummy in a leather jerkin and underpants and boots and all the things a man of those times wore beneath the metal. They do the same thing with the horses. The animals are seen encased like armadillos—'barded' is the correct word—but they also wear all their gorgeous undergarments as well, the embroidered housings, richly and romantically emblazoned, falling to their hoofs, indeed so near the ground that one would imagine they must have got in the way when they galloped.

I was amused by the expressions upon the faces of a group of visitors who strolled into the central hall, prepared to be bored, when they saw before them twenty armed knights on horseback, facing each other in two rows, their tall jousting lances pointing to the ceiling. They look so real that one expects them to clatter into motion, to see one of the horses toss its encased head, or a rider to turn and lift a visor or adjust a helmet. They lead the imagination to a field where little pointed coloured tents are pitched upon the grass, where the trumpets are sounding and the crowds shouting and jostling, and where the ladies are excitedly leaning from the grandstand as the heralds enter the lists.

It is interesting to see that while most of the knights are shown riding *la brida*, or with long stirrups, the usual knightly European seat, a few ride *à la gineta*, with short stirrups, the seat which the Spaniards copied from the Moors. Spanish knights rode with short Moorish stirrups when bull-fighting on horseback and when performing that picturesque ride with lances known as the cane tourney. This was the entertainment once staged in the tiltyard of old Whitehall Palace by Philip II and his gentlemen for the amusement of the English court.

The armour to be seen here, made at a time when the famous armourers of Augsburg and Milan were in rivalry, is, I suppose, the best in the world. A first-rate armourer must have been as celebrated among kings and knightly circles of that time as a first-class tailor in the age of the Prince Regent. And how these armourers flattered the male body: what slender waists, flat thighs and beautifully moulded calves! Many a poor little creature must have looked his best in armour; and many a girl must have had a shock after the tournament, when she saw her perfect knight in ordinary clothes! One hardly thinks of armour as flattering, but it undoubtedly was. We learn too that a first-class armourer signed his suits and dated them as an artist signs a picture, and an expensive suit was delivered with a box of extras, or spare parts, which could be screwed or bolted on to give additional protection if required. One learns a lot about armour in this wonderful exhibition.

A good question for a quizz-team might be: on what side did knights pass each other when jousting at a tournament? I am inclined to think that many people would say they passed right side to right side, and I am fairly sure that I have seen pictures in which they are doing so. But this is wrong, and the figures in the Madrid Armoury, some of which are shown with lances levelled in the correct way, prove that a knight levelled his lance over the left ear of his horse and passed his opponent left side to left side, or bridle arm to bridle arm.

It is quite startling to come upon the Emperor Charles V just as you see him in Titian's portrait, riding out spear in hand before the battle of Mühlberg. This is the suit of armour which Titian painted in that magnificent picture. The small suit of armour made for Don Carlos, the son of Philip II, whose death is one of the mysteries of Spanish history, shows that the boy was slightly deformed, which has so often been suspected, because there is a difference in the size of the paldrons, or shoulder-pieces, of this suit.

I think one of the most memorable sights in the Armoury is a dog in armour, perhaps the type of mastiff that was trained to attack men and stampede horses. To protect his head he wears a small, flat steel cap in which is set a red ostrich feather. His neck, chest and shoulders are covered with chain mail held in place by a steel gorget that passes between his front legs and is attached to the underside of a saddle on which there are several steel spikes. Except for his legs he appears to be invulnerable. Anyone who has tried to make a coat for a sick dog that will remain in position will admire the ingenuity of those who contrived this dog suit. I was reminded of the delightful story told by Bernal Díaz of the war dogs which Cortés had with him during the conquest of Mexico. Once, when a party of exploring Spaniards had dropped anchor in a little bay near a desert island, they were astonished to see a dog rush down to the beach and run up and down in an ecstasy of delight. They found he was a Spanish war dog which had been lost on the island by a previous party eighteen months before. He was fat and well and, like most Robinson Crusoes, had evidently been scanning the horizon for a friendly sail.

The shabby old sedan chair, or litter, in which the Emperor Charles V was carried when his gout was troubling him, is one of the great sights of the Armoury. It is believed to have found its way to Madrid from the monastery of Yuste where the Spanish Diocletian, having renounced the world, spent his last years mending clocks and watches and growing flowers. Two of the most important members of his court were a cat and a parrot. After the Emperor's death these pets were placed in the imperial litter and sent in charge of a trusted servant to the court, which was then at Valladolid; and one can imagine how astounded the towns and villages on the way must have been to see such strange passengers in the litter of the man who had once been master of the world.

I was puzzled at first by the bullet holes which I saw in much of the armour, both of man and horse. If I had not been so enchanted by the wonderful and beautiful things to be seen there, I should at once have tumbled to the fact that kings, princes and knights had come under machine and rifle fire during the Civil War. The modern bullets have torn through the finest steel of Augsburg as if it were cardboard.

§ 7

The policeman wore a white helmet, a white belted tunic like a bush-shirt, and blue trousers. He opened a gay beach umbrella and, having fixed the end of the pole to a socket in the road, drew on a pair of white cotton gloves. He was now ready to begin work. Taking a whistle from his pocket, he blew a shrill blast and all the traffic stopped. Several hundreds of Spaniards, who had been waiting on both sides of the road, now crossed. There was another shrill note and the traffic moved again. Sometimes an ignorant foreigner or a disobedient Spaniard would try to cross the road at the wrong time; then the whistle was blown in anger and the offender would slink back into safety. There was a remarkable difference between these two sounds, one was long, soothing and protective, the other sharp and oath-like, yet both were only whistles.

I would observe this scene every morning from the American café where I could get, without question or explanation, bacon and eggs, always my first act in a foreign city. The Spanish breakfast is as deplorable as the French: rings of batter fried in oil called *churros*, and a cup of coffee or chocolate. The result is that all morning Spaniards are nibbling shrimps, prawns, little bits of ham, anything they can get to stave off hunger until luncheon at two o'clock.

After breakfast I would wait for the Prado to open—strange that the cinema, while it has taken the names of the Alhambra and the Plaza, has not, so far as I know, adopted that of the greatest picture house in the world—or I would just walk about the streets. Behind the Puerta del Sol I found a Madrid more attractive to me than that of the main boulevards, a seventeenth century Madrid of tall, balconied houses, now either slums or converted into shops, many of them belonging to the Madrid of Velázquez and all of them to that of Goya. The heart of this old city is a superb seventeenth century square, the Plaza Mayor. Though it has descended in the social scale, it is still intact, and all four sides are composed of tall, dignified houses built over an arcade, each one with an iron balcony. From these balconies the court and the aristocracy gathered to witness bull-feasts, cane tourneys, and the *auto-de-fe*, for the offices of the Inquisition were conveniently round the corner. Nowadays the balconies of the Plaza Mayor are hung with washing and sometimes you may see bedding hung out to air in the sun. Upon the north side of the square is a building that looks rather more important than the others. It is decorated with frescoes and crowned with two little towers with thin spires. It is still called the House of the Bakery, for it stands on the site of the municipal *panadería* of old Madrid, and here was the royal box from which the kings and queens of Spain witnessed public spectacles. In the centre of the Plaza Mayor is a fine prancing statue of Philip III, in whose reign the square was made, and there are several massive stone seats upon which one may sit and look at this glorious piece of seventeenth century town planning and reflect that the parent of the Plaza Mayor was the Place Royale—now the Place des Vosges—in Paris, and that the Spanish Plaza, if not the father, was, by the oddest of circumstances, certainly the godfather of old Covent Garden.

Henry IV of France built the Place Royale in 1610. It was the first great piazza outside Italy, a huge open space surrounded by uniform houses for the courtiers, and by arcades, and the open space in its centre was used for parades and tournaments. Ten years later Philip III copied this square in Madrid. Thirteen years later the first royal bull-feast in the Plaza Mayor was given in honour of Charles, Prince of Wales—afterwards Charles I—who was paying his romantic visit to Madrid to court the Infanta. When Charles became King of England, and Covent Garden was formed in 1631, he often went to watch it in the course of its building, no doubt with memories of the Plaza Mayor in his mind.

After a morning spent in such delightful reflections it was pleasant to find a café in one of the main streets and order a *granizada*, a drink composed of shaved ice with sweetened lemon-juice or coffee. The consistency of the ice determines whether a *granizada* is excellent or just good. It should be like snow during a thaw when you can squeeze it into a hard ball of ice, but if too watery the result is an unpleasant kind of sorbet. It cannot be easy to make and varies greatly from place to place. However, while spooning a *granizada* upon the Calle de Alcalá, the stranger's eye will be attracted by the crowds.

I do not know whether the human race is becoming uglier or whether I am more critical, but I find it rarer than I used to do to see a really striking human being. The Spaniards are on the whole a small, dark race though there are burly, blue-eyed Spaniards as well, men from the north. As Madrid is more a national capital than international cities like London and Paris, you can be sure that out of a hundred people who pass you in the street, ninety-nine are Spanish; and I think they show a remarkably wide range of racial variation. As you look at the faces in the streets you are perhaps struck by the few who might have been painted by Velázquez and the great number of El Grecos and Goyas. Ten minutes in any café in Madrid will prove how wonderfully El Greco caught the tall, thin, pallid Spaniard of the Black Legend, at his best the gloomy grandee, at his worst the villain of melodrama. Goya found his models everywhere, indeed there seem to be many more Goyas than El Grecos. There could not be a greater difference between two national types than the sad-looking Spaniard who appears to be thinking of his own funeral and the chubby, rotund man who seems to have come from someone else's. I suppose they are the two fundamental types: the knight and the man-at-arms, the Don Quixote and the Sancho Panza.

Then the Spanish woman. One wonders how the tradition has grown up in other countries that she is tall, slim and serpentine. She is usually small and nearly always dark, she runs easily to plumpness and her most photogenic age is between fifteen and twenty. Her three chief beauties are her eyes, which are full of intelligence and vitality, her hair, which is always beautifully kept, and her walk, which is perhaps the most notable feature of all. She is always perfectly shod. But whenever I think of the Spanish woman it is the walk I remember, the head held high, shoulders back, and the feet placed confidently forward with no mincing steps and no glide.

The least observant visitor in Spain must notice that women and feminine affairs do not dominate the landscape as they do in England and America, where a stranger to our planet might suppose that the chief activity of our civilization is to clothe its women and provide them with rival brands of cosmetics. The secrets of the female wardrobe

are not revealed on hoardings or in shop windows, a display which
Spaniards would consider indelicate, and frankness between the sexes,
which is supposed with us to lead to understanding, is not apparent.
On the contrary, it is obvious that men and women inhabit their own
separate worlds. Mr. V. S. Pritchett says in *The Spanish Temper*:

> The women of Madrid, as they go by in their twos and threes, and so rarely
> with a man, have a militant, formal, prim appearance. Sociable and talkative—
> for all Spaniards love talking for its own sake—they are trained to a double
> role: they display themselves, they have great personal pride; yet never for one
> moment do they allow their eyes to meet the eyes of a man as they walk the
> street. The decorum is complete and is distinctly Victorian. . . . As they walk
> by, carrying themselves so well, they are rather a collected, rather severe female
> race. For all this dominant appearance—and they clearly dominate the men by
> having their role in life firmly marked out and mixed with the male role very
> little socially—they have the reputation of being homely, innocent and sensual.
> They are passionate lovers of children: there is marriage and eight children in
> their eyes.

Perhaps the Victorianism of Spain is reflected most clearly in its
children, and the best place to see them is in the beautiful park of its
*El Retiro*, which is the garden of a seventeenth century palace with
stately avenues and its lakeside grottoes. One morning I was sitting
there in the shade, sorting out my first impressions of Madrid and
enjoying the sound of the gardener's hose on the rubbery canna leaves,
when I heard a child's voice, somewhere at the back among trees,
shouting 'Juanita!', then, more imperiously, 'Juan-ɪᴛ-a!', and this was
followed by a rapid object that shot across the path and ended round
my knees. I found myself holding a wooden hoop. I could not remember when I had last seen one. The owner appeared almost at once. He
was a boy of about nine or ten dressed in a white sailor suit with
anchors embroidered on the collar, and upon his head was a wide straw
hat turned up from his intelligent little face. He walked straight up,
made a little bow, took his hoop and saying in Spanish 'Thank you,
sir', disappeared. A most composed young don.
He appeared again in a few moments with an elderly female, obviously Juanita, who held by the hand a delicate little wax doll of a girl,
who was maybe six years of age. She wore a dress of starched muslin,
with little frills over her shoulders and a blue sash tied at her back in a
bow. A starched muslin bonnet was set on her dark curls and she
walked in white kid shoes with pom-poms on the toes. This brother

and sister might have been drawn by du Maurier, and I was reminded of faded brown snapshots in family albums and indeed of my own childhood.

Juanita, too, was interesting. She was an aged peasant whose nut-brown face had been worked over by time and sun. There can hardly have been two inches unscored by lines and wrinkles. She wore a lace cap and a bunchy black dress, and I should say she was an old family nurse who had returned to end her days in domestic service.

The little boy with his hoop, his sister in her muslin frock, and the old nurse, formed a group old-fashioned enough to be a period picture and, to an English eye, reminiscent of Kensington Gardens about 1900. You see hundreds of such groups in Madrid, hundreds of small white sailors, hundreds of muslin dolls, and one is filled with wonder to think that Spanish children will consent to wear clothes which would start a mutiny in any English or American household. Then look at a Spanish toy shop. There you will see hoops, beautiful marbles of coloured glass, monkeys that run up and down sticks, cardboard theatres, and golliwogs—all the toys of yesterday.

Old men and women wheel through the streets little trolleys to which coloured balloons are anchored, and these handcarts are stocked with all kinds of old-fashioned sweets that I imagined to be obsolete: aniseed balls, liquorice, boiled sweets shaped like gooseberries, pink and white sugar pigs, marzipan beach pebbles, and little muslin bags full of chocolate money. It is delightful to see the children running up to these trolleys in their sailor suits and muslin dresses to stand on tiptoe and gravely make their purchases, then going off with the bags tightly held and unopened in their hands, for in Spain it is bad manners to eat in the street, as it once was in England.

But of all the sights that charmed me in Madrid I liked best the little girls in their first communion dresses. You come across these tiny bridal figures in the crowds, generally on a Sunday, always dressed with the same meticulous care and each one like all the others—a white veil, a starched white dress falling to white kid shoes, a Mass book bound in white grasped in a little pair of white cotton gloves and, looped over the right forearm, a rosary with a silver cross. These enchanting little figures trip along among the full-sized human beings, conscious of this important moment in their lives, their little faces a perfect study in Spanish gravity and decorum.

## § 8

I went about Madrid looking for the House of the Seven Chimneys, —the *Casa de las siete Chimeneas*. None of my friends had ever heard of it. At last I found it in the Calle de las Infantas, which is the second street on the right, where the Calle de Pelayo joins the Avenida de José Antonio. The street is narrow and the old buildings have now been converted into shops and offices. The house, whose seven chimneys probably made it something of a landmark in the seventeenth century, is still known by its old name today. It was the house of the English ambassador in the time of Philip IV.

Here on the evening of March 7, in the year 1623, a servant went in to tell his master, John Digby, the Earl of Bristol, that an Englishman who called himself Thomas Smith wished to see him. Though he would not state his business, the stranger was eventually shown in to the ambassador. He was a tall man muffled in a cloak and carrying a valise. When he uncovered his face the Earl of Bristol was astonished to see the handsome and unscrupulous features of George Villiers, Duke of Buckingham, the favourite of his master, James I. Infinitely worse was to follow. Buckingham said that he had left the Prince of Wales (afterwards Charles I) down in the lane outside, holding the horses. The ambassador hurried into the street and 'in a kind of wonder' took the Prince up into the house and listened to the fantastic story the travellers told him. It appeared they had left London in disguise a little over a fortnight before, Charles calling himself John Brown and Buckingham, Tom Smith—a wonderful flight of the imagination! They had crossed the Channel and ridden to Paris where, mingling with the crowds in their disguises, they had witnessed the rehearsal of a masque in which the beautiful young Queen of France, Anne of Austria, had danced with Henrietta Maria, then a girl of fourteen. Charles looked on with no idea he was watching his future queen. Accompanied by two companions, they had ridden across Europe, averaging sixty miles a day, and when within a day's ride of Madrid the Prince and Buckingham had spurred on ahead, leaving their companions to follow. The object of their journey was only too obvious to the ambassador. Charles had come to woo the Infanta of Spain in person, led on by Buckingham, and the two 'sweet boys', as doting old James I called them, had the royal sanction for their mission. Charles was twenty-three and Buckingham was thirty-one, both old enough to have known better.

The visit of Charles to Madrid is the only amusing episode in the life of a tragic king, and it is a queer reflection that the most Quixotic act in Anglo-Spanish history should have been perpetrated on Spanish soil by a Prince of Wales! It began about twelve years before when James I, egged on by the Spanish party in England and also by the Spanish ambassador, conceived the idea that a Spanish marriage would be a profitable political investment. To the amusement of other countries, he saw himself the father-in-law of a happy Europe. The scheme dragged on through the reign of Philip III, when it was made clear that such a marriage would depend upon the return of England to the Roman Catholic fold, and when Prince Henry died, his brother Prince Charles inherited the marriage plan. Advisers then suggested that the diplomats would effect nothing, and that young Philip IV, who had succeeded his father, would be unable to resist the compliment of a personal visit from Charles to ask for the hand of his sister. The Infanta Doña María was then twenty-one and had threatened to become a nun if she were forced to marry a heretic.

Such was the situation when Charles and Buckingham put on their disguises and decided to go to Spain. James wrote fatuously of them as 'sweet boys and dear venturous Knights worthy to be put in a new romanso'. And considered not as a political blunder but as a piece of human behaviour, it was indeed a romantic and unusual event. Only in fairy-tales did a prince set out to win the love of a princess; in real life he accepted without question or enthusiasm the bride selected for him by the foreign office, and often did not see her until the wedding-day. There were few exceptions to this rule, but, oddly enough, one had occurred in the Stuart family not a century before, when James V of Scotland went to Paris in disguise to inspect a possible bride. Though he believed his disguise impenetrable, and went shopping in the markets, we learn that 'every carter pointeth with the finger, saying "Là voilà le Roy d'Écosse!" ' Maybe this was the precedent for another Stuart's visit to Madrid.

When the Earl of Bristol had recovered from his bewilderment he realized that the only thing to do was to announce the arrival of the prince to the Spanish court. He knew the secret could not have been kept in Madrid even for a day. The arrival of the Prince of Wales caused consternation. Such a thing had never happened before in the history of Spain. That an Infanta should be courted like an ordinary woman was unheard of, and Count Olivares, the Prime Minister, sat up all night devising schemes of procedure. It is said that when Philip IV heard the news, he was going to bed. He went over to a crucifix that hung at the bed-head and, kissing its feet, cried that even the Pope should not make him consent to the marriage of his sister to a heretic. But a good face had to be put on in public, and when the Prince's arrival was announced the Madrid crowd went crazy with joy, believing that Charles had come to Spain to become a good Catholic and that wedding bells would succeed where the Armada had failed.

Charles seems to have been in a state of emotional tension and could not wait to see the Infanta. He had to be told that nothing could be done outside the deliberate framework of Spanish etiquette, that, in fact, he was not yet officially in Madrid at all! The first thing was to arrange a meeting between Buckingham and Olivares, then between Charles and Philip. The curious fiction of a chance meeting was fixed upon. It was arranged that Buckingham and Olivares should drive out at a stated time and that their coaches should stop at the same moment, when Buckingham and Olivares would descend and advance to the centre of the carriage way and exchange compliments. Accordingly, on the evening of the next day loungers and others on the banks of the Manzanares, beneath the old *Alcázar*, saw the huge gilded coach of the chief minister, drawn by six mules in splendid harness and attended by a crowd of pages and lackeys, come swaying along while from the opposite direction appeared the coach of the English ambassador, in which sat the Earl of Bristol and Buckingham.

The procedure was observed, then Buckingham entered the Spanish coach, and after driving about for an hour or so both coaches trundled up the steep road to the *Alcázar*, where Buckingham was granted an unofficial meeting with Philip IV. This over, Olivares entered the English coach and was driven to the House of the Seven Chimneys, where he was presented to Charles. Contact had been made, and the formalities and decencies of life observed.

During his meeting with Olivares the Prince broke all the rules by asking bluntly when he could see the Infanta. He was so insistent that the Minister had to do something, and therefore another little plan was devised. On the next day, a Sunday, it was the habit of the royal family to drive out in the afternoon and join the *paseo* in the Prado, and Olivares arranged that the Infanta should wear a blue ribbon on her arm and that Charles should watch the procession from the ambassador's coach, drawn up in a side street. This happened as arranged. The gilt coaches came trundling along, and the King bowed to the

Earl of Bristol while Charles sat quietly and eagerly watching, though officially invisible.

The next event was the state entry of the Prince into Madrid and his removal from the House of the Seven Chimneys to the palace, where a suite of rooms on the ground floor had been redecorated for him. Before this took place, however, he was given a private interview with Philip. Buckingham wrote to James I:

The next day your Baby desired to kiss the King's hand privately in the palace, which was granted and thus performed. First, the King would not suffer him to come to his chamber but met him at the stair-foot, then entered into the coach and walked in his park. The greatest matter that passed between them was compliments.

Couriers galloped across Europe with letters to the 'dear Dad and Gossip', as James liked to be called, from 'Baby Charles' and 'your dog, Steenie', as Buckingham signed himself.

A little over a week after his arrival Charles entered Madrid in state, and the capital, as it was always ready to do, gave itself over to rejoicing. The solemn, glittering splendour of the Spanish court poured itself through the streets to the sound of drums, trumpets and pipes. At the end of a cavalcade that took three hours to travel one mile came Philip and Charles, riding side by side under a white canopy whose silver poles were carried by six officers. They were both admirable horsemen, both young, handsome and regal. A Spanish reporter noted that Charles had a gallant shape—*bizarro en el talle*—and the crowds noted with pleasure that whenever Philip doffed his hat as he passed a church or a shrine, Charles did so too. Having arrived at the palace, Charles was presented to the Queen, pretty Isabel of Bourbon, daughter of Henry IV of France and Marie de Medici, and the sister of the girl he was eventually to marry—Henrietta Maria. The Earl of Bristol, upon his knees, acted as interpreter, and later that night the Queen sent her guest a useful but unusual present—a quantity of underwear, table linen, and a scented box full of toilet preparations.

The next day Charles was to be the guest of honour at a royal bull-feast in the Plaza Mayor. The grand old square was then new. The balconies were gay with cloths of crimson and gold and with heraldic escutcheons. The crowds gathered under the arcades, the aristocracy at the balconies above. The grandees arrived in their state coaches, drawn by six mules or horses, with outriders and footmen, pages and attendants. The Queen's procession, with its line of heavy coaches swinging on their leather straps, the leather blinds rolled up to reveal the painted and powdered beauties inside, drew up opposite the *Panadería*; and Queen Isabel with the Infanta María, both dressed in brown silk with diamonds sparkling in their hair, ascended with their ladies to the royal box.

More colour poured itself into the square as the King's procession entered. The Prince of Wales, dressed in black with a white plume in his hat, sat a magnificent bay horse, and knee to knee with him rode Philip IV, dressed in brown, tall, thin, with that long, plum-shaped face and protruding Hapsburg jaw, a face that was not yet decorated with the famous upstanding mustachios. Behind them rode grandees, ministers, ambassadors, generals, admirals, and beside them marched halberdiers, musketeers, and archers of the royal guard. The King and Prince Charles took their places at a balcony next to the Queen. The square was cleared of coaches, the water-carts laid the dust, and the entrance barriers were closed. Immediately beneath the royal box a company of the King's guard stood ready to present their pikes to the bull, if in danger, but never to give way an inch.

The bull-feast which Charles then witnessed was the mounted tournament from which the modern bull-fight has developed and of which it is a vulgarization. It had not then been made into a solemn ritual nor given esoteric significance. It was just a mounted tournament in which noblemen pitted their skill and horsemanship against a wild bull. They were attended by their servants on foot, who handed them fresh spears and performed other menial tasks, and it is from these servants that the modern *cuadrilla* has developed.

A trumpet sounded and into the empty Plaza rode the Duke of Cea mounted upon a grey Andalusian charger. His servants wore a livery of brown and silver. The Duke rode up to the royal box, uncovered, bowed and retired. He was followed by the Duke of Maqueda and other nobles, attended by their servants, and when all had made their bows and the square was empty again, the bull was let loose. Each nobleman tackled the bull alone, riding *à la gineta*, with short stirrup leathers and wearing the single-pointed long gilt Moorish spurs. Another Moorish memory was the eastern costume sometimes worn by the servants who handed up spare javelins to their masters or drew off the bull. We know nothing about this particular bull-feast except that no one was killed and that the spectacle ended in a torrent of rain and bedraggled finery as pages rushed about in the gathering twilight calling for grooms and coachmen.

Although Charles was living in the palace and had daily opportunities of seeing the Infanta, he was never allowed to speak to her in private. He believed he had fallen in love and several observers wrote home to that effect, including Buckingham, who told the 'old Dad and Gossip' that 'Baby' swore that unless he married her there would be trouble. (He meant war with Spain.) But the difficulties were immense and the conditions laid down would have caused a rebellion in England. The Pope wrote to Charles and suggested his conversion, and Charles replied indiscreetly. At one time things seemed to be going so well that James fitted out a fleet to bring the bride to England and ordered Inigo Jones to design expensive chapels for her. At this period Charles began to learn Spanish and the Infanta to study English. Then new difficulties cropped up and the marriage was as far off as ever.

Charles seems to have conducted himself with dignity save for one foolhardy exploit for which a man of lesser rank might have lost his life. Learning that the Infanta was going alone to gather May-dew one morning in the gardens of the *Casa de Campo*, on the banks of the Manzanares, the frustrated lover decided to go there too. With the help of Endymion Porter (whose jolly Here's-a-health-unto-his-Majesty face, painted by Van Dyck, is in the Prado), the Prince climbed a wall and dropped down into an orchard. He saw the Infanta coming towards him along a garden path. He started towards her with affectionate words, but she gave a loud shriek, turned, and ran. An aged nobleman came hurrying up and begged the Prince to go away or he, as the guardian of the Infanta, might lose his life or liberty. He unlocked a garden gate and Charles retired.

It is extraordinary to think of Archie Armstrong, James I's Scottish fool, in Madrid! He arrived with a band of noisy young English courtiers who came from London with new clothes for Charles and Buckingham, including their Garter robes, and a spectacular collection of jewels to be given away as presents. Incredible to relate, Archie, with whom one might imagine the Spaniards would have had nothing in common, was a great success. It was said that he was granted more privileges than anyone. He was invited more than once to entertain the unapproachable Infanta and one day is even said to have twitted her on the defeat of the Armada! While the Spaniards seem to have loved him, the English could not endure him, and on one occasion Buckingham threatened to have him hanged. This caused Archie to make his famous reply that 'no one has ever heard of a fool being threatened for talking, but many dukes have been beheaded for their insolence'.

Royal art collector

Archie is a wonderful instance of the shattering effect of a grain of truth in a peck of lies and deception. With the licence of his calling and the bluntness of his Scots tongue, he said exactly what he thought about the Spanish Marriage; and no one could silence him. He seems to have been a chilling blast of candour throughout the negotiations. The Spanish court was, of course, fond of dwarfs and jesters, and Archie, probably with a few comic words of Spanish which he managed to pick up, actually seems to have struck up a friendship with Philip IV. Some years later when he had a son, he called him Philip for the 'King of Spain's sake'.

Charles became the greatest art collector in English history and it may be that he learnt much, or even drew his first enthusiasm for pictures, from Philip IV. Though the Spanish King was only eighteen, he had inherited taste and judgement and had already marked down Velázquez as a genius. The year of Charles's arrival in Madrid was that in which Philip brought Velázquez to the capital and gave him an appointment at court. Charles, fresh from the boorish court of James I, where even masques were considered highbrow, must have been impressed by Philip. There were perhaps moments when they stood together in admiration before the canvases of Titian—in later life Charles acquired forty of them. One fancies them strolling up and down the corridors and galleries of the old *Alcázar* talking, not of religion or politics, but of paintings and painters. It was by their patronage of painters, Philip of Velázquez and Charles of Van Dyck, that these two rulers have impressed themselves upon the mind of posterity.

Their conduct was remarkably similar. Philip in later life could not tear himself away for long from the studio in the palace where Velázquez worked. He loved to watch him, and such a moment has been preserved in the Prado's great picture *Las Meninas*. Charles behaved in the same way with Van Dyck, dropping in to watch him at work at all manner of times, and so constantly that a special landing stage was constructed for the royal barge at Blackfriars.

Whether Charles ever met Velázquez is not known, though it has often been said that he sat to him in Madrid. Such a picture was sold by Lord Fife in 1809 and is now, I believe, in the United States. But whether Charles sat for his portrait or not, it is certain that he revelled in the art world of Madrid and in the auction sales. While he was there the great collection of the Duke of Villa Mediana came under the hammer and the young Prince bought a great number of canvases.

27

Lope de Vega tells us that the Prince of Wales 'collected with remarkable zeal all the paintings that could be had, paying for them excessive prices'. Among the treasures he failed to buy were the two volumes of Leonardo da Vinci's drawings, which eventually came to England and passed from the Arundel Collection into Windsor Castle.

At the end of six months Charles and Buckingham returned to England. The Spanish Marriage would not take place. There was a return to good manners and many rich and beautiful presents were exchanged. Though Charles did not get his bride, he received a *Virgin* by Correggio, a *Venus* by Titian, an elephant, an ostrich, and five camels.

The English visitor with a few moments to spare may like to walk along the narrow Calle de las Infantas and reflect upon the interesting early Stuart characters who assembled there when Charles was in Madrid. There was John Digby himself, the Earl of Bristol. He received his first chance in life when, as a young man, he was sent to tell James I the news of the Gunpowder Plot. James liked him and advanced him and he became a distinguished diplomat. He wrote an exquisite little poem called *The Earl of Bristol's Farewell* ('Grieve not, dear love, although we often part'), which years ago, before radio was born, was sung in drawing-rooms by throaty young tenors.

There were the two companions who had galloped across France with Charles and Buckingham—Endymion Porter and Francis Cottington. You have only to look at Porter's picture in the Prado to know what kind of a man he was, bluff, good-hearted, humorous, loyal, the kind of man whom we have all met and admired. Though he looks so typically English, his maternal grandmother was Juana de Fi gueroa y Monte Salve, a relative, it is believed, of that Duke of Feria who was Spanish ambassador at the court of Mary Tudor. Porter was always travelling about with an eye for a good picture for Charles's gallery in Whitehall. He was a friend of Rubens, Van Dyck, Herrick, and that playwright who was supposed to be a natural son of Shakespeare's, William d'Avenant. Like many another cavalier, Porter lost everything during the Civil War and died penniless, dependent upon the kindness of an Irish barber who had once been his valet.

Cottington was equally typical of his age. He was Charles's secretary at the time of the Madrid visit. He lived in a state of theological perplexity, turning Catholic when he was ill and Protestant when he had recovered. He had a distinguished career under Charles I and became a peer and Chancellor of the Exchequer. After Charles's execution he tried to help Charles II, and was in Spain again as an old man, attempting vainly to interest the Catholic powers in a Restoration. Here his final attack of Catholicism struck him and he retired to die with the Jesuits at the English College in Valladolid; but the last word remained with his relatives, who removed his body to Westminster Abbey.

Among many others were James Howell, the author, who was there on business concerning a ship's cargo, and that charming and attractive young man, Sir Kenelm Digby, who had been sent abroad by his mother to separate him from the beautiful Venetia Stanley, whom nevertheless he eventually married. There was also Sir Edmund Verney, who nineteen years later died for Charles and was found on the field of Edgehill still grasping the Royal Standard in his dead hand.

Such were some of the Englishmen who gathered at the House of the Seven Chimneys in that bright age. They formed a chorus of cavaliers to that strange episode known as the Spanish Match, which seems to have had all the elements of a good comic opera.

# Chapter II

*To the Escorial by coach—the tragedy of the Hapsburgs—the room where Philip II died—the royal vaults—Don John of Austria—the markets and sweet-shops of Madrid—a glance at faces in the Prado*

§ 1

WHILE I was walking along the Calle de Alcalá one morning I saw a superb touring coach labelled 'Escorial' drawn up outside an office. Coaches today have become incredibly regal. If civilization has anything to do with the extension to the many of the comforts and the luxuries once enjoyed by the few, then these coaches are among the most civilized objects of our time. The people inside looked so jolly and cheerful that I went into the office and bought myself a ticket for the Escorial.

I joined a varied company. There were a few English, some French, and Americans from the south and the north, also two bright, talkative little nuns with a blue-chinned Spanish priest who had evidently been told to look after them and obviously disliked the task. Torquemada could not have looked more sombre in the presence of a couple of Lutheran dancing-girls. I don't know why, but I was surprised to hear the nuns speaking with a strong American accent. I suppose it sounded rather odd to hear a nun say, with an enthusiastic flash of spectacles, 'Why, I guess we're just thrilled to death to be in Spain!', and 'Oh, padre, we simply can't wait to see the Escorial!' The priest shrank a little from their girlish enthusiasm and, giving them a glance containing a certain amount of brimstone, said something polite.

I found myself sitting next to a heavy, rich-looking American who was already smoking the first cigar of the day. He had just returned from Seville, he told me, and had been around quite a bit. He was friendly, shrewd and inquisitive. He confessed that he felt rather let down by the tourist posters, for Spain was not living up to them. He had expected a continuous performance of *Carmen*, with swirling, polka-dot dresses, mantillas, and castanets; and these things existed, he had discovered, only in the night clubs and cabarets.

'Where are all these beautiful *señoritas* you read about?' he asked. 'Have you found any of them?'

I pointed to a few sleek early typists.

'Oh, shucks!' he said wearily, and threw his cigar out of the window.

'Did you go to a bull-fight in Seville?' I asked.

'Yeah, a bunch of cissies in coloured pants,' he said. He was evidently difficult to please. The conflict between the real and the ideal is one we must all face in our own way, I reflected, and what was this business man from New York but a Don Quixote who expected life to be a gallant out-of-date poster? No one had flung a carnation at him. To a real Quixote, of course, any missile would have been a carnation enchanted in transit.

A dark little guide climbed in, counted us as if we had been school-children, and the coach moved magnificently through the early morning, the most splendid vehicle in Madrid. We sat inside, comfortable in our mutual foreignness, with nothing to do, no effort to make, no Spanish to try to speak, but just to sit on superb foam rubber seats and, as my companion would have put it, be taken places.

The Sierra de Guadarrama for which we were making was visible thirty miles away to the north as a range of dark mountains against the sky. The country through which we passed was flat, gaunt and treeless, but the sky was a heavenly blue and invaded by two or three little wing-feather clouds. In a few miles we came to a road that branched off towards the palace of El Pardo, where General Franco lives among seventeenth century tapestries, pictures and frescoed ceilings. There also are the barracks of his famous Moroccan guard.

The road became more interesting as we began to climb. I am told that those who, like my American friend, have been led to think of Spain as a land of guitars and castanets, are surprised in winter to see upon this road young Spaniards with skis and toboggans hurrying to the snowfields of the Guadarrama; and upon the Pico de Peñalara, which is nearly eight thousand feet above the sea, the snow lasts often until June. We swung into a grand mountain scene where fir and pine climbed the foothills, and we looked into gloomy valleys and up a the granite summits, which lifted their fangs into the sky, dramatic and threatening even on a fine day.

The small village of Galapagar was the last resting-place for the royal coffins on their way to the vaults of the Escorial. Richard Ford tells us that when the cortège was ready to depart in the morning, a high official of state would advance to the coffin and inquire whether his majesty would move on. A few more miles of mountain road brought us into a village where little boys offered post-cards of the immense grey and threatening building we saw before us.

What we saw was, of course, the Escorial.

## § 2

It lives up to its reputation magnificently; it is all the things that have been written about it—gloomy, majestic, sombre, austere, chilly and dignified. It stands upon the side of the mountain, Calvinistic in its severity, and each window, and there are many hundreds, is an acute and probing eye. I believe that no great building has ever more clearly revealed its builder. It would be a simple matter to write a life of Henry VIII without going to Hampton Court, or of Louis XIV without seeing Versailles, but the biographer of Philip II must visit the Escorial, because it is an expression of him in granite, and no picture or photograph gives one a true idea of it.

We were all chilled a little by this building. The bright chatter which had filled the coach died away and we stood, a forlorn little group, in a grey entrance court while the guide—and he was a competent guide—came up and put the English speaking people on one side, the French on another, and began to address us first in English and then in French. He told us how Philip II had decided to build this monastery-palace as a tomb for his father, the great Charles I of Spain and Charles V of the Holy Roman Empire, and how he also wished, in the building of it, to propitiate St. Laurence for the sacking of St. Quentin, in France, when Spanish troops had committed the sacrilege of burning a church dedicated to that saint. We remembered of course that St. Laurence had been grilled on a grid-iron. We all nodded. Well, Philip II built the Escorial in the form of a grid-iron, the four terminal turrets were its feet—it was a grid-iron upside down —the palace buildings were its handle and the rectangular courts and buildings the grids. I believe this is a later fancy, but everyone is told this story.

All the granite came from the neighbouring hills, and for twenty years Philip II lived with this dream of the great monastery-tomb in which he intended to retire and end his days. He used to sit at a window in the old *Alcázar* at Madrid and watch the building through a spy-glass. A road at the back of the village led up to a granite rock in which a seat had been cut called the Chair of Philip II, and there the King would sit, watching the Escorial take shape. All this we learnt from the guide who, amazing to relate, told it vividly and with enthusiasm, though I suppose he does this every day.

I thought what an achievement it was for one man in his lifetime to have conceived and executed such a massive expression of his piety and his unbending will to dominate the faith of Europe. The building has strength and majesty, and also beauty of proportion, but all its charm could go into a tea-cup. One surely has a right to expect a little charm in so much granite, but evidently Philip had none to give. Nowhere in the world at that time was there such an architectural giant, and while it was rising upon these grey hills in Spain, country houses were being built in England, some with profits from disbanded monasteries—Longleat, Penshurst Place, Haddon Hall; and Jesus College, Cambridge, and Middle Temple Hall, London, also belong to this time.

The Spanish schoolboy has a more involved history to learn than any other European, and the English boy does not know how fortunate he is in having a perfectly straightforward story to learn, with a single line of kings and a country that can be called England from an early time. From the moment the Arabs invaded Spain in 711, the country ceased to be the Spain known to the Romans and the Visigoths and could not be called Spain again for nearly eight hundred years. During these eight centuries the country became a Christian north and a Moslem south, living in a state of border raids and guerrilla war that flared up into a crusade when a Christian king could persuade the other Christian kings to be his allies. The crusade over, the situation relapsed until the next flare-up, perhaps a century later. During these long intervals the Spanish Christians and the Spanish Moslems had a great deal in common, almost everything except religion.

So for a period which in English history separates the Saxon from the Tudor ages, there were not only two ways of life in progress in Spain at the same time—a Christian and a Moslem—but in Christian Spain there were several kings reigning over the various states in the north, which ultimately resolved themselves into two, Castile and Aragon. The great moment arrived in the year 1469, when Isabel of Castile married Ferdinand of Aragon and Christian Spain was at last united. These were the 'Catholic Kings'—*los reyes católicos*—whose names the stranger hears all over Spain. With the combined strength of their united kingdoms Ferdinand and Isabel inspired a ten year crusade that eventually drove the Moors out of Spain. The bells of

Europe rang and a Te Deum was sung in St. Paul's Cathedral in London, and in all European capitals, when the news came that Ferdinand and Isabel had accepted the surrender of Granada, the last stronghold of the Moors, and had planted the Cross upon its ramparts. This happened on January 2 in the year 1492, and among those who watched this stirring scene was Christopher Columbus.

Now came Spain's Golden Century, the Spain of the Hapsburgs. It had been the policy of Ferdinand and Isabel to build a strong block of influence against France by marrying their daughters into the right families. One became Queen of Portugal; another, Catherine of Aragon, Queen of England, the first wife of Henry VIII; and the third, Joan the Mad, was married to Philip the Fair of Burgundy, heir to the Hapsburg Maximilian I, Emperor of the Holy Roman Empire. This poor woman was fated to be the tainted source through which the ancient Hapsburg line was to continue.

The sons of Philip I and Joan shared between them the mighty Hapsburg inheritance. Charles I of Spain, who became the Roman Emperor Charles V, founded the line of the Spanish Hapsburgs which, after lasting two hundred years, petered out in madness with Charles II of Spain; while Ferdinand, who followed Charles as Emperor, carried forward the Austrian line, which did not disintegrate until the first world war of 1914-1918.

It is to the unhappy Joan that the projecting Hapsburg jaw and lips have been traced, as well as many of the other unfortunate characteristics of this family; and in order to understand the haunted faces of the Spanish Hapsburgs which gaze at us from the walls of the Prado, we should know something of her terrible story. She was seventeen when she was sent to Flanders to marry Philip I of Burgundy, who was eighteen. She is said to have been an attractive and beautiful young woman. He never pretended to love her, but she fell passionately in love with him. She was self-willed, possessive and hysterical and her husband's frequent infidelities flung her into fits of appalling rage and despair which a Flemish chronicler described as 'amorous delirium'. She would lock herself up and go on hunger strikes; she would become violent and uncontrollable, and conceived such a loathing for her own sex that she drove all the women from her household and sometimes insisted on following Philip in the field, the only woman among ten thousand men. She would do nothing to abate her jealousy and after some years of marriage she was on the borderline of sanity, if not across it.

# Joan the Mad

Her mother Isabel died when Joan was twenty-seven, leaving her the crown of Castile. Philip and Joan were in Flanders at the time and left by ship to go to Spain and take up their inheritance. A gale blew up, the fleet was scattered, and it was feared that the ship would be lost. Their conduct in the face of death was interesting. Philip buttoned and tied himself into a leather garment that was then inflated with air —a sixteenth century 'Mae West'—and knelt in prayer before a sacred image: Joan exhibited no trace of fear but put on her best dress and clung to Philip, saying that if the ship went down she would cling even closer. When the seamen sent round a bag for offerings to propitiate the Virgin of Guadalupe, Joan calmly hunted about until she had found the smallest coin she could give, saying that she was not in the slightest degree alarmed, because kings never drowned. They rode out the storm, but the battered fleet had to put into Weymouth for repairs.

Learning of the distinguished visitors, Henry VII invited them to visit him at Windsor, and Joan being ill, Philip went alone. He was given a state progress through London and was received at court. A pretty glimpse of Catherine of Aragon, then a young woman of twenty-one, has been preserved. Wishing to entertain her brother-in-law one evening, we learn that 'my lady Princess Catherine danced in Spanish array, with a Spanish lady for her partner'. Joan, having recovered, arrived at Windsor some days later, where the sisters met. Some folk-lorists connect this visit of Joan the Mad with the pretty but enigmatic rhyme:

> I had a little nut-tree, nothing would it bear
> But a silver nutmeg and a golden pear;
> The King of Spain's daughter came to visit me
> And all because of my little nut tree.
> I skipped across the water,
> I skipped across the sea,
> But all the birds of the air
> Could not catch me.

When eventually they arrived in Spain, Philip attempted to thrust his wife into the background as mentally unfit. This did not please either the Castilians or Joan's father, Ferdinand of Aragon, who was still alive and had been appointed regent in Isabel's will should their daughter be incapable. Within a year of having landed in Spain Philip the Fair died suddenly, perhaps of typhoid fever, perhaps of poison, and his death thrust Joan into permanent mental darkness. Her mania took the form of refusing to allow her husband's body to be buried or to be approached by women. She set up the corpse on a throne, clothed in brocade and ermine, and after it had been embalmed she refused to leave the coffin, which had to be opened every night for her to kiss the dead man's face. In the depth of winter, with snow upon the Castilian plains, she decided to take the body from Burgos southward to Granada, and one night, halting at a building and finding that it was a convent of nuns, she immediately ordered the coffin out of the church and into a field, where she and her attendants spent a night in the wind and the rain. To make things worse the poor woman was pregnant, and the funeral party halted in the little town of Torquemada, where she gave birth to a daughter. Her two famous sons, Charles, who became Charles I of Spain (and is known as the Emperor Charles V), and Ferdinand, who was to succeed him as Roman Emperor, were then small boys in Flanders. Charles was seven and Ferdinand was four.

For some years the mad Queen roamed about the country accompanied by a hearse and the coffin of her husband. She travelled at night with her face covered. At length her father Ferdinand managed to persuade her to enter the fortified mansion at Tordesillas, still accompanied by Philip's corpse, and this became her prison for forty-seven years. She did not leave it until death released her at the age of seventy-six.

Such was the mother of the great Emperor Charles V and the grandmother of Philip II. When her father Ferdinand died, the regency of Spain fell to her son Charles, then a young man of sixteen, who had not yet been elected Roman Emperor. He visited her in her fearful cell, where she spent days crouched upon the floor in rags, surrounded by plates of uneaten food. Almost until the end of his life Charles V, so powerful and glorious in the eyes of the world, lord of so much of Europe and of the new lands of America, had the awful vision before him of the room in which his mother lay upon the floor or else stormed and raved, even, it is said, refusing the consolation of religion. Like some monster of Glamis, the mad Queen of Spain was revealed by Charles to his son Philip when the boy was old enough to understand. While on his way to Coruña in great pomp to embark for England for his marriage with Mary Tudor, Philip called upon his grandmother; it was the last time he saw the ancestress of the Hapsburgs alive.

The moment Joan was dead and Charles could hand the crown of Spain to Philip, he put into operation a plan he had cherished for years. Although only fifty-five, he was prematurely senile, almost toothless, and suffering from gout and other ailments. His mother died in April, 1555, and in October Charles summoned Philip from London to Brussels to take part in one of the most dramatic scenes in European history. In the ancient palace of the Dukes of Brabant, and in a hall covered with splendid tapestries and guarded by halberdiers and archers of the guard, the deputies of the Netherlands took their places in a half-circle before a dais upon which three chairs stood beneath a canopy. The Emperor then appeared, walking with a staff and leaning upon the shoulder of William, Prince of Orange, while behind walked Philip, followed by members of his family and a brilliant throng of cardinals, ambassadors, nobles, and the Knights of the Golden Fleece. It was a moment charged with great emotion, for everyone knew that the Emperor had decided to abdicate and end his days in a monastery. He made a short dignified speech of farewell and begged any whom he had wronged to forgive him, but before he had finished his audience was in tears. The Emperor also shed tears and had to sit down and rest. He rose again and addressed his son Philip, who knelt in front of him, telling him of the fair heritage to which he now succeeded and bidding him 'to be a strenuous defender of the Catholic faith, and of law and justice which are the bulwarks of empire'. He embraced his son in front of the assembly. Thus, at the age of thirty-two, Philip II became the most powerful monarch in the world.

The next year the Emperor settled himself in the little monastery of Yuste in Extremadura, with a talking parrot and a favourite cat, with clocks and watches, which he liked to mend, and a garden where he grew flowers and vegetables. He had renounced everything except his appetite. His doctors tried to control him, but he continued toothlessly to devour food he was unable to digest. Gifts of rich delicacies began to pour in from all parts of the kingdom, and his devoted steward watched with dismay long trains of mules approaching the monastery 'laden, as it were, with gout and bile'. This faithful steward, though he considered plovers harmless, now 'interposed himself between his master and an eel-pie as, in other days, he would have thrown himself between the imperial person and the point of a Moorish lance'. Charles became so crippled by gout that he could not open an envelope, and the man who had once galloped all over Europe was unable to sit a pony. Such a man, of course, cannot really retire and his quarter at Yuste became the whispering gallery of the world. But not for long One day he had the fancy to rehearse his own funeral. Dressed in mourning he attended the solemn Requiem Mass, while a catafalque stood before the altar and the church blazed with candles. He retired thoughtfully to his little garden in the afternoon, where he caught a chill that developed into a fatal fever. Calling for his wife's crucifix, he expired with the word '*Jesús*' upon his lips.

When his will was read two personal documents were discovered. One requested Philip to erect a worthy tomb for his remains; the other admitted the paternity of a small boy named Jerome, who had been brought up secretly by his steward. The Emperor hoped this boy would be a monk: he grew up to be the great Don John of Austria.

Philip revered his father and ruled his life by his precepts, and, of course, the Emperor's last requests were a command. The worthy tomb that Philip erected was the Escorial. It was a tomb, a monastery and a palace, and something more: it was a retreat from which Philip, who had inherited the Hapsburg melancholia, ruled the world. And perhaps one might say too that it was a consummation of Spanish history. Eight hundred years of steadfast Christianity lay behind it. The hills of Spain are covered with the mouldering remains of the castles from which the war against Islam was carried on. The Escorial is the castle of the new crusade: the crusade against Protestantism. All the elements of Spanish history seem therefore to be concentrated in the granite headquarters of the Counter-Reformation.

§ 3

We plodded after our little guide, whose ability to be keen and interested aroused my wonder, along endless corridors and cloisters and up granite steps into tall apartments hung with tapestry. The figure of the pale, neat Hapsburg in his black doublet and hose, with the collar of the Golden Fleece about his neck, seemed everywhere, just slipping round the next corner in black velvet shoes.

The thing that fascinated me about the Escorial is the contrast which is to be seen there between the seventeenth century and the eighteenth, between the Hapsburgs and the Bourbons who succeeded them. The French kings did their best to achieve the impossible, to introduce a note of cheerfulness and of gaiety into the Escorial, but the old building resisted with all its strength. The contrast between the stark, solemn seventeenth century and the frivolous, tinkling eighteenth is extraordinary. You suddenly enter rooms where Goya's bright tapestries hang upon the walls, where French clocks tick upon mantelpieces and simpering little gilt chairs and couches, which remind you of a sale at the *Salle Drouot*, stand round the walls; and a passing official, just to amuse the tourists, touches off a musical box and sends a trickle of sound dancing through the rooms like some ghost fluttering startled from behind a curtain. Then a flight of stairs or a corridor and you are back again in the seventeenth century, among hard chairs of walnut and chestnut, and instead of little satin couches there are hard benches and stools. The ticking of the clocks fades and the musical boxes are forgotten. Flemish towns are on fire and the Duke of Alba is on the march, and in these quiet rooms the man in the black doublet, with the Golden Fleece at his neck, rustles papers with his white fingers and reads the report of a spy from London or Paris. Here for the first time one seems to draw a little closer to Philip II. By great good fortune the rooms he worked in and the bedroom, hardly larger than a ship's cabin, in which he died, have been preserved and remain in much the same condition as in his lifetime. They could not be simpler: a crucifix to pray at, a chair to sit on, a writing desk, and a stool to support a gouty leg. That is all that Philip, the heir to much of Europe and of America, wished when he made his own background. It is in effect the cell of a monk, a version of the rooms at Yuste in which his father died.

This is the room from which he used to say he ruled the world with two inches of paper. In addition to his desk and chair there is a steel cabinet that belonged to his father, a book-case, a gilded armillary sphere, and a lodestone found near the monastery which can hold a weight of eleven pounds. As Philip knew nothing about magnetism, he cherished it as a great wonder. So strong is the power of personality that after all these years the room does not seem to be uninhabited. It is an inquisitorial, watchful room; and, after all, is that so strange? How many people, how many countries, have been watched from it. Philip's spies were everywhere. He often knew more about the private happenings in foreign countries than his own ambassadors. All the secrets of Europe came on tiptoe into this room and were diligently filed away. Philip could turn up a dossier in a second. Once when a distinguished churchman had been mentioned for preferment, the King listened in silence to a recital of his virtues, then, opening his private file, quietly remarked, 'But you have told me nothing about his amatory exploits.' In contrast to his father, who was always on horseback, Philip was a great clerk and in another walk of life would have been an admirable civil servant. He loved to pore over his papers and to store away information. He was the junior partner of Spain; the senior being the Deity.

When embassies came they were received not in this private room but in an adjacent throne-room whose simplicity must have astonished those accustomed to the splendour of lesser monarchs. Flemish tapestries covered the walls, a huge leather carpet lay upon the floor, and beneath a canopy backed by a shield of the royal arms sat Philip II of Spain, a brimless tall hat upon his head, a ruff round his neck, a stick in his hand, and his left leg propped up on a folding gout stool. That is how he was seen by many from all parts of the world.

The impression he created was one of fear. He had surrounded himself with an oriental screen of tranquillity which many of his visitors found embarrassing. His habit of staring straight into their eyes was disconcerting, even to St. Teresa. He spoke in a low voice that was sometimes difficult to hear, and all this, combined with the absolute power he represented, caused even hard-bitten ambassadors to quail in his presence. He knew perfectly well the effect he was causing; it was part of the defensive shell he had built round himself. 'Calm yourself,' he said to his visitors, '*Sosegáos*'; this, of course, must have had the opposite effect. Once, it is recorded, a papal nuncio, overcome by the chilly atmosphere or maybe afflicted by a stammer, began his speech, then halted and fumbled for words. 'If you have brought it in writing,' said Philip kindly in his *sosegáos* voice, 'I will read it, to save time.'

This was Philip in later years. In youth he was fond of dances, masquerades and love affairs. His affections were warm and each of his four wives found him to be a good husband. His conduct in England was irreproachable as husband of the faded Mary. He wrote the most charming and paternal letters to his daughters, and although it was said at the time that a good volume could have been made of his dry sayings, there are fewer stories about him than of any man of similar eminence in history. One story that shows he had a sense of humour has been told by Kate O'Brien.

The Archbishop of Toledo was in the sanctuary, proceeding with the confirmation of certain of the royal children and with them, as Philip always insisted in such things, of any children of the village or surrounding farms who were prepared to receive the sacrament. The occasion was one of immense splendour and ritualistic pomp, as Philip adored such occasions to be. The choir performed with a perfection which outdid Rome itself; all the brilliance of the Spanish hierarchy was in the canonical stalls; Philip, his family, and the Court were in their stalls. Incense, flowers, candles, silence—and the Archbishop proceeded to confirm the children. But one little peasant boy had apparently not been told what to expect when the sacrament was administered to him, and when the Archbishop, great prince of the Church, gave him the ritualistic slap on the cheek—perhaps he overdid it—the little boy, true Spaniard of the Spaniards—sprang to his feet and shouted at the prelate—'You son of a bitch!' All things taken into account, that made a good situation, and the Court and the priests knelt paralysed. (No one seems to know what the Archbishop did.) But Philip II, most pompous of ritualists and devotees, burst out laughing. And the ceremony went on without further disturbance.

Philip was at his best as a husband and a father, when he dropped the mask he wore in public and became a simple, kindly and likeable human being, as the charming letters prove which he wrote from Lisbon to his young daughters. He asks them in one letter whether they can see the Escorial from the *Alcázar* at Madrid. 'I don't know whether you can see it from your windows, but you ought to be able to see it. Yes, I believe your brother would look very well in short skirts, but he shouldn't try to outdo the usual custom in this regard.' Evidently the young princesses, one thirteen and the other fourteen, wanted to take the four-year-old Philip (afterwards Philip III) out of baby clothes.

There cannot have been anything terrifying about Philip in the family circle, for the two motherless young princesses often consulted him about their dresses. On one occasion he is glad they are not going to wear toques and on another he grants them permission to wear gold on their frocks, but not too much, when they attend a wedding. One looks in vain for the sinister Philip of the Escorial in these letters. He describes with dry amusement the doings of an elderly and drunken dwarf, Madalena Ruiz; how fond she is of strawberries, how one day she went aboard a galley and was sea-sick, how Philip scolded her and how angry she was with him. They are the letters any devoted parent might have written to his daughters. Incidentally, there is a charming portrait in the Prado of one of the princesses with this same dwarf, Madalena Ruiz, who looks anything but a toper. She is more like a serious little old nun. She holds a couple of marmosets in her arms and the princess stands, magnificently clothed, with her hand affectionately upon Madalena's head.

One day Philip sent his daughters a small box.

> Some one gave me the other day what is enclosed in this box [he wrote], telling me it was a sweet lime. In my opinion it is very plainly a lemon, nevertheless I decided to send it to you. If it is a sweet lime, I have never seen such a large one. I don't know whether or not it will arrive there in good condition. If it does, taste it and let me know when you write, what it is, for I can't believe a sweet lime can be so large. The small lemon that goes with it is only to fill up the box. I am sending also some roses and orange blossoms, so you can see what they are like here; and so all these days I have had the Calabrian bring some bunches of the one or the other, and many days there have been violets. There are no jonquils here. If there were I believe they would be up by now, for other things are already out.

This is a Philip unfamiliar to history, a man fond of flowers, enchanted by the song of nightingales heard from his window, anxious for his children's welfare and excited to know that young Philip had cut his first tooth. But nothing will ever dispel the traditional picture of the bigot of the Escorial, a man who trusted nobody, who never revealed his real feelings, whose whole life was ruled by the conviction that he was the man chosen by God to fight, with or without the Pope, for the Catholic faith. His impassivity was a legend even in his own time. The French ambassador once remarked to the Venetian envoy: 'The King is such that he would not move or show the slightest change of expression if he had a cat in his breeches!'

The latest account of him by Dr. Marañón does nothing to dispel the sombre picture. Like all other kings and princes of the time, he authorized state murders, known as executions, and this should surprise and shock us less than it did former generations, for in our time the same murders have been called 'purges' or 'elimination'. I found it impossible to conjure up the picture of an ogre, as so many have done in these rooms. Indeed I think some people go there as they might go to the Chamber of Horrors, determined to be shocked. Instead, I thought how this age with its witch hunts, its ring of spies everywhere, its melodrama, its propaganda, and the division of the world into two camps, should be better able than most generations to understand the age and the problems of Philip II.

One turns away from the room where Philip sat at his desk and ruled the world with scraps of paper to the little alcove where he died like a Christian martyr. It is a dark little alcove, just large enough to take the four-poster bed that stands in it. While he was lying in bed he could look through a window and see the priest officiating at the high altar of the church beyond. Like so much in his life, this was a reflection of his father. The Emperor's room at Yuste had the same outlook to the altar of the church.

When he knew that he was dying, Philip gave thanks to God and ordered that a skull with a gold crown upon it should be placed where he could see it. Although he was in the greatest physical agony, and remained so for more than a month, he continued to fuss about his death and funeral, making all the arrangements and even ordering lengths of black cloth for draperies in the church. His habit of doing everything himself remained until the end. He had already had his outer coffin made from the timbers of a broken-up old galleon called the *Cinco Chagas*, or, the Five Wounds, a ship which had fought against the Turks. The wood was a South American timber called angelin, so weathered and salted that it was like steel. He now had the inner, leaden coffin carried into the Escorial and placed where he could see it.

His pain and humiliation were protracted and were such that he was unable to move or to bear the weight of a sheet on his ulcerated body. Sometimes the friars read to him all night while continuous services were held in the church. As his pain and fever increased he was given Vaiticum, and a few days later, when death seemed near, Extreme Unction. One reads with surprise that Philip, such a student of liturgy and one who went through life with the thought of his death always before him, knew nothing about Extreme Unction, and had never seen the sacrament administered or read the ritual. This was now done for his benefit, and the last rites carefully rehearsed so that he should know what to expect. This melancholy and painful scene was, at Philip's request, witnessed by his son.

'Look at me,' said the dying king. 'This is what the world and all kingdoms amount to in the end. Some day you will lie here where I lie.'

His agonies were prolonged almost beyond human endurance. Sometimes he smiled through his pain and prayed or recited the Forty-second Psalm. At length, during a spell of consciousness, he asked for the old wooden crucifix which the Emperor Charles had held on his death-bed and for a box of candles from the shrine of the Virgin of Montserrat, which he had saved for this moment. The Archbishop of Toledo helped him to hold a lighted candle, while in his other hand he grasped his father's crucifix. He died as the monks in the great church beyond his cell were preparing the altar for the Mass of Dawn.

43

## § 4

The Library with its curved, frescoed ceiling is as splendid as a gallery in the Vatican. I think the most impressive literary anathema in the world is inscribed over the door, threatening anyone who removes a book without authority with excommunication, and by the Pope himself! Strange how violent book anathemas have always been, from the curses on monastery manuscripts to the schoolboy's 'Steal not this book', ending with a threat that if you do so, 'the Lord will cast you down below'. Philip II was reluctant to lend books and hated to see them leave the library, not because he was a book-lover but because he was a collector of books. Apparently he collected because it was the fashion for a king to do so, but he liked to get libraries on the cheap. Though he would hesitate to spend money on a rare and important book, he would buy magnificent bindings and sumptuous choir books, which he loved to see lying on the music desks.

The books in the library are arranged with their titles to the wall and their gilt fore-edges outward, a method, I was told, that has existed since the Escorial was built. The effect is that of a wall lined with gold. But it is a system that would worry most people, for not only is it impossible to find a book without reference to a list and its numbered place on the shelves, but a thief could also easily abstract a book and replace it by any book with gilt edges and the theft would not easily be discovered. Beautiful as they look, books with their faces to the wall appear to me as if in disgrace.

There are many fine things to be seen in cases down the centre of the room: the breviaries of Philip II and Charles V, some beautiful illuminated manuscripts, and, most interesting of all, the original manuscripts of several of St. Teresa's works, with the little wooden box containing her ink-stand.

In the Baptistry I saw the famous St. Maurice by El Greco, which the art critic Julius Meier-Graefe thought the 'most beautiful picture of mankind'. His book was the first popular appreciation of this painter and helped to launch the cult that has now reached such notable proportions. Meier-Graefe went to Spain to study Velázquez, but instead fell in love with El Greco, and his book is a fascinating account of an artistic conversion. He said a striking thing about El Greco. Describing the mixed feelings of one faced by El Greco's work

44

for the first time, he wrote: 'The picture stood there like a spirit whom you are trying to kill with a pistol.' It is believed that El Greco went to Spain in the hope of getting work at the Escorial, but Philip II did not care for his painting. It is odd to think of Philip dreaming of saints and martyrs and the way of the spirit, yet turning down El Greco, for no other painter was so attuned to the soul of Spain during the time of the great mystics.

In the great Basilica which, like everything in the Escorial, resembles a granite fortress built to last until Domesday, I saw upon a tombstone let into the pavement the name one sees all over Spain—José Antonio Primo de Rivera. No greater honour has ever been paid to any Spaniard.

There are two arches on either side of the high altar and beneath each are groups of kneeling figures so life-like that at first, as one catches sight of them, one pauses afraid of interrupting their devotions. One group shows the Emperor Charles V in his imperial mantle, with his wife, daughter and sisters; the other shows Philip II with three of his four wives. The missing wife is Mary of England. I asked why she had been omitted, but no one could tell me.

When Lady Holland visited the church in 1804, she saw two monks praying in the choir and was told that ceaseless prayer for Philip's soul had been observed since his death two hundred years before, the friars being relieved every six hours, day and night.

§ 5

We descended a flight of marble steps into the royal vaults and entered an octagonal underground chapel encased in black marble and adorned with pilasters and gilt capitals. The two little American nuns crossed themselves, the saturnine priest looked gloomier than ever, and the rest of us glanced about chilled and rather shocked to see lying upon shelves massive marble sarcophagi which held the remains of the kings and queens of Spain.

The vault is constructed beneath the high altar of the church so that when the priest celebrates Mass, he does so immediately above the dead monarchs. They lie in tiers of four, one above the other, in the marble grandeur of their last court.

Only three kings are missing since the time of Charles V. They are Philip·V, the first of the French Bourbons, who could not bear the Escorial and its royal vault and was buried near Segovia; his son

Ferdinand VI, who was buried in Madrid; and Alfonso XIII, who lies in Rome. The little guide tapped an empty sarcophagus and said that it was waiting for his late majesty. Then, in an aside, he added that before the revolution which drove Don Alfonso into exile, he often used to motor out to the Escorial and pray in this gruesome place. Who would have believed it of that debonair figure, as gay and careless, it seemed, as a Stuart, who left so many stories and *bon mots* scattered among the hotels and turf clubs of the Côte d'Azur?

Yes, they were all there; we diligently counted them. The Emperor Charles V, his son Philip II, and Philip's feeble and unworthy son Philip III, pale Philip IV with his upturned moustaches, then the poor, demented Charles II, his son, with whom the Hapsburg line ended. Then we started to count the Bourbons. As we read the names of Charles III, Charles IV and Ferdinand VII, cheerful memories of Goya filled the vault and I seemed to see men astride prancing horses, or standing importantly, with the ribbon of an order across a satin waistcoat.

There is a curious Spanish propriety in the ranking of kings on one side of the vault and queens on the other, but the only women admitted were those who had produced male heirs to the throne. This was their final reward. Isabel II, who died in 1904, is buried among the kings because she was a queen regnant, while her husband, only a king-consort, is over the door.

This awesome vault has been in the mind of Spanish kings since the time of Philip IV, who began the custom of retreating into it to pray beside his own tomb. That melancholy king, a not unknown mixture of rakishness and piety, performed some strange acts in this vault. Upon one occasion he had the coffin of his ancestor, the Emperor Charles, opened so that he might see him, and he described this to a nun, Sister María of Agreda, who was his confidante.

I saw the corpse of the Emperor [he wrote], whose body, although he has been dead ninety-six years, is still perfect; and by this it may be seen how richly the Lord has repaid him for his efforts in favour of the Faith while he lived. It helped me much, especially as I contemplated the place where I am to lie when God shall take me. I prayed to Him not to let me forget what I saw there.

His attendants, finding the King still absent at the end of two hours tiptoed into the Pantheon and saw him kneeling in prayer upon the marble floor before his own sarcophagus, his face bathed in tears.

More dreadful and macabre was the arrival there of his half-witted son Charles II, at the age of thirty-nine, the year of his death, to seek comfort from the spirits of his ancestors. This last of the Hapsburgs was the result of a long line of almost incestuous marriages. His wretched reign was merely an intrigue between France and Austria for the succession to the Spanish crown. The poor creature's mental state was made worse by the wicked suggestion that he had been bewitched, in which his confessor was one of the main culprits, and all the horrors of his stumbling progress through life culminated in the royal vaults, when he insisted upon opening the coffins of his predecessors. He collapsed at the sight of the body of the once beautiful Marie Louise, the wife of his youth, and, promising to join her soon, the mad king stumbled up the marble stairs, to linger on in darkness and melancholy for a few more months.

We were all a little chastened by this last audience chamber of Hapsburg and Bourbon. Upstairs, with the sun slanting through the windows, we had heard their clocks ticking away, we had seen the tapestries against which they had moved and lived, the chairs they had sat on, the fireplaces round which they had drawn to warm themselves when the snows lay upon the Sierra. We had also seen them in the Prado; they were real to us, we could have recognized them in the street. It was easier to believe in them in the Prado than in this sumptuous underground vault where marble and jasper attempted to disguise the dustiness of death.

Like a true Spaniard the little guide was not going to allow us to escape the last morbidity. As we followed him up the steps, he paused at a grille on the left and tapped it with a finger. 'This is the rotting-place,' he said. 'We call it in Spanish the *pudridero*. Here the royal bodies are left for ten or twelve years. . . .' Then he turned and added in a whisper, 'María Christina is still in there.'

§ 6

Those who hoped that our ordeal was over and that, our serenity restored, we should soon be sitting in the hotel eating *langostinos*, were distressed to find that our tour among dead royalty had only just begun. The first landing on the way up leads down again into a series of vaults which were slightly more cheerful in appearance. The marble is white and artists have been allowed to exercise their sepulchral fancies. After the uniform state and gloom of the royal mausoleum, a white angel in tears or a drooping figure of Grief was a relief to the nerves. In a succession of vaults those queens of Spain who had failed in their dynastic duties, or had produced only daughters, lie with princes and princesses without number. Then come a numerous company, the natural sons and daughters of kings, known as 'the Bastards of Spain'.

In an alcove all to himself we came upon one of the handsomest men of his time, Philip II's illegitimate brother, Don John of Austria. His fine face, his noble brow and straight nose are carved in life-like marble, a little ruff touches his tufted chin, and he lies as if asleep, in full armour with a sword between his hands. As we filed past, I heard a woman whisper to another, 'What a wonderful man!' I thought it interesting that a face which had appealed to a great number of women in its time could still catch a woman's eye and inspire a compliment which Don John would no doubt have appreciated. The guide told us nothing about him, but hurried us away, and I heard people whispering and asking each other who his mother was and how he came to die.

She was a German girl named Barbara Blomberg, the daughter of a merchant. Charles V met her when he was at Ratisbon, in Germany. The Emperor was never proud of the affair and took the child away as soon as possible, sending him to Spain to be secretly brought up by his favourite steward, Quixada. Young Jerome, as he was then called, was brought up as a village lad; he went bird-nesting and orchard-robbing with the other boys, and no one, except Quixada, knew his origin until after the Emperor's death. It speaks well for Philip II that as soon as he knew of his young half-brother's existence —there were eighteen years between them—he arranged a meeting and gazed with pleasure at a handsome lad, fair and blond like himself, with a fine straight body, a contrast to his own unfortunate heir, Don Carlos. Philip told the boy who he was, took him to court, and gave him a household befitting his rank. He named him Don John of Austria.

Don John grew up to be the handsomest man in Europe and the most admired; he was gay, reckless, a great gallant and a bold and lucky soldier. A touch of common blood had toned down the Hapsburg melancholy which nevertheless was there under the smiling surface. 'Some of his letters to his half-sister, Margaret of Palma, relating his amours, seem to ask for the music of *la donna e mobile* to accompany them,' remarks Dr. Marañón. The great moment of his life was the day when, at the age of twenty-six, he led a combined fleet fitted out by the

Pope, Spain and Venice, into action against the Turk. As the galleys passed the mole at Messina the papal nuncio in full pontificals blessed each one on its way. There were two hundred war galleys and six lumbering Venetian galleasses, which were the Dreadnoughts of the day. Grains of the True Cross had been sent by the Pope, and each ship carried one of these sacred relics. Don John's flagship, the *Real*, was flying the blue banner of Our Lady of Guadalupe, while the Standard of the Catholic League, which had been blessed by the Pope, was ready to be flown at the moment of action.

For weeks the fleet cruised among the Greek islands and at last, on Sunday, October 7, 1571, made contact with the Turkish fleet in the Gulf of Patras, near Lepanto, which is the Italian name for the Greek Naupaktos. The Turks were in great strength and some of the Christian commanders were inclined to be cautious, but that was not Don John's way. He decided to give battle. The Turks were sighted before noon, with the sun in their eyes, moving slowly against a slight head wind, an enormous half-moon, or scimitar, of galleys, with thin pennants flying, the oars rising and falling, the sun glinting on brass and steel. Stepping into a light brigantine, Don John sped up and down the lines of his fleet to cheer and encourage his men. Anticipating another sailor in the distant future (or did the other sailor remember him?), he cried out, 'Whether you are to die or conquer, do your duty this day, and you will secure a glorious immortality!'

Back in his flagship in the centre, or battle, of a line three miles long, of warships moving abreast, Don John watched the approaching enemy. He had sent the great galleasses ahead to break the Turkish line with their broadsides, and their guns were the first to sound. As the Turks came within hail, a blood-curdling war-cry rose from them, but the Christian fleet moved in silence as every officer and man knelt when the Pope's banner, with the image of Christ Crucified, was seen to break from the mainmast of the *Real*. Monks and friars who accompanied each galley gave absolution, and the men rose to their feet and awaited the impact. As the fleets moved together a soldier in the Genoese galley *Marquesa* rose from a bed of sickness and took his place. His name was Miguel Cervantes and though he was to lose the use of his left hand before sunset, he took a fine right hand out of the battle with which he was to write *Don Quixote*. One who was there at the time happened to look up towards the flagship as she moved rhythmically forward, the papal banner blowing ahead of her in the wind as if anxious to meet the infidel, and there he saw, upon the gun platform, Don John of Austria in a suit of gold armour dancing a galliard with two of his officers to the music of the fifes.

For the next three hours smoke hid the sea. Peasants in the mountains beyond Patras listened to the sound of the guns. When the smoke cleared the Turkish fleet was smashed. Only forty ships escaped. The rest were on fire or beneath the waves, or were seen floating helpless upon the water. That was Lepanto, one of the most decisive naval victories in history. The story is told that as the battle was being fought Pope Pius V interrupted his treasurer, who was discussing financial difficulties, and, opening a window, gazed as if astonished at the sky. Then, turning with a radiant face, he said: 'This is not the time for business, but to give thanks to Jesus Christ, for our fleet has just conquered.' He hurried to his private chapel. Two weeks afterwards the news reached Rome.

The splendid young victor of Lepanto had only six years more to live. The whole world seemed to lie at his feet. He was younger than Alexander the Great had been at the time of his Asiatic conquests, and the Pope, whose admiration for him was boundless, was anxious to help him to a kingdom and a wife. But nothing could be done without Philip's consent. It may be that Philip enviously saw in his half-brother all that he would like to have been, for methodically and relentlessly from his study in the Escorial he stamped out Don John's dreams one after the other. The most romantic of these dreams was the landing of a Spanish army in England from the Low Countries, the rescue of Mary, Queen of Scots, from prison, a march on London, in which Queen Elizabeth was to have been driven from the throne, the marriage of Don John and Mary Stuart and their coronation as King and Queen of England! That was Don John's quixotic dream. It found approval in the Vatican, but none at all in the Escorial.

Instead, 'the Last of the Knights' found himself with the most thankless job in the Spanish dominions—the governorship of the Netherlands. He languished for two years in camp and council chamber while his appeals for money and support were carefully filed away in the Escorial. One autumn he fell sick of fever. His men carried him on their shoulders to a disused pigeon-loft in a farm-yard, which was hastily cleaned and hung with tapestry to make it into a sick-room. He grew worse and in his delirium he imagined himself on the quarterdeck of his flagship at Lepanto. During one of his conscious moments he remarked to his confessor that he possessed nothing in the world, not even a hand's breath of earth, and asked, 'Is it not just then, father, that I should desire the wide fields of heaven?' He was barely conscious when he received the last rites and, as his confessor said when writing to Philip, 'he slipped out of our hands almost imperceptively, like a bird vanishing in the sky'.

Veterans were seen to weep as the body, clothed in armour with a coronet upon its fair hair and the Golden Fleece upon its breast, was carried through regiments standing to attention on the mile long road to Namur Cathedral. It was whispered that he had been poisoned and the murderer was said to be his brother, but history has acquitted Philip of this crime. It is believed that the cause of death was typhoid fever. When Philip heard of his brother's wish to be buried in the Escorial, he sent orders for the body to be sent to Spain. This was done in a shocking way. The body was cut up into three portions and placed in three leather saddle-bags and in that way smuggled across France with a party of returning Spaniards. Some historians have suggested this was necessary in order to avoid the expense and difficulty of taking a royal body in state across Europe; but surely a ship could have been spared to take home the victor of Lepanto.

Our tour of the vaults was over. We hastened with pleasure into a first-class hotel and ordered sherry and dry martinis. We had become unnaturally bright and cheerful. We were like a band of pilgrims which has emerged from a dark and frightening wood. The little nuns had stretched the priest's knowledge of English far beyond breaking-point, and now, disregarding them, he sat with his napkin tucked into his collar, attacking *entremèses*, red mullet, veal, cheese and fruit, with the pleasure of one whose penance is over. Rather to my surprise my New York friend had enjoyed himself. He thought the Escorial was the finest thing he had seen in Spain.

There was coffee on a terrace that overlooked the Escorial. We could see it lying below, so grey and indestructible, the dome of the church and the pepper-pot turrets rising in the afternoon light.

## §7

There is an extraordinary neatness and precision about Spaniards, about their dress, their manners, and their famous courtesy. One hardly expects this neatness and precision to be extended to street markets, but it is. In most countries markets are a noisy and dirty chaos where food is dumped on stalls and sold to the sound of shouting and screaming. But tucked away in the side streets of Madrid are the most decorous and beautifully arranged markets in the world. They are the sort of ideal market that you might see in a ballet or a musical comedy.

I often visited one in the early morning that lay between the Calle de Velázquez and the Calle de Goya. It was a small, covered market with lock-up stalls round the four sides and a line of them down the centre. Housekeepers with baskets, servants with shopping-lists, and even a *señora* herself, would be going round ordering the day's food from stalls whose owners seemed to be competing together to compose the most attractive still-life groups. Never have I seen fish, fruit, vegetables and meat displayed with a finer sense of the attractiveness of common things. Every time I visited this place I was struck afresh by the beauty of a scene that changed in colour with the gastronomic year. Even the butchers' stalls, which are everywhere a strong argument in favour of vegetarianism, were not offensive. No bloodstained man advanced with a knife to a suspended corpse; one might almost have believed that a leg of lamb had grown upon a tree.

This market art must be peculiar to Spain, for I have never noticed it anywhere else and I always haunt the markets of a strange town. The fruit looked as appetizing as the cold buffet in a restaurant. Cherries, which were then in season, were displayed in deep wicker baskets, both whitehearts and black cherries, all graded in size, every stalk removed and each cherry appearing to have been polished. There were trays of wild strawberries from Aranjuez, and here for the first time I saw and bought some of those delicious but odd-looking flat little peaches, called *paraguayos*, which are grown round Madrid. It was a revelation to see how interesting and beautiful vegetables can be when arranged with a sense of their shapes and colours; the bright green peppers and the paler asparagus with its purple stalks, the chillies, red as a guardsman's tunic, and the bronzed metallic aubergines, were composed, with the help of the homelier cabbage, the leek, and a bed of spinach, into something as fine as a flower-piece.

The fish stalls were as brilliant in colour and as beautifully arranged as the fruit stalls; indeed the fruits of the orchard, the garden and the sea rivalled each other in colour. The fish were arranged on a bed of vine leaves in flat wickerwork trays. There was often a pink edge, or trimming, of shrimps, followed by a silver ring of sardines, rising to a pile of red mullet, hake and cod, culminating in a turret of crayfish. The effect of the colour and the composition of such a group recalls those elaborate confections known to our ancestors as 'subtleties', designed for the eye and not the stomach, which was placed upon the table at the end of a medieval feast.

The Spaniards must be among the greatest eaters of shell-fish in the world, and one of the best-organized things in Spain is the rapid transport of fish from the coast to all the inland places. Madrid, a mountain capital far from the sea, is served with fresh fish daily, and the nightly race of icy lorries from the coast is almost like a public service, and is maybe a good deal more popular. Even during the height of summer one eats shell-fish in Madrid that was landed only the day before at some coastal port. It is amusing to see the stranger carefully extracting the odd clam or mussel from his *paella* in the belief that it cannot be safe to eat shell-fish so far from the sea.

The grocers' shops in Spain have frequently the look of a medieval spicery, but are chiefly remarkable for their exquisite name—*ultramarinos*. What a word this is! How truly gross is our own word. Whenever one sees the word *ultramarinos* written above a little shop one seems to see ships moving towards green islands where pepper and cloves are being carried down to an emerald bay. To be the grocer, and own a shop called *Ultramarinos*, in Madrigal de las altas Torres— Madrigal of the High Towers, a town not far from Madrid—would be to live in the very poetry of language. (It is even only slightly disappointing to learn from Professor Trend that *madrigal* here does not mean a song, but a tangle of bushes and briars!)

One would like to know, when gazing with wonderment into a confectioner's window in Madrid, how much of the oriental lusciousness displayed there is a legacy of Arabian Spain. There is a Byzantine belt of cookery, in which I think one must include Spain, stretching from Istanbul southward across Asia Minor, where it peters out in the eating-houses of Aleppo and Damascus, then westward across Macedonia, Greece and the Balkans. And the honeyed sweetmeats with which the Sultan fed his favourites were not Turkish or Arab, for these races never invented even a sugared almond, but Greek or Byzantine. I have seen confectioners' windows in Madrid which I feel sure must reflect the sweetshops of Constantinople in the days of the Palaeologi.

I imagine that the Arabs brought these Byzantine delicacies with them when they came to Spain, and the taste for them has existed ever since. The convent and the monastery are wonderful repositories for a recipe, and it is interesting to be told that some of the favourite nougats and marzipans are still made and sold by the nuns. But who buys the daily consignment of sweetness, the honey cakes, the crystal-lized cherries, the oranges boiled in syrup, the candied greengages, the little cakes dripping with cream, the nougat, the marzipan? Enough of this is renewed daily in the windows of Madrid to fatten a hundred harems.

I found myself falling into the insidious Spanish habit of shrimp-eating in the morning. There was a charming café where coloured umbrellas were set out in a garden in the business part of Madrid. There were little tramcars jangling past on one side and on the other towered Madrid's cathedral-like general post-office, some-times referred to as Our Lady of Communications. There are few things more delightful than to have nothing to do in a strange city and enough money to do it pleasantly, to sit and watch people and to wonder about them and to have one's shoes polished by a young Murillo. The Spaniards can sit for hours just talking, or, if alone, doing nothing, with the mind's engine shut off, just coasting pleasantly. This immobility is a wonderful gift, like the ability of a dog or a cat to go to sleep at any time.

I realized how small Madrid really is when I began to notice the same people time and again. While I was sitting at this café I saw the two little chatterbox nuns go past, more eager and thrilled than ever, and this time, I was glad to see, they had been given as guide a hand-some and courtly priest who smiled down at them with an air of impersonal gallantry.

§ 8

I often went to the Prado to see the kings and queens I had been reading about: Philip II and his contemporaries, painted by Titian and Coello; Philip IV, by Velázquez; and the Bourbons, by Goya.

I suppose the portrait of Charles V by Titian is one of the greatest pictures ever painted. We see the Emperor wearing the armour he wore at the battle of Mühlberg. The artist has not attempted to disguise his air of gaunt illness. He was so gouty and weak on the morning of the battle that his enemies mocked him as Charles the Moribund; yet this invalid found strength enough to arm and lead his troops to victory and even to ford the river Elbe. Titian was seventy when he painted this masterpiece, and still young, while his sitter was old and worn out at forty-seven. What a picture it is! The horseman rides out of a dark wood under a streaked and threatening sky, grasping a spear.

His face under the steel helmet is old and tired, and we, who know his story, realize that he is longing to retire from the world and to make his peace with God.

A book should be written about great invalids, men and women whose spirits conquered their bodies, and such a book would not be complete without the Emperor Charles V. It is said that before a battle this bold warrior used to tremble violently as his armour was buckled. One looks into his face conscious of a warm and human personality which he failed to hand on to Philip, but, in the queer way these things happen, he was able to bestow in full measure upon Don John of Austria.

Philip II was good-looking as a young man, rather haughty and priggish perhaps, but still a princely figure with a well-shaped leg. One can well believe the story that Mary Tudor fell in love with Titian's portrait of him. There is also something faintly rakish about Philip at this age, a glint in the eye maybe, that no doubt explains Mary's coy hesitations at the thought of marrying a man of such dangerous possibilities, who was eleven years her junior. The poor woman must have gone through agonies of indecision before they culminated in that strange and touching scene when the imperial ambassador, having assured her time and again that Philip was a good young man who was not likely to deceive her with other women, was suddenly summoned at night to the Queen's apartments. There he found Mary red-eyed with weeping, alone with her old nurse, and the Sacrament exposed upon an altar. She said that, having asked God's help, she had decided to marry Philip and now swore in the presence of the Blessed Sacrament to make him a good and faithful wife. Then the Queen, the ambassador and the nurse knelt down and prayed, and the ambassador rushed off to send messengers galloping to Charles V with the news.

A wonderful companion picture to Titian's Philip II is the famous portrait of Mary by Moro. One's sympathy goes out to her. She was never good-looking, but now her youth has faded and her face has hardened into primness and obstinacy. All the years of neglect and frustration, when she and her mother, Catherine of Aragon, were swept into the background by Anne Boleyn, seem to be written there. Outwardly she is a queen in her splendid brocades, but at heart she is a frightened, hurt and soured little spinster whose chances of happiness had always been sacrificed to politics. The Spaniards, who from the earliest times have admired fair skins, praised her complexion, which was the milky kind that goes with red hair and freckles; but there was nothing else to praise. Her almost non-existent eyebrows remind one of her father, Henry VIII, and her russet hair, parted in the middle, is dead-looking. She gazes out with the fearless frankness of the near-sighted, for her vision was so poor that she had to hold a book a few inches from her face. And has any woman ever held a rose more reluctantly, pinching it by the stem as if it might sting her? (Maybe it was a Protestant rose!) One looks at Mary Tudor with the feeling that one has met her before. Is she not the prim and rather frightening aunt of one's youth whose life has been wrecked by an unhappy love affair or a selfish mother, and who in middle-age spreads her suppressions over a numerous company of god-children, cats, dogs, pet birds and philanthropic societies?

To return to the portrait of Philip. We can now sympathize with this young man of twenty-seven who for the sake of duty and the Catholic faith married this difficult wife of nearly forty, who was also his second cousin. Nothing reflects more credit upon him than his behaviour to her during the brief period of their marriage. Never for a moment did he let her see by word or glance that he felt his marriage to be a martyrdom, that in private he had said to a friend that he must drain the chalice to the dregs; on the contrary he gave her, for the first and only time in her life, an illusion of love, affection and security. As one looks at this solemn young man, whose expression was one of habitual melancholy, it is amusing to remember that his father and the Spanish ambassador had impressed upon him the need for outward jollity and bluffness when among the English, and how he went about forcing himself to smile, to slap people on the back, trying to be a good chap, and how upon one occasion he appeared before his startled grandees after dinner and asked them to join him in a tankard of beer!

So we pass from picture to picture and observe how the Hapsburgs become paler and more peculiar with every cousinly marriage until we arrive at Philip IV, with his jutting chin, his uptwirled moustaches, and his miserable, haunted eyes. The glimpse Velázquez gives of the decadent court of Spain is as vivid as the word pictures which Evelyn and Pepys were painting at the same time of the Whitehall of Charles II. During his career as court painter, Velázquez completed at least forty portraits of his patron, which works out at more than one a year, as well as portraits of queens, princes, princesses, nobles, and, perhaps most appealing of all, the court dwarfs and buffoons. It is startling to enter the little room in which *Las Meninas*—The Ladies-in-

Waiting—is shown by itself. You face a mirror in which the picture is reflected. The figures seem to be alive. You expect them to move. You have the feeling that you have eavesdropped in the painter's studio in the old palace at a moment when he is painting the King and Queen. To amuse their majesties as they stand motionless, their small daughter, the Infanta Margarita, has been brought there, and she stands, a strange little figure in a tight white satin bodice and a farthingale, her pale hair looped up on one side. A lady-in-waiting kneels, offering a cup to her on a gold salver, and another lady-in-waiting curtsies on the other side. There are two rather solemn dwarfs, and a mastiff just dozing off in the quiet of the studio. Velázquez stands at one of his enormous canvases, his head slightly on one side, his brush poised, having just completed a stroke, as he studies some detail of the royal couple. It is a scene that must have been witnessed a hundred times by court officials. It is a moment stolen from eternity.

The self-portrait of Velázquez in this picture is one of the great things in the Prado. We see a man of deep sensibility and strength of character and we can readily imagine how the pale, weak King loved the society of his court painter, why also he made him a Knight of Santiago, an unheard-of distinction for a mere artist. Velázquez led one of the most tranquil lives in the history of art. He was content to spend his life in his studio, experimenting with light and the third dimension, devoted to his wife, content with his salary and absorbed in his work. It is a little ridiculous to think of this great man as a royal quartermaster, whose duty it was to see to the decoration of the palace on state occasions, but it was a court appointment of some note. It was while engaged on such work that Velázquez caught a fever which proved fatal. Ford commented that 'Spain's greatest artist was sacrificed on the altar of upholstery'.

We come to charming Isabel de Bourbon, the sister of Henrietta Maria, and the first wife of Philip IV. He loved her devotedly, although he was never able to remain faithful to her. She was the mother of that adorable small boy, perhaps the best known royal child in art, Don Balthasar Carlos, who, dressed as a little general with a baton in his hand and a feather in his hat, comes prancing along upon his fat pony. How solemn and important he looks as he sits that 'little devil of a stallion pony', a gift from his uncle, the Emperor Ferdinand. The young prince was adored by his parents, but, alas, he was not to inherit the Hapsburg crown: he died at the age of twenty-five, probably of meningitis.

All his trials were attributed by Philip IV to his own sins. It is the pale face of Philip, with its lank fair hair, that one remembers, no longer the smooth face of the young noble who greeted Charles, Prince of Wales, in Madrid, but the disillusioned, weak face of a voluptuous and guilty mystic. No stranger letters have ever passed between a monarch and one of his subjects than those between Philip IV and Sister María, the nun of Agreda, to whom he confessed his faults and confided all his temptations. This highly improper literature passed regularly into the convent and inspired outgoing correspondence in which sometimes the nun chided the King for his wickedness and always tried to give him strength. It is extraordinary to think of a monarch who was surrounded by such pomp and ceremony, who sat for hours on official occasions like a graven image without the faintest smile or sign of humanity, abasing himself before this humble nun.

Then we come to the strange little Mariana of Austria, who was the second wife of Philip IV and also his niece. She was fifteen at the time of the marriage and he was forty-two. As Velázquez painted her in her fantastic wig with its salmon-coloured ribbons and the enormous hooped farthingale, there is already in her hard little eyes and her tight mouth a promise of the tough, competent woman she was to become. The nun wrote to the King at the time of his marriage begging him 'to fix your whole attention and goodwill upon the queen, without turning your eyes to other objects strange and curious'. And Philip obeyed the nun for a little while, but a man who had fathered at least thirty illegitimate children was by that time set in his habits and before long was once more weeping for his sins.

So we pass on to the last of the Hapsburgs, the half-imbecile Charles II, the son of Philip IV and his niece Mariana. The portraits of him, in which the artist has obviously struggled to be kind, show a degenerate face, unbalanced, lop-sided, the protruding jaw no longer a family distinction but a physical deformity. His teeth did not meet and he had to gulp his food like a dog. His mental development was retarded and even when almost adult he used to run about the palace and play like a child. This was the final result of those consanguineous marriages for which the House of Austria was famous.

Though it was assumed that he would be unable to have children, a merry French princess was sacrificed to him and to politics, and after her death a placid young German shared his throne and dominated him, no difficult task. So for thirty frightful years, while Spain sank into squalor and misgovernment, the court of the half crazy Charles II became a maze of intrigue as various powers schemed to obtain the succession to the crown. The King drifted through life with a pack of cards, a couple of dwarfs and a following of friars, two of whom had to sleep in his room at night. When he died at the age of thirty-nine it is said that he looked like a man of eighty. His bedroom was cluttered with the skeletons of saints, with arms, legs, skulls, and hands in their gold and silver reliquaries, and still, with the obstinacy of the half-witted, he had put off the problem of his successor. It is said that the Primate of Spain, who favoured the French faction, had the last word when he told the frightened King that unless he named Philip, Duke of Anjou, grandson of Louis XIV, as king, he would die in sin and go to hell. The wretched Charles then dictated his will and when it was produced he burst into tears and added in his scrawling childish writing, *Yo el Rey*—I, the King. And so the Hapsburgs, who had ruled Spain since the deaths of Ferdinand and Isabel, bequeathed the sceptre to the House of Bourbon.

Philip V, the first French Bourbon, inherited Spain as if it had been a silver candelabra, and Europe inherited the War of the Spanish Succession. We are now well on the way to the bright satin world of Goya and a Bourbon family almost as sad and melancholy as the Hapsburgs, to a Spain of imitation French palaces and waterfalls, of French ways and fashions, and of a reaction in the form of an idealization of common Spanish types like the *majo* and the *maja*, wrapped in a Spanish cloak and delightfully unaware of Europe.

It all looks so bright and gay seen in the glossy colours of the great painters, and all day long people pass before these figures of the past, gazing up from their catalogues and passing on, without the slightest idea that they have looked into the eyes of human tragedy and failure.

# Chapter III

*The Pastrana Tapestries—the Princess of Éboli and the murder of
Escobedo—Goya—the tragi-comedy of the 'Earthly Trinity'—the
palaces of Aranjuez—strawberries beside the Tagus*

## § 1

PASTRANA is an old town about forty miles to the east of Madrid,
famous for some of the finest tapestries in Spain and as the place
where the one-eyed Princess of Éboli was imprisoned in her own palace
by order of Philip II. The lady was mischievous and talkative and knew
too much of a certain state murder.

I decided one morning to run out there by car and see what Pastrana
is like, and I left Madrid at that fresh hour which many *madrileños*
spend in bed. Women were going to Mass. The milkmen were delivering milk in Ali Baba cans, slung one on each side of a mule or pony,
and the morning air was delightfully flavoured with the smell of new
bread. The road soon left the city and plunged across country to Alcalá
de Henares. I passed a barracks where I read Franco's slogan above the
main gate, *Todo por La Patria*—All for One's Country—and had a swift
vision of recruits in shirt-sleeves on the square; an elegant young officer,
booted, spurred and wearing a sword, took my mind back to days so
far away that they might be of another world.

The road to Alcalá de Henares is not the most beautiful in Spain. You
see on either hand a treeless, rocky upland with a hint of far-off villages.
Some lorries passed me, rushing into Madrid, there were a few cyclists,
and occasionally a man riding a mule or a donkey. Although the
last Moors were driven out of Spain centuries ago, they did not
take with them the Moorish habit of sitting back on the hindquarters
of asses with legs almost touching the ground. Now and then these
*caballeros* would, seemingly on the spur of the moment, turn off the
highway and strike straight across the featureless landscape into a
world where no stranger's imagination could follow them. They disappeared into dips, emerged again diminished in size as they rode on,
maybe to a group of stone houses and a church, where the smell of
wood smoke and frying *churros* would be lying in the air, where hens,

60

geese and goats would be strolling about, and women with piercing dark eyes would be waiting to stand no nonsense from any man.

I came to the old university town of Alcalá de Henares where Don John of Austria was educated. It was the birthplace of Cervantes and also of one of England's unhappy queens, Catherine of Aragon. Princesses are usually born in palaces, but the children of Isabel of Castile were born wherever their crusading mother happened to be at the time. I saw Cervantes standing thoughtfully on a plinth in the main square, and I went on, thinking that, like many another immortal, he would have sacrificed fame gladly for a little hard cash in his lifetime.

So suddenly that I cannot remember where it happened, I found myself moving through rich country; the whole landscape was golden with wheat and barley, and the fields sloped down towards beautiful green valleys where poplar trees outlined the courses of streams. It was as surprising as if I had suddenly, in half a mile or so, descended from the heights of Dartmoor into one of the Yorkshire dales. Consulting my map, I saw that I was travelling in country where a number of small rivers converge on the Tagus, which here is about eighty miles from its source and at the beginning of its long journey to the Atlantic. Water is the very source of life, as the Romans knew and the Moors after them. Wherever rivers flow and rains fall there are these rich fields moving in the wind like that golden lake which Spaniards sought so far from home; and there are also hares and partridges, and people look less gaunt. Although it was only early in June they were already reaping the harvest. The first sign I noticed was the appearance of perhaps ten haystacks, one behind the other, moving towards me along the narrow track; then I saw that beneath each golden mass twinkled a donkey's legs, and last of all came a little barefoot boy with a straw hat on his head and a stick in his hand. As he passed me, he did not gape like a yokel, neither did he glance at me acquisitively, but he looked as if I might perhaps have been either a saint or a devil in disguise, and giving me the benefit of the doubt, he gravely wished me good-day.

The sun was now warm and the heat began to tremble over the curved acres of wheat. The dirt road led upward and then downward, with enchanting views everywhere. I paused to watch a row of reapers advancing through a field of corn with sickles in their hands. I saw the tasselled heads bow to them and fall as they passed on, and, though it may be imagination, I thought that a countryside tended by hand, as Spain is, ploughed by oxen and reaped with the sickle, looks better, and in some way more contented and cared for, than a country which is driven over with tractors. But that may be the sheerest sentiment, and Spaniards would gladly renounce all their biblical attitudes for a few tons of agricultural machinery.

My first glimpse of Pastrana was of a great cluster of roofs some distance below, roofs at all angles and levels and covered with those long tiles which turn every shade from red to black and are common to all those countries which once formed part of the Roman Empire. You find them in the South of France, throughout Italy, Greece, and across Asia Minor, and when they are dug up in Sussex they are carefully washed, labelled and placed in museums. Rising from the centre was an ancient church, its nave and side chapels capped with the same tiles, and as I went downhill, this church appeared to rise until its tower, containing a great bell, was outlined against the sky. At the bottom of the hill was an old gateway through which hundreds of sheep were noiselessly pressing, and the arch framed a vista of stone houses nodding together across a cobbled street, each one with an iron balcony. A little market-place was flanked on one side by a low wall overlooking a ravine, and opposite rose the imposing Renaissance gateway of the Pastrana palace, with the ducal arms carved in stone. A narrow street led up into the town and there was another vista of old houses and balconies. The surprising arrival of the telephone has covered the slit of sky above these streets with a precarious network of thin wires, and upon some of the balconies are rows of porcelain insulators that look like swallows preparing to migrate. There is a little Renaissance fountain which might have come from Rome, battered and decayed but still working as well as ever it did. From the centre of the fountain rises a stone column upon which is a large, melon-shaped stone basin with four human heads round it, and from each mouth pours a jet of water which falls in a graceful curve into the well. There was not a moment while I was there when the fountain was not surrounded by women and girls with water jars, and while they filled them, muleteers would lead up their animals to drink, and donkeys with wooden saddles on their backs would come and lower their gentle little faces to the water.

The double gates of the palace still hang on their original hinges and they are studded with nails the size of half-a-crown. The air of decay outside prepared me for the scene of desolation within. An enormous courtyard, where the ducal retainers once mustered, and where the litters and the wagons and travelling coaches once assembled before a journey, is now a dust heap. The windows of the palace, their shutters gone or broken, gave upon a scene that only Time can stage. So frightful was the reek of bats and goats inside the palace, that I did not climb the dark stairways to the upper floor.

I walked on to the church, which the casual stranger might think is dedicated to Don José Antonio so large is his name written on the wall. In the dark interior I met a priest who knew the history of the town. He told me that its greatest moment in history was four centuries ago, when Ruy Gómez de Silva, Prince of Éboli, decided to start industries there. He collected together various Moorish craftsmen, the descendants of those scattered after the fall of Granada, and settled them in their own quarter of the town. Among them were silk-weavers, goldsmiths, silversmiths, and weavers of tapestry. When Pastrana had just achieved fame for its beautiful products, the edict went forth in the reign of Philip III that all those of Moorish blood must leave the country.

'But you must see the Pastrana tapestries,' said the priest. 'They are unique in Spain.'

I followed him into the sacristy.

## § 2

I found myself in the middle of an ancient battle. From a fleet of caravels an army of knights and men-at-arms had just landed before the ramparts of a walled town. The King's ship was nearest to me. I could have stretched out my hand and touched the ropes that ran up in a V-shape from the gunwale to the top-castles. I could tell it was the royal ship because it was larger and grander than the others, and a royal standard flew from the peak of the top-mast, while the main-topsail was dressed with the King's personal pennon, or *pennoncelle*, a slender flag, perhaps thirty feet in length, which flew and dipped in the wind like the tail of a kite. Everywhere was the apparent confusion of armed men landing in little boats. The noise was frightening; trumpeters in red caps and blue doublets pointed thin silver trumpets to the sky and blew fanfares; knights in steel armour moved forward with drawn swords; men-at-arms wound up their cross-bows; lances were pointed upward, at the slope and at the ready; and in the centre was the King himself, in full armour, covered with Florentine brocade, a diadem encircling his plumed helmet, a lance in his hand, moving forward seated upon a huge *destrier* fully barded, a plume tossing upon its head to match that of its rider. And as this noisy forest of spears and lances moved forward to the town, startled faces beneath turbans gazed down from the walls and javelins were sent hissing towards the steel helmets.

The priest smiled at my amazement. Could this be tapestry? By what magic had coloured silk and wool revived this old battle so that a man looking at it today knew what it felt like to move stiffly in armour and to hold a sword in a hand sheathed like an armadillo, knew what it was like to hear the trumpets sounding and to see a king in armour riding into battle with his banner carried before him? But this was not all. Glancing round, I saw that the whole sacristy was covered with such tapestries. Each one carried the story a step further. The second was perhaps the most interesting of all. It pictured the siege of the town, which the invaders had not been able to carry by force of arms. In order to blockade it, they had brought with them in their ships a pre-fabricated palisade, which in this second scene has been erected round the town except on the seaward side, where the fleet is at anchor. The palisade is made of tough wooden beams planted in the earth and bolted together. There are openings in it closed by a bar, and at each opening an armed sentinel is stationed. I was reminded of the pre-fabricated fort which William the Conqueror is said to have taken across the Channel when he invaded England. Here again the splendid King is seen escorted by his trumpeters, his standard bearers and his bodyguard, and while he glances towards the town, where an influential-looking infidel seems to be making signals of distress, the men-at-arms work their bombards behind wooden gun-shields, and one bombard has actually been mounted on wheels. The scene, like all the others, is one to fascinate a student of medieval warfare, while others less technically interested will find themselves transported from the modern world into the strangeness and beauty of the Middle Ages. Those of us who have seen a carpet of flowers growing over the scars of war, even in the heart of London, will notice with a fellow feeling that the medieval artist has crowded every scrap of ground not occupied by the ironmongery of medieval war with the freshest and the sweetest of flowers, which spring from the grass.

The priest told me that these tapestries illustrate the Moroccan expedition of 1471, undertaken by Alfonso V of Portugal, and I was all the more interested because this king was the grandson of Philippa of Lancaster, the daughter of John of Gaunt, and a good touch of Plantagenet blood ran in his veins. Philippa must have been a fine woman, for she had three splendid sons, and there can be no better tribute to any mother. There was Duarte, or Edward, named in honour of England's Edward III; there was Pedro, a chivalrous knight who died tragically; and the immortal Henry the Navigator, whose life's work in his maritime college at Sagres inspired the navigation of half the globe. It is good to remember that Henry the Navigator was partly English. Alfonso V, the King of the Pastrana tapestries, was the son of Philippa's eldest child, Edward, and he is seen in these tapestries with his son John, who succeeded him and was at the time of the expedition a youth of sixteen out to win his spurs.

The priest told me that it is believed the tapestries were made on the looms of Paschia Grenier at Tournai, from the designs of Nuño Gonzálvez, who was the court painter in Portugal at the time. They are supposed to have been made immediately after the expedition in 1471 and to embody the impressions of eye-witnesses. How they came from Portugal to Pastrana is not so obvious. It is conjectured that they were hung in the war pavilion of the King of Portugal and during warfare between Portugal and Spain fell as booty into the hands of the Mendoza family and thence to Pastrana. As nothing has been written about them in English so far as I know, with the priest's help I did my best to sort out the crowded and involved happenings depicted on them.

The first tapestry shows the landing of the Portuguese army before Arzila in Morocco. What makes these tapestries so puzzling at first sight is that the artist has broken the unity of time and action in an attempt to show various incidents of the siege which did not occur simultaneously, so that one tapestry contains perhaps five or six incidents which took place at different times, but with the chief actors, King Alfonso and Prince John, in the leading parts. The clue to these scenes is the extraordinary personal standard of the King, for wherever you see it, there he also will be found. This emblem looks rather like a small parasol with the covering removed to show the ribs, but with the fringe still left in position; and I doubt very much whether anyone could guess what it is meant to be. It is supposed to represent a water-wheel shedding drops of water as it revolves, a sign that the King's tears would never cease to fall for the loss of his beloved wife, Isabel. We see the King leading the way through the waves, for a storm blew up and it was difficult to land the troops; but Alfonso, plunging in fearlessly, was followed by the army, with the loss of two hundred lives. These unfortunate men are to be seen in another part of the tapestry, struggling in the water. We notice the King mounted on horseback, and again on foot, approaching the town.

The next tapestry is the siege itself, with the palisade erected. Here again the King is seen apparently in several places at once. The third tapestry, the most crowded and noisy of the whole lot, shows the final assault, with the King on horseback directing the attack, while the trumpets blow and knights and soldiers pour into the town through breaches in the walls or climb to the ramparts upon scaling ladders. Overlarge and distressed Moors fight on the battlements and fly to other positions as the sanguinary hand-to-hand conflict develops. This is perhaps the best picture of the King as he sits his charger, his red velvet surcoat matched by the red brocade covering of his horse, which is almost as completely and as richly armed as his rider.

The scene changes with the fourth tapestry. We see the entry of the Christians into a deserted Tangier. In the centre of the tapestry is a typical Flemish walled town with its towers and battlements and a few minarets thrown in to give a Moorish touch; the sea washes the walls and there are beautiful little star-shaped flowers growing at the foot of the towers. On the left the knights approach the silent town on foot and on horseback, and the stiff attitudes of these men in plate-armour, grasping swords and lances, are admirably portrayed. A knight in armour enters the main gate of the city with the royal banner, which he will plant on the ramparts above, and in the background the presence of a great army is wonderfully suggested. The hero of this tapestry is neither king nor prince, but an earnest young man in armour who rides a splendid war horse armoured and plumed like himself, and this is Don Juan, Chief Constable of Portugal, and son of the Duke of Braganza. While this is happening on the left of the silent town, the Moorish inhabitants are seen on the right in a dignified and unhurried flight. Those who made the tapestry were living about thirty years after the Turks had captured Constantinople, and no doubt the costumes of Byzantine refugees were more familiar to Europeans than the dress of Moors, and this may explain why we see a brilliant crowd in shimmering brocades and cloth of gold, wearing every type of headdress from turbans to little conical hats tipped with fur, while the unveiled women in their draperies are entirely Greek in appearance. Once again the crowd in its coloured shoes treads down fields of flowers.

There are two more tapestries, I imagine by a different artist and from different looms, depicting the siege of Alcázarquivír on the Moroccan coast, and though they would be outstanding anywhere else, they are not in my opinion in quite the same class as those I have described.

The priest then produced some of the church treasures, but my eyes wandered from gold reliquaries and processional crosses, magnificent as they were, back to the tumult and the shouting, where the trumpeters blew their fanfares and the King rode among the silver daisies.

'Would you care to see the burial vaults?' asked the priest, leading the way back into the church.

## § 3

We descended steps to the left of the altar and entered a limewashed crypt, where I saw by the crude light of unshaded electric globes that a great deal of worldly splendour had come to rest there. Upon a shelf were small, ancient coffins bound with bands of tarnished metal, and each coffin was provided with a key-hole as if it were a travelling trunk. These were the remains of children who had stumbled and fallen along the first steps to grandeeship. The rest of the vault was occupied with the tombs of the Mendoza and Pastrana families, lying in two rows facing each other. I came to the tomb of Doña Ana Mendoza y de la Cerda, the one-eyed Princess of Éboli.

The priest knew, of course, the stories which linked her name with that of Philip II, but he believed them to be gossip, and he talked of her in a gentle and kindly way as a great and imperious woman who by this time had answered for her sins before a higher tribunal and was immune from earthly censure.

In a picture at Pastrana the Princess is seen kneeling piously beside her husband while St. Teresa invests two Carmelite friars with their habits; and she is a young woman of obvious charm and beauty. She wears the waisted, puff-sleeved and high-necked fashion of the day, and her tight pleated ruff frames an oval face, perfect save for a black patch over the right eye. I asked the priest if it were known how she had lost this eye. He replied that the stories current in Spain for many centuries are that she met with a hunting accident, or that she lost the eye while fencing with one of her pages. Her most recent biographer, Dr. Gregorio Marañón, disbelieves both stories and thinks she may merely have had a squint.

She was married in her youth to Ruy Gómez de Silva, the favourite of Philip II, and in the course of their fourteen years of married life she became the mother of a large family. Gómez, who was the soul of tact, was able to control his imperious wife, but a flash of her temper came out now and then, particularly in her dealings with St. Teresa, in her own way an equally great autocrat. The Saint has described how she travelled to Pastrana to found a Carmelite convent there.

The Princess was charming and persuaded St. Teresa to show her the manuscript copy of her *Life*, of course in the strictest confidence. The book was then handed round the palace and, as some of the Saint's experiences seemed fantastic to those with no experience of the spiritual life, she was mocked at behind her back and, worse still, someone informed the Inquisition that the book should be inspected. Always ready to descend like a sledge-hammer upon would-be saints and hysterical nuns, the Inquisition took up the matter, and it is sometimes said, quite erroneously, that the action held up the publication of this famous work for ten years. What really happened was that the Inquisition found no fault with the book and St. Teresa herself left it in their keeping for safety until she should need the manuscript to copy for the use of her other convents.

Nevertheless this incident did not make for good feeling between the two women and when the Princess began to harry and dominate the Carmelites of Pastrana, St. Teresa was extremely angry. The Princess stopped at nothing to get what she wanted. Desiring an image of proved sanctity for the convent, she is said to have kidnapped the sacred statue of *Nuestra Señora del Soterraño*—Our Lady of the Underground Passage—from the chapel of the Castle of Zorita in Extremadura. She wrapped it in a white cloth and decamped with it in a bag. Such actions were bound to lead to an explosion between the Saint and the Princess, which occurred when the Prince of Éboli died and, in the first excess of her grief, the Princess decided to become a nun in her own convent. The Carmelites were dismayed by the thought of this distinguished novice. 'The Princess a nun!' cried the Prioress. 'Then in my opinion this house is doomed.' And she was a good prophet. The Princess turned the convent upside down. She insisted upon the use of her titles when she was spoken to and she expected the nuns to serve her on bended knees. After several months of uproar, St. Teresa sent two monks to Pastrana with orders to close the convent and take the nuns to Segovia. The rage of the Princess was so fearful that a convoy of five carts full of nuns had to steal out of Pastrana at midnight to avoid her wrath.

The Princess then returned to the world much refreshed to plunge into political intrigue. Dr. Gregorio Marañón, in his book *Antonio Pérez*, does not believe in the stories of her amours, which are still current in Spain, but thinks she was just a headstrong woman with an insatiable desire to dominate and command. She formed an association which may have been only a business one, with Philip's chief Secretary of State, Antonio Pérez. He was a self-made man of outstanding ability and defective moral sense, a scented dandy who knew all the dark secrets of the Escorial. He was the man who made up the King's mind for him. He and the Princess became so involved in dangerous intrigues that the moment came when they felt that, in order to preserve themselves, they had to murder a man who knew something of their schemes—Juan de Escobedo, the agent of Don John of Austria. Pérez craftily worked on the King's suspicious mind and persuaded him to order the execution of Escobedo for reasons of state. In modern autocracies murders of this kind are known as 'purges', but in the sixteenth century they were termed 'executions', and a king who ordered such a murder, and they were common events, had no difficulty in receiving absolution.

The interesting thing about Escobedo's murder is its clumsiness. I have always imagined that poison to drop in a cup of wine or inject into an orange was as easy to obtain in the sixteenth century as aspirin in this; but not a bit of it. First, the murderers sent a man to Murcia to gather poisonous herbs, and a brew was concocted which was tried out on a cockerel. The bird was unaffected. The murderers then used 'a certain water' on Escobedo but, like the cockerel, he remained unshaken. They tried a powder which only made him sick. Finally, becoming impatient, they decided to use a stiletto. Here again one would have imagined that a stiletto, and a bravo to use it, might have been picked up at any street corner in old Madrid; but apparently this was not so. One of the conspirators went to 'his own country' to find a friend who had a stiletto 'with a very fine blade', and others went off to Aragon to hire desperadoes. So it happened that Juan de Escobedo was stabbed to death one night in the streets of Madrid, as he was on his way home.

Gossip at once associated Pérez and the Princess with the crime. The King soon knew that Pérez had lied to him about Escobedo and that he had obtained permission for the 'execution' of an innocent man. Philip at once arrested Pérez and the Princess. Pérez was charged with the murder, but managed to escape to France and later to England, where he became a friend of Roger Bacon and the Earl of Essex. He was a great social success and, strange to relate, he was the first pioneer of dental hygiene, in an age when, as Dr. Marañón says, nearly everyone over forty was toothless. He had always been devoted to scents and lotions, which he used to mix himself, and his dental washes, and the quills and feathers with which he cleaned his teeth, were much sought after by the French aristocracy. 'A tooth is worth more than a diamond' was one of his sayings, which a modern tooth-paste manufacturer might not perhaps scorn. Pérez died at last alone and neglected and, like so many Spaniards, in exile.

The Princess of Éboli had the humiliation of spending the last thirteen years of her life in one room of a palace in which she had once lived in royal state. Her room was secured by locks and bolts, the window with iron bars, and the poor woman communicated with her gaolers by means of a grating like that in a convent. One feels that her sins must have been much greater than any surviving evidence shows. Her husband had been the King's great friend and she had been a lady-in-waiting to the gentle and beautiful young Queen of Spain, Elizabeth of Valois. Yet none of these old memories softened the King's heart. He was deaf to all her complaints. Even her powerful relatives were unable to plead for her. On the face of it she was savagely punished.

I said so to the priest. He shrugged his shoulders. He was used to hearing sins and imposing penalties and, like a good lawyer, would not commit himself unless he knew all the facts, which I suppose nobody will ever know. I took a last glance round the vault where the stormy Doña Ana lies near the only man she probably ever cared for, her elderly and tactful husband, and certainly the only man who knew how to control her feudal wildness. As the priest switched off the light and we went up into the church, I thought what a strange association it was, the great lady, the descendant of kings, as she proudly claimed in her dedicatory inscription in the convent, and the scented parvenu, Antonio Pérez. We said goodbye. I went back to look at the palace. It would be a wonderful place to reconstruct and a perfect background for the Pastrana tapestries. I asked a villager if the room in which the Princess was imprisoned is still known. He led me to the front of the palace and pointed up to a tower to the right of the gateway, where I saw a heavily barred window.

I went to a little bar up some steps off the market-place, where the owner, quite metropolitan in a white apron behind the counter, gave me an iced beer and, as I was a stranger, fished some anchovies out of a tin and handed them to me on a saucer with toothpicks. There were two flour mills and three olive mills in the town, he told me, and the people from hamlets for miles around came in to Pastrana to do their shopping. The main crop was olives. Had I come all the way from

Madrid to look at tapestries? I could see him thinking what a strange world it is. I had also come to see the palace of Doña Ana, I told him.
'Oh, *La Canela!*' he said.

This is the Spanish for cinnamon, and is still used to describe a most delectable lady.

I found my way back to the main road and reached Alcalá de Henares as it was growing dark. In the *Hostería del Estudiante* I had dinner in a hall full of dark old beams and fully conscious of its atmosphere. There was a row of pigskins on a rack, fat, black and bursting with wine. The proprietor carefully untied the neck of one and skilfully eased a jet of wine into a jug, and brought the jug to my table. I had *moje*, which is a soup of La Mancha, seasoned with tomatoes and pimentos, then they brought me a great hunk of roast lamb, brown and crisp from the oven. A girl who might have been Dulcinea's sister placed a cheese on the table and a plate of oranges.

All the way back to Madrid I thought of that old town in Castile where the great ones of their time are sleeping in the neat white vault under the church.

§ 4

One afternoon I walked along the cool avenues of the Paseo del Prado to spend an hour with Francisco Goya y Lucientes. In England and in France there is no way of knowing how great a painter Goya was, for neither the National Gallery nor the Louvre contain any of his finer paintings and I fancy that his work reproduces badly, even in colour. At any rate it is not unusual for those who are familiar with photographs of his pictures to be struck with astonishment and delight when they stand before the originals. That was indeed my own experience.

Goya was an Aragonese peasant born in 1746, and he grew into an extremely ugly bull-frog of a man. His was that mixture of ugliness and vitality which is immensely attractive to some women. He had a good voice and could play a guitar, and as a young man soon found it prudent to fly from Madrid. Being penniless, it is said he joined a *cuadrilla*, or troupe, of bull-fighters and wandered from town to town with them until he came to the Mediterranean. He found his way to Rome where he studied painting, and here again he is said to have climbed into trouble—there was a rumour of a convent wall—and he returned to Spain. He married the daughter of the court painter and

71

in his thirties found himself a fashionable artist to whom the King, Charles IV, his scandalous Queen, María Luisa, their mean and unpleasant heir, Ferdinand, and Manuel Godoy, the Queen's lover, as well as many of the grandees of Spain and their wives, were proud to sit. His supposed love affair with the wealthy young Duchess of Alba, when he was in his forties, has been much written about, but it depends on a series of veiled allusions, conjectures and rumours. Her sudden and mysterious death is believed to have brought on those moods of depression verging on madness which lasted for the rest of Goya's life. He became stone deaf before he was fifty, yet he painted at this time some of the noisiest scenes that can be imagined, the terrible events of the *Dos de Mayo*—the Second of May—when the Madrid mob turned on the French troops and began the War of Independence, known to us as the Peninsular War. I wonder if Goya's deafness had anything to do with his almost frantic determination to make his colours scream, as they do in these ghastly pictures, especially the yellow and white clothes of the kneeling Spaniard who is about to be shot by a firing squad of French soldiers. The deaf man saw these scenes, but he has made us hear them. You almost brace yourself for the volley of musketry which is about to sound in this picture.

In his old age Goya lived with a relative in a pleasant house outside Madrid whose walls he covered with a series of haunted and frightful pictures painted in whites, greys and blacks, pictures of witches, apparitions, hideous spooks and spectres, a giant devouring a naked body whose head it has bitten off, and such like subjects, the visions of a hysterical child who was frightened of the dark, and these have caused many people to believe that he ended his life in madness.

'There are moments when I am so furious with everything', he wrote at this period, 'that I hate myself as well.' His ghastly dreams have been skilfully peeled off the walls of the old house and now occupy a whole room in the Prado. They seem to have been splashed on to the walls with the hate he felt for everything. He died at the age of eighty-two, in self-imposed exile in Bordeaux.

Goya had a violent temper. His portrait in old age is that of a terrifying old man in a Bolivar hat, an incorrigible old Scrooge. The story that he threw a plaster cast at Wellington during a sitting in Madrid is not generally credited, but there seems nothing improbable about it. Wellington disliked sitting to artists, who, he believed, could never be trusted with military details, and he once called back Sir Thomas Lawrence and briskly ordered him to correct a sword. If he had behaved in this way with Goya the aged curmudgeon, who in his day had painted the Bourbons in all their decaying splendour, would not have received lying down a disparaging comment from a trumpery foreign general! Unfortunately for the story, a note in the handwriting of a member of the Goya family on the back of the strangely ethereal Wellington in the British Museum suggests that this sketch was the basis for the three oil paintings of Wellington by Goya: the equestrian portrait which can be seen in Apsley House, Piccadilly; the portrait with the hat, now in the United States; and the hatless portrait on loan to the National Portrait Gallery. In all these we look at a delightfully novel Wellington who might have had a Spanish grandmother.

I made for the rooms where the work of Goya's earlier years is to be seen, the royal portraits. Here the thunder of the nineteenth century is yet unheard. The nightingales are singing in Aranjuez, and the tinkle of the minuet mingles with the whisper of the fountains, for the eighteenth century has a few more years to run. The complacent Charles IV is shooting sparrows behind a hedge at San Idelfonso, María Luisa is hanging yet another Grand Cross upon the bull-like shoulders of her hero, the young Ferdinand is filled with hatred for his mother and her lover: and far from these domestic scenes a poor young Corsican lieutenant of artillery has just written an essay on happiness in which he rather priggishly notes the dangers of ambition. Napoleon, with Mars as his ally, was only a lieutenant in 1791, but Manuel Godoy was far better off with Cupid, for he was already a general.

As I look at these portraits of Charles IV and his family, I wonder how it happened that Goya alone among court painters was exempted from the need to idealize and flatter. Such paintings are always ordered by the sitters, and painted by the artist, with an eye to posterity, and it is therefore understood that an attitude should be struck, that a plump, unsoldierly hand should be stretched towards imaginary brigades and that, if beauty cannot linger upon a queenly brow, at least it can be arranged that a fair amount of regal charm may repose there, but not with Goya. He painted what he saw, with the result that the royal family, in the words of Gautier, look as if they were a grocer's family who had won the big prize in a lottery. Charles IV comes out best from the ordeal, a blunt, stupid, but kindly old squire, who might have hunted with Jorrocks; but what are we to say about that aged Aphrodite, María Luisa? She is like one of Cinderella's ugly sisters, a greedy termagant, with thick arms, bare to the shoulder, which, however, a visitor once found irresistible. 'I cannot refrain from praising the beauty of the Queen's arms, which really were quite perfect,' wrote Mme Junot, whose husband was for a time French ambassador. I also recalled the words of Napoleon who, having seen María Luisa for the first time, wrote to Talleyrand: 'The Queen bears her history in her face and need I say more?'

But there is something missing in the Prado. Where is the 'incomparable Manuel', where is the favourite who was really King of Spain and whose scandalous association with the Queen created the riot after Charles IV had abdicated? What a pity that Goya's superb and impudent study of Godoy could not be brought to the Prado from the *Real Academia de Bellas Artes* and thus complete the earthly trinity. It is well worth while to go there to see him in his marshal's uniform, not standing as a soldier should, but reclining appropriately enough in a love-seat, or *dos-à-dos*, his fat legs stretched out as if breeches and boots were too tight, his plump hand pendulous over the back of the seat, suggesting not the swords it had drawn but the cheeks it had patted, and his whole air one of fat and pampered sultanhood.

Godoy was the son of impoverished gentlefolk of Badajoz, and he must have been a striking figure at the age of eighteen when the Queen first saw his large thighs in tight buckskin breeches and his broad chest in a guardsman's tunic. María Luisa was then thirty-four. In twelve years' time Manuel Godoy was not only one of the richest men in Spain but was also Prime Minister, and, of course, the most powerful and hated man in the country. The King was as devoted to him as the Queen, and this mutual attraction remained unbroken by disaster, exile and poverty. It is true that Godoy was an adventurer, but he also had a talent for affairs, a geniality and a bursting vitality which shone in the pale and sombre Bourbon court as if he were the infant Bacchus. French and Spanish writers—for little has been written in English about Godoy—have often speculated on the degree of marital astigmatism from which Charles IV suffered. It seems that he had developed a curious and original theory: that kings were fortunately relieved from the anxiety which beset certain ordinary husbands because it was impossible for queens to demean themselves with men of lesser rank to themselves. His Majesty obviously knew more about hunting than history. Nothing could shake this view and attempts to open his eyes were always cut short, although the whole of Europe was discussing his wife's conduct.

Disaster at last stole upon them among the groves and gardens of the summer palace. Godoy was in a perilous dilemma when he gave right of way into Portugal to the French armies, who came clattering into Madrid in 1808 with Murat at their head. The mob went mad with joy, believing they had come to destroy Godoy and to make Ferdinand king. Shouting for Godoy's blood, the crowd surged to Aranjuez, thirty miles away, where the court then was. As night fell Godoy's palace was stormed. The portly favourite took refuge under a pile of rugs in an attic and remained there for a day or two until, driven out by thirst and exhaustion, he gave himself up to a startled sentry. Running between two troopers, who tried to save him from those who wanted to lynch him, bleeding, his clothes torn to rags, he was flung upon the straw of a stable. And there the triumphant and vengeful young Ferdinand, who for years had hated him and had watched his mother lavish the wealth and honour of Spain upon him, came and enjoyed his victory. Meanwhile the King had decided to abdicate, but his real worry was—what had happened to dear Manuel? But at this point history seems to have taken a wrong turning. Godoy should now have perished at the hands of Ferdinand and his party, and no doubt he would have done so if Murat had not stepped in and rescued him. For a Voice had spoken. From far across the Pyrenees came a precise command from a little man in a green coat with a lock of hair across his forehead: the King and Queen, Godoy, and Ferdinand were to be sent at once to Bayonne.

The Voice was a cynical Voice and it had never boded any good to persons in such circumstances; but how astounded the owner of that voice would have been to know that he had decreed another forty-three years of life to Manuel Godoy! The Favourite was then forty-one. He was to live for thirty years after Napoleon had died on St. Helena, a third of a century after Charles and María Luisa were dead, and ten years longer than young Ferdinand. He was to live on in a world that had forgotten his name, a queer old survivor from an age of candlelight and minuets. When he died the streets were already lit with gas; locomotives with high smoke-stacks were puffing everywhere; for he was eighty-four years old, and it was the fourteenth year of Queen Victoria's reign, the year of the Great Exhibition, 1851.

However, such remote thoughts worried nobody on April 30, 1808, when several antique Spanish coaches covered with dust trundled into Bayonne, while French troops presented arms and the guns of the citadel fired a royal salute. Out stepped old Charles IV, grey-haired, rheumatic, but regal and confident even in defeat, then María Luisa, looking apprehensive; but both saw among the dignitaries assembled to greet them the 'incomparable Manuel', and they flung themselves into his arms. God was in his heaven—the three of them were together again!

The last act was the handing back of the crown of Spain and the Indies by Ferdinand to his old father, who passed it on, with a courtly gesture, to Napoleon, who took it quickly; for he had already arranged for his brother Joseph to wear it.

Their pensions arranged, which were never fully paid, and their residences settled, the old gilded coaches and a long line of berlins and wagons moved off to the north, taking Charles IV, María Luisa and Godoy into lifelong exile. All indeed except the sombre and disgruntled Ferdinand, who eight years after was to be recalled by his brave, loyal country to reign as Ferdinand VII. But before they departed and the curtain fell upon this solemn farce, it rose immediately upon an epic. A messenger covered with dust galloped into Bayonne with the news that the people of Madrid had risen and were fighting Murat's troops. It was the *Dos de Mayo*. The common people of Madrid suddenly realized that their rulers had been duped. Swarming into the Puerta del Sol and the surrounding streets, armed with iron spikes, knives, pokers, bull-branding irons, and anything they could find, they slew every Frenchman they could see. Murat called out his cavalry and among them were the Mamelukes, whose curved scimitars and turbans, no doubt lighting ancient memories of the Moors, increased the fury of the mob. Goya was there and left his account of it in the Prado. It was the moment when Spanish pride was touched and Spanish hatred roused, and no one, least of all Napoleon, knew how important that moment was to become. The first shots of the Peninsular War had been fired in Madrid, and they were to grow and swell to a great cannonade that ended only on the field of Waterloo.

The 'earthly trinity' continued to live together as true and devoted friends into old age. Little pictures of them in their exile crop up frequently in the memoirs and diaries of the time. We see them as three elderly inseparables under a French or an Italian sky. We hear that the old King enlivened his exile by collecting watches and mending them, and in playing his violin. Baron de Bausset tells how one evening Charles tried to play the Boccherini quintet with four Italians and finished well ahead of them. He came into the room where the Queen and Godoy were listening to the race, wiping his head with a red cotton handkerchief. 'You see, you see, you hear!' he exclaimed.

'They can't follow me. Ah, if I had my 'cellist Dupont with me! He used to follow me. But these Romans can't manage it: it is too much for them.' Regal as ever, music was a matter of precedence and, as he once put it when he was a few bars ahead, 'Kings never wait.'

Godoy used to row with the old Queen on a little lake in the gardens of the Villa Mattei, while the King stood on the bank beaming with pleasure. And once a French nobleman, who visited them when they were living in the Villa Borghese in Rome, was asked by María Luisa if he had ever seen Godoy in his uniform as Prince of the Peace. When he said that he had never had this pleasure, the Queen exclaimed, 'Oh, you must see him in his fine clothes: you will see how they suit him!' 'Yes, yes,' cried the King, delighted with the idea. Uniforms were brought in and the ageing favourite, quite unabashed, solemnly dressed up. 'Walk up and down, Manuel,' said the Queen. 'Yes,' said the King, 'walk up and down.' And Godoy proudly paraded about the room. 'Qu'il est beau!' said the Queen. 'Qu'il est beau!' said the King. 'Mon Dieu, qu'il est beau!' echoed the attendants. And Godoy was then dressed up in turn as Grand Admiral, Generalissimo, and Captain-General, and no one could tell who enjoyed it most, the King, the Queen, or Godoy himself.

When the Queen died only Godoy was with her. The King had gone away on a shooting trip. It was a bitter winter and it was impossible to heat the marble rooms of the Palazzo Barberini, in which they were then living. The icy Tramontana entered the Queen's bedroom and even pierced the damask curtains of the bed upon which she lay dying of pneumonia. Godoy sent hurriedly for the King, and wrote the day she died: 'I have fulfilled the duties of friendship, and she has made her peace with our Redeemer.' The King received news of her death some days later and wrote: 'Friend Manuel, I cannot describe to you how I have survived the terrible blow of the loss of my beloved wife, after fifty-three years of happy married life.' María Luisa was sixty-eight years of age and Godoy was fifty-two, with another thirty-two years of life ahead of him.

He attended the impressive obsequies of his mistress in Santa Maria Maggiore. Twenty-one cardinals were present, for María Luisa was a faithful daughter of the Church and was treated in Rome with all the honours of queenship. Then, strangest of all to relate, her body was taken by orders of the Pope and placed in the vaults of St. Peter's, to await its transfer to the Escorial, surely the only woman who has ever lain among the Pontiffs. How that would have amused her.

§ 5

I crossed a little suspension bridge into Aranjuez, which is a town thirty miles to the south of Madrid, famous for its summer palace, its nightingales, its strawberries and its asparagus. It stands upon the banks of the cloudy Tagus. The river moves beneath an umbrella of elms which, it is believed, Philip II brought from England four centuries ago, and of the mightiest plane trees I have ever seen; there are also oaks and sycamores and miles of gardens, woods and orchards. Castilians who have never travelled believe that Aranjuez is the lushest spot on this planet and a faithful replica of the earthly paradise. It is, in effect, a little corner of France beside the Tagus. Here the Bourbons erected a palace in imitation of Versailles, with grottoes and fountains, with endless avenues and shady places, where it seems that the music of the last *fête champêtre* has only just died away, indeed, one might fancy that footmen are only just packing up the remains of cold partridge, and the musicians putting away their flutes. There is even a costly little imitation of the Petit Trianon in which princesses might play at dairymaids with silver pails.

How delightful it was to have this strange little eighteenth century backwater to myself on that fresh morning. Behind its railings, and among trees and fountains, rose the palace, with its blinds drawn as if the court were sleeping late that morning after a masquerade. The great range of stables stood silent, but it seemed that at any moment the gates might open and the air be full of the hissing and the whistling of grooms, and that coachmen would trundle gilded coaches on to the cobbles. Why do things in Spain never die? What is there in the air of this country that preserves the past not as a mummy but as a living thing? In Aranjuez I had the illusion that it was still 1754 and all the inhabitants were sleeping late or in hiding.

In front of the palace gates I met a little girl of perhaps twelve or thirteen, who wore a huge straw hat and showed her teeth as she smiled. She asked me to buy a punnet of strawberries, which, of course, I did. Goya, who was so cruel to men and women, painted children with love and affection, and this little face with its dark, almost almond-shaped eyes and its ivory teeth might have been painted by him in his gentler moments. When I said how quiet it was, she smiled all over again and replied that it would be *muy ruidoso* when the coaches came in from Madrid. Every day, she said, the tourists came to walk through the palace and to have luncheon by the river. When I said

78

goodbye she tilted her head to one side and gave me a flash of her eyes, and I walked on thinking that medieval children, who were often reigning queens at an age when a modern girl is not yet in the fifth-form hockey team, were probably rather like her.

I walked along avenues of enormous trees whose branches met overhead, down little paths leading into gardens and shrubberies. I came to an old boathouse beside the river, where long ago princes would come to row upon the Tagus with princesses and perhaps to picnic and read Rousseau in some leafy backwater. I came to tall hedges and to fountains standing silent in green shadows. There was no sound but the piping of birds in the branches, and once again I had the feeling that the real inhabitants, the people who had made this place long ago, were playing at hide-and-seek with me and perhaps, turning a corner suddenly, I might hear a burst of laughter and see a flurry of silk petticoats and red-heeled shoes. So at last I came to a little palace standing gravely with a Roman air all by itself in the sunlight. It was called the *Casita del Labrador*.

The word Labrador calls up in the English mind a picture of sleigh dogs straining into a blizzard, or caribou stretching their heads to nibble the frozen birch bark in a sheeted land, but in Spanish it has no topographical significance: it means simply a peasant or labourer. This Peasant's Cottage, so whimsically entitled in the malaise of the period, was built by Charles IV in one of those moments of real fantasy which have enriched the world with some of its most peculiar constructions, and delightfully links Aranjuez with Brighton. Inside, an incredible collection of costly frippery is crowded into what, speaking palatially, is quite a small space. There is a staircase of gilded bronze, marble everywhere, a table of onyx, frescoes, tapestries, enamels, glass chandeliers, little rooms like golden birdcages, clocks everywhere, most of them indifferent specimens, and nowhere to live or even to sit down. What did they do in this place, indeed what could they do but posture in their silk and satin and drink little cups of chocolate or sip sweet champagne? It hardly seems to have been worth it. Only two things interested me. One was an exquisite fresco on a back landing, by Zacharías Velázquez, who painted his charming wife and good-looking family gazing over a balustrade. He did it so realistically that I expected her to smile or wave a hand and for one of the delightful children to come running down the stairs. The other was a travelling chapel, also in an upstairs room at the back. This was an enormous triptych which could be locked up and transported on pack horses or mule back. It was the same sort of altar which our Plantagenet kings took with them from castle to castle, and no doubt the great lords had them too, as they migrated round the country from manor to manor, eating up the produce of their lands. Downstairs is a preposterous cellar painstakingly decorated as a peasant's room, the plaster carefully peeled from the walls and a general air of grinding poverty most expensively achieved. In the sentiment of the time, I suppose the monarch would descend into this squalid apartment from the finicky grandeurs abovestairs and, having eaten a rustic *olla* served to him on bended knees, reflect how much happier he would have been if a peasant. It was fashionable to do that.

It was all absurd, and I was reminded of a weekend I once spent years ago with a wealthy and popular actor, who invited me and some other guests to his 'little place in the country', warning us to come in our oldest clothes. When we arrived, we saw a sumptuous fake Tudor mansion in which each bedroom had its own Hollywood bathroom. While our host was modestly explaining that the house was originally a woodman's cottage, a guest remarked: 'I suppose the poor chap used to wash his axe in my bathroom.'

I walked back to the palace gates, where I saw that the coaches from Madrid had indeed arrived. Aranjuez was no longer asleep. My little rogue with her boxes of strawberries was smiling to a dozen cameras and the waiters stood about gazing speculatively at the day's assembled stomachs. I entered the palace at the tail end of a party. We swarmed up the grand staircase as if we were storming it, and wandered through rooms hung with tapestries, lustres and gold cupids. We gazed at ceilings which could not possibly be admired without a camp bed, and were shown flamboyant clocks, again of the kind which no collector would envy, not a Tompion or Graham in the whole assembly. There was one delightful moment when the guide wound up a musical clock and set it going; then we heard a faint enchanted tinkle go dancing under the painted ceilings, and it was as though an invisible Watteau shepherdess had glided in and was pirouetting round us and hiding behind the satin curtains.

The guide described the riot in Aranjuez which caused Charles IV to abdicate and which brought down Godoy in disaster. The tourists listened intently, anxious to learn something. I left them and went on, for I was hungry and it occurred to me that I ought to get to the restaurant by the river before the crowd arrived. I chose a table on a balcony overlooking the Tagus. I ordered cold asparagus with mayonnaise sauce, a grilled sole, more asparagus, this time hot, with melted butter, and finally those small wild strawberries that grow in the woods. As I drank a white wine of La Rioja, I thought the Tagus looked quite impressive flowing so majestically towards Portugal. A Frenchman at the next table was talking about Godoy. Poor Godoy, cursed with years like the Wandering Jew, lingering alone and impoverished in a Paris lodging, a mystery to his neighbours who thought him to be an old actor—perhaps they were not far wrong. The children in the park loved him and called him 'Monsieur Manuel'. He tasted to the full the bitterness of those who outlive their contemporaries. Even his *Memoirs*, which he thought would shake the world, caused no sensation, for the matters which were so important to him were no longer of interest: they belonged to a dead world. I thought of telling the Frenchman that, if he cared to do so when he was back in Paris, he could seek diligently in that portion of Père Lachaise known as *L'Îlot des Espagnoles*, and there he would come across the humble tomb of the man who once ruled Spain.

In the late afternoon I drove thoughtfully back to Madrid.

# Chapter IV

*By autobus to Toledo—the Cathedral—the notorious Ana Bolena—the tomb of John of Gaunt's daughter—Toledo blades—the Arab invasion of Spain—the Mass of the Mozarabic Rite—Richard Ford*

## § 1

A SPANIARD was standing on my feet and I was holding a small child: in other words the autobus was almost full. In some amazing way more people managed to force themselves in, driving those who were already standing into even closer intimacy. The small brother of the child I was holding had once been standing near me in the aisle, but now he had been swept forward and I could see his mournful little face drowning in a sea of serge.

Sitting in front of me were two nuns who wore immense wimples of starched linen, but they were more architectural than wimples: they were really a survival of those elaborate and laundered headdresses of the Middle Ages, like the *hennin*, or steeple, which towered, slanted and drooped in infinite variety through the fifteenth century, with many a reproach from the pulpit and many a compliment from the troubadour. They were designed not for a small motor-bus but for an ample world of gateways, and I noticed with admiration how skilfully the nuns wore them from force of habit and, like cats, which know the exact width of their whiskers, were aware to a fraction of an inch how much they might move their heads without causing a linen collision above them. It was curious to think that a naughty headdress which was designed as a provoking piece of coquetry should have come to rest at last upon the heads of nuns.

Even the good manners of the Spanish travelling public were shaken, and a few protests were made, as a huge barrel of a man tried to board the 'bus with a basket from which protruded, with an expression of fiery indignation, the head of a cockerel. Holy saints, couldn't he see that there was not even room for a *langostino*? All right, but perhaps— just perhaps, *señores*—there might be room for one more *sardina*! This sally made him popular, and people drew in their breath and crushed even closer as this amusing *hombre* entered with his bird and soon had those at the back of the 'bus laughing at his jokes. How like the Irish the Spaniards can be! At last the 'bus began to vibrate. There were several reports like pistol shots. A girl crossed herself. A box in the roof announced that we were going to hear the *Waltz Emperador,* and, to a gay lilt of Strauss, we took the road to Toledo.

Spain is penetrated to its inmost recesses by motor vehicles which become smaller and more venerable as you leave the main highways. There are first-class coaches which cruise along at sixty miles an hour and there are humbler 'buses, with and without radio, in one of which I was now travelling. Like all things in Spain, the 'bus service recalls an older world. Coach travel must have been like this in the time of Dickens. The objects roped on the roof had the look of luggage in a coaching print, and one's fellow travellers somehow created the atmosphere that one was not a stray bit of matter being transported from here to there, but a member of a band of pilgrims engaged upon the adventure of journeying about the world, with a stock of food which was to be shared, together with opinions on life in general. When the 'bus drew up steaming in a village, there was usually time to get out and smoke a cigarette or visit the local inn.

The mother whose child I was holding was a pretty young woman dressed in black, with a string of Majorcan pearls around her ivory throat. She held her youngest child, I was holding the middle one, and the eldest was, as I have said, standing. They were all boys, she told me, with the smug air of a fulfilled and successful female, then she added, with a little smile for the contrariness of men, that her husband wanted the next to be a girl. I asked if they had a name for this dream child, who, I suspected, was perhaps with us in more than spirit, and she said, yes, they had decided to call her, as so many thousands of Spanish women are called, Pilar, in honour of *Nuestra Señora del Pilar* at Zaragoza. She thought I was an American. It is a sign of the absence of British travellers in Europe that the English are always being mistaken for Americans. She told me that she had a cousin who had emigrated to America and lived in Rio de Janeiro. To her, as to most Spaniards, America meant South America. Her husband was a minor official in the *Ayuntamiento,* the Town Hall, in Madrid, and she was going to Toledo because her old parents, who lived there, wanted to see their grandchildren. I could imagine the kissing and the hugging when *los niños* were greeted, for the gravity of the Spaniard deserts him on these family occasions.

The road to Toledo is not a particularly interesting one. At one point our journey became exciting and dangerous. Our driver decided that it was a point of honour to pass a stubborn small car that held the road in front. He challenged the car with his horn and then the duel began, with feints towards the side of the road, thrusting and withdrawing, the gears roaring and clashing, until, with a final *suerte*, we lurched victoriously past and had a swift, satisfactory glimpse of our opponent crouched over the wheel, apparently motionless, with his foot down on the accelerator.

The 'bus became half empty at Illescas and we could breathe again. Illescas, where white-robed nuns preside over several splendid and pristine El Grecos. I wished there was time—the usual regret of the stranger in Spain—but already the driver was blowing his horn and the passengers, emerging from *ventas*, *posadas* and *caballeros*, were converging on the 'bus.

The brown landscape unwound itself, with a hint of browner hills on the sky. Men rode mules beside the road; in the fields the grain, stacked in small stooks as in Scotland, was being loaded upon the backs of donkeys, and piled upon wagons drawn by black oxen. We would swing into white villages where a tall church towered over the cottages and men in shirt-sleeves would be waiting for us at the 'bus stop. We would throw them a bag, or a mysterious bundle sewn in sacking, and our mission of civilization completed, depart. Women sat on low stools at cottage doors, sewing or making lace, gravely lifting their eyes to watch us on our way.

We stopped at last at the foot of a mighty hill and I got out of the 'bus and glanced up. I saw the city of Toledo sitting in the solemnity of the late afternoon, like an old knight with a sword across his knees. The city rose in tiers, a rising mass of roof tiles from which the towers of churches were lifted against a blue sky. It was like a hill town in Italy, but much starker for no cypresses rose from the terraces. The 'bus appeared to gather itself for the supreme moment of its day and, turning at a Moorish gateway, began to grind up the hill into Toledo.

We came to rest in an ancient plaza where Toledans were sipping coffee and eating ices at cafés beneath an arcade. Happy, happy Spain, where there is always time to sip coffee and where to be busy is not a virtue! In line with us against the pavement were other 'buses, one from Seville, and all with the air of coaches waiting for the ostler to lead out the new team. There, sure enough, were grandpa and grandma in their best black clothes, waving handkerchiefs at the coach windows in an ecstasy of family piety, and when *los niños* descended the old people enveloped their small descendants with cries of delight.

*The Escorial and (below) bedroom of Philip II at the Escorial*

Gate of the Éboli
Palace, Pastrana

The Fountain,
Pastrana

*Nuestra Señora la Blanca,*
*Toledo Cathedral*

*Our Lady of Guadalupe,*
*Extremadura,*
*in procession on her feast day*

*Puente de San Martín*

*A shooting trip (J. F. Lewis leading, R. Ford with striped mantle)*
*By J. F. Lewis, 1833*

*Richard Ford in Majo costume*
*By K. Becquer*

*Richard Ford*
*By J. F. Lewis, 1833*

*By courtesy of Mr. Brinsley Ford*

*The Giralda Tower, Seville*

*Printed in Great Britain*

There was no nonsense about a taxi. The hotel boots shouldere.
bag and led the way across the plaza down a street as thin as a k.
where the balconies almost met overhead. The boy led on and up ov
the cobbles to a hotel in a street as narrow as the rest. Groaning, I
climbed five flights of stairs, but my reward was a room from whose
balcony I could see, beyond the roof of a tenement opposite, a great
brown slice of Toledo, its towers and domes gilded by the setting
sun. Then church bells began to ring, not sweet bells or chiming bells,
but deep-throated, rather angry Catholic bells. A girl in an attic
opposite, with coils of glossy jet hair about her shoulders, drew a curtain, smiled at me and coquettishly drew the curtain back again. I heard
from somewhere below one of Nature's unmistakable sounds, strange,
I thought in Toledo, the cry of a Siamese cat. I found it at last on a
balcony to the left, sitting there sending out its harsh, infantile cry. And
the sound of angry bells continued to boom over Toledo and to flow
in an urgent, vibrating river through the canyons of its streets, saying
clearly: 'Attention, you miserable sinners, remember the Glory of
God!'

§ 2

It was now dark, and I thought I would walk up to the Plaza de
Zocodover for some coffee. I found a table on the edge of the pavement and gazed round at the crowds who were circulating in the
nightly *paseo*. Who would have dreamt that Toledo contained so
many dark, flashing little girls in bright summer frocks, their hair
beautifully done, their feet neatly shod, or so many hatless youths and
young men. They perambulated in twos, threes and fours, the girls
together, the boys together, and here and there I noticed a girl and a
boy who had achieved *novio*hood—a *novio* is a sweetheart—walking
together, not arm in arm—certainly not—but with a modest air of
submission on her part and a manly proprietorship on his.

The whole population of Toledo seemed to be congregated in the
plaza. Now and then a couple of soldiers or a Civil Guard would
mingle with the crowd; or a couple of those furry shovel hats worn by
Spanish priests would come sailing by slowly and majestically like a
couple of sable barges borne along on a sea of glossy hair. It is amusing
to watch Spaniards talking in the street. They are unable to walk along
and talk without looking at each other. They must stop every few
yards and gaze at one another. They must touch a shoulder or gently
tug a lapel. But the important thing is to study the effect of their words

upon another human being. The national sense of drama demands an audience; and they change roles every few minutes.

I decided to stroll down to the cathedral. Only a few yards from the lighted square where all this life was in movement, I found myself in descending tunnels of darkness, eerily lit by lamps in brackets where the streets intersected each other. The light fell in shafts, illuminating a few yards of cobbles where cats throbbing like dynamos were holding their more static but franker *paseo*. High walls of massive stone enclosed me, and the sky above, only slightly lighter than the darkness below, was no more than a couple of fingers wide. The cheerfulness of lighted windows was absent, for these old buildings are turned inward to a courtyard. Indeed, though Toledo may remind one of Damascus or Aleppo, most European towns were like this in the early Middle Ages. It was difficult to believe that behind those massive gates studded with rusty nails, each one like the gate of a prison, lay a bright *patio* with a well in the centre, a relic of the Roman impluvium, with geraniums in flower pots, a few palms, and perhaps even our old friend the aspidistra, which in Toledo severs its last link with Laburnum Avenue.

I had been walking for some time before I realized that I was lost. There was no one from whom I could ask the way. The only thing to do was to go on and keep to the wider streets. There was a man standing just out of the light of a lamp near a murderous-looking alley, and there was something about him and about the smell of the place, and also the way the old houses looked, as if they were pretending to be asleep, that forbade converse; so I went on. But I became aware that this individual was walking behind me, and in that place, and at that time of night, it gave me a creepy feeling which was, of course, absurd. However, I stepped abruptly into a gateway and lit a cigarette while I waited for him to get ahead. I wandered on until I came to a large, dark building with an open gate, where a faint light was burning in a courtyard. I went inside hoping that there might be a nightwatchman, but there was nobody. I saw a bell rope near the door and gave it a gentle tug, unprepared for such a violent reaction, for a deep, angry bell began to clang in the interior. It was then that I noticed that this place was a convent. Beside the door was one of those revolving hatchways upon which letters and groceries can be placed and swung inside without revealing the inmates. It was stupid of me not to have noticed it before. And now I had probably awakened a nunnery.

It was an embarrassing situation. It would have been craven to have tiptoed away like a boy playing a practical joke, and also life teaches us that we should always stay and face our follies. As the minutes passed I hoped against hope that the holy women had not been disturbed, but, alas! I soon heard the sound of slippers approaching along a stone corridor and a grille was shot back. A voice asked who I was and what I wanted. I apologized most humbly for ringing the bell and explained as well as I could that I was a traveller who had lost his way to the cathedral. The invisible nun, having pondered this for a moment and having savoured my Spanish, said in tolerable English: 'You are quite near. Just go round the corner and take the second on the left and then you will see the tower.'

In a little square at the side of the cathedral, and beneath a spreading tree, an old peasant was arranging hundreds of water melons in a green pyramid. He had brought them in from the country and was getting them ready for the morning market. He arranged boards to prevent them from rolling away and then, satisfied that they were safe for the night, he spread a rug on the ground, covered himself with a blanket and curled up in the lamplight to go to sleep. I walked back to the Plaza de Zocodover, where the *paseo* was still in progress. I had a large cold drink and then I went to bed.

§ 3

The roots of Toledo Cathedral descend into the age of poetry, when strange and beautiful things might suddenly happen to anyone. It was the time when, in England, St. Cuthbert was Bishop of Lindisfarne and Caedmon was a monk at Whitby; when a little chapel that became the Minster in the West had just been consecrated near the Thames by Mellitus, the first Bishop of London, and when another small church dedicated to St. Paul had been built on Ludgate Hill and endowed by Ethelbert, King of Kent. In that far-off time in Spain the Roman cities were still intact and the Gothic kings, encrusted with jewels, rode through the sunset of the Eastern Roman Empire dressed like the Emperors of Byzantium.

At this time there stood in Toledo one of those little churches which are still to be found tucked away in the north of Spain, massive, round-arched, arcaded, and covered with the stiff figures of Gothic saints; and the bishop of this church in the year A.D. 666 was St. Ildefonsus, or Ildefonso. They say that one night at Matins, for in those days they

87

sang Matins at midnight, a woman suddenly appeared in the Bishop's place, and it was seen at a glance that the Blessed Virgin had descended from heaven. St. Ildefonsus had just written a powerful treatise to confound those who had questioned the virginity of the Queen of Heaven, and it was assumed that she had come down to earth to bless and reward her champion. Just at the moment when the candles are lighted before the ninth lesson, when the celebrant must put on his vestments, the Virgin rose from her place and invested the Saint with a rich chasuble, telling him that it 'came from the treasury of her Son'.

Those who disbelieve this story have pointed out how often the gods and goddesses of Greece suddenly appeared in the midst of their worshippers and how sometimes they also left gifts of clothing behind them, such as the *peplum* of Minerva and the *cestus* of Venus; which suggests, of course, that the Blessed Virgin was following a well-worn precedent. Those who believe the legend, however, and many do to this day, go to Toledo Cathedral to touch a fenced-in marble column which stands on the place where the high altar of the first church stood thirteen centuries ago. A black hollow has been worn in the marble by millions of believing fingers, and while you stand looking at this stone someone is sure to come along, kneel, touch the marble, cross himself and go off into the vastness of the cathedral. Through all these centuries the memory of the small place on the pavement has never been lost, although the first church was pulled down by the Moors in 712 and a mosque erected in its place; though the mosque was pulled down in 1086 and a church built there, which in its turn was demolished in 1227 to make way for the present cathedral. Before these enormous sweeps of time the mind grows dizzy, and one marvels at the tenacity of Christian memory.

I went to early Mass in the cathedral, where the ancient sacrifice was offered in a side chapel which blazed with gold in the enormous emptiness of this silent church. On another day I went to High Mass. I saw a procession come from the sacristy led by the mace-bearer in a red robe and a tufty white wig, and behind came the cross-bearer, walking between two acolytes, the choir, the canons, walking two by two, then the subdeacon, the deacon, and the celebrant wearing an embroidered cope. The choir and the canons, turning to the right, entered the *coro* and went to their stalls beneath contemporary carvings of the Fall of Granada; the celebrant turned left to the high altar, passing through the exquisite wrought-iron screen made in 1548 by Francisco de Villalpando, a screen once so richly silvered, I was told by a sacristan, that it was painted black to save it from Napoleon's army; and High Mass began.

By a careful calculation the Mass is timed to end just before an agonized creak of the great door indicates that the first group of eager and inquisitive heads from Madrid has been thrust into the darkness. A polite but inexorable official stands near the door to see that women's heads, arms and legs are decently covered. He is known officially as a *Silenciario*, and popularly as an *Azotaperros*, or dog-beater, but more trying than these two functions is the censorship of dress. It happens a score of times every day that a woman is obliged to borrow her husband's coat to cover her arms or to extemporize a church veil from a scarf or handkerchief.

'But what can you do about their legs?' I asked, while exchanging a pinch of snuff with the *Silenciario*. He lifted his shoulders until his neck had vanished, and spread out his hands in the apostolic gesture of prayer, and so stood transfixed for a moment. 'Nothing can be done about legs,' he replied, 'but to prohibit entry to the cathedral.' It is, perhaps, surprising that the worst offenders are not Protestants but French Catholics.

An immense twilight fills these Spanish cathedrals, and in some of them this is deepened into a blackness almost like night. Toledo is one of the brighter cathedrals and at midday is almost as light as York Minster or Westminster Abbey. With its *capilla mayor* at the east end, and something like twenty chapels stretching in an almost unbroken sequence round three sides of the building, each one a complete little church in itself, it is so crowded with carving and with memorials of different periods that it is difficult to know where to look. It is not, I trust, irreverent to think, as I did, that a great medieval cathedral in its heyday, blazing with its double arcade of chapels, was not unlike a celestial market-place whose merchandise was immortality and whose coin was faith. Those familiar only with Gothic cathedrals which have passed through the Reformation and the French Revolution must be astonished when in Spain they come face to face with these intact memorials of the age of faith. Toledo has been enriched by the artists of Europe: French, Flemish, German, Italian, and even English, for I am told that the six superb candlesticks upon the high altar were made in Protestant London during the eighteenth century.

I spent ten minutes every day sitting between the *coro* and the high altar, looking up at the tremendous *retablo*, or altarpiece, which rises in tiers dripping with gilded medieval stalactites, each division of which enshrines a scene from the Passion. These exquisite works, and there are hundreds of them in Spain, in which carvers, painters and gilders have grouped a great number of their contemporary townsfolk into sacred tableaux, are most exhausting to look at; indeed I believe it might be a good thing to be a little short-sighted, when the effect might perhaps be one of rich tapestry. But each little division or scene is such a charming glimpse into the life of the Middle Ages that one sits on enduring much discomfort in puzzling out a form of art which, in trying to interpret a series of related events, was not perfected until the invention of the cinema. In the Middle Ages people who could not read must have gazed at a *retablo* much as we look at an illustrated paper.

Three ancient kings of Spain are buried in the sanctuary as well as the great Cardinal Mendoza, the 'third king' as he was called, of the time of Ferdinand and Isabel. But it is a little difficult to forgive His Eminence for insisting in his will that he should be buried in this place, for to do so the exquisite north wall had to be pulled down and probably an orchestra of angels perished. Half the orchestra fortunately still stands, crowning the pinnacles of the existing south wall, and what a charming orchestra it is! Each angel is a little painted figure about two feet in height, and they all wear white gowns that descend to their angelic toes, their wings are neatly folded, and they are waiting for the tap of some heavenly conductor before they begin to play the flutes and trumpets which they hold to their lips, to clash the cymbals, sweep the harp strings, and thrum an instrument which I like to believe is a *viol da gamba*.

Among the statues of saints and bishops near the high altar is a peculiar intruder; indeed, it hardly seems possible that he should be there at all. He is a Moor, a hated infidel, standing upright among the men of God in one of the most honoured niches in the cathedral. A verger explained him in a fascinating story.

When Alfonso VI accepted the surrender of Toledo in the year 1085, the news went flying round Christendom and men rejoiced to know that the ancient capital of Gothic Spain would once again be a Christian city after a Moorish history of three hundred and seventy years. It had a mixed population of Arabs, Christians and Jews, and to pacify the Arabs, Alfonso entered into a gentleman's agreement with the Moorish potentate, promising that the great mosque would be respected and that Moslems would still be allowed to worship there. Alfonso was almost immediately called away and no sooner was his back turned than a powerful combine, a French queen and a French bishop, cancelled the King's promise. The Queen was Constance, daughter of Robert, Duke of Burgundy, and the Bishop was Bernard, a Frenchman, who became the first Archbishop of Toledo. When the King returned and found soldiers occupying the mosque, he was so angry that he threatened to burn the Bishop at the stake and, so the story goes, might have done so had it not been for the eloquent pleading of the learned *faqíh*, Abû Walîd, who begged successfully for the Bishop's life. The royal anger, however, did not go to the length of restoring the mosque to Islam, and when it was pulled down and Toledo Cathedral erected on its site, a statue of the humane and magnanimous Abû Walîd was placed among the saints; and I imagine he is the only infidel so honoured in the whole of Spain.

Among the many statues of the Blessed Virgin in Toledo, there is one really lovely medieval French statue in marble known as *Nuestra Señora la Blanca*, the White Virgin. She stands, life-sized, crowned, and wearing the dress of a lady of the fourteenth century, holding Jesus in the crook of her left arm while she steadies His small body with her right hand, the fingers spread against His chest; an attitude which any-one who has ever held an infant naturally adopts. The Child places His right hand under His mother's chin and the effect is utterly charming. Always the first Mass of the day is said before this Virgin at her altar in the *coro*. But the most venerated Virgin, indeed the Virgin of Toledo, is not this exquisite White Virgin in the *capilla mayor*, but *La Virgen del Sagrario*, the Virgin of the Sanctuary, who has a chapel all to herself in the north aisle.

She is seen above the altar, clothed in stiff jewelled vestments of old brocade and wearing a domed silver crown; the Child wears a little cope of brocade and a small crown. All you can see of this statue, which is one of the famous miracle-working Virgins of Spain, is the tiny oval of her face, darkened by centuries of incense. I have seen a photograph of the statue without the vestments and it is an extremely archaic work; indeed the Christ, with His short hair, toga and sandals, might almost be Roman.

The *Virgen del Sagrario* is probably the first truly Spanish Virgin, robed and crowned in the traditional manner, which many travellers see, but as they go about Spain they will find others, in cities and towns, and sometimes in village churches, all dressed in the same stiff vestments, which descend outward from the shoulders in a broad cone shape. Every town in Spain likes to believe that its Virgin is the most splen-didly dressed in the country, and it is always with pride that monk or priest pulls out drawer after drawer in a press to show visitors the contents of her wardrobe. In Toledo I listened to a priest who gravely explained to a group of tourists that the mantles of the *Virgen de Sagrario* were the most precious and exquisite in the country, and that nothing so fine existed anywhere else, then he paused a moment, except maybe in the Monastery of Our Lady of Guadalupe, in Extremadura, he concluded regretfully.

'How extraordinary!' I heard an Englishwoman whisper to her companion. 'All these embroidered clothes—for a statue!'

I have noticed that many English Catholics are made vaguely uneasy by the Spanish practice of 'dressing up Our Lady as if She were a doll', but if it is the object of a sacred image to inspire awe and reverence, then I consider the practice wholly justified; for these mysterious Virgins are, I think, among the most impressive and unforgettable sights in Spain. The custom has also the sanction of an incalculable antiquity. The ancient Egyptians not only clothed the statues of their gods, but rouged and painted their faces, and we know that the deities of Greece were decked out with magnificent robes of state: there were even special officials whose task it was to dress the ancient statue of Athena Polias on the Acropolis. The statue of Hera at Samos possessed a large wardrobe of many coloured robes—white, blue, crimson, purple and pied—whose names and colours have been preserved in inscriptions. It should be said too that those queens of Spain who made mantles for statues of the Virgin from their own state robes were also following a custom practised in the ancient world. It is therefore with some truth that one feels, as one looks at these dressed Virgins of Spain, that the stiff Byzantine-looking mantles and the crowns invest them with a timeless atmosphere, and it is not always easy to arrest the mind at the Christian era as it goes rushing down the centuries.

I visited the Treasury with its gold and silver, its El Greco and its Goya, its Gothic chests studded with enormous uncut stones, and I was told, as everyone is, that the large monstrance, which weighs something like twenty-seven stone, was made from the first gold brought from America and given by Columbus to Queen Isabel. What a misleading story this is. Inside the great monstrance is a small one, just large enough to hold a chalice, and this is it which was made of gold whose origin may or may not have been the gold-mines of America; at any rate it came from the Queen's treasury at a time when the first American gold was beginning to pour into Spain. A canon told me how during the Civil War the priceless treasures of the cathedral were taken in the greatest secrecy and hidden away in rock tunnels which extend in a labyrinth beneath the so-called House of El Greco. In that eerie tomb —for one of Toledo's many famous wizards used the tunnels for his experiments in the Middle Ages—the treasures were so well hidden that it is said some still remain underground. The canon mentioned casually that seventy or eighty priests were murdered by the Communists in Toledo.

I went to the upper part of the cloisters and asked an old woman who was knitting in the sun where I could see the Gigantones. She shouted the name 'Amelia!' at the top of her voice, and shortly a jolly-looking woman came round the corner with a bunch of keys. She unlocked the kind of room in which carpenters store stage scenery and I saw, lining the walls, the figures, some of them about twenty feet high, of the giants and giantesses which are carried out at popular church festivals, such as Corpus Christi. The chief characters were Ferdinand and Isabel, crowned and wearing royal robes, and Moors with turbans and carrying enormous scimitars. Some of these figures are beautifully modelled and the bodies are always made of light cane or basket-work, so that they can be carried through the streets by a man standing inside the framework. The old Gog and Magog which perished when the Guildhall was set on fire during the raids on London also had bodies of basket-work, in order that they could 'walk' in a procession, but the new Gog and Magog are made of solid wood. The giants of Toledo have a varied court of *Cabezudos*, or Big-heads, which are huge papier-mâché masks that slip over a man's shoulders. They are generally caricatures of types or people, always brilliantly coloured and often smiling in a rather frightening way; the clothes that go with them are sometimes beautiful suits and dresses of eighteenth century brocade. During the feast the Big-heads go among the crowd and chase them, while some carry bladders with which they whack the girls. What makes these *Cabezudos* infinitely more terrifying than any horrific film is their ghastly semblance of life and their inexorable smiles.

Thousands of these highly inflammable figures must have gone up in flames in many countries during the early days of the Reformation, for Corpus Christi was one of the first Church festivals to be banned by Luther. Here and there one comes across a stray giant in a Protestant country, left over from the Middle Ages and spared probably because its home was the town hall and not the church. I remember a wonderful giant of the heroic type in the old Weigh House in Amsterdam.

Amelia proved to be a talkative and informative guide and she told me the names of the giants and their wives. I asked if she had ever heard of Anne Boleyn. She shook her head. I tried again, but this time I gave it the Spanish pronunciation—Ana Bolena. Oh yes, of course, she knew Ana Bolena! Everybody in Toledo knew Ana Bolena! If I were interested she would show me Ana Bolena at the end of the room. She led the way to a canvas dragon and, sitting upon the back of this creature, was a hideous little doll with tousled hair, dressed in some old piece of flowered material. This was Anne Boleyn. In order to show me how the dragon and Ana Bolena behave in the procession, Amelia stepped under the canvas into the framework. There was a loud creaking sound and the dragon suddenly elongated its neck while a flickering tongue slipped in and out, and at the same time Ana Bolena jigged from side to side on the creature's back. I asked Amelia if she knew who Ana Bolena was. She replied that she had always heard she was a wicked woman who had to ride upon the back of a devilish dragon because she had committed so many great sins. So this memory of the divorce of Catherine of Aragon and the Reformation lingers on in Toledo in the form of this ugly little doll! But Amelia also told me that this was not the original Ana Bolena. The old Ana Bolena had not been ugly, indeed she had a very pretty face, but during one of the processions her head came off and someone, probably a tourist, stole it while it was lying on a shelf waiting to be repaired. Anyhow they could never find it. Poor Ana Bolena had lost her head, and so they found an ugly one from somewhere and stuck it on instead.

Calderón chose Anne Boleyn as the villainess of his play, *La cisma de Inglaterra*, and Spaniards with whom I have discussed the survival of her name in Spain seem to think that in some parts of the country it is still used as a term of abuse for an ill-tempered woman, and one told me that in Puebla de Sanabria in Galicia it is the name given to a witch. But modern Spain has either forgotten such old and painful memories, or it prefers to think of Henry's second wife in her role as a seductive female; for one day, while sitting in a cinema in Madrid, I saw an advertisement flashed on the screen telling women that if they wished to be beautiful they should use 'Ana Bolena' lipsticks and face creams.

§ 4

Until I began to investigate the tombs of Spain I never really grasped what a good claim Philip II had to the English throne. I suppose a

Catholic genealogist at the time of the Armada would have infinitely preferred his blood-relationship with the House of Lancaster to Elizabeth's tenuous Tudor connexion with the House of York; and perhaps had the Armada been invincible we might have heard a great deal about this.

The tomb that provokes this reflection is to be seen in a side chapel of Toledo Cathedral called the *Capilla de los Reyes Nuevos*—the Chapel of the New Kings—a place which is generally locked; but it is well worth while for the English visitor to study its rather capricious times of opening. On each side of the doors stand weeping life-sized heralds in emblazoned tabards. It is not often one sees a herald in tears; they are usually proud and defiant, blowing trumpets and arrogantly issuing challenges. However, these heralds are absolutely heart-broken, frozen in attitudes of sorrow. The chapel is small, and beneath sepulchral arches are four tombs, those of Henry II of Castile, 'the Bastard', and his wife Joan, and their grandson Henry III, 'the Infirm', and his wife Catherine Alencastre, a spelling that may easily put one off the scent; for this is the tomb of Catherine of Lancaster, daughter of John of Gaunt, that son of Edward III, who, though never a king himself, was the ancestor of so many kings and queens.

John of Gaunt's adventures in Spain are an odd and fascinating little chapter in Anglo-Spanish history. They began in the year 1366 when Pedro the Cruel was driven from the throne of Castile by his half-brother Henry of Trastamara. He fled with his daughters to Bordeaux, which was then English, and persuaded the Black Prince to interest his father, Edward III, in his misfortunes. While at Bordeaux the daughters, Constance and Isabel, met the Prince's two brothers, John of Gaunt and Edmund of Langley. All three brothers took part in the English expedition that crossed the Pyrenees and successfully replaced Pedro on the throne. But in two years' time the illegitimate Henry appeared in Spain again, there was a scuffle in a tent, Pedro was stabbed to death, and Constance and Isabel of Castile took refuge with the English.

John of Gaunt, whose first wife, Blanche of Lancaster, was dead, married Constance of Castile, while his brother, Edmund of Langley, married Isabel. In twelve years' time John of Gaunt and Constance took an English army to Spain to claim the throne of Castile, though the expedition ended not in war but in wedding bells. They gave up all claim to the throne upon the marriage of their daughter Catherine to Henry III of Castile. This is the 'Catherine Alencastre' who is buried in Toledo, a woman who, as a little girl, lived in the Savoy and saw the Strand in those days when London was

> *. . . small and white and clean,*
> *The clear Thames bordered by its gardens green.*

She knew Geoffrey Chaucer, who must have taken her on his knee many a time, and she probably had as governess that loyal and much-maligned woman, Catherine Swynford, Chaucer's sister-in-law and her father's mistress. She would have remembered the turmoil of Wat Tyler's rebellion and the sacking of her father's palace in the Strand. She would have been told how brave young Richard of Bordeaux had ridden out to meet Wat Tyler and the rebels, and before she left England she would have seen the young king in his brief happiness with his beloved Anne of Bohemia. Strange thoughts in Toledo Cathedral, where one might be supposed to be thinking only of Alfonsos and Mendozas!

Catherine could not have had a happy life in Spain. Her husband was an invalid, and like so many queens of Spain she was left with an infant heir and lived in terror that he might be taken away from her. But he was not. He became John II of Castile and the father of Spain's greatest queen, Isabel the Catholic. It is interesting to think that Isabel's grandmother was the daughter of John of Gaunt. On her mother's side also Isabel had English blood, for her maternal grandmother was John of Gaunt's other daughter, Philippa, Queen of Portugal.

Important as this marriage was, it is surpassed in interest by that of Pedro the Cruel's younger daughter, the flighty Isabel, with John of Gaunt's brother, Edmund of Langley. They became the ancestors of Edward IV, Edward V, Richard III, and Elizabeth of York, who was eagerly married by Henry VII to bolster up his weak claim to the throne by linking himself with the House of York. So the Spanish blood, fairly thin by this time no doubt, passed to Henry VIII and Elizabeth. Should you feel curious enough to see the tomb in England where Edmund of Langley lies beside the daughter of Pedro the Cruel, all you have to do is to go to the parish church of All Saints at King's Langley, in Hertfordshire; and there you will find them. As you stand there you may reflect, as I have done, on the strange chain of events and the interwoven lives which link Hertfordshire with the dynastic wars of Castile.

§ 5

You often hear an insistent tapping in the streets of Toledo, and if you follow the sound you come to a workshop where a man in a leather apron is standing at a forge with a pair of tongs. He draws out a red-hot sword blade and carries it to an anvil where a companion begins to hammer it. This tapping of swords is a sound which has been heard in Toledo since Roman times.

One afternoon the sound led me to the city wall, where steps rose to a little house and a garden full of marigolds and geraniums. Next door was the sword factory of Vicente Martín Bermejo, who happened to be at home and was delighted to hear that I wanted to see how swords are made. He took me first to a small room where buyers are shown the products of the workshop, from swords to nail-scissors, all made and damascened on the premises. There were modern military swords, rapiers, presentation swords, antique swords for tourists, who actually buy them and somehow manage to introduce them into their respective countries, and, of course, the bull-fighter's *estoque*, a sword whose hilt is bound with red tape and whose blade tapers for the last four inches into a downward curve.

To show me how finely tempered are Toledo blades, Señor Bermejo bent one into a circle until the point touched the hilt. These fine blades, he said, were made of Bilbao steel. This is what Falstaff meant in the *Merry Wives of Windsor* when he compared himself bent double in the buck-basket to 'a good bilbo, in the circumference of a peck, hilt to point, heel to head', for that was how Toledo swords were often exported in the old days, and evidently how Shakespeare had seen them. The poet Martial, who was a Spaniard born at Bilbilis in Aragon, now a Roman site near Calatayud, knew something of sword-making, which was one of the industries of his birthplace. He tells us in one of his epigrams that in his day the smiths took the sword blades hissing from the forge and plunged them into the ice-cold waters of the Jalon. This is probably the origin of Shakespeare's line 'a sword of Spain, the icebrook's temper', spoken by Othello, who kept such a weapon in his bedchamber. Martial refers again to the tempering qualities of Jalon water in that descriptive epigram addressed to his fellow Spaniard, Licinianus, in which he recalls the scenes of his youth and the happy countryside of Roman Spain.

We passed through a door and found ourselves in the forge, where piles of good 'bilbos' were lying in bundles like sticks against the wall,

97

ready to be made red-hot. With exquisite skill the sword-makers neatly nipped the red blades from the fire, giving me the impression that they could have tossed them in the air and have caught them with their tongs as they came down. I was not surprised to be told that sword-making is an hereditary occupation in Toledo and goes back in families as long as memory can tell. Catching up these red-hot blades, the sword-makers carried them to anvils where they began to hammer at them with a series of blows measured by instinct. They know how hard to hit a blade, just as they can judge from the colour of the red-hot metal the right moment to withdraw it from the forge. They talk about the Tagus just as Martial wrote about the Jalon. They say it is the Tagus water that gives the Toledo blade its superb flexibility, but you know perfectly well that what made the Toledo sword the best weapon of its kind was a superb tradition of craftmanship, which goes back beyond even the oldest Gothic church in Spain and was an ancient craft when the Romans built the theatre at Mérida. I have no doubt in my own mind that if you could substitute a few gallons of the Thames for the Tagus, the blades would be just as good! The easiest way to temper a sword is in oil, but that is not the right way or the old way. Hot steel and cold water is the recipe, and that is the way they do things still in Toledo. They make swords for the slaying of bulls, for the American souvenir hunter, and for members of the Diplomatic Corps when in evening dress, as if they were making them for the Cid.

In another room we came upon rows of young women and girls damascening scissors, paper knives, cuff-links, tie-pins, and the dozens of other objects which the steel trade of Toledo now makes for tourists, for after all men must live. This art of damascening, which I dislike, came to Toledo with the Moors in 711, and it seems to me strange that it should have survived. What we see today is the art in its cheapest and most debased form. A pattern is cut in the metal and a black pigment rubbed over it so that the pattern stands out against the black. The real damascening, which was so highly valued in the Middle Ages, was the beating into metal of gold and silver wire.

A curious sidelight on the conservatism of Spanish sword-makers is given by Don Pascual de Gayangos in his notes to Al-Makkari's history. It is that at Albacete, in the Province of Murcia, several manufacturers of scissors, daggers and knives had retained the Moorish decorations exactly, perhaps believing them to be purely ornamental. He saw a knife in London which bore on one side of the blade the words in Arabic, 'I shall certainly kill the enemies with the help of God', and on the reverse, 'Fábrica de Navajas de Antonio González, Albacete, 1705'.

As I said goodbye to Señor Bermejo, I saw that an expensive American limousine had miraculously managed to find its way there through the narrow streets, and was surrounded by a crowd of people. They had come to gaze with adoration at a sallow, over-dressed young man with raven hair plastered down upon his head and rudimentary side-whiskers against his brown cheeks. He stepped from the car and languidly acknowledged the gasp of awe with a slight nod, then slowly ascended the steps of the sword factory. He was, I was told, a famous *matador*.

## § 6

The wall which still partly encircles Toledo is a medieval wall, but it contains Roman stones, Gothic stones and Moorish stones, so that it is really a visible epitome of the city's history. I thought, as I walked beside a stretch of it one blistering hot afternoon, that it exactly matches in colour the temples, churches and castles of Syria. Baalbec has the same golden glow, tawny as the desert, and so has Kala'at Sim'ân, the church where St. Simeon sat upon his pillar, and also the great crusading castle, the Krak des Chevaliers. Toledo's wall is still strong and arrogant wherever it exists, and I saw many a section from which a bowman could loose his shaft and dodge back behind the machicolation. My path led down to the Tagus, which casts a brown arm round Toledo on all sides save the north. Here on the south-west it passes through a dramatic gorge which has been bridged by a slender path of golden stone, the Puente de San Martín, whose arches curve gracefully to the water a hundred feet beneath.

As I stood on this bridge, I saw the pink shapes of naked boys below, plopping like frogs into the Tagus every now and then from boulders, while envious younger children watched them from above and listened to their shouting and splashing. On the far side of the bridge the land rose in hot brown ridges, and there was a row of white cottages running parallel with the river. At a similar bridge El Greco painted his view of Toledo, now in the Metropolitan Museum, New York, a strangely green Toledo to my eyes, for in June everything was burnt brown, and a cloudy Toledo too. The storm which El Greco painted was obviously the work of an enchanter and in this eerie light the city stands out whitely, the abode of saints and wizards.

At chairs and tables outside one of the cottages sat a merry group of Sancho Panzas playing some gambling game with the metal caps of mineral water bottles. I found a vacant table and was given a jug of white wine for which I was charged only five pesetas. Sitting in the shade, I gazed at the city climbing its hill in every shade of brown culminating in the proud ruins of the Alcázar, where during the Civil War a Christian soldier defied the Communists though he knew the price was the life of his son, who was a hostage in enemy hands; at the pinnacles of St. John of the Kings, whose walls are hung with fetters struck from the limbs of Christian slaves; at the slender bridge itself, whose legend is the first story the visitor hears in Toledo. It is a story of wifely loyalty and ingenuity, and they say that before the bridge was finished the architect fell ill and confessed to his wife that he had miscalculated the stress on the arches and consequently feared that when the scaffolding was removed the structure would collapse into the gorge, taking his reputation with it. His wife told him not to worry and that everything would turn out well. One night, perhaps under cover of an El Greco storm, she stole out and set the timbers alight and the bridge crashed down, as it was believed by accident. The architect then revised his arithmetic and the re-built bridge soon became the pride of Toledo. At this point the wife's conscience pricked her and she confessed her sin to Archbishop Tenerio; but the primate, instead of condemning her, congratulated the husband on the loyalty and resourcefulness of his wife.

There is another story about a mass of masonry near the river and not far from the bridge. Here an exquisite maiden named Florinda used to bathe during the reign of the last of the Gothic kings, Roderick. Her father was Count Julian, the Governor of Ceuta, on the opposite shores of Africa, and she had been sent, as the custom was, to be educated in the Queen's household. One day the King, surprising her at her bath, took her by force, and the girl in her distress sent messengers begging her father to come to her. Julian arrived, but gave the King no hint that he intended to be revenged. As he took Florinda and prepared to depart, the King asked that a particular breed of hawk might be sent to him from Africa, and Julian agreed affably, saying that he would send hawks such as the King never dreamt of. Back in Ceuta he plotted a raid on Spain with the Arab governor of Africa, holding out the bait which no Arab has ever been able to resist, easy plunder. Under the command of the Arab general Tarik, the promised 'hawks' arrived in Spain in 711 and Roderick, like Harold at Hastings, fell in battle and was never seen again. And in this romantic way, says legend, began those eight centuries of Arab and Moorish civilization which are Spain's unique experience in Europe. It is the event which distinguishes her early history from that of other European countries; it has placed a dark, enduring gleam in the eyes of her women and has given that plaintive eastern undercurrent to her music; among many other things it has possibly planted that streak of cruelty in Spanish hearts which is regularly sated on Sunday afternoons.

Few scholars now believe the story of Florinda and King Roderick. It is true, however, that Roderick's conduct in usurping the crown led a section of the Visigothic aristocracy to invite the Arabs to come over as allies and drive him from the throne. It was assumed that when this was accomplished the Arabs would return to Africa, well paid by loot. The Visigoths were rough Teutonic warriors, proud of their long hair and addicted to massive jewellery studded with gems as big as boiled sweets, and, like the Anglo-Saxons, they preferred the country to the town. They formed an alien aristocracy that mixed little with the Romanized Spaniards, but lived on its fortified farms and estates. The bulk of the population continued to live in the Roman towns and walk the pavements as Spaniards have been doing ever since, though one imagines that Roman Spain must have been rather knocked about by that time. A great authority has said that it existed in a state of intellectual squalor, for 'hardly anyone could read or write; there were no materials for doing so. Parchment was too expensive, slate too difficult to manage, and the supply of papyrus had stopped when the Moslems conquered Egypt in 639.'

Nevertheless, shocking as Visigothic Spain might have seemed to Martial and Seneca, who remembered a civilized age, the old legend of golden Spain, the rich province, still existed, and there was at any rate sufficient brilliance about it to arouse the liveliest expectations in the minds of the Arab invaders, as the talk given to the troops on the eve of their venture seems to show.

'You must know,' said the Arab general, 'how the Grecian maidens, as handsome as houris, their necks glittering with innumerable pearls and jewels, their bodies clothed with tunics of costly silks and sprinkled with gold, are awaiting your arrival, reclining on soft couches in the sumptuous palaces of crowned lords and princes. . . . You know that the great lords of the island are willing to make you their sons and brethren by marriage.'

Far from bearing the light of a superior civilization into Spain, as many people may have been led to believe, the Moslems were evidently awed at the thought of setting foot in a wealthy and luxurious country. The reference to the Spaniards as 'Grecians' shows that the Arabs grouped the inhabitants of Spain with the Byzantine Greeks whose luxurious cities had filled their ancestors with amazement when they set out upon their career of conquest and plunder.

The same note of awe is repeated in the account of the great battle which settled the destiny of Spain, in the course of which Roderick, the last Visigoth king, disappeared and no one knew what had happened to him. 'The Moslems', wrote Ibn el Athir, 'found his white horse, which was mired in a slough, with its saddle of gilded buckskin adorned with rubies and emeralds. They found also his mantle of cloth of gold, adorned with pearls and rubies. . . .' Not far off they found one of his shoes, of cloth of silver. The care with which these costly details are enumerated seems to me to prove that, apart from the usual Semitic love for such inventories, the Arabs were acutely aware that they, whose ancestors had lived in tents of goat-hair, had entered a world of undreamed of richness. So Visigothic Spain ended with a king who had vanished no man knew where, a jewelled saddle, a gold mantle and a silver shoe, and a riderless horse on the edge of a marsh.

At the time of the Arab invasion the Omayyad dynasty was in power, with its capital at Damascus, and there the Caliph held his court. I have often heard people talk about a caliph as if it were an ordinary title interchangeable with that of sultan. But there can be, in theory, only one caliph at a time, the head of Islam, the descendant of the Prophet, although in practice there have often been several, with rival claims, as there have been rival popes. It was under the rule of this mighty potentate that Spain now fell, and the Arab generals had to report to the Caliph at Damascus and to set aside for him a fifth part of all the plunder. One is reminded of the Spanish conquest of Mexico and Peru where the same procedure was followed, for Cortés and Pizarro were always careful to set aside 'the royal fifth' of all the looted gold for Charles V before they shared out what remained. Cortés, too, was in the habit of reporting to the monarch in Spain, just as the Arab emirs did to the Caliph at Damascus.

The Arab generals were dependent upon Damascus for something like forty-five years until, in a terrible upheaval, the Omayyads were overthrown by the Abbasids and the seat of the Caliphate was moved from Damascus to Bagdad. This is the famous dynasty which produced Hârûn-al-Rashîd, who is known to most people from the *Arabian*

*Nights.* The Abbasids slew every member of the Omayyad family except one, a young man named 'Abd-ar-Raḥmân, who escaped and, after many romantic adventures, decided to risk crossing into Spain in the hope that some there might still be loyal to his fallen dynasty. He was fortunate. He found supporters and overthrew the reigning emir in a battle in which it is said he rode the only serviceable horse and, as a banner, used an unwound green turban tied to the head of a spear. Then, as Emir of Córdoba, he naturally had no intention of paying allegiance to the Abbasid murderers of his kinsmen, and Moslem Spain became an independent country for the first time. The only attempt of the Abbasids to bring 'Abd-ar-Raḥmân to order was defeated by him and, having decapitated the rebels, he packed their heads in salt and camphor and sent them in boxes to the Caliph of Bagdad. He was succeeded by six independent emirs in the course of thirty years, then the greatest of his descendants, 'Abd-ar-Raḥmân III, proclaimed himself Caliph by virtue of his Omayyad blood, and Moslem Spain became known as the Caliphate of Córdoba. This was the time of its greatest grandeur, for upon the structure of Roman Spain, which the Arabs had inherited, was superimposed the brilliant civilization of the Byzantine and the Moslem East. This was the golden age of Islam. The Caliphs lived in the greatest splendour, guarded by five hundred lancers of their bodyguard. They were clothed in robes of brocade with their names and titles woven in gold upon them, and they lived in palaces and gardens which seem to have brought the Bagdad of the *Arabian Nights* into Spain. Every ship that docked in Seville brought them something new, an artist, a poet, a box of manuscripts, a learned man from Bagdad, a group of singers, exquisite Coptic embroideries from Egypt, a gold fountain from Constantinople; indeed European pilgrims who saw Córdoba at that time thought it was the wonder of the world —'the pearl of the universe'.

But no matter how brilliant the Arab world looked in Spain or elsewhere, it was always rotten with schism and feuds, and it might truly be said of the Arab as it is so often said of an individual that he was his own worst enemy. The brilliant period of the Córdoban Caliphate lasted only a little over a century, then crashed in the usual violent and contentious confusion. There was never another Caliph in Spain. Instead there were sultans of Córdoba, of two different dynasties, whose rule ended in 1225. When Ferdinand III captured the city he found it a mere shadow of the once splendid capital of the Caliphs. The Moslem power then shifted to Granada, where for two hundred and fifty years or so a long line of sultans followed each other until their final defeat by Ferdinand and Isabel in 1492.

So the stranger in Spain will possibly find it easier to understand Moorish Spain if he thinks of it as an occupation that went through four phases: approximately forty-five years as a Moslem colony; a hundred and thirty years as an independent emirate; a hundred years as a Caliphate; and two hundred and fifty years as a greatly shrunken territory ruled by minor kings or sultans.

Against the story of the Moslem Goliath we must put that of the Christian David. There was a time when the resistance movement was reduced to a few warriors in a cave. Then with their first success the movement grew, the Christian kingdoms developed in the north— Asturias, León, Navarre, Aragon and the counties of Barcelona and Castile—ruled by kings and nobles who often spoke Arabic, wore turbans, and married Moslem women: but no matter how often they fraternized, they had at the back of them the Church, a law and language derived from Rome, and the fellowship of Europe. Internal dissensions, almost as bad as those which helped to deliver the enemy into their hands, prevented the Christians from wiping out an isolated and self-indulgent pocket of Islam centuries before they actually did so.

The Arabs in Spain seem to have been the most agreeable and tolerant conquerors. It is true they could be violent and cruel, especially to one another; that they could decorate their terraces with flowers planted in the skulls of their enemies and could command the muezzin to call to prayer from a 'minaret' of piled corpses, as they did at León; but they never systematically tried to stamp out Christianity or to force Christians to wear humiliating and distinctive clothes, or forbid church bells and crosses, as they did in other parts of the world. They even allowed their Christian foes to dig up the bones of saints which lay in their territory.

The Arabs, who had brought no women with them, found the Spanish ladies to be all they had hoped for; and history, so far as I know, does not tell of one woman who jumped out of a window rather than marry an Arab or a Moor. An example which was rapidly followed was that of the first emir, 'Abdu'l-Azîz, who married Egilona, the widow of King Roderick. She is said to have rebuked her husband for the lack of respect shown to him, for all Moslems were equal under the law. 'Why,' she asked, 'do not thy subjects bow down to thee, as the Goths used to do before my late husband, King Roderick?' The emir replied, 'Because such practices are contrary to our religion.' But the lady was persistent, and in order to satisfy her without making any change in procedure, he had a very small door cut opposite his throne, so that his callers had to bend down before they could approach him.

In a few generations those sultans whose harems were well stocked with Galicians had produced a race of fair-haired and blue-eyed Arabs, and it is said that some of these fair Moslems were so sensitive about their appearance that they were in the habit of dyeing their skins brown. Naturally the Arab rulers were frequently influenced by a Christian wife or a concubine A beautiful Basque named Aurora dominated the Caliph Hakam II and continued to control affairs after his death with the help of a great warrior, al-Mansûr. A strong aroma of the *Arabian Nights* pervades the story of the King of Seville, al-Mu'tamid, who fell in love with a young woman named Romaiquia: Arab annalists say that they remained devoted to each other all their lives and when a palace revolution led to the downfall of al-Mu'tamid, she accompanied him into exile. Some believe that she was a Christian slave girl, and that the King first saw her one evening when he was strolling with a friend beside the Guadalquivir during the evening *paseo*, composing verses about the river, each capping the other. Romaiquia, who was passing in the crowds, overheard them and is said to have joined in so cleverly that she attracted the young prince's attention, which led to her purchase and her arrival at the palace as a royal concubine and, eventually, wife. Al-Mu'tamid took the greatest pleasure in ministering to her caprices, and the pretty story is told that one winter, when snow had fallen upon the plain of Córdoba, Romaiquia was so delighted that she made her husband promise it should fall every year. In order to keep his word, he is said to have planted the plain with almond trees. Another story, which is perhaps more likely to please Arab minds than ours, is that Romaiquia once saw some women with milk pails walking up to their ankles in mud, and returned to the palace demanding that she and her girls should also be allowed to do this. The indulgent al-Mu'tamid ordered a courtyard of the palace to be strewn ankle-deep in a paste made of ambergris, musk and camphor dissolved in rose-water, then he let loose Romaiquia and her girls in it, equipped with milk pails slung on ropes of the finest silk!

Arab life, with its luxury and its polygamy, had powerful attractions for many Christians. The early kings and queens of Spain wore garments woven on Moslem looms, and they did not object to borders edged with Arabic slogans. In a bilingual country, as Spain became, Arabic literature was widely read by Christians, and even the national hero, the Cid, often wore Arab dress and sang Arab songs. There is an amusing story of a tough Norman count who went to Spain to fight the Infidel and was discovered to be missing after the taking of Babastro in 1064. He was found at length in an Arab house, which he had appropriated, lounging on a divan dressed in Arab robes, surrounded by singing girls. Jewel boxes were lying open, the furniture was draped with costly silks and brocades, and the Count was having the time of his life in surroundings which no one in Normandy could have imagined!

The Reconquest of Spain was not a simple black and white struggle between stern-faced crusaders rallying round the Cross and eternally vigilant adherents of the Prophet. Most of the time both sides rubbed along pleasantly together and there were many exchanges of courtesy; but when war did break out it was carried on with the utmost vigour and no holds barred. In the early days, and into the time of the Caliphate, the Moslems carried out spring and autumn manoeuvres in the north, ruining the crops in the spring and the harvest in the autumn, raiding towns and monasteries, then returning to their own territory. This gave the Christians a breathing time for recovery, and both sides settled down until the next raid. War, in the sense of a crusade, or a united effort, had to wait until the young Christian kingdoms had healed their internal disputes and were ready to fight side by side.

In this strange country the Jews, who had been an important part of the Spanish nation since the Temple was destroyed by Titus in A.D. 80, were generally valued and trusted by the Arabs. The most interesting people were the Spaniards in occupied Spain who remained true to their faith. They were called Mozarabes, or would-be Arabs, and the Moslems refrained from persecuting them, for the poll-tax was one of the principal sources of revenue. These Christians, sealed up as it were in occupied Spain and untouched by outside influences, observed a ritual that to those of the north, who had come under Cluniac and other French influences, seemed almost heresy; and it was not without a great struggle that they were at last persuaded to discard their liturgy. The Mozarabic Mass is one of the greatest liturgical curiosities of the Western Church and there is still one church in Spain in which it is said every morning, less maybe as a curiosity than as a link with those Christians who observed it in the far-off days of emir and caliph. The church is Toledo Cathedral.

## § 7

I went to the chapel in the cathedral, where at nine-thirty every morning the Mozarabic Mass is celebrated. A small acolyte in a red surplice rather too large for him was standing at the door, looking angelic, as all these little Murillo-like boys do in Spain, until, suddenly lifting his robe to the waist, he ran rapidly inside the chapel, exposing a pair of patched trousers. The only other attendants were five young French priests who told me they were studying ancient liturgies and had come to Spain just to see the Mozarabic rite. To French people it had a peculiar interest, they told me, for it is the sister rite to the Gallican liturgy, which was abolished in France by Charlemagne eleven centuries ago in favour of the Roman rite. When Charlemagne's grandson, Charles the Bald, wished to see for himself the ancient rite of his ancestors, he sent to Toledo for priests to celebrate the Mozarabic Mass in his presence. This was the extraordinary relic of Western Christianity we had come to see.

We filed into a chapel which was large and dark and looked vaguely neglected. It is used only for the Mozarabic Mass for an hour or so every morning and is then locked up. We found that those who attend the Mass take their seats on benches round the walls within a few feet of the altar steps, while the choir is behind them on the other side of an iron grille. I thought it was an uncomfortably exposed position for one who, like myself, had no idea when to kneel or stand and I determined to keep an eye on the French priests, but they turned out to be as ignorant as myself.

A server came in, prepared the altar and lit the candles. The priest entered, carrying the veiled chalice and the paten, and there began a long interchange of prayer and response between the priest and the choir at the back, which reminded me of interminable Eastern liturgies. The priest then placed wine and water in the chalice and blessed them before beginning what corresponded to the Introit of the Roman Mass. The Gloria was the same as in Latin, but the resemblance soon faded and there were more long prayers. The priest then offered the chalice and, after more prayers, washed his hands, and the Mass of the Faithful began. Then the Diptychs were read, which have been shortened in the Roman Mass to a single prayer, but these, as in the Eastern Church, continued at great length, mentioning by name innumerable saints, martyrs and archbishops of Toledo. I caught such names as Saturninus and Raimundo, which took the mind back to Roman and Visigothic days. Another primitive custom which we saw as the Mass proceeded was the giving of the Pax before the Preface, as in remote times and as in some of the oriental churches today. The Canon began with the words which come almost at the beginning of the Roman Mass, 'And I will go to the altar of God, to God, the joy of my youth,' and passed to a prayer that corresponded to the Preface of the Roman Mass. The words of consecration were the same as in the Roman Mass, but the priest broke the Host in a completely oriental way into nine small fragments, seven of which he laid out on the paten in the form of a cross, with two over, which he placed under the right arm of the Cross. So this ancient ritual moved to its close.

It was primitive and beautiful, but very long. To the monks of Cluny, who encountered it when Alfonso VI captured Toledo from the Moors in 1085, it must have seemed more like the Byzantine liturgy than anything in the West, and one can understand their anxiety to bring the Spanish Church into line with Rome. On the other hand, how well one can also understand the passionate love of the Mozarabes for the rite which they had faithfully observed for centuries while under foreign occupation. The story goes that they would not consent to a change until the Roman and Mozarabic rites had been tested, first by combat between two champions appointed to represent them, and then by trial by fire; and it is said that on both occasions the Mozarabic rite was victorious. The Roman rite had to be imposed by royal authority.

The French priests were as fascinated as I had been. In return for their information I was able to tell them something—and I think the most remarkable thing I know about the Mozarabic missal—that they did not know. It is that the Mozarabic rite lives again in the English *Book of Common Prayer*. It seems that when our prayer book was being compiled Cardinal Ximenes had just published the Mozarabic liturgy, and a copy is believed to have come into the hands of Cranmer, who was impressed by the beauty of the prayers. Many of these he, or his collaborators, lifted bodily from the Mozarabic rite into the Prayer Book. The exhortations beginning 'Dearly beloved brethren, the scripture moveth us . . .' are pure Mozarabic, while innumerable collects are straight translations of the Mozarabic or are adapted from them, notably the collects for Christmas Day, for the first Sunday in Lent, and for St. Andrew's Day. The French priests were astonished, and brought out their notebooks as I described how this primitive and perhaps even apostolic liturgy has, by the strangest destiny, lived again

108

in a Protestant prayer book and has become a part of the mental and literary heritage of the English people.

§ 8

I paid a last visit to the cathedral, to the *Burial of Count Orgaz* in the church of Santo Tomé, to the cafés in the plaza, and, having bought a damascened paper-knife, caught a train back to Madrid. Among the letters and parcels which had assembled there for me was a copy of Richard Ford's *Gatherings from Spain*, for which I had sent to London, having the fancy to read it on the spot. In spite of Ford's habit of writing as if he were a splenetic old gentleman, I found it a perfect bedside book in Spain.

The name of Richard Ford crops up sooner or later in every modern book about Spain, and he is quoted as having said something wise, witty or caustic about subjects as far apart as Spanish church architecture and the use of garlic in salads. Who, the reader may ask, was this pontifical Ford and how did he become an unquestioned authority on Spain? He lived in that delightful age when a thousand pounds a year was wealth and two thousand pounds a fortune. In 1830, when Richard Ford was thirty-four, the doctor ordered his pretty wife, Harriet Capel, daughter of the Earl of Essex, to winter abroad. Ford was that glory of the nineteenth century in England, an educated amateur who had no need to earn his living. His father, Sir Richard Ford, was at one time chief police magistrate at Bow Street and was the creator of London's mounted police.

Spain was 'in the air' in 1830 when Mrs. Ford was advised to seek a warmer climate. The Peninsular War was a recent memory, Washington Irving's *Conquest of Granada* had just been published, and Ford was friendly with Wellington, Washington Irving, and also with Henry Unwin Addington, who was then British Minister at Madrid. It was with the advice and encouragement of these friends that he set off for Spain in the autumn of 1830 with his wife, three children and three maidservants.

For the next three years Spain was his home. He lived in hired houses and for a time, as Irving had done, in romantic quarters in the Alhambra at Granada. When he could leave his family he went off on long excursions, mounted upon a fine-looking Cordobesan pony, sometimes alone, or with such friends as the artist, J. F. Lewis, who stayed with the Fords while he was painting his *Sketches of the Alhambra*.

There is not an aspect of Spanish life which this affluent and scholarly dilettante did not explore. And speaking Spanish, as he soon learnt to do, dressed in Spanish costume, ready always to talk to a duke or to bed down on straw with muleteers or bandits, he learnt more about Spain from personal observation and experience than any foreigner has ever done. How Ford managed to acquire so much knowledge and cover so much territory in only three years will always be something of a mystery.

He returned to England and lived at Heavitree House, Exeter, a house which has just been pulled down. He terraced the gardens in the Spanish fashion, making a Moorish tower and planting cypresses and other trees which he ordered from Spain. The corner of his bathroom had once adorned the Casa Sánchez in the Alhambra. One day when dining with John Murray, the publisher, he was asked to recommend someone who could write one of Murray's handbooks on Spain, and replied, half jokingly, that he would do it himself. He was taken at his word and for five years this task, which he optimistically believed he could complete in six months, became the pleasure and the bane of his life. One of his friends has described how Ford was to be seen working away at the *Handbook* in a garden house at Heavitree, dressed in a Spanish sheepskin coat and surrounded by a huge library of Spanish books, by pigeon-holes crammed with notes, and with piles of manuscript on all the chairs and upon the floor. He complained loudly of the slavery to which he had condemned himself; and how well we can imagine his complaints! He had a superb gift of invective.

But the pain of composition was merely the beginning. No sooner had the first edition of the *Handbook for Spain* been printed than Addington, becoming alarmed by its discursiveness and its outspoken comment—the two great charms of Ford's writing—managed to persuade his friend to cancel the edition. Only twenty copies are believed to exist and these are, of course, great rarities. Ford sat down to rewrite and re-shape the book, and at length produced the first revised edition. He was such a perfect traveller that he seems to have conveyed this quality to his manuscript, for when it was complete—it filled a large portmanteau—it was lost in a London railway station and was next heard of in the north of Scotland! When the book was printed it was a success, and indeed could not fail to be so, for Ford's acute and pungent personality was in every word of it. It is a surprising work to find disguised as one of Murray's guide-books, and no great book has ever made a more prosaic-looking bow to the public. The *Handbook* made Ford's reputation and it was soon followed by *Gatherings from Spain*, which contained a lot of the suppressed first edition.

Ford's fame as a writer has obscured his skill with brush and pencil. About five hundred of his best works are now treasured by Mr. Brinsley Ford, his great-grandson, and with the passage of time these now have an added interest as a glimpse of Spain in 1830. Several portraits of Ford exist and all show him to have been a notably handsome man. One of the best is a sketch by J. F. Lewis which reveals him in perhaps a soulful moment, Byronically collared, his regular features clean-shaven except for the then fashionable soft side-whiskers, seen at their best in all pictures of nineteenth century divines. A delightful water-colour by J. Becquer shows Ford wearing a tall sugarloaf hat, an Andalusian jacket, a sash, and breeches sewn with buttons all the way down the seams; still he looks a typical Englishman.

All his contemporaries speak of Ford's charm as a companion, and he was welcome everywhere in literary London. He advised and helped George Borrow—strange that two such writers on Spain should have stepped on each other's heels—and greatly admired *The Bible in Spain*. Among his many enthusiasms was the art of cookery and he shone as brightly in the kitchen as in the dining-room. Sometimes he would arrive at a friend's house to cook a Spanish meal with a couple of bottles of wine in his pocket and the right ingredients for a salad in a bag. It was he who introduced two fine things into England: Amontillado sherry and Montranches hams, whose fat when properly boiled he compared to 'melted topazes'.

Ford was married three times, and Thackeray used to say that he could always remember the number of his house, 123 Park Street, by the number of his wives. He died at the age of sixty-two, leaving to his descendants a great number of treasures and personal relics. Mr. Brinsley Ford tells me that he owns 653 letters written to friends by his great-grandfather, of which only a small selection, those written to Addington, were published some years ago. Ford's passports, of which a complete series exists, prove how widely he travelled as a young man before he visited Spain. Only two of the famous notebooks from which the *Handbook* was written survived a fire which Ford made of them shortly before his death.

His caustic wit and his readiness to lash out at anything he disliked, particularly the French, have made some believe that he did not really care for Spain, but that is to misread him completely. He loved Spain as an artist and a scholar, but he hated misery, indolence and mis-government, all of which he frequently encountered, and when he did so he wrote down exactly what he felt. It is not often that the spirit of a country takes possession of a foreigner and seems to speak with his voice, and this the always fascinating but sometimes unhappy Spain of the eighteen-thirties did through the mind of Richard Ford.

# Chapter V

*A visit to Our Lady of Guadalupe—a man in a silk hat—Extremadura
—memories of Cortés and Pizarro—Roman Mérida—Jane Dormer*

## § I

THE unfenced rocky land stretched away on both sides, dotted with patches of stubble where some peasant had managed to grow a little wheat in a pocket of subsoil. The air had that Grecian quality which reminded Plutarch of spun silk, and far ahead the white road ran on to meet the Castilian sky. It seemed to me all of a sudden that this road was the whole of Spain. The man on the mule with a wide hat shading his face represented all the Spaniards who had ever been born, and the woman standing at the door of the white cabin, who exchanged a word with him as he rode past, all the women. I had the feeling that I had been there before and had seen the man on the mule and the woman at that particular place, then the flash of recognition passed and there was nothing but the white road running on to meet the sky. It is strange how, because of some trick of light or maybe the mood one is in, the spirit of a country appears to alight on some ordinary scene as softly as a bird and as briefly, and is up and away again before one can grasp it.

There was the tall tower of a brown church in the distance, and as I drew nearer a great bell outlined against the blue sky. There were mud walls, old streets winding up to the church, a sudden noiseless rush of black goats shaking their beards like a group of lecturers, a girl filling a brown jug at a decayed fountain, an old priest in a dusty soutane, and two mules standing under an archway with wooden saddles on their backs. Then the white road going on again across the plain.

Upon the outskirts of Talavera de la Reina I stopped to look at a church and a bull-ring standing side by side. Inside the church was an old man who turned at the door, genuflected to the Sacrament, then rose and dipped his finger in holy water. He told me, nodding towards the bull-ring, that the great Joselito had been killed there in the 'twenties. He had been there and had seen it. His old eyes searched my face to make sure I appreciated the terrible tragedy of which he had been an eye-witness, probably the greatest of all his memories. I found myself thinking that he had had his money's worth that day. There had been only one Joselito and to see Death stretch out a bony hand on a sunny Sunday afternoon must have been a stupendous experience. No Spaniard could ever forget it.

On the other side of the road, upon a wide space of level ground, I saw a sight which must have been ancient when the Pyramids were built. It was a threshing-floor of the sort seen on the wall paintings in the Theban tombs and described in the Old Testament and in Homer. Several farmers had brought the produce of their fields to the floor and the corn was stacked round about ready to be threshed. This was done by threshing sledges moving slowly round on a circular path, driven by boys and men who stood upright, leaning slightly backward as they grasped the reins. The sledges were pulled by mules and as they described their slow circles, crushing out the grain and cutting the straw into chaff, the drivers seen through a cloud of dust had the appearance of charioteers. In Spain, as in the Old Testament, these threshing-floors are well-known places and are used every year at harvest time, indeed they probably have local names that are as familiar in the countryside as the threshing-floor of Ornan the Jebusite, where the Lord halted a pestilence. I was shown one of the sledges, which resembled in every detail the primitive agricultural implement called in *Job* a 'threshing wain'. It was simply a heavy board whose underside was studded with flints or with iron teeth. 'Behold I will make thee a new sharp threshing instrument having teeth,' we read in *Isaiah*, 'thou shalt thresh the mountains, and beat them small, and shalt make the hills as chaff.' This Biblical instrument was known as a *morag*; in Spain they call it a *trillo*. I asked an old fellow whether they ever used a *trillo* with rollers fitted to it, but I have an idea he could not understand me. He replied that they used them in Extremadura, but he may have been trying to please me. It would not, however, be surprising if such a Roman province still used the Roman *tribulum*, which is the Latin name for an improved version on rollers of the more primitive threshing sledge. I was glad to have seen such a Homeric spectacle, for who knows how soon it may be before the *trillo* is replaced by those tall, vibrating towers which devour a harvest like starving giants.

I stopped at a garage to buy some petrol. A man covered in grease emerged from a repair shop and worked a hand pump. His appearance spoke of the horrors of decarbonization and of an unending struggle with the entrails of antique engines. Garages in Spain have not yet been streamlined, and petrol is sold not by persons in spotless overalls but by any mechanic who happens at the moment not to be lying on his back under a dying car. I asked the man the way to the monastery of Our Lady of Guadalupe, and he pointed a sable forefinger and told me to go through Oropesa to Navalmoral de la Mata and then turn left along a dirt road across the mountains, which, he said, was really quite good in the summer-time. He said he would like an American cigarette and so I placed one between his lips, and he gave me the smile of a Christy Minstrel as I drove away.

More white road, with the Sierra Gredos on the right, led me to Oropesa. I glanced up at a hill where I saw a chapter of Malory firmly seated upon the summit, walls, towers, ramparts and gates, apparently complete. This was the old castle of the Dukes of Frias and is now a *parador* managed by the State Tourist Department. I was tempted to go there, but I was afraid of getting stuck on the long mountain road to Guadalupe and so went on, consoling myself with the thought that the castle was probably full of earnest Germans with Leicas.

I soon crossed from Castile into Extremadura, that ancient district which was once part of Roman Lusitania. This province, with its long tradition of poverty and agricultural collapse after the Moors were driven out, is the land that produced the crews of Columbus, and the conquistadores, a land whose impoverished inhabitants were only too glad to exchange their native surroundings for the golden dream of the Indies.

I turned south on the dirt road and for the next hour or two found myself faced by an unending series of zigzags and blind corners. The landscape was dotted with olive and cork trees and every inch that could grow was cultivated. From the high mountain road I looked out over a superb panorama of hills leaning together and folded one upon the other, the bunchy little olive trees sometimes climbing precipitous slopes and each one standing in a pool of its own shadow. The switchback was fantastic. With true Spanish politeness the radiator boiled most considerately opposite a thin jet of water which flowed down to the road through the rock. The landscape spoke of the hand of man, yet hardly a human habitation was visible. Enormous distances must have to be trekked on mule and donkey to reap the small handkerchiefs of golden wheat and olives, and here again the words 'made by hand' could have been printed on the well-kept countryside.

The Virgin of Guadalupe to whose shrine I was going is the presiding deity of Extremadura, a Virgin of tremendous intercessionary potency at the Throne of God. She has a unique place among the hundreds of Spanish Madonnas as the first Spanish Virgin whose name occurs in the history of the New World. Years before Cortés and Pizarro sailed the seas, Columbus himself named the island of Guadeloupe in her honour, a sure proof, if any were needed, that his seamen came from Extremadura. When he arrived in Spain after his first voyage, Columbus himself came to her shrine with a wax candle weighing five pounds to give thanks for delivery from the terrible tempest which nearly wrecked his frail caravel on the homeward voyage. He tells the story himself in his *Journal*, under the date February 14, 1493. They were some distance from the Azores as it proved, though they did not really know where they were. The waves broke over the ship, the wind increased, and Columbus resigned the vessel to the storm. All night they ran before the wind and with the rising sun both the wind and the fury of the waves appeared to increase. At this moment, when death seemed to be the inevitable end to all their adventures, Columbus called the crew together and ordered that a pilgrimage should be vowed to Our Lady of Guadalupe and that if they escaped the storm some member of the crew, chosen by lot, would take with him to the shrine of Our Lady a wax candle five pounds in weight. He commanded that chickpeas should be brought, one for every member of the crew and one pea to be marked with a knife in the form of a cross. This was done, and in the midst of the hurricane the peas were placed in a cap and well shaken. The first to put in his hand was Columbus and he drew out the marked pea, 'and from that moment he regarded himself as a pilgrim and as bound to go to fulfil the vow'. The vow was made on a Thursday and the storm continued to drive the ship all that day and for two more days, until after dark on the evening of Saturday they reached an island they were unable to identify, which turned out to be Santa María in the Azores.

It became the custom to apportion part of the spoil of the Americas to Our Lady of Guadalupe. Her name was spread by Cortés and his *Extremeños* all over Mexico, and from Mexico all over South America. When Cortés returned from his conquests he went to Guadalupe and prayed at the Virgin's shrine for nine days. Don John of Austria also went there to return thanks for the victory of Lepanto and he dedicated to Our Lady of Guadalupe some of the relics of the battle.

My first glimpse of Guadalupe was from a hilltop where, glancing down, I saw on the slopes of a hill what looked like a fortified castle with a village grouped about it. The countryside was dotted with olive trees which marched almost up to the walls of the monastery. The size of the building surprised me, for it was almost as startling as it would be to come upon St. Paul's Cathedral in open country. I was reminded of St. Catherine's Monastery in Sinai, and of the monasteries of the Wadi Natrûn in Egypt, for though Guadalupe is much later in date, it was clearly built with the same eye to defence.

In half an hour I was standing in a tiny plaza in the heart of a completely medieval village. A melon-shaped fountain spouted four jets of water into a circular basin where girls were filling water-pots and a few yards away an impressive flight of steps led to the church of Our Lady of Guadalupe. Above a medieval gateway were iron balconies and the doors of living-rooms, for the church was submerged by the monastery buildings which had impinged upon it in every direction. Hawks had their nests among the turrets and the air was filled with their hovering and sudden gliding.

§ 2

I rang the bell at the door of the monastery, but nothing happened. I lifted a heavy knocker and the reverberations echoed down a stone passage. I rang again and eventually heard the approach of sandals. Bolts were shot, keys turned, and a middle-aged Franciscan was standing there. He seemed to be in a great hurry and kept glancing over his shoulder. Could I stay in the monastery? *Si, si*, I could certainly stay, he said impatiently, casting another swift glance down the passage, but first I must put the car in the garage, which was the first gate to the left round the corner, then I must return. He listened, glanced over his shoulder again, and shut the door. I wondered what on earth was agitating him.

The garage was unforgettable. It was a disused Renaissance church with the dust and débris of at least two centuries thick upon it. I drove the car through the west door and parked it under the arch of the north aisle. The pavement had been taken up, the altar had been removed and in its place had been erected a stage! Who, I wondered, could have performed plays in this remote spot. I returned to the monastery and pulled the bell-rope. The same Franciscan shot the bolts and opened the door. He invited me to step inside and to place my suitcase in the passage; then, with the same hunted expression, he darted away, promising to return in a *momentito*, that delicious word which means a 'little moment'. However, the *momentito* became a full-grown moment and then five minutes, and I was becoming impatient. I was standing in a stone passage which opened on my left into a hall where a flight of steps led upward, I assumed to the church. I walked forward to investigate and nearly collided with a young man in morning-dress, with a white carnation in his buttonhole and a silk hat in one hand, who, without a glance at me, darted up the steps two at a time and vanished. I watched him with memories of *Alice in Wonderland*, thinking that now Guadalupe had no further surprises for me; but I was wrong. There was a room opposite the steps and, hearing the sound of voices, I tiptoed forward and looked inside. A young woman was sitting there in her wedding-dress, holding a bouquet of white flowers tied with satin ribbon. Her muslin veil was thrown back and a number of fashionably dressed women with painted finger-nails were fussing round her. One glance told me that they belonged to the upper circles of Madrid. So this was the cause of the excitement! I had evidently arrived after a nuptial mass.

Beyond the room where the bride was sitting was a small courtyard with a palm tree growing in a corner. Here male members of the wedding-party, their silk hats on chairs beside them, were drinking a jug of monastery wine. One of them, glancing round furtively to make sure he was unobserved by the guest father, drew a flask from his pocket and poured something a little stronger into a glass. He was only just in time for at that moment Padre Jerónimo Bonilla, no longer flustered, came up and asked me to follow him. He led the way up a flight of wooden stairs and I followed, carrying my bag. There were bamboo tables on the landings, covered with pious little embroidered mats edged with red pom-poms, surely the gift of some reverent sisters, and up we went until we came to a long gallery with doors opening to the left. He paused at one and led the way into an immense bare room with four beds in it. I wondered whom my companions were to be. One of the beds was modestly placed in a wall recess curtained with a strip of quite sumptuous brocade which looked good enough for a minor feast day. The floor boards were scrubbed white, there were washstands and basins, a hat rack, an unflattering oleograph of the Blessed Virgin, and a little wrought-iron balcony which looked down over the purple roof tiles of Guadalupe.

Padre Bonilla told me the rules, and said rather sternly that the gates were locked at ten. I asked him about the wedding, and he replied that it was a great privilege to be married in the Church of Our Lady of

Guadalupe. People came from Madrid and from all parts of the country, but especially from Madrid and the cities and towns of Extremadura, to be married here. The couple I had seen were *Madrileños*. They had arrived the previous afternoon and had spent the night in the monastery. They had made their confession, had gone to Mass, and were now married. They were returning to Madrid that evening. He remarked that it was now half-past three and that I could get some luncheon in the little room near the courtyard. The usual guest dining-room was occupied by the wedding-party.

I washed and stood for a moment on my balcony watching the hawks wheeling and gliding, then went down to the little room. An old peasant woman gave me a jug of sharp red wine, eggs *flamenco*, a pungent stew of beans with garlic sausage and meat swimming in olive oil, and a plate of cherries. I smoked a cigarette under the palm tree and then thought I would ask the way to the church; but there was no one about. The monastery was wrapped in the profoundest silence. Even the old peasant woman had vanished. I explored stone passages like tunnels and by the purest chance found my way to the church through the sacristy.

It is one of the dark Spanish churches and looks smaller than it really is because of the immense *coro* occupying the centre of the building, like a church within a church. When my eyes became accustomed to the gloom I saw Our Lady of Guadalupe above the high altar, wearing her silver crown and a cope of gleaming brocade. Steps led into the *coro* and I sat there for a time, looking at the enormous hymnals on huge revolving lecterns. I became aware that someone had entered the church. Glancing towards the high altar I saw two figures, a man and a woman, kneeling on the altar steps. The woman rose, and, ascending the steps rather timidly, genuflected to the Sacrament and placed upon the altar a bouquet of flowers tied with ribbon. Then she knelt and prayed a moment before rejoining her husband. Bride and bridegroom then rose and silently left the church. They had no idea that anyone had witnessed that touching and beautiful beginning of their life together; and I found myself praying that the snares and delusions which sometimes haunt the holy state of matrimony would not trip or hurt them; and that they might always look at each other as they did at the moment when they rose up from the altar steps of St. Mary of Guadalupe.

## § 3

The village of Guadalupe is a medieval community in working order. Nobody has ever tried to improve it or plan it, or tell the inhabitants how much happier they would be with hot and cold water laid on, indoor sanitation, electricity and radio. Consequently the people appear cheerful and contented. Hens, chickens and small dark pigs live on terms of friendship with the cottagers and they too seem contented. Most of the houses have balconies of wood or iron and some of them are covered with Morning Glory and scarlet geraniums; some have projecting upper stories; and as many of the streets are only a few yards wide and twist up and down hills, the effect could not be more picturesque. In the evening women and girls bring chairs to the cottage doors and sit sewing together or making lace on circular frames; and as they sit they tell stories and gossip, missing nothing that goes on around them. It is a delightful sight to see an old grey head and a glossy young one bent over the same piece of work, and sometimes four feminine generations are assembled in these chattering groups.

In one of the streets I came upon some women and girls who were erecting a little shrine outside a house. They had decorated it with sheaves of corn and were trying to make the cheapest kind of celluloid dolls look like angels. They had sewn beautiful little garments for them and had cut out wings and haloes. Everything was perfect except the expression of the fat celluloid faces, which were hardly saintly. A little arbour had been made with boughs of trees, and wildflowers had been placed in jugs and bottles. I asked what this was for and an old woman told me it was the Eve of St. John; and then I remembered that it was the twenty-third of June.

The old woman, seeing my interest (and she had indeed set a dozen bells ringing in my memory), invited me to attend the *fiesta*; and when I did not at first understand she ran out like an aged maenad and performed a few dance steps, saying to me, '*Música . . . música . . .*', while she held imaginary pipes to her lips. '*Flauta . . . flauta!*' she said, still playing the pipes with one hand and beating an invisible drum with the other. 'Thrub-thrub-thrub,' she cried, imitating the drum. She was a wonderful old woman, who would have been the life and soul of any party: but learning that the *fiesta* did not begin until eleven o'clock, and remembering Padre Bonilla's stern warning about the locking of the gate, I said with genuine regret that I could not accept her invitation. It would have been a wonderful thing to have seen this survival of the rites of St. John's Eve, and I wondered if I could possibly escape from the monastery.

Dinner was served in the refectory of the guest-house, the padre at the head of the table. It was a long room hung with the delightful pottery made at Talavera, plates and dishes charmingly coloured and decorated with animals and flowers, glazed thickly like Byzantine or Arab pottery. There was a beautiful little seated figure of Our Lady of Guadalupe, and I promised myself that if ever I passed through Talavera again, I would go to the factory and buy one. There were six other guests, a sombre French couple, three elderly Spaniards who were on pilgrimage, and a talkative and amusing young man who, finding the French couple and myself a poor audience, addressed himself exclusively to the padre. His stories must have been good, for the padre, who began dinner looking like a Zurbarán, ended looking rather like Friar Tuck, rocking with laughter. We had vermicelli soup, lamb cutlets, followed by a dish of cherries, and we drank the same local red wine I had had for lunch. I thought it was excellent, but the French couple turned up their noses at it and drowned it in water.

I was thinking all the time of the pagan festival slightly converted to Christianity which was to take place in the village, and the more I thought of it the more pagan it seemed and the more difficult to ask leave of absence. It was, of course, Midsummer's Eve (Old Style), the night that bonfires were once lit all over Europe; the night when maidens saw the faces of their future husbands; the night that watchers at a church door would see those who were to die in the next twelve months approach and knock; the night cattle were protected against witches; and the night—I believe I heard this once in Ireland—that the souls of sleeping people left their bodies and sped off to that spot on land or sea where they would one day perish. I felt that a whole chapter from *The Golden Bough* was to be enacted in the village that night—and I should be locked up in the monastery!

Dinner ended, the padre plied a toothpick with true Spanish zeal and lapsed into melancholy. I knew that I should not have the courage to ask him to leave the door unlocked. We said good-night and I found myself alone in my large room, with a choice of four beds. It was a warm night and I took a chair out to the balcony and looked at the stars. The village lay below in a dense pattern of roof tiles. I could hear the water splashing into the fountain in the plaza. Bats were flickering round my balcony. Candlelight shone in a few windows; sometimes a dog barked. A man crossing the plaza shouted good-night to a friend, and then silence descended upon the village. How strange it was to hear no mechanical noises, no car cranking up, no wireless, no gramophone, nothing but this glorious silence and the beauty of the northern constellations burning in the night. Suddenly a quick thread of fire shot up into the darkness and a rocket exploded above Guadalupe. There was another and another, all from the direction of the little shrine. Midsummer's Eve had begun. I thought of the peasants with their sheaves of wheat and their boughs of greenery who were celebrating a rite older than Christianity, and I longed to be able to go and see what was happening. I smiled to think of the old maenad who had pretended to play the pipes and had promised me *música* as if I had been a priest of Pan. I wish I could say that I made a rope of sheets from the four beds and descended the steep walls of the monastery, as better men have done on occasions sacred and profane; but the church had me in its safe keeping and after a moment of regret I turned away from the starlight and went to bed. I chose the one nearest to the window and was soon asleep.

I was awakened by a noise and glanced at my watch. It was three o'clock. All the dogs were barking. I went to the balcony and saw Guadalupe lying in a wash of moonlight. Every roof tile was clearly visible. Then I heard the sharp notes of a pipe, the sound that must have awakened me, a quick running up and down the scale, loud and strong, the voice of the pagan world. It sounded again nearer, as into the moonlight of the plaza walked the piper. He had a drum slung round his neck and as he walked he brought the pipe to his lips and sent a few notes into the moonlight, just to keep him company on his way home.

§ 4

The story of the discovery of the statue of the Virgin of Guadalupe is not unusual. She was buried during the Arab invasion and discovered centuries afterwards, as other statues were discovered in various parts of Spain. They say that during the time of Alfonso the Wise—the thirteenth century—some herdsemn were watching their cattle near Alia, when a cow belonging to a herdsman from Cáceres was found to be missing. He sought her for three days in vain and then decided to seek her where the monastery now stands. There he found the dead body of the cow.

He drew out his knife and began to skin the animal. As customary

in Extremadura, he made the first incision on the chest in the form
of a cross, but no sooner had he done so than, to his fright and bewilderment, the animal rose up and was alive and well. As he was transfixed in amazement, he saw the Blessed Virgin standing there and
she spoke to him. 'Do not be afraid,' she said, 'I am the Mother of
the Saviour.' After telling him to take the cow back to Cáceres, she
commanded him to bid the priest come and dig at the spot where
the cow had been lying, for there, concealed in the earth, was an
image of her. She said that the image when discovered must remain
where it had been found, for in time to come it would be a sanctuary
upon which she would shed grace and mercy. Then she vanished.

The cowherd returned to Cáceres, where he found his wife in great
sorrow. One of their sons was lying dead. The man, with many tears
and deep devotion, prayed to the Virgin to give back his son's life as
she had given life to the cow and it would be a sign that would enable
him more easily to perform the task she had set him. He arranged for
the boy to be buried near the place of the apparition, but as the priests
were preparing for the burial the boy awakened, as if from sleep, and
asked his father to show him where Our Lady had appeared. The
priests were immediately convinced by this miracle and began to
dig at the spot indicated by the herdsman, and there, in an ancient
tomb, they discovered the statue of Our Lady of Guadalupe.

At first a humble little shrine was erected over the statue, but its fame
spread all over the land and countless pilgrims came to worship from
far and near. Among those who visited the shrine was Alfonso XI, and
he ordered that a monastery and a church should be built on the spot
and made the necessary grants of land. He came again in triumph in
1340, after his victory over the Infidel at Salado, bringing with him a
part of the spoils and trophies to be dedicated at the shrine. So began the
royal connexion with Guadalupe which continued throughout history.

In the few days I was at the monastery I was able to see this famous
statue as near as it is possible to approach her. The figure is carved of
wood, but is so concealed by vestments that I could only see the
almost black oval of her face and one beautifully carved hand, which
holds a sceptre. She is about three feet in height, and one assumes,
because of the clothes that cover her, that she is standing. But this
is not so; she is seated and holds the Child Jesus on her left arm. She
wore a jewelled skirt beneath a cone-shaped vestment stiff with pearls
and diamonds, which concealed her feet in the traditional Spanish
manner. Her headdress was composed of two rows of huge pearls

attached to a frame of golden roses and diamonds made from a seven-teenth-century necklace which had belonged to the Countess de la Roca. Archaeologists who have seen the statue without its vestments say that it may be Roman, and some believe that it may have been a gift from Pope Gregory the Great to Archbishop Leander of Seville in the sixth century.

The Virgin is enthroned at a considerable height above the high altar; and at the back is a superb baroque hall in jasper, marble, walnut and cypress wood, where the statue can be withdrawn from her throne for a procession or to be dressed in other vestments. This apartment, called the *camarín*, was a typical baroque reconstruction, and when it was designed in the seventeenth century an opening was made in the wall above the altar and a rich little box, or throne-room, with a glass door, fitted for the Virgin so that she could be removed from the church into the *camarín*. In many churches this sumptuous little apartment is the Virgin's dressing-room, where she is clothed for festivals.

The *camarín* at Guadalupe is obviously associated with the robing of the Virgin, for a door leads from it into her jewel-room. This is furnished with chairs, tables and cabinets, all of the seventeenth cen-tury, and the walls are lined with crimson silk. Here is to be seen an amazing collection of jewels and crowns, headdresses and all kinds of valuable objects given at various times to the Virgin. And indeed this preoccupation with her wardrobe, and the amount of jewellery that can be hung about her, must strike some as odd and others as an interesting link with remote antiquity. It is a curious form of piety, indeed it fascinates me and I could watch monks for hours as they lovingly withdraw shelves from presses and point out the beauty of the oddly shaped garments, with an expert eye for embroidery and needlework. The monk who displayed the Virgin's wardrobe at Guada-lupe was one of these enthusiasts, and it was strange to see him in his rough habit and sandals fingering the brocades with almost sensuous enjoyment, and telling me which dress the Holy Virgin wore for Corpus Christi and which on other great feast days. The most spectacu-lar and valuable dresses have names. There is a superb piece of em-broidery known as 'the One from the Infanta', which was sent from Flanders by the daughter of Philip II, Doña Clara Eugenia, in 1629; another is called 'the First of the Community', and a third 'the Rich Robe of the Community', both embroidered and sewn with thousands of pearls by monks in the eighteenth century. What a strange occupation for men who had turned their faces from womankind to sit year after year making these rich and flashing gala dresses for the Queen of Heaven. The monk drew my attention to the coats-of-arms in enamel and gold, with diamonds and pearls in the centre of each crest, which form the border of one robe, and to the great cape sewn with thousands of pearls in such a way that from every direction they spell the words 'Ave Maria'.

'There is nothing richer in the whole world,' whispered the monk as he closed the press.

I was taken through a long gallery where hundreds of vestments and altar frontals were displayed in glass cases. I saw one labelled 'Frontal of the Queen of England, sent to the monastery in 1621'. This was rather puzzling, for James I was then king and there was no Queen of England, Anne of Denmark having died in 1619. May the gift not have taken some years to reach Guadalupe and be an interesting proof of Anne's long flirtation with Rome?

I was taken to the library which contains, I was told, the best collection of choir books in Spain; and indeed here one could study Spanish illumination from the fifteenth century to the eighteenth, in books beautifully bound and in perfect condition. Among the greatest treasures of Guadalupe are the eight pictures by Zurbarán, illustrating the life of St. Jerome, which line the long wall of the sacristy. Hanging above the altar is a Turkish lantern. It is the stern lantern from the flagship of Ali Pasha and was given to Our Lady of Guadalupe by Don John of Austria after the battle of Lepanto.

§ 5

I was looking forward to Extremadura, for I had been reading Prescott again for the first time since I was a boy, and I was anxious to see the countryside which had produced Cortés and Pizarro. Padre Bonilla shook hands with me and told me to be sure and return some day. I drove my car out of the nave of the derelict church as if I were one of Cromwell's troopers, and took the road to Trujillo.

I found myself in a countryside greener and less austere than that of Castile, but lonelier and also poorer, for the villages were far apart and the corn was desperately thin. There were bare miles strewn with gigantic boulders, and, alternating with glades of oak and cork trees, a few acres of wheat or barley were tilted against the hillside. There were pigs everywhere, small and active, rather the colour of blue-black ink.

They were running about the villages on terms of friendship with the inhabitants; they were rooting beneath the oak trees; and industriously roaming the hills in charge of small boys who held long sticks in their hands. My eyes swept the landscape from granite hill-top to gentle valley, and I thought how astonished the men from this part of Spain must have been to find themselves in jungles where the trees were laced together with lianas, where humming-birds were poised above hibiscus flowers and macaws flashed and screamed among the branches. I thought too that the discovery and conquest of South America, particularly of Mexico and Peru, is perhaps the world's best adventure story. I doubt very much whether a space ship to the Moon would give Mankind quite the thrill of hearing, as the fifteenth century did, that the world known until that moment was only half of this planet; and that beyond the Western Ocean lay another hemisphere, new lands, new men, new flowers, new fruits and animals and, even more startling, great cities whose limestone walls shone like plates of silver as the conquistadores, climbing up through green forests, gazed at them in awe and wonder. It is not easy for us to imagine how in those days marvels were piled one on top of another, and, as I say, I do not believe it would be quite as wonderful if some day we are told what it is like to stand upon the rim of Tycho, or how deep the dust lies on the Mare Imbrium.

What an odd accident it was that this new world should have been offered to Spain the moment her long contest with the Moors was over, that men whose forebears had been trained in the Moorish wars should have crossed the Atlantic, and, with the same old battle-cry, '*Santiago y cierra España!*', should have spurred their horses *á la gineta* at the Aztecs and the Incas, and have besieged the lake city of Tenochtitlán as their fathers had so recently besieged Granada. Only twenty-nine years separated the fall of Granada from the fall of Tenochtitlán, or Mexico City.

I was delighted to find that *The Conquest of Mexico* and the companion book on Peru were as readable as I had found them when I was a schoolboy. It is astonishing that this massive output was the work of a man who was almost blind. Prescott's life is one of the most heroic in the story of authorship. He was born in Salem, Massachusetts, in 1796, and was well off and well connected. When he was at Harvard a rag took place in the Commons Hall in the course of which he was struck in the left eye by a piece of stale bread. He lost the sight of this eye and was threatened all his life with the loss of the other. Many a man of means would have become an invalid; Prescott not only triumphed over his defect, but actually turned it to advantage. His partial blindness trained him in mental discipline and gave him a remarkable memory; perhaps it also strengthened the pictorial quality of his writing, for his descriptions of the strange civilizations of the Aztecs and the Incas, and the scenes in which the Spanish conquerors found themselves, are full of light and colour. One of his secretaries has left an account of him at work in a darkened library fitted with screens, which had to be adjusted with almost every cloud that passed across the sky. He wrote on a now obsolete instrument called a noctograph, designed for the blind, which was a frame with lines traced in wires on which words were written with a stylus on carbon paper. How a man so handicapped, who had to use other people's eyes, who had to have his authorities read to him, and in a foreign language, who worked in America, far from the European sources of his works, how such a man could have slowly and painfully marshalled such an enormous mass of historical detail is a shining example of courage and genius. When he was writing *The Conquest of Mexico* he was limited by his failing sight to one hour's work a day with his remaining eye, and this hour was divided into two widely separated periods of thirty minutes. How did he find the strength and the courage to plod on at this snail's pace, year after year, book after book? He answered this himself in his diary, where he wrote: 'After all, regular composition of a great historic work is the best recipe for happiness—for me.' And all the time he strengthened his spirit as he fought his body. 'If I could only have some use of eyes!' he wrote in 1848. In the following month he wrote: 'I use my eyes ten minutes at a time, for an hour a day. So I snail it along.' The next year he wrote: 'I must make my brains—somehow or other —save my eyes.' And so it was all his life. It must have been balm to him when the critics said that he had missed nothing. This great American died at the age of sixty-three, with sixteen weighty volumes to his name, having done more with half an eye than most historians have done with two.

If Prescott has a fault it is, I think, that he idealizes the civilization of the Aztecs and the Incas so that many a reader must have put down his books with the feeling that the conquistadores were evil men, and that the civilization destroyed was a relic of the Golden Age and finer than the Christianity which replaced it. While there are admittedly moments when the unhappy Montezuma appears to have been the only Christ-like character in the story, and while it is difficult for us to understand how Cortés could piously attend Mass and then put a whole village to the sword, the fact remains that the Aztecs, in spite of the exotic and superficial splendour of their civilization, were really a race of barbarous cannibals. No matter what we may think of the conquistadores themselves, the missionaries who accompanied them were men of the highest and most noble principles; and Spain has the right to be proud of them.

Bernal Díaz del Castillo, that tough old soldier, and one of Prescott's most-quoted authorities, was the author of one of the grandest books of adventure ever written. It is the story of the conquest of Mexico as seen by one of the men who followed Cortés in the wars and at the end could write: 'In this beautiful voyage of discovery we had spent our all, and returned to Cuba covered with wounds, and as poor as beggars.' They were poor; they were wounded; but it had been a 'beautiful voyage of discovery'!

Díaz was born in the small town of Medina del Campo, between Valladolid and Salamanca, the town where Isabel la Católica died in the castle, which may still be seen, and he went out to the Indies when he was a young man. He was still young when he joined the expedition to Mexico, but his name would never have been known had he not in old age been stung into what Fitzmaurice Kelly has called 'a first-rate example of military indignation' by the publication of a history of the conquest of Mexico. By that time only five of the original conquistadores were alive, and Díaz, anxious that the deeds of his old comrades, and also his own, should not be forgotten, sat down on his farm in Guatemala to tell the true story—*historia verdadera*—as he saw it happen. He had an excellent memory. He even recollected the names and colours of the eighteen horses with which they started out and whose appearance terrified the natives, who had never seen a horse before. He remembered the nicknames of his comrades and wrote of them: 'We lived like brothers. . . . I remember all of them so well that I could paint all their faces if I knew how to draw.'

His most interesting description is that of Hernán Cortés himself, the greatest of all the conquistadores, a man who had some magic of leadership and also incredible luck, whose very name inspired his followers; a man who with a handful of fellow-adventurers plunged into unknown jungles and brought an ancient civilization down in ruins. He reminds one of Hannibal, of Alexander, of Ulysses, with a touch of Cromwell and Bill Sikes. (And also of Don Quixote, but then he exists to some extent in all Spaniards.)

Cortés came from Medellín, near the Roman Mérida, in Extremadura, and was the son of an impoverished *hidalgo*. Landing in the Indies at the age of nineteen, he became a colonial administrator. He was thirty-three when Díaz met him in Cuba, and he was, we are told, 'a devil among the women'. But by that time he had met his match in a husband-hunting mother, and Cortés soon found himself firmly saddled with a pretty and charming young wife, who, he was heard to declare in the first flush of his defeat, might have been a duchess. Her name was Catalina Xuárez and she appears only once again in history, when she followed her husband to Mexico to enjoy the state of a great lady, and after a few months to die in the fantastic capital of Montezuma.

In 1518 Cortés was appointed commander of an expedition which the Governor of Cuba had decided to send down the almost unknown coast of Mexico. Although his estate was lucrative, Cortés was hard up because, as Díaz explains, he needed all his money 'for his own person and the dress of his young wife'. Therefore he sold his property and it is characteristic of his grand manner, and also typical of the conduct of a would-be grandee in those days, that the first thing he bought as a preparation for the invasion of a savage and unexplored region of the earth was 'a state robe with golden trains, and ensigns bearing the arms of our sovereign, the king'. The plan was to explore the coast of Mexico and to exchange glass beads with the natives for gold and silver. These expeditions were organized on the principle which later became usual with the merchant adventurers of all countries. A number of men would sell their possessions, or otherwise provide money, to buy ships, horses, arms, and a good supply of knick-knacks, and would persuade the rank and file to join them on the understanding that the trading profits, or the loot, would be shared on an agreed basis. There was never any lack of recruits, for the islands of the West Indies, which were Spain's springboard for the mainland, were filled with lusty young men who had left Spain to seek their fortunes overseas. There could be no greater misconception than the idea that the King of Spain financed the conquest of South America: all he did was to give legal sanction to the bands of private adventurers, while the Pope added his blessing. One of the most surprising features of the conquest was the way the conquistadores would call the natives together and solemnly read to them, through an interpreter, legal proclamations signed *Yo, el Rey*—I, the King—followed by explanations about the Pope and the Emperor. What the poor natives made of this we can well imagine! However, the invaders had put themselves right with God and the Roman Law, and everybody had been legally cautioned.

Bernal Díaz admits his readers into this fellowship of adventurers, the oddest mixture the world has ever known of piety and violence. Each conquistador was inspired by the determination to win enough gold to make himself a gentleman. They landed from eleven ships in February, 1519, about six hundred men, eighteen horses, and ten small cannon. When they had subdued the coastal natives, Cortés learnt that these tribes hated the dominant Aztecs and he quickly enlisted them as allies. They agreed to march with him to the fabulous Aztec capital and to make war on Montezuma. Among the peace offerings made by the now friendly chiefs to Cortés were small eatable dogs, monkeys, lizards, and twenty young maidens. In a clearing in the forest, with palm trees around them, the adobe houses standing in the sunlight, and the sentinels patrolling the edge of the forest, muskets on shoulder, these maidens were solemnly christened. Grave and copper-skinned and in their brightest skirts, they stood with flowers in their straight black hair and bangles shaking on their slim wrists, while the good friar, Father Olmedo, admitted them into the Christian Church, the first American converts. They were given new names, the names of mothers, sisters, wives and sweethearts in Spain and Cuba, then Cortés shared them out among his captains, who now felt free to live with them in *barraganía*, that form of marriage which was not 'marriage in Latin', or in church, which had existed in Spain for centuries, and was a reflection of the Moslem world. That was how Marina came to the conquistadores, a young woman who was to play a great part in the conquest of Mexico. She spoke the coastal dialect and also the language of the Aztecs, and Cortés found her an invaluable interpreter. It was through her that he was eventually able to speak with Montezuma. She was 'the most beautiful, the most meddlesome and the most enterprising' of the girls, and it is strange, considering the reputation of Cortés, that he should have given her to one of his captains. Later on, however, she became his mistress and bore him a son who grew up to be a Spanish aristocrat. It is typically Spanish that this band of adventurers, learning that Marina was a princess who had been sold in infancy by a wicked stepfather, and conscious of her air of breeding, were such sticklers for etiquette that they gave her the title of *Doña*, which in those days was no empty title, and so bestowed upon her a sign of nobility to which not one of them, even Cortés, could aspire. This is a good instance of their desire to do everything with strict propriety. It was not hypocrisy, but simply Spanish formalism in its most extreme form.

In the meantime Montezuma's spies had been watching from the cover of jungle and forest. They had drawn pictures of the Spaniards in the Aztec picture-writing and these had been rushed by relays of runners through jungle and forest, over mountains, across fibre bridges swinging above torrents and gorges, and up to the plain where Tenochtitlán shone on its lagoon. More terrifying than the bearded men were those apparitions with two heads and four legs, for never having seen a horse before, the Mexicans believed man and animal to be one creature. And when Montezuma saw these pictures he was dismayed. He remembered a prophecy that one day Children of the Sun would come out of the West and rule Mexico. These obviously were the gods. In his innocence he sent them gifts of massive gold and begged them to return to the Sun, hoping in some way to delay the working of destiny. The Spaniards took one glance at the gold and decided to go to Tenochtitlán.

First Cortés, as if he were a Roman, solemnly founded the town of Vera Cruz, La Villa Rica de Vera Cruz was its full name—the Rich Town of the True Cross—which appropriately and honestly bracketed God and gold and so set the keynote to the conquest. Next he burned his ships, but, being Cortés, he took care to save all the iron and the rigging, and this in the months to come was to save the situation for him. Having thus formed a base camp and cut off retreat, he marched away, leaving a small garrison behind. His strength was four hundred men, thirteen horses, and six or seven cannon. The capital of Montezuma was two hundred miles away and it took the Spaniards and their native allies nearly three months to get there. They toiled through steamy forests and jungles. They were frozen in mountains where Díaz felt the cold through his armour. They passed between pine-trees where the delaying charms and amulets of Montezuma's wizards were as thick as spiders' webs. They had to fight, and many were wounded. When the natives had slain their first horse they cut off its head and sent it round the tribes to prove that it was not immortal. At every step the invaders saw the wonders and the horrors of this strange land which had existed from the beginning of human history, cut off from all contact with the world they knew. Upon the summits of pyramids they came to temples whose walls were splashed with human blood. They met hordes of grisly priests in black robes whose hair, which was never cut, was matted with dry blood. When a victim had been dragged to the summit of the pyramids, he was held down by these vultures while one in red garments swiftly gashed his breast with an obsidian knife and tore out the still pumping heart. The dead body was then flung from the *ziggurat*, where priests were waiting to cut it up. 'Indeed,' says Díaz, 'I even believe that human flesh is exposed for sale cut up, in their *tianges*, or markets.' In one temple they found the flayed skins of two of their companions who had been captured, their beards still adhering to their cheeks. Díaz himself lived in dread of being captured. The Spaniards were also horrified by countless young men dressed as women and they forbade them 'to make a livelihood by such cursed lewdness'. These were some aspects of the civilization whose end many writers have deplored.

The truth is that the Aztecs, for all their gold and silver and their superficial brilliance, were really savages. Iron was not known, copper was rare; and a people who had made and policed a system of communications which would have been a marvel in the Europe of that time, who had also created beautiful botanical and zoological gardens, did not know the use of the wheel. The first wheels ever seen in America were those of Cortés' cannon. Sheep were unknown, so were cattle, and so was wheat. But the Spaniards encountered two products which were to invade the Old World just as the horse, the cow, the sheep, and wheat were to invade the New: these were tobacco, which the Mexicans smoked in pipes and in cigar-holders of tortoiseshell, or took as snuff; and cocoa, or chocolate, which the Aztecs prepared in a manner which is said now to have been lost. It was whipped up with vanilla into a froth that was almost solid and eaten cold with a spoon.

The small company of Spaniards reached the plain now known as the Valley of Mexico, some seven thousand feet above the sea, where the city of Tenochtitlán lay like a Mexican Venice upon the surface of a great lake. As the Spaniards crossed one of the stone causeways which was the only approach to this island stronghold, they saw a brilliant gathering approaching, as Montezuma came to meet them in a palanquin of burnished gold whose poles rested upon the shoulders of nobles. Above his head was a silver canopy with a fringe made of hummingbirds' wings and other iridescent feathers. As he stepped from his litter, his court bowed down with averted eyes, for it was not etiquette to look at him; and as he walked, supported by princes of the royal house, attendants went before placing strips of cotton tapestry on the ground so that his golden sandals should not touch common earth. He was forty years of age, tall, thin, with straight black hair, and his skin was lighter than that of his subjects. As he moved the Spaniards noticed with interest that his robes were encrusted with pearls and with precious stones like emeralds, known to the Aztecs as *chalcivitl.* He wore a royal crown of green feathers. Cortés flung the reins of his horse to a page and, dismounting, went to meet the Emperor. Montezuma looked at the bearded solemn face beneath its casque and believed it to be the face of a god.

What are we to make of what followed? Was it the basest treachery and villainy or was it an inevitable act of self-preservation? A royal palace in Tenochtitlán large enough to hold all the Spaniards was given for their use. Montezuma treated them as if they were truly gods. He was delighted to have them as his guests and he showered gifts upon them. Their position was false and they knew it. They had come with conquest in their hearts and they were treated as honoured guests. In four days' time Cortés asked leave to ascend the great pyramid, or *teocallis*, and see the temples of the Mexican gods. Montezuma went first in state, followed by Cortés on horseback, attended by his cavalry and a guard of infantry, among whom was Bernal Díaz. It was their first sight of the city, for Cortés had confined them to the rooms and gardens of the palace. They were amazed by the crowded streets—the population is said to have been three hundred thousand—by the squares, one of which was larger than the Plaza Mayor in Salamanca, and by the markets where merchants were selling goose-quills full of gold dust, and tubes of amber, cocoa, chocolate, maize, furs and feathers, and beautiful cotton like the finest silk. When they had climbed the hundred and fourteen steps to the summit of the temple, they stood horrified by the hideous gods and by the priests with their matted hair. 'This infernal temple . . . this temple of hell,' wrote Díaz. He saw the awful Uitzilopochtli, the god of war, an idol, 'with a very broad face, with distorted and furious-looking eyes, and covered with jewels, gold and pearls, which were stuck to it with paste'. In front of the god, smoking in a pan, they saw the hearts of three men who had been slaughtered that morning. The floor and the walls were almost black with dry blood, 'and the smell was worse than in a slaughter-house in Castile'; they also saw the great drum of serpent skin which later on they were to hear throbbing day and night without cease. Against the advice of Father Olmedo, who was also there, Cortés bravely rebuked Montezuma for his idolatry and asked for a shrine in which to place a statue of the Blessed Virgin. The Emperor was shocked and offended. 'In our eyes these are good divinities,' he said. 'I beg

133

of you not to insult them.' Cortés apologized and led the way down the pyramid, while the Emperor remained behind to propitiate the offended idols. Cortés might have been an early Christian in a pagan temple, and from that moment the battle for Mexico seems to be the battle of Christ against the bloodstained gods from the beginning of time. As the Christians descended the pyramid they saw the city below, intersected by canals, and the lake lying in the beauty of the morning, bearing upon its water floating islands covered with flowers. Like most things in Mexico, beauty stood hand in hand with demons.

Díaz was one of those who attended Cortés when he and Marina visited Montezuma in the palace where the Emperor lived in semi-divine state. Before they entered his presence, great nobles had to cast a robe of sackcloth over their rich mantles and carry a small pack, representing a burden, upon their backs; and thus symbolically humbled, they approached with averted eyes. Three hundred dishes were prepared every day for the Emperor to choose from and he ate alone behind a golden screen, served by beautiful girls who never looked at him. At the end of dinner, after he had been served with the royal chocolate, the girls 'presented him with three beautifully painted and gilt tubes, which were filled with liquid amber, and a herb called by the Indians tabaco . . . one of these tubes was lighted and the monarch took the smoke into his mouth, and after he had done this a short time, he fell asleep.'

The Christians received permission to build in their quarters a chapel to the Blessed Virgin, where, as long as their wine lasted, Father Olmedo said Mass. Noting that a door had been walled up, they removed some stones and found themselves in a large room stacked to the ceiling with gold and jewels. They walled it up again. As time passed they sensed a change in the manner of their hosts. The old cordiality and reverence had disappeared. News had come that Montezuma's vassals on the coast had attacked Vera Cruz and killed some Spaniards. Cortés and his men began to feel trapped and feared that the Aztecs might rise and massacre them. After taking counsel together, they resolved on perhaps the boldest plan ever put into operation by a small band of soldiers in the heart of a warlike nation. They decided to seize Montezuma, to take him suddenly from his palace and keep him as a hostage for the good behaviour of his nation. 'The whole of that night', says Díaz, 'was spent in prayer with Father Olmedo, to ask the Almighty's support in the holy cause.'

In the morning Cortés, with Doña Marina as his interpreter, and with his captains armed, went to the palace; and in an hour's time the populace saw the royal litter moving towards the Spanish quarters, the Emperor's attendants in tears. That a few bold men could abduct a great king in his own palace would appear incredible, unless the king were a willing captive, but it seems that Montezuma felt himself a helpless puppet on the strings of fate. Cortés bowed low before him, all the soldiers removed their caps in his presence, yet even to the most foolish Mexican it must have been clear that the real power in Mexico was no longer the Emperor. Cortés had the nerve to demand the person of the high official who had ordered the attack on Vera Cruz. This man came in due course in his litter and with the state of a high officer. Cortés burned him alive in the market-place. While the execution was in progress Cortés himself fastened fetters on the legs of Montezuma, presumably as a punishment. When the Spaniards returned, they found that the Emperor's attendants were holding up the fetters so that they should not chafe the royal limbs. Cortés himself knelt down and unlocked them. In spite of such humiliations, their relations remained almost affectionate. Montezuma won the hearts of his captors by his melancholy acquiescence and by his affability and his willingness to reward them with gold and girls. The next step was Montezuma's formal oath of allegiance to Charles V, which was drawn up by a notary in true legal fashion, signed, sealed, and sent to Spain. This was followed by the usual tribute of vassal to lord. For centuries the Aztecs had been hoarding gold, and it was this rich hoard that was now taken over by the Spaniards and melted down into gold bricks. A fifth of this was set apart for the King of Spain and the conquistadores shared out the rest. It should be interesting to those who believe that equality of wealth is possible to know that in a few days many of the soldiers had gambled away their share, and consequently some were as poor as when they had started out, while others were richer.

Having captured the Emperor and acquired his wealth, Cortés next demanded and received permission for a Christian shrine to be maintained on the top of the pyramid, alongside the idols. Ascending the pyramid one day to supervise the cleaning of the shrine, Cortés suddenly lost his temper with the priests and seizing a bar of metal, he leapt up and struck the idol Uitzilopochtli in the face and between the eyes, breaking off his golden mask, crying as he struck, 'We must risk something for God!' He reminds us of St. Paul. Yet even Paul did not strike the image of Diana of the Ephesians. Many a Christian has been canonized for less than the act of Cortés upon the summit of the pyramid in Mexico. It was the greatest moment in the conquest of Mexico, and it places Cortés in a category apart from all the other conquistadores. Naturally he paid the penalty. Such an insult to the gods brought to a head the revolt which had been simmering for some time. Montezuma begged his friends to escape while it was possible; but as they were making plans to do so, they heard that eighteen Spanish ships had put into Vera Cruz and that a commander named Narváez had landed with nine hundred troops, including eighty horsemen, eighty musketeers, eighty crossbowmen and a number of formidable cannon. The rank and file rejoiced, believing them to be reinforcements, but Cortés knew that they were enemies who had to be fought at once. He rightly guessed that the Governor of Cuba had sent a force to subdue him for having taken upon himself the style and authority of a conqueror. Surrounded now by foes, Cortés acted with his usual speed and brilliance. Leaving a small force in Mexico to hold the city, he made a forced march with a miserable little army, all he could muster, of two hundred and sixty-six men, only five of whom were mounted. But they were tough commandos trained in jungle warfare. While Narváez and his Spaniards believed Cortés to be miles away, they were set upon at night in a torrent of tropical rain and utterly routed. Narváez was blinded in one eye and his force surrendered. Diaz gives us the delightful information that a swarm of fireflies assisted the smaller force by making their opponents imagine them to be the burning fuses of innumerable musketeers.

No sooner had Cortés defeated Narváez than he learnt that Mexico had gone up in revolt. Back he marched, this time reinforced by the newcomers, who readily joined him in the hope of plunder. They found the garrison they had left besieged by the Mexicans. The fury of the Aztecs was indescribable and seems to have surprised even Cortés. Montezuma was hurt when Cortés repulsed his friendship. One day the Emperor put on his royal mantle of white and blue, and his golden sandals, and with the diadem upon his brow appeared in royal state upon the tower of the palace. Silence fell when the furious mob recognized the Emperor. He ordered them to cease from fighting and that if they did so, the white men would leave Mexico. A murmur of rage was heard as he mentioned the Spaniards. An arrow was loosed at him; stones were flung, one of which struck him senseless to the ground. Montezuma had now touched the depths of humiliation and in three days he died. Father Olmedo knelt beside him with a crucifix, but he turned away. 'I have only a few moments left,' he said, 'and at this

time I will not desert the gods of my fathers.' The Spaniards wept for
him. 'We all loved him as a father,' says Díaz, 'and no wonder, seeing
how good he was.' I have wondered more than once how it was that
the hideous faith to which he remained constant, the most bloodthirsty
ever recorded and the most primitive, could have produced a character
so full of Christian meekness.

Cortés now found it necessary to retreat from Mexico. He decided
to lead his small army by night over the shortest of the three causeways
across the lake. First an astonishing scene took place in the palace. A
few horses, all wounded or lame, were loaded with gold, part of the
share set aside for the King of Spain. Then the soldiers were admitted
to the apartment and told they could take what they liked. The
prudent, like Díaz, seized a handful of jewels, but the greedy and the
foolish loaded themselves with chunks of gold, which were soon to
be their death. In darkness they set out across the causeway. Suddenly
the great drum of serpent skin was beaten from the *teocallis* and the
Spaniards were assailed by thousands of warriors in canoes. Stuck full
of arrows, hit by stones, wounded by spears thrust upward from the
water, they dropped into the lake, to be captured by the Aztecs, while
those behind fell into confusion. Gold, horses, a train of cannon, all the
baggage of Cortés, several hundred Spaniards and several thousand
native allies, were lost in the savage confusion of the night. When a
miserable few without arms struggled to the mainland, Cortés looked
at them and wept.

They retreated south into the country of their old allies, the Tlaxcalians, who, surprisingly enough, remained loyal to them. They had
no muskets, no cannon, and no gunpowder. They were nearly all of
them wounded. As they retreated, they fought the terrific battle of
Otumba, which was saved from disaster by Cortés, who galloped
straight at the enemy commander and cut him down. Healing their
wounds among their native allies, the incredible Cortés began to plan
the reconquest of Mexico. And slowly his luck began to turn. Ships
arrived with reinforcements for Narváez, for the Government at Cuba
was unaware that he had been defeated. These were decoyed into the
service of Cortés. Thus he got cannon, horses, bowstrings, muskets and
gunpowder. But he was developing an idea as bold as his capture of
Montezuma. He had no ships, but he had observed during the retreat
that in order to advance into Mexico ships were necessary to hold the
causeways. He set his native allies cutting timber for thirteen brigantines under the supervision of a ship's carpenter, Martín López, and

used all the ironwork and rigging salvaged from the ships he had burnt soon after landing in Mexico. He had his ships built in sections so that they could be carried over the mountains and assembled at the lakeside. Six months after his defeat he was ready to move on Mexico again. His army now consisted of five hundred and fifty soldiers, forty-two horsemen, eight small guns, and a horde of Tlaxcalians who were anxious to see the downfall of their hereditary foes. Among those who dined at his table was a young Aztec prince of the blood royal, who had become a Christian and had taken a Spanish name. Cortés rarely forgot anything.

As they marched back to Mexico they came across grisly evidence of the fate of those Spaniards who had been captured by the enemy. In one native town, says Díaz, 'the blood of our unfortunate countrymen was even then sticking to the walls of the temple. Here were likewise found on an altar the entire skins of the faces of two Spaniards with the beards still hanging to them. The skins had been dressed in the same way as the leather we use for making gloves.' In another temple were found the skins of five horses 'as beautifully stuffed as anywhere in the world, with their feet and shoes'. They had been offered to the idols with the clothes of sacrificed Spaniards.

'Having heard Mass and commended ourselves to God,' the army took the most difficult and the steepest road to Mexico, the prefabricated brigantines following on the shoulders of eight thousand natives. So they came again in sight of the lagoon and the city in which they had dared and suffered so much. The siege lasted for nearly three months and proved the warlike valour of the Aztecs. The streets were blocked with dead, and the starving women and children who tottered out of the town and wandered about, gnawing the bark of trees, roused the pity of the Spaniards and moved Cortés to call again and again, but vainly, for surrender. The 'drum of hell' was almost continuously beaten; and upon the pyramid, visible to all, the dark priests bent over the sacrifices. Cortés himself narrowly escaped capture, and those Spaniards who were slain in battle were thought fortunate. Sometimes the besiegers glanced up towards the pyramids, where flames burned day and night, and saw with horror their captured comrades decked grotesquely in feathers and made to dance in front of the idols before they were forced backward on the sacrificial stone. At length Cortés, to his sorrow, for it was 'the most beautiful city in the world', decided to burn down the Aztec capital; and his army advanced behind a wall of fire. Finally a starving city capitulated in its ashes and Mexico had been conquered.

138

Cortés began almost at once to build what has become Mexico City. The present Royal Palace in the Plaza Mayor stands upon the site of the residence he erected on the ruins of Montezuma's palace. The modern cathedral stands near the site of the awful *teocallis*, but the area of the great lake has now shrunk, and there is now dry land where the first Spaniards saw thousands of canoes.

Hardly had the conquest been consolidated than Doña Catalina arrived to join her husband. She was not a welcome guest, but he was able to give her the state and dignity of a queen. She is said to have been extremely jealous, and while Doña Marina was no longer a rival, there were perhaps others. She was discovered dead in bed within a few months of her arrival, in circumstances which the many enemies of her husband did not, in their malice, forget.

Cortés was thirty-six when Mexico was conquered and was possibly the greatest Spaniard of his time, a king in all but name. But he was doomed; his success had made too many enemies. He was fêted in Spain and overwhelmed with honours. He became the Marquis of Oaxaca and married the beautiful and aristocratic Doña Juana de Zúñiga; but Mexico was handed over to the Colonial Office and Cortés, grand and titled though he was, had to make way for viceroys from Madrid. His last years were spent in battles against unequal adversaries—Malice, Envy and Jealousy: and the time came, it is said, when he could not even gain admittance to the King. He died near Seville, unhappy and frustrated, at the age of sixty-two. His remains were taken to Mexico, but secretly removed on the eve of national independence in 1823. It is believed that they were shipped to Sicily, where the head of his family then lived; but where they are today is unknown.

Among sidelights on the invasion of the New World is a book, *The Horses of the Conquest*, by that fine horseman R. B. Cunninghame Graham, who, on long-vanished mornings in the nineteen-twenties, I remember seeing in Hyde Park sitting an ambling Mexican pony. He says that the first horses in the New World were descended from the famous breed of Córdoba, long since extinct. It was a breed said to have been formed during the Arab Caliphate by four sires brought from the Yemen of the Hedjaz and crossed with the native mares. Cortés and Pizarro and the other conquistadores bought their horses from breeders in Cuba and the West Indian Islands, who had developed a thriving horse trade, breeding horses specially for war. The horses imported from Spain by these breeders were probably of the same type as the horses painted by Velázquez: short-backed and without too much daylight showing underneath their bellies. The terror inspired in Mexico by the first horses was such that many accounts of the conquests contain the sentence, 'For, after God, we owed the victory to the horses.' The Aztecs were never able to conquer this fear, but the Incas of Peru, on the other hand, quickly learned to ride. So did the Patagonians. Within fifty years after Don Pedro de Mendoza had abandoned his seven remaining horses, when the first occupation of Buenos Aires failed, the Patagonians had become horse Indians and hardly walked a foot. In 1580, when Don Juan Garay went there, the province was full of wild horses, the descendants of the seven mares and stallions abandoned in 1535. The New World with its wide plains and its cultivation of maize was an ideal breeding-place for horses, which under these conditions rapidly evolved a natural type bearing slight resemblance to the original.

Cunninghame Graham mentions the strange destiny of the black horse, *El Monzillo*, which Cortés rode during the exploration of Yucatan in 1525. This animal went lame so badly that Cortés was obliged to leave him, to his sorrow, at the lake of Peten-Itza, with an Indian chief who promised to look after him. A hundred and seventy years passed before white men returned to that district. In the year 1697 two Franciscan friars came paddling down the river Tapia into the lake of Peten-Itza. They were attached to an expedition which soon arrived with its horses. The Franciscans were surprised by the delight shown by one of the natives, a chief called Isquin, at the sight of the animals. He leapt and pranced round on all fours, neighing. It seemed to them remarkable that he knew so much about horses! The Franciscans, who found these natives difficult to convert, heard about their great god Tziunchan, the god of Thunder and Lightning, and eventually they were taken out on the lake to an island where the temple of the deity was situated. To their astonishment they found that the god Tziunchan was a stone statue of a horse. They pieced the story together and found that the god was *El Monzillo*, left there by Cortés so long ago. The Indians had apparently treated him with the utmost kindness, indeed they killed him with it. He refused to eat the fruit, and even the chickens, placed before him, and so languished and died. His body was buried on the island; soon a cult sprang up, and *El Monzillo* rapidly took precedence over the other local deities. It is a great pity that the friars in their indignation broke the statue into pieces.

The conquistadores, like their ancestors in Spain, rode with short stirrups after the Moorish style, but, as horses became wild in South America, it was necessary to lengthen the stirrups. The modern gaucho rides with long stirrups, but he still sits in the Moorish, now called the Mexican, saddle originally brought over by the conquistadores.

§ 6

As I approached the hill town of Trujillo I saw that the ramparts, which appeared intact from a distance, were crumbling walls, and that the Moorish *alcázar* was an empty shell. Steep streets containing many a fine Renaissance palace, now in decay, ascend to the upper level of the town. I saw a coalman filling his sacks from a dump in the once splendid entrance to a palace; the delicious smell of new bread led me to another where, by the glow of wood fires, I watched a woman with an iron rake drawing loaves from an oven constructed in a once palatial courtyard. All these palaces had been built with the wealth of Peru. Their foundations were the gold of the Incas and the mortar that binds their stones was blood and luck. Yet how few of the conquistadores made anything out of their adventures. They were killed in battle or else found, when the sharing-out time arrived, that their portion would hardly buy a new horse or a sword. But the palaces of Trujillo prove that a few, at any rate, managed to get their hands on gold that did not vanish at a touch.

The magnificent plaza in the lower part of the town contains a splendid row of medieval houses built above stone arches; and on the opposite side is the most ornate palace in the town, with a coat-of-arms about two stories high carved on the façade. I was told that this is the palace of the Marquesa de la Conquista, the present holder of Pizarro's title. The history of this title is unusual, for Pizarro never married and the title lapsed after his death. He had lived, however, with an Inca princess, the daughter of the Inca whom he had murdered, and by whom he had a daughter. This woman married her uncle, Hernando Pizarro, who survived Francisco, and the marquisate was revived in favour of their descendants. If the title has descended in the direct line, its holders can boast the blood of the great Pizarro and also of the Inca, Atahuallpa. Many visitors are told that this palace was the house of Pizarro, but this is not so. He never retired to Trujillo, but remained in Peru, where he was eventually murdered.

Storks nest all over Trujillo, on church tower, convent and palace.

They fill the air with the dry clattering of their beaks—*crotonasia*, the ancients called it—and as they stand poised on one red leg, gazing intently into the street, secure in having captivated mankind for centuries, they might be the spirits of the town's most benevolent citizens. I sought refuge from the heat in the Café Victoria, which faces a romantic statue of Francisco Pizarro. He rides forward in full armour, grasping a drawn sword, plumes waving from his helmet, the very soul of noble knighthood. The statue is the work of the American sculptress Maria Harriman Rumsey, and a replica stands in front of the cathedral in Lima. As I sipped a glass of *manzanilla*, I thought that Trujillo, like many a town in the Midlands and the North of England, reflects the wish of the newly rich to model their lives on those of the nobility. The self-made conquistadores and their descendants used the wealth of Peru to construct palaces which were modelled in every way on the knightly palaces of Spain, just as rich brassfounders and others during the industrial revolution patterned themselves on the county families of England. We can imagine with what pride the self-made peasants and swineherds of Extremadura returned as rich noblemen to their home towns, and how the presence of a coat-of-arms over the main gate must have seemed to them more miraculous than anything that had happened to them in the Indies.

The ruin of an old palace on the top of the hill in the ancient town is known most misleadingly as the home of Pizarro, for he never had a home in this grand sense of the word. It is a nobleman's palace, with a coat-of-arms above the gate, and is probably the home of his father, but not of his mother. Colonel Gonzalo Pizarro, a retired officer, was guilty of what the Spaniards call so lightly a *desuedo*, or negligence, with a young woman of humble circumstances in the town, the result of which was the future conqueror of Peru, Francisco Pizarro. The boy was never educated and until the end of his life could neither read nor write. Like most boys in Extremadura, he herded swine, and then went off to the Indies at an early age to seek his fortune. The colonel was guilty at least twice again of similar negligences, who were named Gonzalo and Juan. He also had a legitimate son, Hernando Pizarro, who was older than his three half-brothers. Hernando was a haughty aristocrat and, although Francisco was the founder of his fortunes, he seems to have looked down on him just as Francisco looked up to him in envy and admiration. These were the four Pizarros who galloped about Peru like the Four Horsemen of the Apocalypse and brought down a civilization which appears to have had much to recommend it.

## Gardens of the Inca

The Incas were not cruel like the Aztecs, neither were they cannibals. They propitiated their gods with roast llama and, helped by a docile peasantry, evolved an early form of the welfare state.

One of the remarkable things about the Pizarros was their relatively advanced age. Cortés was thirty-three when he landed in Mexico, but Francisco Pizarro was over fifty when he conquered Peru, and his half-brother Hernando was even older. None of the Peruvian conquistadores are as attractive as Cortés: they were a brutal crowd, cruel, treacherous and vengeful. The death of Montezuma was a pathetic tragedy for which Cortés was of course to blame; but it was not a foul crime like the judicial murder of the Inca. Pizarro invited this monarch to dinner, captured him, slew his unarmed followers, and agreed to release him if he would fill a room with gold. When the Inca had done so, Pizarro sentenced him to be burned to death on a trumped-up charge, and remitted this to strangulation when the poor creature accepted Christianity at the stake—a horrible parody of the Inquisition and surely the foulest act in the history of the New World. These Pizarros and their followers were the first American gangsters and their bloody disputes with each other seem to have set the pattern for all South American revolutions.

Still, adventures such as have befallen few men came their way. They gazed in wonder at the jewelled gardens of the Inca at Cuzco, where flowers of emeralds and precious stones shone amid branches of gold and leaves of silver; they saw the royal mummies of Coricancha, crouched each on his gold-embossed throne, dressed in jewelled robes; they saw the great Temple of the Sun as it was before they stripped seven hundred plates of gold from its walls and took down the cornice of pure gold which encircled it. These men, who had never had a penny to bless themselves with, now gambled away golden discs and emeralds and set off like a pack of wolves to seek more wealth. They were also the first to hear the fantastic story of the Gilded One—El Dorado—a dream which eventually lured Walter Raleigh to his death. This Gilded One was believed to be the king in a city of gold called Manoa, who every day stripped himself and, having covered himself with gum, rolled in gold dust. In the evening he was rowed out on a lake by his nobles, where he plunged into the water and washed off the gold dust. The lake was said to be filled not only with gold dust but also with gold offerings flung into it by the followers of El Dorado. Gonzalo Pizarro was one of the many who tried to find this wonderful city, and encountered instead appalling and unbelievable hardships.

All three illegitimate Pizarros died violent deaths. Juan died from wounds received in battle. Francisco, when an old man of sixty-five or seventy, was set upon in his house in Lima by armed men and slain. Gonzalo, defeated during a rebellion against the viceroy of Peru, was beheaded. Thus these three violent characters perished as they had lived. Only the haughty and arrogant Hernando, the eldest and the only legitimate Pizarro, survived, probably because he was safe in a prison in Spain, pending one of those Spanish lawsuits which have all the elements of eternity. He was kept in prison for twenty years. It was obviously a technical confinement, for he was allowed, while incarcerated, to marry his niece, the daughter of Francisco and the Inca princess, and by means of this unlikely union the Pizarro line was, as I have said, continued. When released, he was a venerable figure of over ninety years of age. All his enemies and contemporaries had passed from the scene of life, and his grievances and troubles mattered no longer to anyone, for he belonged to a past age. It is said that the old man lived to be a hundred.

I climbed the streets of the old town and by the light of matches saw the figure of a kneeling knight in the church of Santa María de la Concepción, and the word 'Pizarro' carved in stone. It is remarkable that guide-books and many recent travellers, possibly repeating one of the few errors of Richard Ford, call this the tomb of Francisco Pizarro. But Francisco is buried in Lima Cathedral, and his gruesome remains may be seen there in a glass coffin. After his murder his body was hastily taken by faithful domestic servants to the old cathedral and interred in an obscure corner. When the new cathedral was built they were transferred to a sumptuous tomb, where they lie side by side with the remains of the great viceroy, Mendoza.

§ 7

The people of Mérida took pride in telling me that the town has the reputation of being the hottest place in Spain. Most of the travellers in the *parador* lay prostrated in the darkened lounge or sat about listlessly in the courtyard, which was covered by a huge awning. This was drawn across early in the morning by a skilful arrangement of ropes and pulleys, then withdrawn after sundown to allow the space to fill with night air. I was interested to meet such a good example of a Roman *valeria* in everyday use in the Roman Emerita; and I was to find other living relics of Rome there.

I decided not to admit that it was hot, and went exploring as usual. I saw a lot by hovering prudently on the shady side of the streets. A notable sight of this city is the railway where big, black locomotives puff westward to Badajoz and the Portuguese frontier through the arches of a Roman aqueduct, while storks stand reflectively above. They resemble railway officials who are timing the trains, and they are unaffected by the sudden gusts of steam and the clouds of smoke. Not far away the finest Roman bridge in Spain strides for half a mile across the Guadiana in a series of splendid arches. Summer had dried up the river, which split into two arms as it neared the bridge, leaving in the centre of its bed long eyots, or islands, where herds of the blue-black Extremenian swine were busily nosing the river stones. From water level I gazed through one of the arches and saw, framed in the ancient masonry and reflected in the water, the turreted walls of the Roman *castrum* beyond; a building which was turned by the Moors into their *alcázar*, and after the Reconquest into a convent by the Knights of Santiago. It is a scene that drips with age and romance; and if I could paint, I should choose the moment when a few pigs herded by a little bare-legged boy occupy the foreground and a group of muleteers, with a dash of red about them, are crossing the bridge above.

I went often to sit in the Roman theatre, which is one of the most complete I have ever seen. The sweep of seats, divided into seven divisions, is intact almost to the top rows, and the proscenium with its stately columns and its statues is very nearly perfect. We consider this age standardized, but cities of the Roman Empire were almost as repetitive as cars from the same factory. The sameness of Roman municipal architecture must have been boring, repeated as it was with relentless monotony in province after province. It is, however, a pleasant thought that possibly Hadrian or Trajan, perhaps Seneca or Martial, all Roman Spaniards, may have sat in the theatre at Mérida and watched a play. I have read somewhere that the first foreign town outside of Italy to adopt the Roman law and language was Cádiz, which the Romans knew as Gades. The dancing-girls of Gades were famous in Rome, indeed wherever there were Trimalchios who gave banquets; and some believe, among them the erudite Ford, that a memory of their stampings and posturings is to be recognized today in the dances of the Andalusian gipsies.

A·few steps from the theatre is an amphitheatre where gladiatorial fights were held. It was also possible to flood this arena for water tournaments, and the arrangements for doing this are clearly visible. Many people imagine that these spectacles took place on an artificial lake upon which the galleys could freely manœuvre and give an idea of a naval action, but, in these provincial theatres at any rate, the sight must have been much less exciting. You can see at Mérida how the water filled certain channels and it must have been through these canals that the ships moved, rather like punts waiting to go through a lock. Evidently the fight was the main thing. Even more interesting were the underground dens in which wild animals were kept before they were taken up in a lift to the arena above. The doors of their dens opened to a heavy openwork cage, which was then cranked up to the level of the floor above by men working a windlass. Having reached the level of the arena, the top of the cage was lifted, and out leaped the lions and the tigers. Except that it is oblong instead of circular, this Roman amphitheatre is like any provincial bull-ring in Spain and about the same size.

But I think the most extraordinary relic of paganism I saw in Mérida is the apse of the little church of St. Eulalia, which stands in one of the main streets. Built against the wall is an outside shrine looking exactly like a small Roman temple: columns, architrave and stones have all come from the ruins of the Roman town. But what is so remarkable is that it is hung everywhere with female hair. It looks as though a dozen girls' schools have been shorn and have left plaits of black, brown and auburn hanging round the image of the youthful saint. There are tresses, too, dusty from the road, some long and curly, others thin and lifeless. Could there be a more pagan survival than this sacrifice of hair to a deity, or rather a saint?

St. Eulalia was a girl of about twelve whose parents were rich citizens of the Roman Emerita. She lived during that deplorable chapter in the history of martyrdom under Diocletian, when Christians committed suicide in their anxiety to become saints. They publicly insulted the emperor, the gods and the law, until the reluctant magistrates, having exhausted their tolerance, were obliged to order their execution; and they went off to the most hideous deaths singing hymns. The Church took the view that, devout and fearless as they were, they still risked a reprimand from the highest quarters upon reaching Heaven. Young Eulalia was determined to be put to death and behaved rudely to the magistrate, who tried to save her from herself. Prudentius, a Spaniard who lived in the fourth century and wrote of martyrdoms, left in his third *Crown-song* an account of her behaviour. After describing the magistrate's attempt to pacify the child, he says:

> *Never a word the martyr spake,*
> *but roared aloud for wrath,*
> *and even as the tyrant sat,*
> *right in his eye Eulalia spat,*
> *next, scattered all the idols round,*
> *and flung the censers on the ground,*
> *and spurned them from her path.*

Eulalia was roasted, and it is believed that the shrine occupies the site of the oven.

After a few days of the heat I awakened with a headache and, feeling rather dizzy and extremely frail, I realized that I had acquired a well-deserved touch of the sun. Too depressed to read, I lay all day in a hot dark room in the *parador*, with a jug of iced lemonade on the side-table. I had plenty of time to reflect on the problem which occurs to few travellers in Spain: the fate of an heretical corpse. You cannot be cremated here, and until modern times a Protestant was buried on the seashore at low tide. What happened inland I do not know. Ford tells us that there were only three Protestant cemeteries in his day, at Madrid, Málaga, and Cádiz. He also says, referring to the seashore burials: 'even this concession offended orthodox Spanish fishermen, who fearing that the soles might become infected, took the bodies up in the night and cast them into the deep to feed sharks withal.' I have come across incidents in many books of travel in which a heretic on his death-bed in Spain is visited by a priest, who does his best to snatch a soul from the burning.

There was a plump young chambermaid, whom I had vaguely noticed as someone to smile at on landings, who now entered my life with bowls of soup. Not to hurt her feelings, I tottered to the bathroom and disposed of the soup as soon as her back was turned; and my luck still held when she brought me a steak, for there happened to pass beneath the window at the right moment what turned out to be the most astonished dog in Spain. I was amused to notice this girl's gradual air of proprietorship as she punched my pillows and smoothed the sheets and treated me as if I were about eight. She was a peasant girl with a maternal torso, a sturdy little pony whose female ancestors had borne water-jars on their heads century after century. She did not lurch about; she glided as you see the women gliding along the roads of the Congo, with immense baskets on their heads. She was not pretty, but she had grace and the large-eyed tranquillity of her race. She also had the self-assurance which comes to women in a country where it is a convention that they are all beautiful. It amused me, ill as I was, to notice how most women of whatever nationality enjoy having a helpless man at their mercy. When I was better, she brought her friend to see the Americano—I was too tired to go into this—whom she had nursed back to life; and it was delightful to watch them chattering, but so quickly that I was unable to follow them. Then, speaking slowly as if to a small child, they would tell me the news of the *parador*. A French family from Morocco had brought their car and were motoring through Spain into France. The wife wore too much lipstick and the daughters—here they exploded with laughter—wore blue trousers! There was also a distinguished Portuguese with his grown-up family, who were staying for two days on their way to see the big *corrida* at Seville. They were rich—millionaires! The wife was a beautiful Brazilian, but her bedroom! You should see her bedroom, with nothing put away and everything lying on the floor! You would never believe it, to see her in an expensive black gown at dinner, so perfect, yet so untidy. The girls laughed and one said: 'I should like to be rich enough to be untidy!'

One day I was brought a delicious cold soup, *gazpacho*, which is a regional dish of Andalusia, but is to be found in most parts of Spain in hot weather. It is made of sieved tomato juice thickened with bread-crumbs, flavoured with garlic, and served ice-cold together with little dishes of chopped ham, sausage, cucumber, chillies, indeed almost anything you like; and these you mix with the cold soup in whatever proportion pleases you. The *gazpacho* described by Ford was olive oil, vinegar and water, in which vegetables and other things were mixed. Ford claims that this was the famous Roman *posca*, which was a ration in the Roman army, and was, maybe, the 'vinegar' offered by the Roman guard to our Saviour on the Cross.

I was up and about just in time to see the departure of the wealthy Portuguese family in an enormous Cadillac. The wife was indeed an elegant and flashing woman, but she had the worn, ill-tempered look of one who keeps Nature at bay with a strict diet. Everyone came out to see them on their way to the great bull-fight, and she departed with a pale smile, like a thin, dark queen.

My first walk took me to the edge of the town, where the ghost of the Roman circus is to be seen on a wide stretch of empty land. The tiers of seats have vanished and the stones were carted away long ago to build houses and churches; but a high mound of earth still surrounds the enormous oval track and even the central *spina*, where the chariots turned, is indicated by a bank of earth several feet high. In the shade of a tree sat a sergeant and about twenty young soldiers, all intently watching the arena. Suddenly in the remote distance four tiny figures appeared, which soon became four military motor-cyclists riding abreast, much as the four-horse chariots in distant times came down the same course. As they approached us, they gingerly shifted their positions, slowly stood on the seats of their motor-cycles and, having established equilibrium, lifted their left legs in the air like trick riders and chugged along to the winning-post, all except one who wobbled perilously and fell behind. Seeing this, the sergeant leapt to his feet and, running down to what in Roman times must have been the back of the dress circle, shouted at the top of his voice words which I translated, from the tone of voice in which they were uttered, as: 'What the blazes do you think you're doing, Number Four? You look like a monkey on a stick! Extend the foot to the full extent of the left leg, head erect and—keep your handlebars steady, you great big useless cissy . . .!'

Four new riders ran down into the amphitheatre and exploded away to the starting-point; and I thought it was a great sight, this Roman race track still being used for the purpose for which it had been built so long ago.

I was describing this to a Spaniard who had turned up at the convent —for the *parador* had once been a convent—a delightful young man who spoke excellent English and had lived in London for several years. He knew Mérida well and had relatives there. 'If you are interested in Roman antiquities,' he said, 'have you seen what I consider the most extraordinary of all our relics, the *Casa del Conde de los Corbos*? It is an old palace built round a Roman temple. No? I will take you there and introduce you to the owner, who is a very rich old man; and I will tell you his story as we go along.'

It was now evening and the *paseo* was just beginning in the main street of Mérida, a delightful promenade from which wheeled traffic had been barred as in so many towns in Spain. As we went along, my acquaintance told me that the owner of the Roman temple had begun life as a poor man, travelling from town to town, but he had grown rich and was now a banker and an industrialist, and indeed everything that was opulent. 'You will see,' he concluded.

We climbed a narrow, crowded street, and just ahead of us walked two small boys like pages bearing banners, holding boards advertising the film to be seen in Mérida that week. It was called *El Final de Una Leyenda*—The End of a Story. We followed them up the street and came at length to an impressive building; and I saw embedded in its façade a row of Corinthian columns about forty feet high. The house stood on the podium of the temple and was approached by a double flight of ancient stone steps. We were brought to a standstill by a silent and watchful crowd and just had time to sense an unusual stillness and solemnity in the air when, through the doors of the house and down the steps, came men in black carrying a coffin covered by a pall. The bell of the church opposite began to toll and everyone in the crowd crossed himself.

'I'm afraid we've come too late,' whispered the young man. 'That was the owner. They say he died yesterday.'

In the forefront of the crowd stood the two little boys advertising *El Final de Una Leyenda*; and all the women from the humble streets round about had put on black and stood with their hair covered by church veils, gazing white-faced at the solemn procession and, like true Spaniards, extracting from it every last drop of drama. They may not have loved the old man when he was alive, they may have thought he was a skinflint; but he was now an immortal soul and that part of him which was winging its way towards the Eternal Judgement Seat inspired only awe and respect. When the coffin had vanished inside the church they continued to whisper in little groups, casting glances up at the Roman temple, while the two boys, still like heralds or pages, lifted their appropriate banners and went back along the street. We entered a small garden where we could see that the Corinthian columns were continued all the way round the house. It was simply a built-up Roman temple, the very thing that had thrilled the Adam Brothers when they saw Diocletian's Palace at Spalato. It was the model of the old Adelphi in London, of the Circus in Bath, and of half the Squares of London.

'We have come at an unfortunate moment,' was the under-statement of my companion. 'It's a pity you couldn't have seen the inside.'

In the morning I left before the sun was properly up; but before I went away I gave my little nurse the best string of Majorcan pearls I could find in Mérida. 'Oh, *señor* . . . how beautiful!': and you might have thought I had given her the Koh-i-noor. She promised to wear them on the day she marries her *novio*, who works on the railway.

§ 8

As I travelled along the road that leads southward to Seville and the coast, I looked out for what I thought was one of the peculiarities of Extremadura, a breed of miniature dogs, full of courage and vitality, which I had noticed only in that part of Spain. They are hardly larger than cats; some look like little collies, others like the smallest terriers. Sure enough, whenever I passed through a village there they were, trotting briskly about, sitting at front doors, or following their masters afield. When I first noticed them I assumed that their size was due perhaps to inbreeding or short rations, then it occurred to me that they might be a distinct breed. Is it far-fetched, I wonder, to imagine that their ancestors may have been those small dogs which Díaz tells us were bred for the table by the Aztecs? These dogs were often among the gifts presented by native chiefs to the Spaniards, says Díaz, and the sentence 'we supped well on little dogs' occurs frequently in his narrative. Is it only a curious coincidence that little dogs should be such a feature of the country of the conquistadores?

About forty miles from Mérida a side road took me in a few minutes to the pleasant little town of Zafra, which looked most picturesque as I approached, with its turrets and towers. I wanted to see the castle of that Duke of Feria who was among the grandees in attendance on Philip II when he went to England to marry Mary Tudor. While there he married Jane Dormer, Mary's great friend and confidante. The Duke was also the Spanish ambassador in London when Elizabeth became Queen; and if he did not originate the idea that Philip should marry Elizabeth, he certainly made that daring proposition to her and to Cecil. He was a wealthy grandee with estates in other parts of Spain, but Zafra was his chief residence and that was where he eventually brought his English duchess.

It is a charming, bright town, with a wide square on its outskirts which leads to a network of old streets and a main shopping avenue closed to traffic. It was so early in the morning that the shops were not open and Mass was not yet over. I walked up to the old palace, which is in the higher part of the town, next to a Moorish tower. It is a rambling, medieval building which had been partly demolished during the Renaissance to make way for the fashionable Italian *palazzo* erected in the centre of it. I saw the five fig leaves, the badge of the Figueroa family, over the gates, and walked into a courtyard with a central fountain and columned balconies, which must once have been lovely. It has now been taken over by the municipality, but marble palaces do not agree with typewriters, filing cabinets, and ill-paid and fretful bureaucrats.

In the little church of Santa Marina next door I thought perhaps I should find the grave of Jane Dormer, for I knew that she was buried in Zafra. But it was not there. Instead I found a tablet commemorating the death and burial of Margaret Harrington (spelt Harinton, as I suppose the Spaniards pronounced it), who was Jane's cousin. The inscription said that 'Doña Margarita Harinton' had died in Madrid in the year 1601. The priest knew no more of Margaret Harrington than that she was an English lady, the daughter of a lord, but he told me that Jane Dormer—known to him as the Duchess of Feria—was buried not far away in the convent of Santa Clara.

I went there and found a pleasant courtyard with shelter from the sun. When I rang the bell nothing happened, so I sat down to smoke a cigarette and to think what an odd little bit of Tudor history had taken place in this remote town in Spain. Jane Dormer had been brought up in the court of Henry VIII, and she was about the same age as little Prince Edward. His tutor often sent for her to dance and sing to the Prince and, as she was a clever little maid, sometimes to read to him. Mary Tudor, who had a passion for children, took a great fancy to her and they became the closest of friends, although Mary was twenty-two years older than Jane. When Mary became Queen at the age of thirty-seven, Jane Dormer was only fifteen. She must have been a girl of notable charm and sweetness, for she was sought in marriage by Edward Courtenay, Earl of Devonshire, the Duke of Norfolk, and the Earl of Nottingham. Mary, to whom anything Spanish was perfection itself, was delighted when Jane was attracted by the Count of Feria, and it was decided that they should marry. Before this took place, Mary died. Jane was at her bedside and it was to her that Mary entrusted her jewels, with instructions that they were to be given to Elizabeth. As soon as Feria scented the changed atmosphere in England upon Elizabeth's accession, he married Jane quickly; and soon afterwards she joined him in Flanders with her cousin, Margaret Harrington, and two of Mary Tudor's old and loyal retainers, Mrs. Paston and Mrs. Clarencieux. These exiles from the Catholic Court of England spent a couple of years on the Continent, then slowly and expensively (for the Count had to borrow fifty thousand ducats) trundled across Europe in almost royal state on their way to Spain. In Paris Jane made friends with young Mary Stuart, who used to write to her and sign herself 'your perfect friend'. Eventually their coaches rolled into Zafra and the young English countess became mistress of a real castle in Spain. Feria was made a duke in 1571, but died many years before his wife, leaving her in charge of all his possessions and with a debt of one hundred thousand ducats. Jane's widowhood was spent in befriending English Catholics, in furthering the cause of the return of England to the Roman faith, and in paying her debts. In this she was so successful that everything was paid off by the time her son, who became the second Duke, was of age. She always kept a coffin in the palace to remind her of her mortality and she hung a little death's head at the end of her beads. Jane lived long enough to hear the news of Elizabeth's death, and it would be interesting to know her thoughts when she heard that the terrifying old woman, whom she remembered as a slighted young princess in peril of the block, was no more. It would indeed also be interesting to know what she and her cousin Margaret and the English exiles, the refugees and the spies, who were continually arriving at Zafra, talked about as they sat together in the old palace on the hill. It is strange and also touching that she willed that her heart should be taken back to England.

I gave the doorbell another pull, and at last a grille was shot back and an invisible nun in the gatehouse beyond asked what I wanted. When I told her I should like to see the tomb of the Duchess of Feria, the little revolving box came round and in one of its divisions lay the key of the church. I found the Duke and Duchess in a dark tomb above a vault which had been rifled by Napoleon's sacrilegious troops.

I went on, thinking that the graves of Englishmen and women that one comes across in foreign places are always lonely and pathetic; why, I cannot say. It does not really matter where a man is buried and many have chosen to lie as far from home as possible. But I have the feeling that it is a sad fate to die abroad, and never to come home to lie under an English sky.

Whichever way you approach Andalusia, you must cross mountains and descend into the fairest and most fertile region of Spain. The road began to rise towards the mighty flanks of the Sierra Morena and to twist and turn, so that at one moment the sun was in my eyes and the next at my back. This country used to be frequented by bandits a century ago and men would make their wills before venturing into it, as they did in the eighteenth century before they entered the Highlands of Scotland. It is said that a few Reds still lurk about the *sierra*, in whose less accessible parts you may remember that Don Quixote underwent his penance.

The southern slopes of the *sierra* led down into a fiery country where the olive trees grew out of red soil and where the Rio Tinto flowed down from the hills. There were pleasant valleys, cattle in the fields, and the limewashed houses looked whiter than in any part of Spain. Then I caught sight of Seville. The city sprawls over the plain and in the centre, like a mastodon, is the cathedral.

# Chapter VI

*Seville in June—the story of the Black Prince's Ruby—a bull-fight—
the modernity of the corrida—the Columbus Library—the monastery of
La Rábida—the port of Palos—a visit to Jerez*

## § 1

M Y room in Seville overlooked a garden intersected by paths of
red gravel, where beds of scarlet cannas blossomed beneath palm
trees. Several little fountains sent up their bright jets into the sunlight.
In the morning I would be awakened by the sound of a gardener's hose
pricking the tough canna leaves and, throwing open the shutters, I
would see that today was going to be even hotter than yesterday.

One approaches Seville with thoughts of grandmamma and great-
grandmamma, who went there long ago with water-colours and painted
those pretty little pictures of donkeys and mules loaded with water-
pots, and handsome Andalusians wearing wide hats and red sashes,
which are preserved in so many family albums. It was in Seville that the
Spain of the tourist poster was born in the nineteenth century; and
it was largely created by the wealthy upper classes of England, who
would arrive by ship at Cádiz or Gibraltar. No doubt if our ancestors
had approached Spain the old way across the Pyrenees or by Coruña,
the romantic Spain of the poster might have been slightly different;
and the Andalusian with his Córdoban hat, his side-whiskers, his
short jacket and his narrow trousers, might not have become the
typical Spaniard for so many the world over. It must be amusing
for the Castilians, the Asturians, the Gallegos, the Basques and the
Catalans, and all the other Spaniards, to see how the world has adopted
the Andalusian, perhaps the least typical of all the Spaniards, as the
prototype of the nation. It is almost as though the nineteenth century
Irishman with his shillelagh had been pronounced a typical Englishman;
indeed it seems to me that the Castilian treats the Andalusian with
much the same affectionate tolerance that Englishmen of the last
century bestowed upon 'Paddy', the delightful, inconsequential, but
always charming and amusing Irishman.

The legend of dancing Spain began after the Peninsular War, when for the first time since Tudor days English eyes were directed beyond the Pyrenees. Southern Spain suddenly became fashionable: Washington Irving, Lane's *Arabian Nights*, *The Barber of Seville*, young sailors and gunners home on leave from Gibraltar, the revival of sherry as a fashionable drink in London, said to have been due to Lord and Lady Holland after their Spanish tour, all helped to attract the English to Andalusia. Fortunately for them, it was as easy for the rich middle-classes of the nineteenth century to reach Seville from Cádiz as it had been in the Middle Ages for the English pilgrim to journey to Santiago de Compostela from Coruña. So with one thing and another —sherry at Jerez, the Rio Tinto mines, and Gibraltar—there was quite a lot of English influence in the south of Spain at that time; and Seville at Easter, when England is often so cold and dreary, was the obvious destination.

Legends grow naturally in the soil of Spain and the legend that it is a sunny land of Moorish fretwork and undulating females has been a profitable one. I was amused when I visited an exalted official of the State Tourist Department in Madrid to find him inspecting future posters, all of which depicted the Spanish scene as it is expected to be; with Spanish dancers, castanets in hand, arms uplifted and feet rapping a *taconeado*, which he knew as well as I did was no more typical of Spain than the Oban Games were of Britain. Still it is a golden legend.

My hotel was a grand one and it was empty, for there are few visitors in Seville in June. It had been built during that brief Restoration period, the reign of Edward VII, when wealth, as if aware of what was in store for it, was having its last fling. The more I looked at my dressing-table the more certain I became that it had once reflected the shoulders of many a beauty painted by Sargent, and I seemed to see too the ghost of a lady's maid heating curling-tongs over a methylated flame and placing the white satin with puff sleeves on the bed. And in the next room dear George, who had been shooting in the marshes since dawn, had removed his Norfolk jacket, his knicker-bockers, his fawn gaiters, and the tweed hat with the ear-flaps and the button on the top, and was bathed, dressed and monocled. The long corridors with their endless rows of mahogany doors seemed to remember such ghosts, who are now as archaic as the Elizabethans.

It was, I thought, with an air of pained resignation that the palatial hall of this hotel welcomed its nightly cargo of modern travellers. First a great coach would draw up under the porch and a little guide would run in and confer with the sleek young man behind the desk. He would be followed by a strange and exhausted assortment of English, Americans and French, all of them carrying small bundles or parcels, and some of them holding red earthenware *jarras*, or leather *botas* which had been foisted on them by the peasantry. The great hotels of Europe have trimmed their sails to this new world and the conducted tour is no longer treated with scorn. No longer are the one-night visitors given an inferior *table d'hôte* and put behind a screen as if they were something to be ashamed of; on the contrary, the wise hotels know that the splendid days of the rich milord will never return, and the individual traveller is now—unless he is on foot or on a bicycle—a complete anomaly.

§ 2

Nothing is more difficult to maintain than a reputation for gaiety. There are moments when the smile must be allowed to fade from the lips, when the bright remark must remain unsaid, and the sparkle die from the eyes. That, I felt, was Seville in June. When Holy Week came round again, I told myself, and the *pasos* were carried trembling through the streets upon the shoulders of penitents, when the hooded *cofradías* drip their candle-grease on the midnight pavements and the wail of a *saeta* sears the darkness, then it would be the Seville I had read about; and the great *Feria* would follow, when the glossy-haired girls would put on their polka-dot flounces and ride pillion behind narrow-hipped young men wearing Córdoban hats; the *casetas* would be set up in the park and the sound of guitars and castanets would greet the dawn. Then, I told myself, Seville would be herself again.

It was surprising to see the city in this out of season mood, for there was more liveliness in a yard of Madrid than in the whole of Seville. The people who had remained in this hot city looked poor and fretful. There were no flashing *señoritas*, no gallant *caballeros* riding by, no flirted fans, no laughter and no whispered compliments, at any rate as far as I could judge. Instead, the crowds of work-people who fought to get on the homeward trams in the evening looked sour and glum, even after making all allowance for the Spanish contempt for work.

I walked down the famous Sierpes, the street where no wheels are allowed. It is a Moorish-looking street and in summer-time awnings are slung across it as in ancient Rome, making a welcome tunnel of shade. I had expected to find its shop windows crowded with delightful and expensive things, but the windows were full of junk for tourists: castanets, little figures of dancers, wooden bulls stuck full of *banderillas*, small china ornaments and imitation Moorish tiles. At intervals along the pavement numbers of well-dressed elderly men were sitting out, almost on the kerb, talking and smoking cigars. Such assemblies are to be seen in most Spanish towns. They looked like a parliament of elders, or members of a stock exchange, and in this narrow Moorish street it seems that they ought to be wearing turbans. They are members of clubs, and it must seem to a stranger a peculiar habit, this passion for the pavement. I remember asking an American woman, who had married a Spaniard, what these men talk about so solemnly as they sit on their kerbside chairs.

'Women,' she replied without hesitation. 'It is the only topic!'

The streets of the old city are among the most picturesque in Spain, and in true eastern fashion the outside of a house is no indication of its interior. Beautiful wrought-iron doors give glimpses into charming courtyards where you can see a fountain, some geraniums in pots, a palm tree, and a dado of Moorish tiles.

I wandered through a labyrinth of narrow streets, coming to unexpected little plazas, then on through more white tunnels which might have been in Africa. Sometimes I heard a voice singing a high-pitched wail in a minor key that ended suddenly, as if bitten off in mid-air. It is extraordinary that though Ferdinand and Isabel expelled the Moors, the voice of Andalusia is still Moorish.

It was in one of these old streets that I came across the perfect curiosity shop. There were baroque saints, old pictures, bits of jewellery, mirrors, swords and daggers, coins, strips of beautifully carved and gilded wood, chairs, tables, glass cabinets bursting with knick-nacks; and the whole place was covered with a sheet of dust. Imprisoned behind this wreckage of another world I saw a pair of sad old Spanish eyes under an aged felt hat. When I spoke the old eyes gleamed for a second, believing me to be an Americano, then filled again with their habitual gloom. In a galvanized tin bath I found a beautiful seventeenth century box lock, complete with its key. The bolt was jammed with rust and for a moment I thought I should buy it for the pleasure of cleaning it and getting the key to work again as once it did—to admit who knows and to whom? Another enchanting and ridiculous object was a musical box that actually worked. Upon the lid sat a mouse in a cage and facing it was an old woman dressed like a witch, with a stick in her hand. As soon as the box gave out its thin trickle of sound, the mouse began to dart in and out of the box while the old witch aimed a blow at it, missing every time. When the music slowed down, the old woman's arm jerked to a standstill and the mouse popped back into the cage.

In the evening a spurious air of brightness seemed to invade Seville with the *paseo*, which, however, had nothing like the vigour of Madrid. Everywhere there were the little dark girls of which Spain has an inexhaustible supply. I saw Goya's *Maja* hundreds of times and would wager that she was never the Duchess of Alba. When I went to a kiosk to buy some cigarettes, a well-dressed man came up and bought a single cigarette. I had never seen anyone buy a single cigarette before.

Later that evening in my hotel I met an Englishman who was motoring round Spain with his wife. They lived in South Africa and had brought their car from Cape Town to Lisbon in a Portuguese ship. They were overcome by the courtesy and kindliness of the Spaniards; though the heat of Mérida and Seville was much fiercer and more exhausting, they said, than anything known at the Cape. He told me of an adventure which had befallen them that afternoon in Seville.

'We were walking through the poorer parts of the old city,' he said, 'when we saw a number of cars parked in the courtyard of a building. It seems ridiculous now, looking back on what happened, but we thought it was a garage and walked in. We found out our mistake at once—we were in a palace! It was too late to retreat, for a footman wearing white gloves came out and asked what we wanted. I was trying to explain to him that we had made a mistake when a middle-aged Spanish lady appeared and spoke to us in perfect English. She laughed when I told her we had mistaken her palace for a garage. "I'm not in the least surprised," she said. "The cars belong to my sons!" She invited us to look over the palace, which was old and interesting. So with two footmen in livery walking ahead of us and opening doors, we entered a palace which reminded us of the *Alcázar*. There were richly coloured Moorish rooms with divans round the walls, there were rooms decorated with coats-of-arms, and the Duchess—for we were certain that she must be one—told us that in the summer the family moved to the top of the palace and only occupied the lower floors in the winter. When we had said goodbye to our charming hostess, we walked out of all this splendour—into a slum!'

§ 3

If you try to imagine St Paul's Cathedral in the centre of a town the size of Bradford, you have some idea of the disproportionate space occupied by Seville Cathedral. Miles away you see this Gothic pyramid rising from the plain, and when you are in Seville its bulk dominates all things. It is like having a mountain in the middle of a city, with little doors in it which men pass in and out, as gnomes enter a hillside.

The guide-books call it the largest Gothic church in the world and the largest church of any except St. Peter's; but it is infinitely odder than that. In order to understand Seville Cathedral you should first see the mosque of Córdoba. More modest than Seville, Córdoba decided to build a cathedral inside the mosque and to leave the mosque standing round it, but in Seville they decided to demolish the mosque and cover with a Christian church the colossal area it had occupied. It is curious to think that the architects of Seville Cathedral were really the Moslems, and that in spite of everything their mosque still shines through in the rectangular shape of this vast church.

When I entered the perpetual twilight of the cathedral, a poor little woman attached herself to me and fluttered shapelessly and noiselessly like a black bat, whining the Christian equivalent of 'alms for the love of Allah'; and when I placed a trifle in her hand she blessed me and faded into the shadows. I stood amazed by the size of this church, not delighted and impressed as one is in St. Peter's, but overwhelmed by this immensity of gloom, by the colossal nave pillars rising to the cavernous vaulting. Upon the great expanse of floor a group of tourists, or a priest and his acolyte, looked like insects as they crawled across the pavement.

The side chapels, where Masses were being said, glowed like little jewellers' shops in some vast deserted market square; and when I came to the tomb of Columbus I saw four giant heralds, representing Castile, León, Aragon and Navarre, bearing upon their shoulders the coffin of the navigator; and these more than human-sized figures seemed, like everything else, out of scale.

But the cathedral is full of exquisite things that shine and glitter. A great deal of South American gold, one imagines, still gleams upon the crowns of Virgins and the limbs of cupids, and the *retablo* behind the high altar seems to hold the population of a fair-sized medieval town; but to appreciate it you need either a step-ladder or a pair of field-glasses.

Every year at Corpus Christi choristers in the dress of three centuries ago dance in front of this altar to the sound of castanets; and if I had to choose, I would rather see this Dance of the Seises than the famous ceremonies of Holy Week. The boys wear satin knee-breeches, jackets hanging from one shoulder, buckled shoes, and plumed hats, and they perform a grave and stately measure. It is a unique survival of the religious dancing which was always popular in Spain, though the Church was more than a little doubtful about it. From what I have read of the Dance of the Seises, it is the last vestige of these ancient ballets. Even so, Rome was anxious to put a stop to it, and Pope Eugenius IV allowed the dance to continue, so the story goes, only as long as the costumes should last. It is said that, in order to keep up the custom, the dresses have been cunningly patched and re-patched until hardly a shred of the original garments remains.

A friendly verger took me into the *capilla mayor* and showed me the silver and bronze casket which is opened four times a year so that the people of Seville may revere the uncorrupted body of St. Ferdinand, who took Seville from the Moors in 1248. To the English visitor this is one of the most interesting relics in Spain. Ferdinand III was the grandson of Eleanor, the daughter of Henry II of England. She had married Alfonso VIII of Castile. Ferdinand's daughter was Eleanor of Castile, the queen of Edward I, who, as every schoolboy knows, sucked the poison from her husband's arm when he was stabbed by an assassin in the Holy Land; she was the mother of the little Prince of Wales who was presented to the Welsh chieftains upon a shield at Caernarvon, and her untimely death caused her sorrowing husband to erect the chain of funeral crosses that end at Charing Cross.

It is strange to think that Edward II had so much Spanish blood, which he handed on to Edward III, and so to the Black Prince and John of Gaunt. The Black Prince's campaign in Spain in defence of the dethroned Pedro the Cruel becomes entirely comprehensible when we think of him fighting for the rights of his great-grandmother's family.

'Come with me,' said the verger, 'there is more to see.'

He led the way down a flight of marble steps to a small crypt, or *panteón*, beneath the high altar, where sacred relics and human remains lie enclosed in beautiful caskets and in glass cases lit by electric light. He pointed out the small ivory crucifix which St. Ferdinand always took with him into battle, and we examined the coffins and caskets, many of which are labelled like museum specimens. Here I came upon two small boxes bound with official red and yellow tape. One contained the bones of Pedro the Cruel, the other those of the only woman who could influence him, his mistress, María de Padilla.

She was the mother of several children, among them Constance, who married John of Gaunt, and Isabel, who married Edmund of Langley. As I have already said, the blood of these women ran on in England to Edward IV and Richard III, and through Elizabeth of York to Henry VIII and Elizabeth. How curious it is to think of a thin trickle of this passionate Spanish blood in the Virgin Queen. On the Spanish side it continued through John II and Henry IV to Isabel the Catholic, and through her daughter Joan to the Hapsburgs.

When María de Padilla died, Pedro convoked a special meeting of the Cortés in Seville and declared that he and María de Padilla had been lawfully wedded for a long time. As witnesses to the marriage he produced his chaplain, his chancellor, and a brother of María. The Archbishop of Toledo took the oaths of these witnesses and the King and his dead mistress were declared to have been man and wife and their children were made legitimate. I read printed upon the labels of these ghastly little boxes proof of the Church's verdict, for María de Padilla was called Pedro's *esposa*, or wife. This decision, incidentally, was also an admission of bigamy, for Pedro had married Blanche of Bourbon while he was already married to María de Padilla!

'Do you have a saying in Spanish about skeletons in a cupboard?' I asked the verger. But he didn't understand me.

Constance was completely devoted to her father, and one of her reasons for marrying John of Gaunt was that he would be a doughty champion to avenge Pedro's murderer. Froissart says that when John of Gaunt and Constance led an English army into Spain to claim the crown of Castile, Constance took the first opportunity to discover her father's remains, which were taken up and conveyed to Seville 'and there most reverently buried'; which is hardly borne out by the box of bones in the little crypt beneath the altar.

'Did you ever hear the story of the big ruby that Pedro the Cruel took from the King of Granada?' I asked the verger.

'Certainly, *señor*, everyone in Seville knows about the great ruby.'

'Do you also know that the ruby was given to the Black Prince by Don Pedro and is now in front of the Crown of England?'

The man was astonished and thought I was inventing it.

'But, *señor*, is this really true?'

'It is perfectly true, and you can see it any day if you go to the Jewel House in the Tower of London.'

I think he would have asked me a great many questions if at that moment a look of sudden anxiety had not crossed his face, and with a 'Quick, *señor*, we must go!' ran up the stairs; and we were only just in time, for the choir and the canons were filing into the *coro*.

§ 4

I remember many years ago being taken by a Syrian merchant through the streets of Damascus to a door in the wall of a slum. On the other side was a court of orange trees, a fountain and a tame gazelle. All round were rooms piled with rugs and carpets which had been brought overland by caravan from Persia. There were silks, brocades, jewellery, pottery, and the usual things which look so wonderful in the Near East and so unsuitable when you get them home. Over several cups of coffee I bargained for two camel rugs, which I still have, and when the deal was concluded the merchant, his blood now up, led me into a series of rooms lit by hanging lamps of tinted glass. The walls were decorated with the customary arabesques, richly carved, gilded and coloured, and some of them were fine and genuinely old.

'I will sell you whichever room you like the best,' said the merchant, clapping his hands for more coffee. 'I will make it very cheap! How beautiful this room would look—or perhaps the smaller one with the gold divans—in your home in England. . . .'

Mistaking my look of dismay for one of interest, he went on.

'I will ship this room for you, sir, with every section clearly marked, so that your carpenter can put it up just as you see it now. And when you invite your friends, sir, and give them coffee, they will think themselves in Damascus. Look, each wall is made in sections that fit together. It all comes to pieces and will pack in boxes.'

As I went away, I thought I had had a good lesson in Arab architecture. It is the architecture of the nomad. Even when made of stone, it has the appearance of having been fretworked in wood that could be taken down, packed away like stage scenery upon the backs of camels, and transported across the desert to be erected somewhere else.

I recalled this as I entered the *Alcázar* in Seville, and thought that

163

possibly most Europeans, if they are honest with themselves, would confess that, the first gasp of delight and astonishment over, they plodded through these Moorish halls with an increasing sense of boredom. The first glimpse is unforgettable; the fantasy, the lightness, the play of light and shade, the clusters of gold honeycombs at roof level, the slender columns matched two by two, the cusped arches, the lace-like arabesques above them; but it goes on and on like an endless Arab anecdote, full of repetition, until you have the impression that the multiplication table has been set to music. At first I thought the *Alcázar* the most beautiful thing I had seen in Seville. It is late medieval Arab architecture and was built for a Christian, in fact for Pedro the Cruel; and you can see an inscription running round the entrance *patio* in which he is referred to as 'the sultan'. What an extraordinary mixture these medieval Spaniards must have been. Even the Cid spoke and read Arabic and liked to wear Moorish robes on occasions, so did St. Ferdinand; while Pedro even observed the Arab custom, if he has not been maligned by his enemies, of preserving the heads of his foes in boxes of salt and camphor.

The *Alcázar* is as curious a sidelight as you will find in Spain of the truth of Professor Trend's statement that 'Spanish mediaeval history cannot be understood in the crude terms of the *Reconquista*'. I am sure many tourists who are shown over this building believe they are visiting a palace of the Moors; but it is more interesting to know that it was built by Christian kings on the site of an older Moorish palace of which hardly any trace remains. It is an extraordinary indication of the way Arab habits and customs had penetrated the life of Christian Spain. It is also strange to know that it is still used as a palace and that Franco, whenever he visits Seville, lives here in a mid-Victorian setting transposed on the arabesques. There are brass bedsteads in this Moorish palace, as you can see for yourself, and crystal chandeliers which hang rather unhappily from the gilt ceilings. I have been told that Alfonso XIII liked the *Alcázar* as well as any of his palaces. It was well suited, no doubt, to a romantic mood, and His Majesty could venture out by night through a little postern gate into the Vera Cruz quarter, where even in the dog days of summer you can sometimes hear a guitar from an upper window.

I asked the guide if he had heard of the Black Prince's Ruby and he said no; when I asked if he had ever heard of the ruby which Pedro stole from the King of Granada, his eyes lit up and he told me this story.

Abû Saïd had usurped the throne of Granada and came to Seville to ask the support of Pedro, attended by a large following and provided with many rich gifts. He rather unwisely took with him a collection of jewels, including an enormous uncut ruby about the size of a pullet's egg; and upon this jewel Pedro set his heart. He greeted the Red King, as Abû Saïd was called, with affection, and lodged him and his suite handsomely; but he had decided to betray his guest and steal the jewels. One day the Red King and his suite were seized, Abû Saïd was stripped of his garments and, mounted on an ass, was led ignominiously to a field outside Seville. Here Pedro and his knights rode at him with their lances. Every time Pedro flung a lance, he cried, 'Take that for the treaty you made me sign with Aragon!', and, 'Take that for the castle you took from me!', until the unhappy infidel sank mortally wounded. That was how Pedro the Cruel came to possess the ruby of Abû Saïd.

Like the verger in the cathedral, the guide did not know the conclusion of the story, which is that after the battle of Nájera, when the Black Prince and an English army had routed the French forces who were opposed to Pedro, the Castilian king in gratitude gave the ruby to the Black Prince. From that time it has had a long and eventful history in England, where it has always been known as the Black Prince's Ruby. The stone was pierced in ancient times and, using this hole, the Black Prince had the ruby sewn to the velvet cap which he wore under his coronet. The stone descended to his son, Richard II, but does not appear again in history until the battle of Agincourt, when Henry V wore it in the front of his helmet. Among the crown jewels sold after the execution of Charles I was 'one large ballas ruby, wrapped in paper'. Who bought it is unknown, but it was mysteriously returned to Charles II. When Colonel Blood tried to steal the Crown from the Tower of London in the reign of Charles II, the Black Prince's Ruby was found in the pocket of Parrett, one of Blood's accomplices. From that time until today the ruby has passed in unbroken succession to the kings and queens of England, and has pride of place in front of the state crown.

It is not a beautiful object. It is irregular in shape and to the uninitiated appears to be a large, oblong piece of dark red glass. It was backed with gold in ancient times, and the stone is so old that court jewellers have declined the responsibility of removing the ugly gold backing in order to weigh the jewel accurately. It is believed that the stone came originally from Burma and was pierced to be worn as a pendant to a necklace.

The *Alcázar* . . . Pedro the Cruel . . . the Red King, Abû Saïd, . . . the Black Prince . . . Agincourt . . . the Crown of England. I suppose it would make quite a good film, except that all the murder and excitement come at the beginning.

I thought the gardens of the *Alcázar* the most beautiful place in Seville, and I never had cause to change my mind. Here was the Seville one reads about: the orange trees, the roses, the hedges of box and myrtle, the cypresses and the fish-ponds. There was a delightfully juvenile water-trap in a little garden, where the king could drench his guests with jets of water from the paving beneath their feet, a typical Arab jest. It reminded me of the distorting mirrors in which the abashed visitor straightens his tie, or used to do so, in the entrance hall of the King of Jordan's palace at Amman. These schoolboy jokes with water became popular in Elizabethan gardens; Spring Gardens, now a narrow little turning near the Admiralty Arch, preserves the memory of one whose water-trap was a feature of old Whitehall Palace.

Centuries of gardening are to be imagined on this site, and many monarchs have impatiently waited for winter so that they could dig up, alter and transform; for gardening is not the peaceful occupation it is imagined to be, but a perpetually restless search for perfection. Charles V and Philip II dug, planted, and improved, made pavilions, reservoirs, and even a maze; and in later times other kings introduced baroque novelties such as dripping grottoes, garden gates, wall fountains, and rusticated stonework. There is a beautiful fish-pond with a little bronze Mercury rising in the centre as if he were in Italy. The flower beds were gay with cannas and agapanthus, plumbago was in flower, so was jasmine; and I sat on a seat covered with Moorish tiles beneath one of the largest *Magnolia grandiflora* I have ever seen. I noticed ten yards away the taut form of a small white cat watching me with suspicion. I made the usual sounds, but one sudden movement would have sent it off at a bound. Gradually I managed to call it to me. Slowly I dropped my hand and touched it, but it leapt away, crouching. It came back and let me stroke it, but it was more puzzled than pleased; for no one had ever stroked it before. If only I had something for it to eat, it might have purred, but a too hasty movement sent it off into the flower beds; and, though I returned at a later time with some meat I had saved, I never saw it again.

## § 5

I was so depressed by Seville the first day that I decided not to use an introduction I had been given, but to slip quietly away to Córdoba. Then I did use it, and my life immediately changed! I was rushed off to cafés, restaurants, bars, public buildings, and even to those queer kerbside clubs; and in a few hours I knew twenty people by their Christian names and many more by sight. They were mostly young and enthusiastic, and this is the way they talked, always against a background of tinkling glass, coffee cups, other people's conversation, and the scraping of chairs and tables on pavements.

'Have you met Don Felipe? No? Well, it can be arranged. He is English and you will like him. Oh, *muy simpático*! He is charming. He is—precious! My dear Aurelio, would you not say that Don Felipe is most precious?'

'Undoubtedly, most precious.'

'But I can't stand precious people. I run miles from them.'

'Ah, but you will like Don Felipe! He is wonderful, he is enchanting, he is the youngest old man we have ever met. Would you not say so, Aurelio?'

It was like living in a verbal soufflé. They accepted me with Irish impetuosity. For them, I had the charm of novelty and I was a wonderful audience. Consequently they performed for me, and I too became precious, incomparable, and—greatest compliment of all—full of *españolismo*! Having lived for some years on this planet, and having met temperamental extroverts before, I knew that there was a time limit to their enthusiasm and that every meeting made me a little less *precioso*, that, once departed, I should be immediately forgotten. This was not insincerity or shallowness: it was just living for the moment, as children do.

They rushed me off to many places, but they were easily diverted. We would start off for one café and go somewhere else on the spur of the moment, or because while we were on our way someone very Andaluz and *precioso* stopped us and insisted that we should change our plans. One of our earliest calls was upon the most famous Virgin in Seville, the patroness of bull-fighters, *Nuestra Señora de la Esperanza*, known also, from the district in which her church stands, as *La Macarena*. All the famous *espadas* revere her and pray to her, and even dedicate their encrusted garments to her. She is a beautiful, drooping and tearful Madonna, but whether she weeps for the bull-fighters, the bulls, or the horses, I cannot say. In the vestry we were shown her wardrobe and, lying next to the state robe she wears in Holy Week, we saw with awe the 'suit of lights' which had belonged to the great Manolete, who was killed at Linares in 1947.

'Ah, how sad, how *emocionante*, and also how precious. . . . Do you know, Don Enrique, that before Manolete went to Mexico he came here and, upon his knees before the Holy Virgin, he swore that if she brought him safe home again he would dedicate his cape to her. He came home, but—only to die. And here'—the verger had unlocked the glass case—'and here, see, touch and feel *his*, the great Manolete's, *traje de luces*. . . .'

They rushed me off to a hospital for the aged poor, where a little old Sister of Mercy showed us a horrible painting, by Valdés Leal, of a dead bishop, robed and mitred in his coffin.

'*Por Dios, hombre*, it's terrible! It's horrible! I can never see it without feeling sick. Murillo said that he held his nose when he looked at it!'

They took me to a peaceful *patio* in a side street where shady colonnades rose round a fountain, and in rooms above were living aged and infirm priests, little men in rusty black with spectacles on their noses; there was a slice of southern blue sky above and a bird singing in a cage. We even walked up the ramps to the top of the Giralda Tower, which used to be a minaret, and from there we saw Seville lying below in the heat of a summer morning, and the Guadalquivir running like a silver thread from the hills. Naturally, after the expenditure of so much energy, we had to go to a café and recuperate with shrimps and olives and the little bits and pieces upon which the Sevillians seem to live; and, as we sat there, more enchanting, precious and sympathetic people would come up and be very Andaluz. I wondered if I had fallen into the lap of some mutual admiration society; surely somewhere in Seville there must be someone who was unsympathetic! And they all talked about the precious Don Felipe to whom they were dying to introduce me. But as he never appeared, I began to think he was an imaginary Englishman.

They were very polite and did their best to talk English or French to me, to save themselves, I suspected, from my Spanish.

'In many books about Spain,' I said, 'you read that at night time in Andalusia the lover may be seen pressed against the iron window screens, whispering to his beloved. I have looked everywhere and not once have I seen this.'

'Ah,' they said, 'it was so even to the outbreak of the Civil War, but, like so many other things in Spain, it went at that time. There is now no need for the lover to whisper through the *rejas*; he can do so elsewhere, for the girls are no longer behind the screen.'

'Yes, that is so true,' said someone, 'and—there are many more illegitimate children!'

'I was talking to a priest the other day,' said a third, 'who was telling me how many more illegitimate children there are, and he said that during the Republic and the Civil War the Spanish girls achieved freedom much too quickly. He told me that recently a girl said to him that she was going to have a child and the father was a young soldier stationed in Seville, who was her *novio*. The priest asked her to bring the young man to see him, and the young man was glad to go. He told the priest he was much troubled in his mind because he had four other *novias* in various garrison towns of Spain, and each one had had a child, and his trouble was that he didn't know which one of his *novias* he ought to marry, because his love for them was equal. He begged the priest to advise him.'

'And what did the priest tell him to do?'

'Well, what do they say in America? He passed the buck. He told the young man to go and confess his sins to his own village priest and ask *his* advice!'

'How interesting,' said a fourth. 'What would *you* advise him to do?'

'Well, it's a question,' said a fifth, 'whether first love or last love is the more enduring, and he must advise the young man to marry either the first *novia* or the last.'

'We must put this question to Don Felipe,' said another.

A young man came over to our table and held forth without any preliminaries.

'I have just heard a story. It is most precious! An American million-aire offered half a million dollars to anyone who could discover a zebra with blue stripes. An Englishman, a Frenchman, a German, and a Spaniard decided to take up the challenge. The Englishman bought a sun-helmet, a rifle and a tent, and took the first 'plane to Africa. The German went to a library and began to read everything that was ever written about zebras. The Frenchman bought a mule and painted blue stripes on it and claimed the prize!'

'Well, and what did the Spaniard do?'

'The Spaniard bought himself an expensive dinner, and while he was smoking a cigar decided what he was going to do with half a million dollars.'

Who were these gay people? I don't know. Nothing is more mysterious to a stranger in Spain than how people, other than the peasants, live, what they are and when they work. As in the eighteenth century, I imagine that many jobs, probably the best ones, are sinecures; others are ill-paid government posts which make it necessary for a man to have several sidelines. There is real wealth, I suppose, in land and in bull-farming; and I was introduced to a young man who drove about in the latest Cadillac, who, I was told, owned a wolfram mine near the Portuguese border and was worth millions.

One night after dinner they took me to a gloomy street in the Triana quarter, where we went down into a basement which no stranger would have had the courage to enter. There was a small room cluttered with chairs and tables, and a wooden stage slightly raised from the floor at one end. There were bull-fight posters on the walls on which legendary bulls of great tonnage and ferocity were charging straight at the on-looker. The room was blue with cigar smoke and full of dark, gipsy-looking Spaniards sipping *manzanilla* or drinking lager beer. My friends slapped the most sinister-looking persons on the back, there was much delighted conversation, much holding of lapels and jocular conversation. A melancholy young stoic came and sat with us for a moment. He was a young *matador* who was on the way up. He was obviously putting on an act, grooming himself and his personality for the great days to come. But I sensed that he was essentially a practical young man with no illusions. He had wonderful control over himself and everything he did was calculated, even the way he lit and smoked a cigarette. I thought he would be a good *matador*. All my friends, of course, said he was wonderful.

I heard the sound of guitars and, glancing towards the little stage, saw four somnolent Andalusians, who had not shaved that day, sitting on kitchen chairs idly sweeping the strings with their fingers while cigarette ash dropped on their waistcoats. They thrummed in a rhythmic coma. Then an old woman, who looked as if she had just left the kitchen for a second, took a chair near the stage and produced a ball of knitting. Like the guitarists, she was completely detached. How eastern this is, I thought; I had seen the same sort of scene in Morocco, in Syria, in Egypt. One of the musicians, emerging from the reservoir of gloom and melancholy which is the birthright of all Spaniards, spoke a word or two to a friend in the audience and went on playing. Then a girl stepped on the stage, and after casually adjusting one of her shoes, clapped her hands once or twice and began to dance. She was small and plump and perhaps sixteen. She wore a long blue cotton frock which fell to her feet in a series of flounces. Her hair was smoothly parted and she wore a flower over one ear. She lifted her arms, the castanets clicked, and she began to dance on the same spot, rapping out a rhythm with her heels. The rhythm became faster; her body obeyed it, her heels tapped more swiftly on the boards; then suddenly, as if frozen, she stopped and stood there poised; then gathering up her skirts, she left the stage. The old woman put the knitting into a bag and followed her.

'A *duenna*?' I asked.

'Her mother,' I was told.

She was followed by other girls who danced *flamenco*, one who danced a quick, merry *alegría*, and another who postured like a bull-fighter in a dance which is called a *farruca*. But none of these dancers seemed to interest the men, who went on drinking *manzanilla*, lighting cigars and cigarettes, talking and casting a glance now and then on the stage. They were a very tough audience. But the girls did not seem to mind. They also were completely detached and might have been dancing in an empty room.

There was a drop in the conversation, however, when a sultry-looking, scraggy, dark girl with enormous blazing eyes and thick dark eyebrows took the stage. Her skin, slightly rouged on the cheeks, was the colour of an Indian's. There was a burst of applause and shouted greetings, to which the girl paid no attention at all. She didn't even condescend to smile. She stood for quite a time in her long, white-spotted red dress, her eyes half closed, waiting to begin while the guitars thrummed in the background. The audience began to clap and stamp their feet in time to the music, still the girl remained motionless as if in communion with far-off spirits. Then suddenly up went her arms, click went her castanets, and the music rushed after her as she moved into a dance which, it seemed to me, had the rare flavour of antiquity. She made the other girls look like beginners. She had tremendous vitality and personality and whatever it is that focuses one's whole attention upon an actor. She had style, elegance, passion. There was hardly a sound now as she danced, only the guitars and the rapping of her high heels; and to me her dress had become the many flounced dress of the Cretan snake-goddess, whose altars were strewn with cockle shells, perhaps the first castanets. There were moments when her body was stationary except for a slight tapping of her heels; but her arms and hands were still dancing, weaving slow patterns in the air. Then she would plunge into her corybantic frenzy again, bending, shuddering, turning and glancing over her shoulder. All the time, above her head, at her waist, in the air around her, like cicadas on a summer day, was the sharp rattle of what Martial called the *Boetica crusmata*. With a swirl of her dusty skirts she had abolished the modern world, and I thought of the Phoenician galleys coming into Gades, of Herod's banqueting hall, of the Greek vases in the British Museum with their dancers. Then, when I least expected it, the guitars broke off, the girl stood as still as coloured marble, hardly breathing, and a volley of *Olé*'s rewarded this living visitor from a world that we are told died three thousand years ago.

Then the spell was broken and I saw that even this panther had her *duenna*. A little old gipsy woman, who must have been her grand-mother, rose from her chair near the stage and followed her Telethusa from the room.

'Come, let us go,' said my friends. 'We shall see nothing better tonight.'

It was now nearly midnight and we went to a café which was crowded. As we were talking, I noticed a small version of the late Field-Marshal Smuts, with a white goatee and the same remote blue eyes, making his way to us between the tables.

'*Ola!* Don Felipe, where have you been all this time? My dear Don Felipe, we have missed you so much!'

And I was introduced to a spry little Englishman who must have been getting on for seventy; I liked him at once; and later on he turned to me and asked, 'How old do you think I am?' It is an embarrassing question and, as I have an unhappy gift of guessing people's ages, I always have to pitch my replies on the right side in order not to give offence; and nothing annoys an old person more than to be told his right age.

'Well,' I said, 'you might be sixty-five.'

'I am seventy-six,' he replied with an air of triumph. 'I sometimes wish I could feel like it.'

## § 6

Having nothing to do on Sunday afternoon, I thought I would go to the bulls. I paid a hundred and twenty pesetas, which is about one pound, for a good seat in the shade, and then wandered round the bull-ring watching the excited crowds find their places and pick up the little flat cushions, at a peseta each, which lie in piles beside each entrance. It had never occurred to me before, but the Greeks and the Romans must have taken similar little cushions with them into their stony arenas. I made friends with a fat little man, one of the attendants, who obligingly unlocked the infirmary for me. It was just as I had seen it on a bull-fight film: a clinically white room with beds made up and ready for gored *matadores*. There was an operating-table and a glass case full of instruments; and a door at the end of the room led into a little chapel where a modern statue of Our Lady smiled sweetly from a dusty altar. When I told the little man that I should like to see the *matadores* pray before the fight, a cynical smile passed across his unshaven face, and I gathered that this happens nowadays only in Hollywood.

'If they cross themselves as they leave the hotel,' he said, with a laugh heavily charged with garlic, 'that's about all that happens!'

I must have looked shocked, for he added.

'In the old days—yes! But then the bulls were big and strong.' His gestures were terrific. Small as he was, he began to look like a *toro bravo*. He tossed his head into the air and crouched savagely. Then he lifted his shoulders, until his neck had disappeared, in the Spanish gesture of despair. 'But, no longer! He would be a timid *torero* who prayed to be saved from the bulls we get these days. . . .'

What an odd point of view this was, yet I suppose entirely practical. You don't bother the Blessed Virgin if you can handle the bull yourself!

As I was finding my way to my seat, I looked through a gate and saw butchers erecting a scaffold with pulleys and ropes and sharpening their knives to cut up the dead bulls. As everyone knows, immediately a bull is slain a mule team jingles in and drags it out by the horns and deposits the carcass with the butchers. I asked what they did with the meat and they gave me the name of a restaurant where I could get a bull-ring steak. John Marks, who has written the best book in English about bull-fighting, says that the cost of a set of six bulls to make up a *corrida* is equivalent to about £1,250. I have read somewhere else that a first-rate *matador* may receive £1,250, or even more, for an afternoon's work, that is to say, the killing of two bulls: and as there are six bulls and three *matadores* in most *corridas*, the cost of the afternoon's ritual, if a good and expensive one, is about £5,000.

I pushed and climbed to my seat through a chattering, shouting crowd, and found myself next to three young girls of the type who adore successful *matadores*. They were looking at themselves in handbag mirrors and putting more red on their lips. Even out of the ring, I thought, the *matador* lives dangerously. Every foreigner in Seville was present; I heard English, French and German within a few yards. Just behind me sat a young priest, which surprised me, for priests are not supposed to attend bull-fights; then I heard him speaking French. The *aficionados* were making a tremendous noise, eating and taking nips from bottles, while boys in white coats stood facing the crowds with trays slung round their necks, shouting '*caramelos! . . . cigarros! . . . limonada! . . .*' For once it seemed the Spanish crowd was not its usual reserved and dignified self.

The clock strikes. There is a roar of applause as the president enters his box, the only proof that Spaniards can keep an appointment to the second. He gives a signal, and as the gates swing wide there enters a bizarre procession which has reminded many observers of ancient Rome. The *matadores* in their gold-embroidered jackets, knee breeches, jam-puff hats, magenta cloaks folded over their left arms, walk across the sand with a swinging stride, indifferent to the applause. There are three of them walking abreast; behind, in file, walk their *cuadrillas*, or assistants, dressed, but not so grandly, in the same style. There are *banderilleros*, who stick darts into the bulls, and *picadores*, who lance the bull in the neck and wheel their horses so that the animal may have something to attack and gore. It seems hardly possible that such miserable horses can walk upright. They are poor, terrified old crocks, black with sweaty fear. They know what is coming to them. Their mouths are drawn back over teeth the colour of tobacco juice. Their right eyes are bandaged so that they cannot see the bull when he comes to tear out their guts. Not everyone knows that their vocal cords are cut, because the scream of a horse is a sound that even a bull-fight crowd would not enjoy. On one side of their aged and bony flanks hangs a quilted mat which, in theory, prevents them from being gored. This is the end and reward of a lifetime of service to Man.

As the *matadores* and their troupes walk forward to make their bow, I notice that every man is out of step. Englishmen or Germans could not do this, or only with difficulty; it would not be natural for them to be out of step as it is for Spaniards. Yet there is something individualistic and impressive about this lack of step; each man puts on his own particular swagger. They bow. They do not lift their hats, but press them more firmly on their heads. They do not look round at the people or curry favour in any way with their noisy fans. Custom demands that they shall look casual and unconcerned, solemn and grave as priests of Mithra about to perform a sacrifice.

## The voiceless victim

The ring is now empty. The president gives a sign. The door of the bull-pen is opened and one would like to be able to say that several tons of black fury hurl themselves into the ring. Instead, a rather small black bull ambles out with the idea that he is free and that in a moment he will catch up with the herd. Then he knows that something is wrong. The noise. The strange smells. As he emerged from the pen, someone, to smarten him up, had stuck a dart in his left shoulder from which flutter the colours of his breeder. The wound begins to bleed slightly and sting as the air gets to it. He is more puzzled than angry. As he is wondering what this can mean, he sees two men running with little tripping steps, their feet in black dancing pumps, as they trail capes. The bull has never seen a cape before. All bulls are fought on this understanding. He looks at them in bewilderment, then, deciding that they are, if not dangerous, at least provocative, charges and misses. Behind the barrier the *matador* is watching to see which horn he uses.

Having sized up his bull, the *matador* appears, the others retire, and he attracts the bull's attention, holding a coloured cape in both hands. He stands still, hardly moving his feet, and waving the animal past him with the cape. Every time he performs one of these beautiful movements, in which grace and courage are equally present, a deep shout, which sounds like 'Allah!', comes from the crowd, and each pass is succeeded by this cry, and 'Allah! Allah! Allah!' comes from every part of the arena. It is spelt *Olé*. Surely it is the voice of Moorish Spain? Where have I heard it before just like this? I remember. It was in the streets of Bagdad one night when, concealed behind a curtain, I saw the half naked *shia* penitents whipping themselves through the streets during a Moharram procession and crying, every time the whips came down on their bleeding backs, 'Ah-Al-lah! . . . Ul-lah! Al-lah . . . Ul-lah!' As I hear this great roar of *Olé!* it sounds to me just the same.

The *matador* retires and a *picador* rides in astride his voiceless victim. The bull must now be bled. It is said that no man could kill a bull on foot with a sword unless its neck muscles had been so much weakened that it lowers its head for the sacrifice. Therefore the first blood is drawn by the *picador*.

Seeing this grotesque intruder, the bull charges. The *picador*, grasping a six-foot lance, drives the point into the bull's neck, and so they stand a moment, the man thrusting, the bull pushing. Suddenly the animal breaks away from the spear and rushes at the horse. There is a leathery bang as the horns hit the *peto*, or protective mat, but the horse is so feeble that he cannot remain on his feet. He falls not because the bull

175

is powerful and fierce, but because he is so old and weak. He falls with all four legs in the air, his belly exposed. There is a confusing scramble as the *picador* rises to his feet, and other members of the troupe come out to help him; but the bull, having at last found something tangible, slashes the horse's belly right and left. The terrified creature lifts a long, stringy neck; its unbandaged eye is bursting with fear; its mouth is wide open, exposing those poor old brown teeth. But no sound comes from it; and the bull goes on lifting and slashing.

Red capes are waved. The bull leaves the horse. A big rosette of blood is bubbling on his shoulder where the lance went in. The horse lies, its mouth open, giving gasping breaths. A man runs up and pulls at the bridle. He aims a kick at the bony ribs, and, with a ghastly effort, the poor framework rises, but it is more a caricature of a horse than ever. Its hind-legs are out of action. It squats in agony, turning its head to left and right. I hope it is dying; but no, suddenly it manages to stagger to its feet. Entrails hang from its stomach in different shades of red. A man takes a handful of tan from the ring and tries to push them back, but they fall out again like red eels. They drag the horse out of sight. He will die behind the scenes or perhaps, if he can stand, straw will be packed into his wound and he may be forced into the ring again.

Now the spectacle moves to act two. The *banderilleros* step forward delicately holding harpoons wreathed in coloured paper. They hold them mincingly by the tips and the ends that go into the bull have fish-hook barbs. As the bull approaches, the *banderilleros* stand on tiptoe and neatly plant a pair of harpoons in the beast's shoulder as he gallops past. The bull is hurt and surprised. He stops and stands miserably in the centre of the ring, shaking his head and trying to lick the blood from his back. Every time he moves, the fish-hook barbs tear his flesh and the wounds begin to froth in pink bubbles. He cannot shake out the darts. He is entirely occupied with his own pain and misery. Then he slowly shakes his head and moos like a cow, a deep, plaintive hurt sound that says, 'Why are you doing this? Let me out. I don't understand.' Immediately in front of him stands another *banderillero*, waiting with two more darts. But the bull won't charge. The man and the bull face each other and nothing happens. The man jumps up and down like a jack-in-the-box to provoke the bull. The crowd begins to laugh. They shout advice. But they soon get angry because the bull won't play. They hiss.

The *banderillero*, alarmed by the cries of disapproval, runs lightly to the bull and plants two more darts in its shoulder. The animal bellows in pain and twists round, mouthing at the wounds and trying to get rid of the things that are tearing him. Blood is now plastered on his flanks in dark streaks. He smells it and it frightens him. He runs to the side of the ring with the *banderillas* shaking and knocking together. He is a piteous object. But the crowd jeer at him because he is not a *toro bravo*. His death is evidently not going to be very exciting. This is the moment when someone ought to have the decency to come in with a humane killer. But the ceremony has to be played out to the end. A handkerchief waves from the presidential box, the trumpets sound as if something tremendous is going to happen, and out steps the *matador* with his sword. The time for sacrifice has arrived.

The *matador* stands with the sword in the curve of his arm and in a loud voice dedicates the bull to someone in the crowd. The trumpets sound again as he advances to the sacrifice. But the sacrifice is thinking only of its own pain and woe. The blood is now running down into the sand. The bull stands with lowered head, lost in misery. I am reminded, as I watch him, of all the tortured Christs of Spain. They wear this same air of spent and hopeless exhaustion. The blood, which Spanish artists accentuate, streaks their bodies in the same way. The dying bull and the dying Saviour. . . .

The bull wants water. He scrapes the hot sand with one foot and drops his muzzle, snuffling. The *matador* stands a few yards off, holding the sword concealed in the *muleta*, a strip of red flannel. He taunts the bull. He calls him names and dares him to charge. Quite surprisingly, the bull does charge. The *matador* is ready for him and slides round as usual as he runs past; but the animal, tired of being deceived, instead of returning to the unequal battle trots over to the same old place in the ring which he has made his own. Three or four times the *matador* provokes the bull to charge; but he just stands there with lowered head exposing that place which is said to be the size of half-a-crown that leads neatly down to the region of the heart. Now the moment has come, the celebrated 'moment of truth'. Here it comes!

The *matador* sights along the blade of the sword and—the bull trots past with the sword sticking up and shaking in his neck! The *matador* has struck bone. The beast now bucks and jumps, trying to shake out the sword. He manages to do so. The crowd hiss and shout insults. The *matador* takes a fresh sword. This time it slides in smoothly up to the handle. '*Ul'lah! Al-lah! Olé!*' And the bull walks off in a quiet, dignified way, with the idea of getting back to his *querencia*, the same spot in the corner, but he never gets there. Half-way he stops. His head goes down. His body sags. He looks as if he is going to be sick. He is. Thick blood pours from his mouth. Slowly, very quietly, he sinks to his knees and stays like that as if in prayer. Suddenly he falls over dead. *Olé!*

The *matador* bows like an actor. The painted girls shrug their shoulders and fumble for their lip-sticks. Three mules harnessed abreast gallop in to a sound of bells, a rope is flung round the bull's horns and the last we see of him is an undignified shape, legs in air, cleaving a red path in the sand. The gates open and shut. The butchers pick up their knives.

More trumpets.

The door of the *toril* opens again and a second bull runs out. In twenty minutes he also is dead. When the sixth bull has coughed up his heart's blood, the day's sacrifices are over. The crowd departs, exhausted with emotion, to sit in the cafés and bars and discuss every moment in the greatest detail, recounting beauties which no one but a Spaniard can ever hope to see.

§ 7

No one brought up on the works of Beatrix Potter can understand, much less appreciate, a bull-fight, and nothing can ever be done about it. The ceremonial slaughter of an animal with all the attendant blood-thirsty formalities does not seem cruel to a Spaniard, at least to those who have grown up with bull-fighting. What those Spaniards would say who had never seen a *corrida* until they had reached the age of thirty is another matter.

Yet it would be wrong to go away from a bull-fight believing that Spaniards are cruel to animals. In their homes and on their farms they are usually kind and considerate, and the dogs and cats of Spain look well-fed and happy. The Spaniard has also always been a great lover and judge of horses and it is a little difficult to understand how a nation of horse lovers, and a nation that respects dignity, can endure the horrible degradation of the bull-ring horses, most of which ought to have been painlessly destroyed years ago. It is not the spectacle of death which revolts a stranger at a bull-fight or the sight of blood, for in these days old ladies in Kensington have seen bloodier sights by far than any witnessed in the most gory of *corridas*, but it is the ceremonial torture which leads to the so-called moment of truth.

## Bull-fighting abolished

Yet how surprising is Spain! Within a few hundred yards of the arena where every Sunday during the season bulls are slain and terrified old crocks are ridden into the ring, A. F. Tschiffely, when visiting a horse-training school called *Los Remedios* in Seville, kept by a gipsy named Francisco Rodriquez, translated the following from a notice posted up in the stables.

### THE HORSE'S SUPPLICATION

MY DEAR MASTER,

Please forgive me for putting before you this my supplication. After the work and fatigues of the day, give me shelter in a clean stable. Feed me unstintingly, and quench my burning thirst. I can't tell you when I'm hungry, thirsty or ill. If I am looked after properly, I can serve you well, for I shall have strength. If I leave the fodder untouched, have my teeth examined. Please don't cut off my tail, for it is my only defence against tormenting flies and other insects. Whilst working for me, speak to me, for your voice conveys more to me than the reins and the whip. Pat me, and so encourage me to work with a good will. Don't hurry me up steep inclines, and don't pull on my bit when I'm going downhill. Don't make me carry or pull too heavy a load. I serve you uncomplainingly to the limit of my strength. If you forget this, I might die at any moment whilst doing my best to carry out your will. Treat me with the consideration that is due to a faithful servant, and if I don't understand you immediately, don't get angry, and don't chastize me, for perhaps it's not my fault. Examine my reins, possibly they don't transmit your orders correctly, because they are knotted or twisted. Look at my hooves and shoes, to make sure that they are not hurting me. Dear Master, when old age weakens me, and makes me useless, don't neglect me, or let me die of hunger. If you can't keep me any longer, destroy me, but do it yourself, so that my sufferings be less. Above all, when I'm no further use to you, please don't condemn me to the torment of the bull-ring.

Pardon me for having taken up your time with this my humble supplication, which I beg you not to forget. This I ask you, invoking the One who was born in a crib. . . .

The tragedy and suffering to which animals are condemned by thoughtlessness and insensitiveness could not be more tenderly expressed than by this Spanish gipsy, and it is good to know that 'The Horse's Supplication' exists in the headquarters of Tauromachia.

I think a great deal of the romance of the bull-ring vanishes when we know that in its modern debased and commercialized form the *corrida* dates only from the eighteenth century. The first French king, Philip V, succeeded in abolishing the old-style aristocratic bull-feast by making it unfashionable, but the pastime then fell into the hands of the grooms and servants, the cattle-men and cowboys. The art of killing a bull on foot as seen today was devised by a carpenter of Ronda, Francisco Romero. He invented the *muleta*. The circus-like costumes worn by bull-fighters date also from this recent period.

How much the bull-fight, having been handed over to the mob, needed formalizing and regulating can be gathered from the accounts of travellers who saw it in the eighteenth century. An interesting book on Spain was written by Captain George Carleton, who took part in Lord Peterborough's expedition to Spain in 1705. He describes in his *Memoirs* how he was captured and spent several happy years with his kindly hosts, who allowed him every liberty. This is his account of a bull-feast.

On the first of the days appointed (for a bull-feast commonly lasts three) all the gentry of the place, or near adjacent, resort to the Plaza in their most gaudy apparel, everyone vying in making the most glorious appearance. Those in the lower ranks provide themselves with spears, or a great many small darts in their hands, which they fail not to cast or dart, whenever the bull by his nearness gives them an opportunity. So that the poor creature may be said to fight not only with the *tauriro* (or bull-hunter, a person always hired for that purpose) but with the whole multitude in the lower class at least.

All being seated, the uppermost door is opened first; and as soon as ever the bull perceives the light, out he comes, snuffing up the air, and staring about him, as if in admiration of his attendants; and with his tail cocked up, he spurns the ground with his forefeet, as if he intended a challenge to his yet unappearing antagonist. Then, at the door appointed for that purpose, enters the *tauriro* all in white, holding a cloak in one hand and a sharp two-edged sword in the other. The bull no sooner sets eyes upon him, but wildly staring, he moves gently towards him; then gradually mends his pace, till he is come within about the space of twenty yards from the *tauriro*; when, with a sort of spring, he makes at him with all his might. The *tauriro*, knowing by frequent experience, that it behoves him to be watchful, slips aside just when the bull is at him; when casting his cloak over his horns, at the same moment he gives him a slash or two, always aiming at the neck, where there is one particular place, which, if he hit, he knows he shall easily bring him to the ground. I myself observed the truth of this experiment made upon one of the bulls, who received no more than one cut, which happening upon the fatal spot, so stunned him that he remained perfectly stupid, the blood flowing out from the wound, till, after a violent trembling, he dropt down stone dead.

But this rarely happens, and the poor creature oftener receives many wounds, and numberless darts, before he dies. Yet whenever he feels a fresh wound, either from dart, spear or sword, his rage received fresh addition from the wound, and he pursues his *tauriro* with an increase of fury and violence. And as often as he makes at his adversary, the *tauriro* takes care, with the utmost of his agility, to avoid him, and reward his kind attention with a new wound.

Some of their bulls will play their part much better than others: but the best must die. For when they have behaved themselves with all the commendable fury possible, if the *tauriro* is spent, and fail of doing execution upon him, they set dogs upon him, hough him and stick him all over with darts, till, with very loss of blood, he puts an end to their present cruelty.

When dead, a man brings in two mules dressed out with bells and feathers, and, fastening a rope about his horns, drags off the bull with the shouts and acclamations of the spectators, as if the infidels had been drove from before Ceuta.

I had almost forgot another very common piece of barbarous pleasure at these diversions. The *tauriro* will sometimes stick one of their bull-spears fast in the ground, aslant, but levelled as near as he can at his chest; then presenting himself to the bull, just before the point of the spear, on his taking his run at the *tauriro*, which, as they assured me, he always does with his eyes closed, the *tauriro* steps on one side, and the poor creature runs with a violence often to stick himself, and sometimes to break the spear in his chest, running away with part of it till he drop.

This *tauriro* was accounted one of the best in Spain; and indeed I saw him mount the back of one of the bulls, and ride on him, slashing and cutting till he had quite wearied him, at which time dismounting, he killed him with much ease, and to the acclamatory satisfaction of the whole concourse: for variety of cruelty, as well as dexterity, administers to their delight.

The feast concluded, says Carleton, with a superior spectacle, when a young nobleman whose name was Don Pedro Ortega, mounted on a fine horse, faced the bull in the old style. It is interesting that this fight of 1708 was apparently a one-man show; and it is curious also that modern experts should say that a man on foot cannot kill a bull until his tossing muscles have been weakened by goring a horse, for it was evidently done with ease in the eighteenth century.

By the time the Rev. Joseph Townsend, author of *A Journey through Spain*, saw a bull-feast at Aranjuez in 1786, the ritual had been laid down and he might be describing a modern event; except, of course, that the bulls were enormous and violent. *Picadores, banderilleros* and *matador* followed each other and the time allowed for the killing of each bull was the same as today, twenty minutes. 'In one morning I saw thirteen horses killed; but sometimes there were many more,' wrote Townsend. Of course in the royal town of Aranjuez he was seeing the best kind of bull-fight and no doubt all the performers had graduated with honours in the royal school. In the country villages and towns, however, some odd spectacles were to be seen. John Macdonald, who wrote *Memoirs of an Eighteenth-century Footman*, was in Cádiz with his master in 1778 and saw a baboon chained to a post in the middle of the bull-ring. 'Sometimes he [the bull] runs at the monkey, and then there is a general laugh.'

An intelligent and observant German, Frederick Augustus Fischer, tells in *Travels in Spain* how he saw bulls baited in the plaza at Bilbao in 1797. The animal was first attacked with pikes, hay-forks and sticks, the crowd having shouted '*los perros!*' Then bull-dogs were let loose on him. These animals savaged the bull, who leapt about with the dogs hanging to him and refusing to let go until eight strong men had thrown down the bull—evidently a young one and not in the same class as those seen by Carleton or Townsend. Six or seven bulls were baited in that way, says Fischer, to the sound of a drum.

Among those who attended a bull-feast held at Cádiz in June, 1793, was Nelson. He went as an official guest with the officers of six British sail-of-the-line. It was a good fight: five horses were disembowelled and two men were badly gored. Nelson, although not unfamiliar with the sight of blood, began to feel sick and wondered if he could sit it out; but he did so. He wrote to his wife that he would not have been displeased to have seen the spectators tossed. The fight over, Nelson and his officers returned to their ships ignorant of the real meaning and beauty of the spectacle they had seen; for, in the usual stupid British way, they confessed that they 'felt for the bulls and horses'.

§ 8

Among the great sights of Seville are the Archives of the Indies and the library where books owned and annotated by Columbus—for he was a great writer in margins—are kept in a glass case.

I was taken there by an American professor who told me that she had been working in the Archives for many years. More than thirty thousand documents relating to the discovery of America and the Spanish American colonies are filed away in this building.

I was shown the autographs of Amerigo Vespucci, Cortés, Pizarro, Magellan, and, most interesting of all, a letter from Cervantes begging to be given a job in America! This letter was written in Seville in 1590, when Cervantes was forty-three and had spent years of drudgery helping to provision the Armada, and, after its defeat, in victualling the galleys. Across his application the clerk to the Council of the Indies had written, 'Let him look for something nearer home.' Would *Don Quixote* have been written, one wonders, if Cervantes had gone to America? It is a sad thought that he might have gone down to his grave, an industrious clerk in the public accounts department of Colombia.

We walked across to the *Biblioteca Colombina*, which is in an old building at the back of the Cathedral overlooking the Court of the Orange Trees. Here in a long book-lined room we came to a glass-fronted bookcase which was unlocked for us. To my astonishment, and rather to my embarrassment, for such priceless treasures should not be handled, the books which Columbus had owned—there are only about ten of them—were placed in my hands. They were in Latin or Spanish. There was a Marco Polo, Plutarch's *Lives*, Seneca's tragedies, Pliny's *Natural History*, printed in Venice in 1489, and *Imago Mundi*, by Cardinal Pierre d'Ailly, in which Columbus had written many a marginal note. It is only afterwards that one is able to appreciate an experience such as this. At the time I could hardly believe that the old brown words in the margins of the books were really the handiwork of Christopher Columbus; I was also unprepared for such a moment, because I had visualized Columbus only on the deck of the *Santa María*, peering into mist and storm, but never sitting peacefully at home reading Plutarch.

I opened a book and saw, written by Columbus, that extraordinary cipher of his.

.S.
.S. A. S.
X M Y

Beneath these mysterious letters he used to sign his name either as 'x.p.o. Ferens', or simply 'El Almirante'. 'This signature has been one of the favourite grounds for mystery hunters,' writes Salvador de Madariaga, 'and the readings of it range from the over-ingenious to the half-witted.' Many have believed that the cipher is a Christian invocation to Christ, the Virgin and St. Joseph, while others (among them Madariaga, who believes that Columbus was of Jewish origin) think it a Cabbalistic cipher and a further indication that Columbus may have been a converted Jew, or *converso*, as nearly everybody of any ability seems to have been in Spain at that time.

What sort of remarks did Columbus make in the margins of his books? They are nearly all related to wealth, to gold, jewels, precious stones and metals. Almost every time he comes across the word 'gold' he underlines it, and in his copy of Marco Polo he underlined such words as 'perfumes', 'pearls', 'precious stones', 'gold cloth', 'ivory', 'pepper'; in other words anything that had a commercial value. And this is very natural. The old caravan routes to the East had been disrupted when the Turks captured Constantinople in 1453, and the rivalry between Spain and Portugal, in which Portugal had the lead, was to find a sea route to India and the fabulous riches of the great Spice Trade. The first victory was the gradual exploration by the Portuguese of the west coast of Africa, culminating in the great achievement of Bartholomew Diaz, who rounded the Cape of Good Hope and found himself no longer sailing south and with India before him. Columbus wrote the most interesting of all his marginal notes in his copy of Pierre d'Ailly's *Imago Mundi*.

Note: that in December of this year 1488, Bartholomaeus Didacus commandant of three caravels which the King of Portugal had sent out to Guinea to seek out the land, landed in Lisbon. He reported that he had reached a promontory which he called Cabo de Boa Esperança [Cape of Good Hope]. . . . He had described his voyage and plotted it league by league on a marine chart in order to place it under the eyes of the said king. I was present in all of this.

Columbus not only had no idea that America existed, and to his dying day did not know that he had discovered it, but was trying only to find a quicker way to India than southward by the Cape route. He thought that, the earth being round, a voyage due west from Spain would be a short cut to India; as indeed it would have been if the earth had been as small as Columbus imagined, and—if the American Continent had not stood in between. However, the geographical error of the fifteenth century has been well perpetuated. We talk about West Indians, meaning the inhabitants of the Caribbean islands, and more absurd still, the error has travelled north into the United States and Canada, the original home of the Red Indian. In the history of exploration few things are more pathetic than the thought of Columbus wandering about the West Indies believing that at any moment he would find himself in Japan.

§ 9

I left the library with my mind full of Columbus, and what better place is there than Seville to contemplate this man's extraordinary story? No one really knows his origin. It has been claimed that he was an Italian, a Portuguese, a Catalan or a Gallegan, and we know that he spoke Castilian with a foreign accent.

He was born in Genoa of a family of weavers and took to the sea as a youth. There is reason to believe an attractive story that he visited England with some Genoese vessels which arrived at the end of the year 1476, when Edward IV was king. If so, this was the year that Caxton left the Continent to set up as a printer in London; and it is a pleasant thought that possibly Columbus and Caxton may have been jostled by the crowds on London Bridge, who would have been astonished to know what strange new worlds they were shouldering.

We are told by those who knew him that Columbus was tall, good-looking, clean-shaven, and with hair that had turned prematurely white. He was a great talker, and some people thought him mad while many considered him a bore; but he had a great opinion of himself and, though he was threadbare, he had the air of a fine noble. He settled in Lisbon, where there was as much talk of reaching India by sea as there is today of landing on the moon by rocket. Some believed that the best route was round Africa, others thought that the short cut lay across the Atlantic, and this attractive theory took possession of Columbus. The main object of his life was to find a sovereign who would back him.

He married a well-connected Portuguese lady, the daughter of a distinguished sea captain, and they had a son named Diego. After a few years of marriage his wife died and, having failed to persuade the King of Portugal to support his scheme, Columbus decided to put the idea before Ferdinand and Isabel. He arrived in Spain, poor but full of enthusiasm, with his boy, who was then five. The monks of La Rábida took charge of the child while Columbus set off to haunt the court, which was then at Seville.

He was forty years of age at the time, quite elderly in those days, and he could not have chosen a worse moment. Ferdinand and Isabel were engaged in the final stages of the Reconquest and the only thing that mattered to them was the downfall of the last strongholds of the Infidel. The scheme of this fanatical white-haired man seemed a piece of luxurious lunacy compared with the expulsion of the Moors. He was kept waiting for six years, which is a long time even in Spain. During this period Columbus had his only love affair, with a woman of whom little is known except that her name was Beatriz Enríquez and that she came from Córdoba. She became the mother of his son Ferdinand,

and one wonders why the emotional, lonely and talkative widower did not marry her, for he was affectionately concerned for her all his life and remembered her in his will. During those seven years Beatriz must have learned all that biographers would like to know about Columbus; he must have poured out his heart to her during this period of frustration, and all this information she took with her to the grave.

To the King and Queen and their advisers, Columbus may have seemed a hare-brained dreamer, but the conditions laid down by him for the westward voyage to the Indies proved that he was also a keen business man. He insisted upon a title, a viceroyalty, and ten per cent of all the profits. Salvador de Madariaga calls him 'a pre-incarnation of Don Quixote'. And surely no stranger character can have been seen at court than this talkative adventurer with his shabby air of grandeur, insisting that among his rewards should be the right to wear gold spurs (an odd preoccupation for a sailor!) and the title of Grand Admiral of the Ocean Sea; and this before anything had been discovered.

The final blow to Columbus was the verdict of a royal commission which had taken four years to come to the conclusion that his scheme was 'vain and worthy of all rejection'. Further argument was impossible. He then decided to offer his scheme to France, and sorrowfully went to the monastery of La Rábida, possibly to collect Diego, who was then eleven. Here occurred the greatest mystery in the story of Columbus. There is, so far as I know, no adequate explanation. He must have confided his troubles to Fray Juan Pérez, who had been interested in him when he had first arrived; and it must be conjectured that he told him something so secret and important that the good friar sat down and wrote to the King and Queen. It must have been a matter of great urgency to have caused the friar to write to the overworked monarchs, upon whom the eyes of Christendom were now fixed on the eve of their final struggle with the Infidel. Stranger still, upon receiving the letter the Queen commanded the friar to go and see her. How extraordinary this is. Columbus had haunted the court for six years; a royal commission had declared his scheme to be moonshine; yet, upon receiving a letter from a friar, the Queen, at a critical juncture in the nation's affairs, decided to hear for herself whatever the monk had to say. As he saddled his mule and rode to court, we may think that good Fray Juan Pérez carried the future of America with him.

When the friar returned it was to command Columbus to attend the court before Granada. Money was sent for him to buy suitable clothes and a mule. So in the January sunlight of 1492 the discoverer of America saw a wave of Christian chivalry riding towards the red towers of Granada, with a silver cross before them. He saw the gates of the city open and a white cavalcade of Arabs ride out, their faces brown and hungry under their turbans. They handed over the keys of the city—the keys of Moorish Spain—the choir of the Chapel Royal intoned the *Te Deum*; the knights dismounted from their chargers and knelt, together with the archers and the pikemen; and no doubt Christopher Columbus was kneeling too.

In seven months' time he sailed into the west. His ships were fitted out in the little port of Palos, below the monastery of La Rábida. Eighty-eight men sailed in the three ships, and the first crossing of the Atlantic took seven weeks. Columbus was the first man to sail out into the open sea steering by the stars. His courage and his faith were rewarded one evening when a gunshot from the *Pinta* indicated that land had at last been sighted. Many believe that this was what is now known as Watlings Island, in the Bahamas. The dream had come true.

Columbus became rich and powerful, then his luck turned. He had discovered a new world, but he could not rule it, neither could he fill its rivers or its mines with gold. He made in all four crossings of the Atlantic. The fame and dignity he had craved came to him, bringing with them no happiness. Fourteen years after his immortal voyage he died, gouty and miserable, still believing that America was Asia.

§ 10

About forty miles from Seville, upon a bold headland which over-looks a salty estuary where the Rio Tinto and the Rio Odiel pour through marshes to the sea, stands the little Franciscan monastery of La Rábida. There is nowhere in the world a building more intimately associated with the discovery of America. It sheltered Columbus when he first came to Spain; it cared for and educated his small son: it comforted the explorer in his despair; and there can be no doubt that Fray Juan Pérez, in his interview with Queen Isabel, caused her to reverse the finding of the royal commission.

As I saw it that morning, low, whitewashed and red-tiled, with a sweep of blue sea at the back and a bed of flowers in front shaking with bees, I thought the monastery could not have changed much since Columbus arrived there. There is a covered porch and a bell. No one answered my ring, so I sat in the porch and watched swallows feeding their young in a nest they had plastered in an angle of the roof. Columbus probably arrived at Palos by ship and had a stiff walk to the monastery, uphill all the way. In his day Palos was a busy little port with its own shipyards and a thriving coastwise trade with Lisbon, but now the sea has retreated, leaving Palos high and dry. It would surprise Columbus could he see it today. Another surprise would be the colossal statue of himself on the other side of the estuary, a mighty memorial in the same heavyweight class as the Statue of Liberty.

The gate was at length opened by a Franciscan, who invited me into a little courtyard. There are only three monks at La Rábida now, he said, but in the time of Columbus there were about forty. We entered the church, where an emaciated Christ hangs above the altar, and in a small side chapel I saw, dark with age, Our Lady of La Rábida. 'Columbus prayed before this statue of the Holy Virgin,' said the friar. His voice sounded like a gramophone record.

He told me the story that he tells all visitors; how one day in the year 1484 a tall man, hand in hand with a small child, rang the bell and asked to be allowed to stay there. The prior, Fray Juan Pérez, 'seeing he looked like a man of another country or kingdom and alien in language, asked him who he was and whence he came'; and it seems that Fray Pérez and other members of the community soon fell under the spell of Columbus, including Fray Antonio de Marchena, the monastery astronomer.

We went upstairs into an austere little cell which tradition says is the cell of Fray Juan Pérez, where so many discussions took place between Columbus, the friars, and Martín Alonso Pinzón, the local shipowner, who eventually crossed the Atlantic on the first voyage. There are unfortunately no traditions at La Rábida which cast any light upon what Salvador de Madariaga has called 'the crossword puzzle of Columbus'. They know no more than anyone else about his origin and birth, the circumstances of his so-called 'flight' from Portugal, or the mysterious secret communicated by Columbus to Pérez which led to his reappearance at the court of Ferdinand and Isabel. I asked the Franciscan if he had any idea why Bernáldez, who knew Columbus well, referred to him as 'a merchant of books of print'. Was Columbus a second-hand bookseller? He shrugged his shoulders. '*Quién sabe?* It is possible! Why not? He had spent years of his life with books and charts. What more natural than that he should have sold them? A man must live.'

In this little stone cell the discovery of America was planned. Columbus and Pinzón must have sat together with charts and compasses, with lists of stores; and, leaning over their shoulders, one may fancy the two friars in their brown habits listening to every word, keen and interested.

The friar unlocked a door and we passed into a room full of little boxes made of different kinds of wood. There were maybe sixteen or twenty of them, arranged on a shelf, and above them hung the flags of the South American republics.

'The republics of South America have sent over some of their soil in boxes made from their own trees,' explained the Franciscan.

I opened a box labelled 'Mexico'. It was full of dark reddish earth. Peru was slightly lighter. I glanced up at the flags and read the names of Mexico, Peru, Brazil, Chile, Argentine, Salvador, Dominica, Paraguay, Honduras, Costa Rica, Nicaragua, Bolivia, Guatemala. I thought it an odd piece of piety, and not entirely free from irony, for the republics which had sent these little boxes of earth had never hesitated to fling mud at the mother country!

The friar darted away to admit a party of swarthy Mexicans in whom I thought Montezuma lived again. They came in reverently, full of the Columbus legend, and tiptoed round the room looking at the boxes. 'Ah, Mexico!', and they bent with interest over a pound or two of their own soil. They did not actually spit when they opened Peru and a few other South American countries, but I felt that their interest had flagged.

I said goodbye to the friar and went down to the old port of Palos. I passed into a grove of tall trees, the descendants maybe of the trees whose timbers made the first voyage to America. Palos is a pathetic little place now. The water which once flowed almost to its doors is now some way off at the bottom of a meadow, but the ancient brick fountain, or well, from which Columbus filled his water casks, is still there, a few yards from the road. There was no one about and I concluded that the population must be out in the fields. I came across some rusty rings in the grass. Were those the rings, I wondered, to which the *Santa María*, the *Niña* and the *Pinta* were moored?

These names are interesting. There is nothing heroic about them. They are the names you will find today on humble little fishing boats in any harbour. *Niña* means the Girl, *Pinta* means the Painted Lady; and a number of those who have studied this question believe that Columbus changed the name of his flagship to *Santa María* from *Marigalante*, which means the *Gallant Mary* or—dare one stretch a point and call her the *Saucy Mary*? I can well believe that Columbus, with his sense of dignity, and inspired by the God-given nature of his mission, would have considered that *Marigalante* introduced a trivial and flippant note into what he believed, and history has proved, was the most significant voyage ever made by man. Even so the names remain charmingly commonplace; we have all seen them in Lowestoft or Aberdeen while the red-eyed herrings rolled in a silver slide from their holds.

While I was thinking of these things, a solitary dark figure came towards me over the grass. It was the village priest. After the usual courteous greetings and hat-raising, I asked:

'Are those the rings . . .'

There was no need to finish the sentence.

'Yes, *señor*, those are the rings to which his ships were moored,' he replied as we walked up the meadow. He was a Columbus enthusiast and was accustomed to meeting all sorts of people who find their way to Palos. We went into the church. He told me that on August 2, 1492, Columbus made all members of the crews go aboard, and no one went to sleep that night in Palos. Lanterns and lamps were reflected on what is now a meadow, and the silhouettes of the three little ships rose against the stars. Then just before dawn on August 3, Columbus and his men attended Mass and took communion. The priest fought a moment with the church door, which eventually swung open.

'There they went, down to the ships,' he said; and there was nothing before us but the meadow and the old rings in the grass.

Half an hour before the sun rose Columbus gave the signal, the wind of morning filled their sails, and the three ships passed out into the Atlantic.

§ 11

On my way back to Seville I came to a white Andalusian town, and crowning a hill at the back was one of those medieval visions which greet the stranger in Spain. It looked like a complete walled city full of knights and fair ladies. One could almost hear the troubadours tuning their lutes and the heralds practising a new fanfare. But, having had experiences like this before, I knew that the vision would disintegrate into a few stretches of crumbling fortifications, dusty streets, tumble-down houses and mule carts. 'How these enchanters hate me, Sancho,' I said, as I left the car in the town below and climbed a dusty track, knowing well that the beautiful scene would soon fall apart into dust and ruins. I passed into the town under a tremendous Moorish gate.

It was just as I had thought. Here was a town that had been great and mighty in the long sweep of the years and now its thousands had departed, its grandeur was forgotten, and a few hundred peasants lived there in small stone cottages. Mules jingled past through the dust, an ox-wagon came up from the town below, while at doorways and in the shade men sat on their haunches, as miners do in Lanarkshire and the Rhondda Valley. A group parted as I approached, one man with a pair of fighting cocks with eyes like angry sparks tucked under his arm. There were empty spaces where buildings had fallen down, and in the centre of the town was the *kasr*, or *alcázar*, a huge place of hummocks and mounds and ruined machicolation, where small boys were playing games among overgrown dungeons.

I heard a church bell and made towards the sound. I saw a little white church whose door was a Moorish arch, and the bell was in a tower beside a Moorish ablution tank. A small boy was tugging at the bell rope and a group of boys and girls stood round the tower. The priest came out of the church and looked at me curiously, for visitors were evidently rare. He told me that the church was dedicated to *Santa María de la Granada*, but the patron saint was *Nuestra Señora del Pino*, Our Lady of the Pine Tree.

'This town,' he said, sweeping an arm towards the ruins, 'was the Roman Ilipa; the Moors called it Liblah, and we call it Niebla.'

While we were talking, I became aware that two Civil Guards in smart uniforms were standing at attention like a couple of young Napoleons in their black patent leather hats, and had obviously come to see me. As I turned towards them, one stepped forward, saluted, and handed me a little pamphlet about the town. I thanked them, they saluted, turned about and disappeared. What could have been politer? They had evidently seen me leave my car in the town below and had followed me with a copy of the town's publicity brochure. When I had time to examine the pamphlet, I found it to be the programme printed in 1951 for the Feast of Our Lady of the Pine Tree. It contained a few pictures of the town but little else, and its cost had been covered by advertisements for bars and *ultramarinos*, *mercería*, and *exquisitos vinos y licores* from places round about.

The priest took me into the church and led me to Our Lady of the Pine Tree, who wears a silver crown much too large for her, while she holds a sceptre in one hand and the Infant Jesus in the crook of the other. The church was full of Moorish tiles of great age and beauty and near the door was a realistic dead Christ in a glass coffin.

'Niebla was once as great as Seville,' commented the priest, 'and both rose against the Moors and slew the garrison; but they were subdued by Mûsâ.'

He spoke of this Visigothic revolt of twelve centuries ago as if it had happened last week. Then, politely excusing himself because he had to take a class of children in the church, he called a small boy and asked him to show me the museum. We walked through the dusty town, the small boy a few yards ahead of me, turning every now and then as if I were an animal he was leading. Having heard me speaking Spanish, he was thoroughly cowed and refused to say a word to me. This put me in my place and I followed dumbly until we came to a small cottage, where he stood aside in a courtly way and asked me to enter. I found myself in a sitting-room crammed with knick-knacks and sacred pictures. There was hardly room to move. The little house was built of great slabs of stone and seemed indestructible. The little boy asked for the key of the museum. Three women began hunting hurriedly for it, looking behind vases and ornaments, asking each other when it had last been seen, and after they had turned the place upside down, they said that the key was lost.

The little boy then beckoned me round the corner and pointed to the window of a semi-underground vault. When I had cleared away the cobwebs and dirt, I managed to see inside, where Roman columns, bits of cornices, Moorish tiles, and all the dusty débris of Niebla's past, were lying piled up in the dark.

I bought the little boy a bag of sweets, confused him with a few words of farewell, and went on my way to Seville.

## § 12

About forty miles from Seville, on the way to Cádiz, is the bright and prosperous town of Jerez, the headquarters of sherry. It is full of palm trees, banks, *bodegas,* and lovers of England, who are delightful at all times and rare in these. Men who appear to be typical Englishmen, wearing well-cut tweeds (and some of them with O.E. ties), transpire, when you are introduced to them, to have names like González. There has been a strong English and Scottish infiltration into Jerez since the seventeenth century and many of the leading families have a great deal of northern blood.

The most interesting non-alcoholic object in the district is about three miles out of the town; it is a beautiful Carthusian monastery whose honey-coloured façade is, I think, the most lovely baroque building I have seen in Spain. Below the monastery is the river Guadalite, where the last Gothic king, Roderick, vanished during the great battle with the Moors, leaving behind only his horse with its splendid trappings.

But only the most determined visitors ever stray so far from the *bodegas* of Jerez, which offer to the stranger more and better sherry than he is likely to encounter again in his life. By the way, sherry is a peculiar word. It is a corruption of the town's name, Jerez (pronounced Hereth), which in its turn is believed to be a Moorish corruption of the earlier Roman name, *Asido Caesaris*. It is an odd thought that every time one asks for a glass of sherry one may be invoking the name of Caesar. This wine is not really a Spanish drink, for the abstemious Spaniard considers it too strong and heavy, though you occasionally see a Spaniard drinking sherry as a liqueur! The first sherry seems to have arrived in England shortly after Catherine of Aragon, for it was usual for trade to follow a royal bride; French princesses frequently resulted in a powerful backwash of burgundy and claret. In the old days Jerez was spelt Xeres, and as the Spanish x was pronounced 'sh' in the sixteenth century, we get the word sherris and sherris-sack, or dry sherry, which was so often, and so affectionately, mentioned by Shakespeare. 'If I had a thousand sons,' said Falstaff, 'the first human principle I would teach them would be—to forswear thin potations and addict themselves to sack.' Although sherry has gone out of fashion from time to time in England, it has always returned. Jerez is full of wine vaults or *bodegas* where the stranger is more than welcomed and where, as the prudent Baedeker remarks, 'It is well to be provided with biscuits or the like.'

I was taken to one of the largest *bodegas* and shown enough sherry to float a fleet. I have never cared for sherry, but I did not dare to say so in this cathedral of *Amontillado* and *Tío Pepe*. They naturally take their sherry seriously in Jerez and to mention port is a kind of blasphemy. The grapes are grown on the surrounding hills in a soil called *albariza*, which is full of lime. The vines are all lime-lovers and are grafted with cuttings of a *Palomino* stock, a vine that produces a small white grape. They prune them drastically and at the vintage in September the grapes are crushed in shallow wooden trays and the juice, having fermented for about two months, is then either stored in casks to mature or is added to old casks of the mother wine, as they call it.

Having been initiated, I was considered fit to taste some sherry.

We were joined at this point by the Bacchus of Jerez, an elderly man in a white coat whose duty it is to ply strangers with wine. He held a metal cup attached to a long handle which he thrust into the darkness of a barrel, and, holding his right hand high in the air, transferred a golden stream of sherry from the ladle to the glass without spilling a drop. This act in itself was proof that he rarely tasted the sherry himself, yet there was about him an air as of revels long ago; round his cap it seemed the ghosts of vine leaves had entwined themselves. The most spectacular barrels were thirteen immense tuns called, with the embarrassing familiarity of the devout, Christ and the Twelve Apostles. He thrust the plunger, or ladle, into the Christ, which contains the mother wine of the vats, and told me that it was laid down in 1862 for Queen Isabel II.

We entered the nave of a cathedral of drinks. Beneath the white-washed aisles the great tuns slumbered in the process known as 'education'. Here Bacchus became lyrical. He thrust the cup into sacred depths and withdrew it full of highly educated vintages. I did not know there were so many kinds of sherry. As we circled the cathedral, Bacchus paused before a cask that was dramatically wreathed with cobwebs. It was almost self-consciously ancient, like the oldest inhabitant who cannot resist the temptation of adding on a few years. This was *Solera*, 1847. What a wine! The highest praise I can give it is that to me it was quite unlike sherry. And as I tasted it, I thought not of its bouquet or flavour, but of its associations. The sun that had warmed it into life in the year 1847 was the sun that had shone on Queen Victoria, a young woman of twenty-eight who had reigned for only ten years; Louis Philippe still occupied the throne of France; the Corn Law Riots were just over in England; it was the year of the financial crisis that followed the railway boom. . . .

Bacchus, noting the gleam of association in my eye and mistaking it for alcoholic enthusiasm, dived his ladle once more into the year 1847; but I was perhaps afraid of remembering too much, and he poured every drop back into the sacred tun. We came to a dark corner where a cask stood alone in the dark and the dust, covered with the Spanish colours.

'It will not be broached,' I was told dramatically, 'until a king comes back to Spain. It was laid down when His Majesty the late Don Alfonso XIII went into exile; it has remained here through the Republic and the Civil War; and some day it will be broached—when a king comes back!'

The moment was *emocionante,* and I said nothing but cleared my throat sympathetically, thinking that it will be a good sound wine when the time comes, for it is already twenty-three years old.

I sat in the sunny plaza of Jerez, where the palm trees cast their shade and the stray breeze brought with it whiffs of *Amontillado, Oloroso* and *Palo Cortado.*

## § 13

I had made friends with Don Felipe, who one day suggested that we might run out to see the ruins of Italica, a few miles to the north of Seville. The more I saw of him, the more I liked him. He was an unusually contented personality and it was difficult to believe that he was seventy-six years old.

'You seem to have found the secret of happiness,' I said to him.

'Yes, I suppose I have,' he replied. 'When my wife died some years ago, I found myself all alone in the world and with enough money to last out my time at any rate. On my seventieth birthday I decided to end the life I had always lived and start another one. It takes a lot of doing, you know—at seventy. I was cluttered up with things: possessions, animals, and two old servants who had been with us for many years. They were the real difficulty. When I told them my decision to sell up and go away, I thought they would never get over it. But I pensioned them handsomely and the happy day came when I hadn't a possession in the world—no house, no furniture, even no books. But I was free to begin my adventures.

'First I went to America and Canada and liked neither. I enjoyed Italy, but not as much as I expected, and Greece even more than I had expected. My money, you will guess, is in dollars! Then I went to Australia and New Zealand and Japan, where I read Lafcadio Hearn for the first time and tried hard to understand the country. I got homesick for England, but on the way back I read a book about Cyprus, and I went there. I liked the island and thought about settling there. Then I came to Spain and at once I felt at home. I have been here a year now and speak Spanish fairly badly. I got to Seville too late for Holy Week and I am staying until next Easter. Then I shall wander on.'

'Where will you go?'

'I don't know. Perhaps India.'

'What attracts you to Spain?'

'I can't analyse it. I like the Spaniards and the way they live. Life here is rather Victorian. It is the kind of life I remember when I was a small boy. I am not religious, but I like the religious atmosphere of Spain, the way the year is strung on the festivals of the Church. I like the climate. I like the food. I like the gay and careless attitude to life. You may say I am seeing the world through the eyes of second childhood, and it might be true. I have not begun to exhaust my curiosity.'

By this time we had arrived at Italica, and I saw a vast and incoherent ruin where once the city stood that had given birth to Trajan, Hadrian and Theodosius. An enormous amphitheatre which had held forty thousand people had been pulled down in the eighteenth century to plug the dykes and river banks of the Guadalquivir. An enthusiastic guide took us all over the ruins and showed us a few tessellated pavements, which he was helping to ruin by splashing water on them from a can which he kept handy. You can trace the line of some of the main streets, but there is nothing left standing. Thousands of tons of marble must have been carted away to Seville.

On the way back we stopped at a little village called Santiponce, where he wished to show me a picture in a derelict monastery. We drove through a farmyard to a large building, the now vacant monastery of St. Isidore. The caretaker, José Bazán, his wife and their family of little boys were delighted to see us. Bazán, I soon realized, was a man with a mission. He felt himself called upon to protect and guard the deserted monastery, and though he received no wages for doing so, and indeed had to work on the local railway in order to live, his life was devoted to the old building. It was his ruling passion. His father had been sexton there for fifty-six years, he told us; he had been born there and he was now fifty-six. He said that he rose three times every night and went round the monastery with a revolver in his pocket, just to see that all was well. In proof of this he fumbled among his papers and produced a firearms licence. He took us first into the beautiful little baroque church of St. Jerome, where life-sized gilded angels were suspended from the roof. He showed us the tomb of Leonor Dávalo, the 'loyal servant', as the inscription recalled; who, when her mistress, Doña Urraca Osorio, perished at the stake in 1327 at the command of Pedro the Cruel, ran up and shielded her with her own body to cover her nakedness, and so died with her. This was also the church in which the body of Cortés rested before his remains were removed to Mexico.

We left the church and wandered round the cold, deserted monastery; and I could imagine the faithful guardian with his revolver padding round those ghostly cloisters and the long, stone passages at dead of night, and a more eerie task I cannot imagine. The place looked haunted and reeked of bats. At length he threw open a door and led the way into the old refectory, pointing to a picture that took up the whole side of an end wall. What at first I took to be a marble bolection moulding was a frame cleverly painted on the flat surface. The subject of the fresco was the Last Supper, the work of some unknown monk of the fifteenth century. The Saviour and His disciples are seen sitting at a long table covered with a cloth patterned like Moorish tiles. The perspective is primitive and the table is tilted towards the onlooker so that everything upon it may be clearly seen. There are no knives and forks, and the Paschal lamb lies ready roasted on a platter. There are little plates of sweet herbs dotted about and the meal is about to be eaten with the fingers. There is a jug of wine and wine cups, and upon a small table nearby a basin and ewer of water. There are little rolls and twists of bread of the same pattern as those made today in Seville. Christ and the disciples have a rather Greek look, and Judas sits opposite Jesus, wearing an expression of the vilest cunning.

While we were admiring this, and saying what a wonderful impression it gave of a meal in fifteenth century Spain, I happened to look at José Bazán and saw him gazing at the fresco, which he must see every day of his life, with an expression of adoration. He pointed out a dozen rare beauties to us and I could see that it was the apple of his eye. I said the right thing when I mentioned the freshness of the fresco and its beautiful condition in that dusty and abandoned hall, for his eyes gleamed and he told us that he regularly cleans it with a feather and rubs white of egg into it. 'Some Spaniards,' he explained, 'who passed this way long ago told my father to do this, and I have continued to do it and shall do so until I die.'

I looked at him impressed and touched. One could write a story about him arriving in heaven and telling St. Teresa how well he had looked after the Last Supper and—was there no way of getting permission to pop down to Santiponce now and then just to see that it was still all right?

I felt, however, that there was something on his mind; and he unburdened himself just as we were going. Would Don Felipe, he asked, write to General Franco and ask him to allow the old mayor of Santiponce to return from France, where he was a political exile, so that he might die in Spain? There was no evil in this man, he said, he was a true Catholic and, although a Socialist, he had saved the monastery from being looted by the Reds. And now, alas! this poor man was dying in France, longing only, as every true son of Spain must do, to return and lay his bones in his own land. Don Felipe gently said that he did not know the Caudillo, neither did he think Franco would pay much attention to him. José vehemently denied this and said that a word from a distinguished and influential stranger would do the trick.

'Has no one written to the Government about this?' I asked. He looked at me with infinite sorrow and dropped his arms with a hopeless gesture.

'The Government!' he said. 'By the time they answer a letter our poor *alcalde* will be dead and buried!'

I was amazed at the man's fidelity and felt that perhaps there is a special corner in heaven for faithful caretakers. As we were on our way back to Seville, Don Felipe said, 'I think we've had a rather Spanish half-hour. Another thing I like about Spaniards is their integrity. When they are good, they are very, very good. . . .'

# Chapter VII

*The mosque of Córdoba—an olive-miller of Jaén—Granada and the Alhambra—ballet by moonlight—north to La Mancha—an afternoon in El Toboso—a Cervantes library—heat in Madrid*

§ 1

I ARRIVED in Córdoba in the dark. I had a glimpse of an ancient bridge and of the Guadalquivir shrunk into its summer bed. There was a mighty arch and narrow white streets where minarets and towers rose into the night. I was immediately surrounded by a crowd of pugnacious young gipsies, who first fought a battle among themselves, then stood back to allow the victors to take me, as they promised, to the best hotel. One said it was 'damned precioso'. I was grateful to them, for without their help I might have wandered round the streets for half-an-hour or so, looking for somewhere to sleep.

The hotel door opened on a lounge furnished with tables and basket chairs, where, like a vision of South Kensington, four elderly Englishwomen sat playing cards. They had all bought Spanish shawls, which lent something bizarre and witch-like to their appearance, but apart from that they might have been sitting in any private hotel in England. They were survivals from the age when England was great, self-assured and unapologetic, an age when old ladies were in the habit of strolling through Balkan tumults with a British passport, prodding sanguinary revolutionaries from their path with the ferrules of their parasols. They sat bolt upright, gazing reflectively at their cards, then firmly and deliberately putting them down in an awesome hush. The rotund Sancho who stood in the background with a tray in his hand began to look almost like the family butler. I suppose Romans of the Augustan Age wore this imperturbable air of rectitude and authority, and were able to command the wonder and respect which, even in these days of decline and fall, are occasionally given to those of the Victorian Age.

At dinner I found myself at the next table to the Englishwomen. One spoke Spanish and was able to indulge in a little dignified cajolery with the head waiter. We fell into conversation and, as I had supposed, they were touring Spain by motor-coach and were on their way to Seville. The old lady who spoke Spanish told me that she had frequently visited Seville when a girl.

'It's wonderful to find a country where people are not always expecting tips,' one of them said to me. 'The other day as we were leaving the hotel the chambermaid came running after us and put the tip we had left for her into our hands, thinking that we had overlooked it.'

'This is the last country where people are courteous,' said the lady who knew Spain, 'though Spaniards can also be very rude. They can forget to answer letters; they can be late for appointments or even forget them altogether; and they can be very inquisitive; but face to face they are delightful. When I was in Barcelona long ago—it was the first time I had been there—I walked down the Ramblas one afternoon and turned into the old city, where I got lost. There was no one about for it was the hour of the *siesta*. I walked on down the winding lanes and became more confused than ever. Then a terrifying bandit turned the corner, leading a donkey. I noticed that the donkey looked fat and happy, so I thought the owner must be a kind-hearted bandit. In my best Spanish I asked the way back to the hotel. He looked at me, removed the huge straw hat he was wearing, bowed, and turning his donkey round, led me back along the way he had just come. Sweeping off his hat again, he pointed to the steps of the hotel. I felt in my bag to give him something, but I had gone out without a farthing! Telling him to stay there, I ran up the steps, where I explained the situation to the concierge and told him to give the man a really good tip and put it on my bill. I watched them talking and waving their hands, then the concierge came back and said, "*Señorita*, the man will take nothing. He asks me to tell you that he has done the only thing the poor can do to help the rich."'

After dinner a young man to whom I had been given a letter of introduction arrived at the hotel, and we went out together. The moon was up and the narrow white streets of Córdoba, touched here and there by moonlight, were the most eastern sight I had seen in Spain. We might have been in Fez. We came to a main street lined with orange trees, to a bull-ring, white and classical like an intact Colosseum, then to a fine square where a bronze statue of the 'Grand Captain' wears an unexpectedly white marble head. We visited innumerable cafés and clubs, in one of which groups of earnest conversationalists sat beneath the horns of bulls and the swords of *matadores*. We found the house where the poet Góngora had lived; then we walked down to the fine Roman bridge and watched the moonlight gilding eddies in the river. Towers, minarets and white buildings were dipped in moonlight, and remembering the greatness of Córdoba in the time of the Caliphate, I sensed an underlying melancholy and the overwhelming weight of the past. The young man talked a lot about caliphs and their favourites, of scents and fountains, murders and conspiracies. Having learnt that he augmented what he called his *salario* by acting as a guide, I had placed our relationship on a monetary basis, much to his relief. No doubt he felt that he had to tell me about the Caliphate to give me my money's worth. He had no particular love for Córdoba, indeed he infinitely preferred Seville, which he believed to be the home of all romance and gaiety.

'The difference between Córdoba and Seville is this,' he explained. 'Seville is a young girl, gay, laughing, provoking . . .' Here he struck an absurd attitude, hand on his hip, his eyes rolling, in an attempt to convey the impression of a dashing *señorita*. 'But Córdoba . . .'

Here he folded his hands across his chest and walked a few paces with downcast head.

'Córdoba,' he said, 'is a dear old lady.'

I did not tell him that it was not at all as it impressed me. Córdoba seemed to me far more like a dead odalisque.

## § 2

In the morning I went to the mosque of Córdoba, with no intention of allowing myself to be carried away by enthusiasm, but in two minutes I was vanquished. Of all the buildings of the Islamic world this is to me the most fantastic. It is not really beautiful and for me it has no more spiritual appeal than the underground cisterns of Istanbul. It reminds me of an immense forest full of zebras. The striped red and white arches stretch away in innumerable vistas, and whichever way you look you see the same view. It is like a trick with mirrors, yet the feeling it roused in me was one of delight. What could be more astonishing than the effect created by hundreds of columns of different marbles, even of different sizes, arranged geometrically and linked by a system of arches. There is something primitive about the arrangement, yet the effect is, oddly enough, sophisticated. I could imagine the Emir 'Abd-ar-Rahmân I contradicting his Greek architects and insisting, with the assurance of a rich amateur, that it did not really matter whether two alabaster columns were of the same height, or even the same thickness; for the love of Allah build up the smaller pillar to match the larger, and make the thinner equal to the fatter with a coat of plaster! Then with a swing he would be in the saddle and away in a cloud of dust, his bodyguard at his heels. What ought to have been a failure was a brilliant success. Indeed when the time came to enlarge the mosque of the first Caliph, the third 'Abd-ar-Rahmân, and his son Hakam II after him, could find no better design and simply enlarged the building to its present astonishing proportions.

As I wandered round this wonderful mosque I thought that I should have been happy in the Caliphate of Córdoba; and I have had the same impression in other buildings of the same period, the Mosque of Ibn Tulun in Cairo and the great Omayyad Mosque in Damascus. Why this should be I do not know, unless it is that the Omayyads reflected a comprehensible Hellenistic world, while later Islam reflected Persia and the Orient. When you stand in this mosque it is easy to believe that the caliphs of Córdoba were reasonable and even kindly people, interested not merely in war and religion, but in astronomy, poetry and gardening. 'Abd-ar-Rahmân I, who began the mosque, was a tall, fair-haired man with only one eye, who had led a romantic life. His family, the Omayyad caliphs, had ruled Islam for generations from Damascus, and he was the only member to escape when the Abbasids exterminated the Omayyads and transferred the Caliphate to Bagdad. After many adventures he arrived in Spain in 755, with a few faithful followers and some jewels, wondering, no doubt, whether he was to meet death or whether Arabs loyal to the defeated Omayyads would come to his rescue, as they did. He founded the fortunes of the Caliphate of Córdoba, though he never dared to take the title of Caliph. He it was who introduced the first pomegranate into Spain from Syria and from his gardens at Córdoba distributed its seed all over Andalusia. He also introduced the first date palm. This was a pathetic act. It suggests most touchingly that, in spite of the triumphant new life he had made in Spain, he felt himself to be an exile and thought of Syria as his home. He wrote a delightful little poem to the palm tree, comparing it with himself as a wanderer in a strange land.

The great 'Abd-ar-Rahmân III, who inherited the splendours of Córdoba in 912 and called himself Caliph, was frankly in rivalry with Bagdad; and it was of his reign that the young man had talked to me under the moon the night before, of its orange blossom and its intrigue, its poets, musicians and artists, its astronomers, mathematicians and doctors; all the things which made Córdoba the fitting scene for a Spanish edition of the *Arabian Nights*.

He built the summer palace of es-Zahrâ in memory of a favourite who bore that name; but the word palace does not convey the right idea of the enormous royal city built in terraces, with its own aqueducts and surrounded by a single wall, which was created three miles or so from Córdoba. Its remains, sad to relate, have almost disappeared, but they prove that it must have been the most splendid palace ever built in Spain. There were hanging gardens, aviaries, zoos, fishponds and running streams, splendid courts and kiosks; and the classical world was made to pay its usual tribute of marble and porphyry columns. Among the many fountains at es-Zahrâ was one of gold brought from Byzantium; and another in which the artist had managed somehow to reconcile the shapes of a lion, an antelope, a crocodile, an eagle, a dragon, and various birds, in one design, the whole menagerie being wrought of gold and set with pearls and jewels. I would gladly sacrifice all the existing Arab remains in Spain to have seen this palace of a great period, with its statues of the beautiful es-Zahrâ and the almost blasphemous frieze that encircled a kiosk, repeating her name; it should have been that of Allah. One of the sights of the palace was the pool of quicksilver in the Caliph's bedroom, evidently an imitation of the quicksilver pool in the Tulunid Palace in Cairo, where the Sultan Khumarameih, who suffered from insomnia, was sometimes rocked to sleep on a floating couch.

In the middle of the mosque I came to the cathedral of Córdoba, which was built simply by carting away a number of columns, to build the church, and carrying its roof higher than that of the mosque. A service was in progress so I did not go in, but it was interesting to stand outside in Islam, as if in the wings of a theatre, and peep through curtains at the preacher in the pulpit, the choir and canons, and the huge organ with its radiating fence of beautiful gilt pipes. Many writers have said how shameful they think it is to find this church in the centre of the mosque, but I cannot see why. Nothing could be more emblematic of Andalusia, perhaps even of Spain, than to see this Christian jewel in its unlikely Moslem setting. Much worse I thought, than building the church inside the mosque, was to build a wall along the north side of the mosque, cutting it off from the Court of Orange Trees. That really is a piece of vandalism, and I went away wishing that President Eisenhower could persuade General Franco to pull it down.

When I returned to the hotel and was preparing to leave for Granada my young friend of the night before appeared to bid me farewell. It is remarkable how Spaniards seem to be able to leave their desks and places of employment at any time they like. While we sipped a glass of *manzanilla*, he told me that there was a music and dance festival in Granada and I should not be able to find anywhere to sleep; and it was upon that depressing note we said goodbye.

I had half a mind to turn south and go to the town of Teba, which lies in a network of secondary roads about seventy miles to the south. But it was too far away. This was the site of the battle with the Moors in which Sir James Douglas was slain when he was taking the heart of Robert Bruce to the Holy Land. Any Scot in Gibraltar can easily get there by train, for it is on the main line from Algeciras to Bobadilla.

The story, which is told by Froissart among others, is that when Bruce was dying his conscience was troubled because his busy life had prevented him from fulfilling a vow to go on a crusade to the Holy Land. Calling his knights round him, he said that when he was dead he wished his heart to be embalmed and taken to the Holy Sepulchre, where his body had been unable to go. The good Sir James Douglas promised to fulfil this mission, and after the King's death sailed in the spring of 1330 with a company of Scottish knights, having Bruce's heart in 'ane cas of silvr fyn, enamalit throu subtilite', which he wore round his neck.

The fleet put into Sluys for twelve days to give Flemish knights a chance to join the expedition. Douglas stayed aboard and kept a running buffet going, where he entertained the local noblemen with 'wines of two kinds and spices'. The ships then appear to have sailed right round Spain, for we next hear of the expedition at Valencia. Here Douglas was told that the King of Castile, Alfonso XI, was at war with the Moslem King of Granada. He consulted his knights and they all agreed that it was a good fight in which they ought to play their part. They turned back and sailed to Seville, where they disembarked their war horses and rode to the camp of the Castilian monarch, who received them with great heartiness and affection. Among the foreign knights who were fighting with the Spaniards was an Englishman famous for his deeds of arms, whose face had been hacked to pieces. Learning of the arrival of Douglas, with whose brave deeds he was familiar, he hurried to meet him in order to compare notes on mutilation. When he expressed surprise that Douglas's face was unscarred, the Scot replied that 'Praised be to God, I have always had hands to protect my head!'

At the end of August, 1330, the Spanish army was drawn up opposite the Moors near Teba, and Alfonso ordered an advance. Douglas, who rode with his knights on a flank, mistaking this for a general attack, ordered his trumpets to sound the charge and galloped forward towards the Moors crying, 'A Douglas, A Douglas!', wearing the heart of Bruce in its casket round his neck. The small band of knights was rapidly surrounded by Moorish horsemen and, seeing Sir William de St. Clair of Roslin in difficulties, Douglas rode to his assistance and was killed. One account of his death says that as he galloped up he took the casket from his neck and threw it into the fight, crying, 'Onward as thou wert wont, Douglas will follow thee!'

The death of Douglas put an end to the expedition. It is said that his body, and also the heart of Bruce, were recovered from the battlefield and taken back to Scotland. Douglas was buried in the Chapel of St. Bride at Douglas, and the heart of Bruce is believed to have been buried in Melrose Abbey.

§ 3

I went on towards Granada through the incandescent glare of a summer's day. The landscape vibrated with heat, the air that rushed past me was as warm as the air in an engine-room, and upon this baked red landscape olive trees climbed the slopes of the *sierra*. Though poets have praised the silver greyness of the olive tree, I often think its beauty has been exaggerated. Except in places like Cyprus, where trees of incredible age stretch wizard arms over the stony land and impress one as ancient monuments, the ordinary olive which is cultivated for its fruit is beautiful and romantic only when you think of its associations with the classical world.

In the whole of Spain there is no sight more luscious than the landscape of Andalusia, and the valley of the Guadalquivir through which I was passing is a good example of it. As the only part of Spain known to the Victorians and to many later travellers, it has been responsible for the legend that Spain is a hot, southern land where the sun always shines. The towns and villages, all wearing their white burnouses of cool limewash, are oases of ease and refreshment along the starkness of the unshaded roads. I came to an exquisite little town called Andujar, which was full of flowers. They dripped down from window-boxes against the white walls, they grew in the streets, they could be seen in patios and in the little plaza. Here I paused to have a cold drink and to watch a young man drinking water in the Spanish way, holding a red clay *jarra*, or water-pot, above his head and letting a stream from the spout curve neatly through the air into his mouth. This feat must be another of those Moorish legacies, for the Arabs loved to take liberties with water. It seemed to me part of that pleasure in looking at falling water which was, and still is, inborn in the Arab. I remember once asking the late King Abdullah of Jordan what had pleased him most when, in the course of a visit to Britain, he found himself in Scotland. Rather unexpectedly, he replied, 'The rain at Peebles.' It appeared that the Government, in one of its moments of inspiration, had housed him in a sanatorium at Peebles when rain fell solidly for three days; and his worried hosts were surprised to find that their guest was only too content to stand for hours at a french window watching it fall.

I went on through the hilly olive country and at length saw on a distant hillside what appeared to be a large and magical city straight out of romance, with greater hills, washed with a blue summer haze, rising in the background. This was the metropolis of the olive country, the town of Jaén. I entered its hilly streets, where a line of prosperous-looking shops led up to a cathedral which seemed only a little smaller than St. Paul's. It was white, dark and cool inside; I had a vision of baroque splendours and a great altar gleaming with gold at the top of marble steps. A sacristan drifted up like an old, dry leaf and pointed to the altar, whispering that there in a coffer lay the holy relic, the *Santa Faz*, one of the handkerchiefs of St. Veronica. I sat for some time too hot to move, then walked out into the whiteness and down the hill to a little restaurant in the main street. It was full of solid-looking men who, true Spaniards, would have felt it beneath their dignity to make any concession to the temperature by unloosening a tie or unbuttoning the jackets which all wore; and with the town outside shimmering in the heat, they attacked enormous plates of *paella* and even huge chunks of roast lamb and roast pork, for which there is no close season in Spain. I remembered the toughness of Cortés and his companions, who wore their steel morions and their quilted armour in the tropics, and thought that Spanish America must have been conquered by men like the eaters of Jaén.

I sat at a table facing a beautiful little wall shrine of *La Macarena*, made of glazed Talavera tiles; and I watched with interest how it is

the custom in the small country restaurants in Spain for a man to
behave with the courtesy which was usual in days when men ate at
a common table. It is good manners to give a little bow to the strangers
near you and wish them a good appetite, which they reciprocate
before you sit down. Spain, I reflected, is the last country of the sword,
that sharp critic of behaviour. Army officers still wear it, the *matadores*
use it every Sunday, and ordinary men behave to each other with the
consideration of an age when any boorishness might be answered at
the end of a rapier.

A plump, jolly person in a dark suit, obviously a countryman up for
a day in town, bowed to me and asked if he might share my table;
then, finding that I spoke a fractured sort of Spanish in splints and
bandages, looked slightly confused. But I limped along with him as
well as I could. This man told me he was an Andalusian small farmer,
a grower of olives and, appropriately enough—for are not all millers
traditionally jolly?—the owner of pressing-mills. He gave me a business
card and invited me to visit him next spring to see the oil pressing. I
should like to do this, for I could fancy the oxen creaking over the
white roads with their antique burden, and the miller, redder, plumper
and jollier than ever, oozing oil like some Dionysiac reveller. I could
imagine him, together with the village priest and the chemist, as the
third member of a powerful triumvirate.

When we had finished, I learnt that he had come into Jaén on the
autobus and would have to wait a long time for one to take him home.
As his village was not much out of my way, I offered to run him back;
and after we had collected his packages and parcels we sped off together
into the hills, with olive trees on each side of us stretching away in their
orderly lines to the very sky. We came to a surprised village, surprised
maybe to have been caught in the act of climbing a steep hill. There
must be some reason, perhaps buried in forgotten Moorish strategy,
why this queer little place had been tilted so uncomfortably among
the olive trees. I looked round with pleasure at the smallest of plazas,
with its fountain, and at the white cottages, all so neat and clean.
By this time an Anglo-Spanish entente had developed and my companion produced me with a dramatic flourish as his English friend.
The strange characters who gathered round us now led the way to a
bar that looked subterranean, though it was above ground, and in the
darkness I could make out barrels on shelves, strings of sausages and
garlic; and there in a great hubbub of conversation, none of which
could I understand, it was so rapid and bird-like and, I concluded, in

the broadest Andaluz, we drank sharp white wine from a red clay pitcher. My friend had to describe in detail how we had met and who I was. That I was an English *turista* made me perfectly comprehensible and they looked at me, smiled and nodded, and seemed delighted that I was there. A young man came in holding a fighting cock beneath his arm. It was a queer-looking object. Its breast had been plucked bare and a ruff of brilliant russet gold and blue feathers fluffed out round its neck; other feathers were cut and trimmed and the long muscular legs with soft down to the knee had the look of black silk breeches. The head on its long aggressive neck gazed sharply about, and in each eye gleamed a drop of golden malice rimmed with an angry orange colour. The creature lay peacefully enough in its owner's grasp, but, as I approached, it aimed a vicious peck at me. When Mr. Sitwell was in Spain he noticed some game cocks in Extremadura which he thought might be the descendants of birds brought into Spain by Wellington's officers; and I wondered if this vicious little Regency buck had had a similar origin. Seeing my interest, the owner took me into a yard at the back of the inn where the twin of the bird under his arm was strutting about in a cage. He opened the cage and placed both the birds on the ground to show me how they moved. First they fixed each other with vindictive eyes, then with their necks extended to the full feinted left and right, raising and lowering their necks and, as it were, fencing with them. Suddenly they were locked together in mid-air, jumping up and down, their ruffs bristling, then up in the air again, their legs kicking and their beaks tearing. The owner separated them with some difficulty and went off with them, one under each arm, the birds still trying to tear each other to pieces. Even if they were not originally English birds, they bore a remarkable resemblance when in action to one of those savage little aquatints sometimes to be seen in the bar parlours of English country inns.

My jolly miller then insisted on taking me to a mill about half a mile away, an old building that reeked of ancient olive harvests. There was nothing to see except a grindstone that was turned by a mule, blindfolded, I was told, to prevent giddiness. At pressing time the olives, stones and all, were cast into the mill and ground into a pulp, the best oil naturally being the first pressing. The pulverized stone is used as a fuel to burn in those eastern-looking braziers seen pushed away in the corners of Spanish buildings to await the winter. The manufacture proceeds from simplicity to simplicity. The oil passed from tanks to jars, each one big enough to take Ali Baba and ten of his companions, which are buried up to their necks in the earth. My friend told me that this is the old way of doing it, but there were also fine modern mills, he said, where the olives were crushed by machinery and filtered under steam pressure; so that side by side in this oily countryside there exist mills which Pliny would have recognized and others where, no doubt, men in white overalls obey dials and temperature charts. The miller said that foreigners like their olive oil clear and yellow, but *nosotros*, by which he meant himself and his friends, prefer it with a bit of body.

Refusing the most charming invitations to stay the night, I said goodbye to the miller and his friends and was in Granada as they were lighting the lamps. An African glow lingered in the west, the air was still and hot, and the streets were filled with gaiety and excitement. The music and dance festival had, it was obvious, filled the city to the brim. I drove up to a large hotel on the Alhambra Hill, which was hemmed in by hundreds of cars bearing the number-plates of cities all over Spain. The clerk in the reception office looked at me, astonished to think that anyone could dare to hope for a room during the *Festival de Música y Danza*, then told me that by the purest chance one of the best rooms was free because only half an hour ago a guest had been unexpectedly called back to Madrid. I could have the room, but only for three days.

My balcony looked from a great height over a large portion of Granada and, by craning my neck and looking to the right, I could see the cathedral rising above the roof line of the city; to the left stretched the Sierra Nevada, drawn in blue lines against the sky, and the summits were dusted with snow.

§ 4

I came down in the hotel lift with a young woman who was carrying over her arm a strange object in this land of shawls, mantillas and castanets; it was a tu-tu, or ballet dress. My glance travelled from this to the owner's face, when I recognized with pleasure that exquisite ballerina, Miss Margot Fonteyn. She told me she had just arrived in Granada and was to dance that night in the Gardens of the Generalife. A stage had been erected among the cypress trees and she was on her way to a rehearsal there.

I suppose one might pay a hundred visits to Granada yet never see the Generalife Gardens by moonlight, or a great dancer performing there, and I went at once to the concierge and asked him to get me a ticket. He looked at me in sorrow and despair. Every ticket had long since been sold. He already had a waiting list of about thirty. They said the same thing at the offices of the *Festival de Danza y Música* and at the tourist offices down in the town. Even Professor Walter Starkie, who had just motored down from Madrid, and for whom all doors open, especially in this stronghold of gipsydom, was unable to get an extra ticket.

I must have spent nearly an hour in the telephone booths of the hotel, trying to speak to the British Consul, the Mayor, the Provincial Governor, the Minister of Fine Arts, and anybody else I could think of; but, of course, they were all out. When I had retired to my room almost defeated, the spirit of Spain decided to take charge of my affairs. A knock on my door was followed by the smallest page-boy in Spain. I vaguely remembered him as the lad who had opened and closed the doors of the telephone booths. I sprang to my feet, believing that the incredible had happened and that one of the influential people I had been ringing up had actually decided to get in touch with me. But something even more interesting occurred. The boy said quietly that he couldn't help hearing that the *señor* wanted a ticket for the dancing at the Generalife Gardens that night. Would the *señor*, he asked, be prepared to pay an extra ten pesetas, just supposing he might hear of a friend who had such a ticket? I looked at the shrimp in amazement. The *señor* would be delighted to pay fifty extra pesetas for a ticket! He gravely bowed and departed. He was back in ten minutes with the ticket.

That is how things are done. Kipling knew what he was about when he said that the important friends in life are taxi-drivers, policemen and hall-porters!

The night was hot and full of spiced scents, and there was not a breath of wind. The full moon was already high when I joined a crowd moving up the steep hill to the Gardens of the Generalife. Floodlights at the base of red towers cast the ramparts of the Alhambra into operatic relief, and Gautier would have been in ecstasies. This was Andalusia as he wished it to be. There was even a sound of guitars in the darkness as we went up the hill. We passed into a scene of complete enchantment. Floodlighting had transformed a natural landscape into an artificial one, and the famous Gardens, lit by lamps sunk in fish-ponds or cunningly hidden to light up a hedge of pomegranates, an archway, or a group of taper-thin cypresses, rose in the night like stage scenery. The full moon sailed above, and the birds and bats, astonished by what was happening, flew bewildered in the lights. From the dusky Gardens stole a scent that in June could not have been orange blossom, but it was sweet and penetrating and aromatic.

I sat among thousands of Spaniards, facing a stage built up to look like a part of the Gardens. The exits and the entrances were box hedges, and at the back the tallest of all the cypresses lifted their thin black spires. A babel of quick bird-like conversation rose around me, but I could still hear that characteristic summer sound of a Spanish crowd, the sharp little raps as women, with a single adroit movement of the right wrist, opened their fans. In the warm darkness hundreds of fans fluttered like moths.

The conductor lifted his baton and the haunting music of Delibes matched the night and the moon. Two limelights met at the back of the stage and into this pool of light stepped Margot Fonteyn, who came forward like a white butterfly. She danced with Michael Somes the *Pas de deux* from Act III of *Sylvia*, and you could have heard a fan drop, which is most unusual with a Spanish audience. It was a moment of perfect beauty and I thought that rarely can ballet have been seen in more exquisite surroundings. I was interested to be told later by Miss Fonteyn that she missed the feeling of the theatre, and felt that her dancing was somehow evaporating and going up towards the enormous night sky and not reaching the audience.

During the second dance, which was the *Pas de deux* from Act II of *Swan Lake*, the good manners of the audience and the self-control of the ballerina were tested to the full. As the swan, pinned in two lime-lights, was fluttering in her last movements, there suddenly appeared upon the stage a bewildered white dog. He was the dog one has so often seen reducing some solemn ceremony or regal occasion to bathos. He probably belonged to one of the gardeners and he was appalled by what was happening to the usually scented darkness of the Generalife. He had come to investigate and find out, like a good dog. He stood braced for effort in the limelight, gazing with interest at the ballerina; and we held our breaths! Then as the dance was ending, feeling that he was completely out of his depth, he trotted briskly across the stage with tail well up and disappeared. But during this embarrassing moment not one titter came from the audience, and I thought I had never seen better manners. The last dance was the *Pas de deux* from Act III of the *Sleeping Beauty*, and although it was nearly two o'clock in the morning, I felt that I could have watched for ever the beauty of that superb young dancer under the full moon of Granada.

As the crowds were finding their way out, I went rapidly in the opposite direction and had a glimpse of that famous little garden where two lines of water-jets curve towards each other behind hedges of box and cypresses; and there was silence except for the sound of falling water, and darkness except for moonlight stealing between the cypress trees. The little garden at that moment looked like something from the *Arabian Nights*.

I thought I could not have had a more beautiful introduction to Granada.

§ 5

The Alhambra rises upon its reddish crag, above elm trees planted, it is said, by Wellington. Upon the spacious parade ground where the sultan once reviewed his janissaries to a beat of kettledrums and a waving of horsehair standards, gipsies try to tell your fortune, boot-blacks try to clean your shoes, and little gipsy girls try to sell you castanets made of pomegranate wood. There is a studio where you can be photographed dressed as a sultan against a painted backcloth of the Alhambra. You can be holding a scimitar or smoking a hookah —or why not both?—and if you have a lady with you she can recline upon a couch and be a member of your harem. It should not be imagined that this is a vulgar pier-head studio of the kind you might find at Margate or Blackpool: it is a genuine survival from late Victorian and Edwardian times and both costumes and backcloths have a delightful air of period. It belongs to the days when so intense were the emotions called up by the Alhambra that visitors liked to take away this certain proof that they had not only been there, but had also entered fully into the romantic atmosphere.

Spain in the nineteenth century was the last country in which you could go about in fancy dress. Those who envied the greater scope offered a little earlier to the Byrons and the Hester Stanhopes could put on sombreros and long cloaks in Spain, and wear breeches sewn with silver buttons from waist to knee. Even the clear-eyed Ford rode through Spain disguised as an Andalusian. This little studio must be considered one of the last inhabited temples of the romantic revival. Surely among its earliest files, if they keep any, must be an old plate of Théophile Gautier.

A convincing proof of the spell of the Alhambra is plate 309 in A. L. Calvert's *Granada and the Alhambra*. Just over fifty years ago Calvert wrote a long series of books about Spain and all of them are noted for their excellent photographs. In the book I have mentioned we see 'the Author in the Alhambra', dressed oddly in what appear to be a pair of rather long running-shorts, horizontally striped socks, a scimitar in his waistband, and his face encircled by a burnous. This photograph has all the charm which distinguishes the products of this studio, the first of which is that the people photographed should look utterly unlike Moors. As I studied Mr. Calvert's well-bred face, with its Edwardian moustache, I had a vision of him, not riding out to slay Christians, still less reclining in his harem, but stopping hansoms in the Strand with a gold-topped cane.

I bought my tickets for the Alhambra in the magnificent palace which the Emperor Charles V never completed. He eliminated many Moorish buildings for the purpose, for which he has been, I feel, unjustly reviled. A step took me into Moorish splendours. I gazed enchanted through little arcaded windows which framed a distant view of Granada, where houses were climbing the hills. I wandered through cool apartments covered everywhere with lace-like decorations, and I did my best to forget the Turkish Baths I had visited and that when young I had been taken to the Crystal Palace.

The Court of the Myrtles, where the reflection of orange trees lies in a pool of unruffled green water, was lovely; and I thought that whenever the Arab can get into the open air and make a garden he often creates the purest poetry.

The Court of the Lions is a thing of light, indeed of weightless beauty. I thought I should go there every day while I was in Granada. It has the look of something which has just alighted upon earth, as the Parthenon has the look of something that is about to fly away. I felt like someone in a story who has passed through a door in a wall to find himself in some *gulistan* of Sa'di; for this is the country of djinn and wizard, the enchanted pavilion of a Scheherazade, where the rose-leaf drops into the porphyry font, where the bulbuls are singing. I walked round beneath the arcades of horseshoe arches, admiring the balance and design of the oblong courtyard, the projecting kiosks with their slender columns, sometimes two by two, and the roofs dripping with stalactites or honeycomb, gilt and coloured; it was a mathematical symphony to be enjoyed by the sultan as he lay upon his divan. The fountain was playing. A tall jet of water rose from the centre and fell into the basin, while from the mouths of twelve lions issued twelve spouts of water that fell into a channel and splashed back over their forelegs. What queer benevolent lions they are, stocky and rigid as the wooden animals of a Noah's Ark, and for some extraordinary reason known only to the artist—was he Persian, Chinese, or Byzantine?— each lion carries his tail behind his left hind-leg, with the end lying against his left flank. They look like a troupe of kindly performing lions who have been taught to support this fountain, as they do, by obediently offering their twelve firm little rumps to twelve stone columns. The colour was as enchanting as the scene; the soft pearly twilight of the kiosks, and the light reflected from the red gravel out-side, flushing the columns pinkly and filling the inverted cups in the roof with the ghost of *vin rosé*.

Anyone who has read Ford's grim account of the decay of the Alhambra will wonder how much of the present building is genuine and how much is restoration. I had the curiosity later to look up the fine engraving in Swinburne's *Travels*, made in 1775, and was surprised to find that the Court of the Lions was practically as it is today. The only differences I could detect are that the Court, instead of being red gravel, was tiled, and the fountain had a rather ugly second basin, also seen in J. F. Lewis's *Sketches of the Alhambra*. Most of the damage was done after Swinburne was there, particularly by Napoleon's terrible looters who, as a parting gesture, nearly blew the whole place sky high.

Beyond the Court of Lions is a satisfactory garden with pools of water, where two even stranger-looking lions squat upon the brink; and at the back is terrace upon terrace planted with cypress, myrtle and oleanders and all manner of scented and flowering shrubs. There are also hundreds of flower-pots planted with geraniums, pinks and carnations. You see flower-pots all over Spain; maybe this also is a Moorish legacy.

Back to the Court of Lions and once again to admire it. Even a building as apparently unanchored to reality as the Alhambra must have a date in history, and it is said that it was begun by Mohammed V in the year 1377. That was the year young Richard II of Bordeaux was crowned King of England; how far away Wat Tyler seems from this stately pleasure dome! Contemporary domestic architecture in England, though a little more solid, lacked the sophisticated luxury of this Arabian Night's Dream. Right to the end of the occupation the Moors of Spain did themselves well. No medieval Christian king lived

214

in such exotic and feminine surroundings, for it is always of women that one thinks in the parts of the Alhambra which have survived. These pretty vistas, fountains and arcades, and these charming little kiosks, designed it seems for the eating of rose-petal jam, for tears, for sighs, provoke the thought that the Alhambra is not unlike a woman who has no other quality than beauty.

Many a visitor to this place has had a vision of exquisite sultanas, but they were not visible to me. Instead, I saw a solemn little Spanish girl, with her tutors and governesses, engaged in writing dutiful letters in Latin to a boy called Arthur who lived in a far country, in a place called Ludlow Castle in the county of Shropshire. After the capture of Granada the Alhambra became the home of Catherine of Aragon, and while she was living there she was betrothed to Arthur, Prince of Wales, the heir of Henry VII of England. When she was sixteen she said goodbye for ever to the Alhambra and sailed away to become Princess of Wales; but many a time in the dark years to come she must have remembered the sunshine and the flowers.

§ 6

I looked down from a window of the Alhambra across a gorge into the Albaicin, where the gipsies have entertained tourists for generations. A pair of field-glasses brought into view little whitewashed houses, some with flat roofs, running uphill together, with narrow lanes between, where many of the gipsies live with hundreds of brass and copper pots and pans in caves lit by electricity.

I noticed in particular one house which had transformed its flat roof into a stage with tiers of seats at one end. While I was looking at this, a large touring-car came gingerly round the corner and stopped opposite the house. Out stepped a guide, followed by six tourists whom I could see from their clothes and their air of polite earnestness were American. The guide was obviously explaining that here was a place where they could see the real thing if they liked. He would introduce them to a very good, honest family of *gitanos*. I could fancy the tourists saying, 'Sure, go right ahead!' While the visitors took pictures of the house, the guide knocked at the door. The whole party trooped inside and the door closed.

In a few moments three American women arrived on the roof, glancing around them suspiciously, followed by the three men, who had their cameras ready. The guide came up with four girls wearing brilliantly coloured flounced skirts, who scattered over the little stage with a swish of red, blue and yellow and took up their positions for dancing. I could hear the sharp snapping of their castanets away up on the hill. They twirled and stamped with uplifted arms while the tourists stalked them with Leica and Rolleiflex, kneeling down to get a low-angle shot, approaching the dancers or backing away to include the whole scene. I hoped they were using colour film. The dance came to an abrupt end, a pocket book was produced, and the guide took the pesetas; and it must have been a generous payment, for all the girls smiled and waved their hands and even the old gipsy who opened the door looked gratified.

Could I, or could I not, hear the voice of some ambitious young man, who wanted to stand in well with the bank president, saying in months to come, as these pictures were flashed upon a screen, 'Gee, sir, you certainly did get under the skin of Spain!'

The big car rolled away in the direction of the tombs of *Los Reyes Católicos.*

§ 7

I made out a list of the great things I had so far seen in Spain: the Prado and the Plaza Mayor in Madrid, the Pastrana Tapestries, the monastery of Guadalupe, the cathedral and city of Toledo, the Roman theatre at Mérida, the cathedral of Seville, the monastery of La Rábida, the mosque of Córdoba, the Alhambra, and last of all the most impressive sepulchre I have ever seen, the tomb of Ferdinand and Isabel in the Chapel Royal at Granada.

A screen, superb even in a land where smiths forge iron as other men carve oak or walnut, separates the nave from the chancel where Ferdinand and Isabel lie upon a bed of white marble. He wears armour, with the Order of the Garter given to him by our Henry VII; she lies beside him, crowned, wearing a long robe and the Cross of Santiago. Near them and enclosed by the same railing are two other recumbent figures, a man and a woman in an attitude of prayer. Who, I wondered, could share the pomp of death with Ferdinand and Isabel? I read the names of Joan the Mad and her handsome Philip of Burgundy.

So here, far from the ornate French chapel which the Catholic Kings had built at Toledo to be their last resting-place, lie the old roots of Spain, Castile and Aragon, entwined at last, together with the Hapsburg graft which produced the great Charles, the sombre

216

Philip, and the inbred kings who ended with the haunted-looking Charles III.

Ferdinand and Isabel . . . Isabel and Ferdinand . . . *Los Reyes Católicos*. Everywhere the stranger goes in Spain he meets their memory and hears people speaking of them, of a gift they made, or of something they said or did; and this is as much of immortality as anyone can hope for. They are always together; to hear about Ferdinand alone is to confuse him with other Ferdinands; and to meet Isabel alone is to wonder for a moment who she is. They remain side by side in one's fancy, a royal Romeo and Juliet, though in fact she was a jealous woman and he a crafty knight who gave her good cause for her jealousy. This Ferdinand was no *el Santo*, but a politician as devious in his methods as his contemporary, our own Henry VII. 'No one', wrote one who knew him, 'could read his thoughts by any change of his countenance.' The dream of his life was to arrange a defensive barrage of marriage beds round France, and he played off his daughters with great skill.

Isabel was a year older than her husband and a finer and greater character. Spain sees her through a rich haze of romance. She was much sought after in girlhood, and some say that among her suitors, when she was fourteen, was Edward IV of England. The story is that he suddenly rejected her because of his love for Elizabeth Woodville; but if there is anything in this, the jilting was not a personal matter at all. It is a fact of history that while the Council were casting about for a good political union—and Isabel of Castile was, of course, in the running—Edward secretly married his pretty young widow and faced the Council with a *fait accompli*. Even so, the thought that Isabel of Castile might have been Queen of England is a strange one.

She was not beautiful, as her portraits prove, but she was good-looking and dignified, with a fair complexion and chestnut hair that was almost red. Her eyes were blue and intelligent. Her excessive modesty lasted until the end; for as she lay dying she refused to expose her bare foot for the oil of extreme unction and a silk stocking was anointed instead. She was a bigot who would stop at nothing to advance what she believed was Christ's Kingdom, and of course she held the odd belief that the God of Love would have approved of the Inquisition and the expulsion of the Jews from Spain. But she had great qualities of faith, determination and vision. She was the most powerful believer in America, for Ferdinand was always rather luke-warm about Columbus. Isabel once said, when supporting the voyage,

'I am ready to pawn my jewels to defray the expenses of it, if the funds of the Treasury should be found inadequate.'

She rode armoured all over Spain like a Joan of Arc, and whenever she appeared the troops felt twice as strong. Her children were born here and there, wherever she happened to be when their arrival interrupted her normal activities. Not one of her five children was born in the same town. She and her husband were a living emblem of the strange thing their marriage had brought to Spain—unity. There was a lively observer of all this at the time, an Italian called Peter Martyr, who set down the events of the reign in a series of interesting letters. Nothing seems to have surprised him more than the sight, at the siege of Granada, of Aragonese and Castilians, and other Spaniards, getting on well together and actually pulling in the same direction.

> Who would have believed [he wrote] that the Galician, the fierce Asturian, and the rude inhabitant of the Pyrenees, men accustomed to deeds of atrocious violence, and to brawl and battle on the lightest occasions at home, should mingle amicably, not only with one another, but with the Toledans, the La-Manchans, and the wily and jealous Andalusians; all living together in harmonious subordination to authority, like members of one family.

Such a thing had never happened before, and for the first time under the Catholic Kings there emerges something that begins to look like Spain.

As Isabel lay dying at the age of fifty-three, the world could show no woman who had been more successful and none more miserable Forty-six years of public triumph had been followed by seven years of personal grief. Fate struck at her in that most tender stronghold of middle-age, her children. When Granada was captured her young family had been with her and had seen the Pope's silver cross planted on the Alhambra hill. There was Joan, who was not yet mad; little Catherine of Aragon, aged seven; and most precious of all, her 'angel', as she called him, Don John, a boy of fourteen, who was heir to the throne, a prince of great quality and promise.

Six weeks after that great moment Joan, who was then seventeen, left Spain to marry Philip of Burgundy, and Isabel felt the parting bitterly, almost as if she had some foreknowledge of the tragedy that was to be this girl's life. She took her daughter to the coast at Laredo, near Santander, where a great fleet of a hundred and twenty ships was waiting to take the Princess to her bridegroom. Isabel slept on board with Joan, and when the fleet sailed she turned away in the deepest grief and rode sadly back to Burgos. Every year after, she was stricken by some new sorrow. In the following year, 1497, the most terrible blow of all fell, when her 'angel', a young bridegroom of nineteen died, as the Spaniards will tell you, of love. At any rate Prince John died and Spain had no male heir to all the glory. The year after, Isabel was stricken with horror to hear rumours that Joan, in Flanders was, lax in her Christian duties. She sent out spies to discover the truth. The next year's sorrow—1498—was the death of her eldest daughter Isabel, Queen of Portugal, who died in giving birth to a prince. Her hopes were now set upon this male infant, but in twelve months he too died. There was only one child now to leave her, the sixteen-year-old Catherine of Aragon, and in the following year she said goodbye and sailed to England to marry Prince Arthur, the eldest son of Henry VII, and heir to the throne. Another twelve months passed and Isabel learnt that Arthur had died leaving Catherine a young widow in a strange land. Another twelve months and Joan returned from Flanders with her handsome and frivolous Philip, and the poor Queen saw that her daughter was, if not mad, strange, eccentric and unbiddable; and death, which had taken away all her bright hopes, had spared this turbulent and disturbing girl to be the heir of Castile.

Joan was insanely jealous of her husband and there were stories of her fearful rages when she suspected him of infidelity. Philip's one desire was to get away from his wife and to escape from the dull, pious court of Spain, which he rapidly did, leaving Joan behind, a prey to thoughts which tortured her and eventually turned her brain. The last twelve months of Isabel's life were spent with her hysterical daughter, who either fell into fits of depression or into rages which Peter Martyr described as 'like a Punic lioness'. Her one thought was to go back to Philip and inflict her love upon him. One night she tried to escape from a castle in her nightdress and, refusing to return to her rooms, clung half naked to the railings all day and for the whole of the next night in a biting November wind. Before an audience of courtiers, soldiers and grooms the poor ailing Queen was violently abused by her daughter as she clung to the iron bars. It was from that moment that Joan became known as *Juana la Loca*, Joan the Mad, or Crazy Jane.

At length in March, 1504, when Spain and France had arranged a truce and it was possible for Joan to make the sea voyage, she was allowed to go to Flanders. Stories of her exploits soon reached Spain and covered Ferdinand and Isabel with shame. Suspecting that Philip was unfaithful to her with a beautiful girl with long fair hair, she attacked the girl and cut off her hair, it was said, in public. Isabel sank under these repeated sorrows and died in the November of that year, worrying about the 'poor Indians in America' and about her mad daughter in Flanders. In a codicil to her will she provided that should Joan be unfit to rule, Ferdinand should act as her regent.

Under a black November sky and in the teeth of the icy winds of winter, the body of the great Queen, robed as a Franciscan nun, was carried from the castle at Medina del Campo, where she had died, across the highlands of Castile and the plains of La Mancha towards distant Granada, where she had asked to be buried. The frightened villagers crossed themselves as they saw the slow procession come winding through the mountain passes, the uplifted crosses, the swinging censers, the tapers of unbleached wax blown out by the incessant wind and rain, the mules and the horses in sable trappings, and the hearse with its wet and muddy velvet shaking over the rough roads. No stars were seen, storm clouds hid the sky, bridges were swept away, men and mules lost their lives in flooded rivers, and it seemed that Nature herself wept for this dead lady. And Peter Martyr, who was there, wrote: 'never did I encounter such perils in the whole of my hazardous pilgrimage to Egypt'.

When the cortège reached Granada, for the Chapel Royal was not yet built, the body of Isabel was placed in the little Franciscan monastery which still stands upon the Alhambra hill. Twelve years passed, then another procession climbed the hill, and Ferdinand and Isabel were together once again. In the following year the Chapel Royal was finished and they were interred before the high altar.

I left the tomb and walked round to the side nearest the altar, where I noticed a short flight of steps leading down below the pavement level. I came to an iron gate and through its bars I looked into a stone vault lit by electric light where, a few feet away from me, I saw the coffins of Ferdinand and Isabel lying on a central stone slab, and on either side were two other coffins, Queen Joan and Philip of Burgundy. There was nothing else in this vault but the four coffins and a crucifix on the wall above a gilt crown.

I knew I should never forget it; it is one of the most startling sights in Spain and one of the most Spanish. Above rises the splendid tomb glorious with all the pomp of high estate; a few steps down is the reality of death. I could not take my eyes away.

> *Death lays his icy hand on Kings:*
> *Sceptre and crown*
> *Must tumble down,*
> *And in the dust be equal made*
> *With the poor crooked scythe and spade.*

How Spanish this is, how utterly and unforgettably Spanish. 'Everything comes to this in the long run,' I seemed to hear a Spanish voice saying. 'What is the point of getting excited about anything when all things end in this?'

## § 8

I left for Madrid one morning at eight o'clock, and though I should like to have gone on to Murcia and Valencia, the heat was so overpowering that I was glad to be travelling north again. Little did I dream what Madrid would be like!

I was soon passing through hilly Jaén, with happy thoughts of my jolly miller, and on through the vine and olive country and the fatness of opulent river valleys where the land, as everywhere I had been in Spain, looked loved and cared for in a way mechanically farmed land rarely does. I thought the countryside of Spain might be compared to hand embroidery, to the still superb work of the Spanish forges, to the innumerable handicrafts which have found their last home in this country.

I came to an extraordinary district where olive trees by the thousand were growing from the brick-red soil, and among the groves I saw strange-looking domes and near each dome a black chimney. These were lead mines, and I suppose, like most of the mines in the south of Spain, have been worked from the remotest antiquity. Although there were hundreds of small mines the landscape was not disfigured by slag heaps, and there were few pit-shafts. I saw some mines which were entered by perpendicular ladders. I met miners, their faces black with grime, riding on the hindquarters of donkeys, each one with an umbrella, and all chattering with Andalusian verbosity.

Then the road began to mount towards the tremendous bastion of the Sierra Morena, and I felt something in the air that spoke of an approaching frontier, something that said I was soon to say goodbye to the plumpness of Andalusia, to the oranges, the almonds and the aloe, and climb into a lean world of rocks where mountain would be folded against mountain to the sky. There was a village on the side of the road with nothing at all notable about it except the name, which springs out of a Spanish history book like Hastings out of ours—Las Navas de Tolosa. Among these mountains in the year 1212—which is just as easy to remember as 1066—Alfonso VIII, who had married Eleanor, the daughter of Henry II and sister of Richard Cœur de Lion, visited the wrath of God upon the Moors with the help of the united chivalry of Europe. He was guided over the mountains by a mysterious shepherd who, it has been suspected, was St. Isidore in disguise.

And now the road was winding into slate-grey gorges designed by Nature for brigandry. Up and on it went, with boulders and rock on either hand, not unlike the road which goes up from Jericho to Jerusalem; a road with the same sinister reputation.

Upon the summit, which is some two thousand, six hundred feet above the sea, the pass reminded me of the Cilician Gates, and here the road dives into a series of tunnels in the rock. Before I went through the *Puerto de Despeñaperros*, as the pass is called—the Pass of the Flinging Down of the Moorish Dogs—I stopped the steaming car and looked back over the beauty of Andalusia lying southward in the morning sun. On the other side of the pass was La Mancha, in New Castile; and, just as if I had been voyaging in a ship from one land to another, I found myself in a different country, a land of hungry distances, of dusty miles and cruising clouds. If you can imagine what it would be like to climb out of Sussex straight on to Dartmoor, you have an idea of the suddenness of the Castilian-Andalusian boundary. I thought how like the south of Spain is to South Africa. Travelling from Andalusia into Castile is not unlike climbing out of the Cape Province, where you leave the lush farms behind you, into the Karoo, where you meet the same skyline views, the same look of sea or desert, and the same treelessness and lack of water. La Mancha and Karoo, by the way, mean the same thing. Mancha comes from the Arabic *manxa*, meaning dry land, and Karoo from *kuru* (with a dental click), which was the Hottentot word for dry, hard land.

I came to Valdepeñas, famous for its excellent wine, where the vines grow at rather inebriated angles on the rocky slopes, and to Manzanares. Upon the outskirts of the little town I saw one of those admirable *albergues* established by that most excellent of all Spanish government endeavours, the State Tourist Department, which to the stranger in Spain is what the policeman is to the foreigner in London. The Department not only befriends the visitor in every possible way and keeps offices for this purpose all over the country, but it also regulates the prices in hotels and maintains a spectacular series of its own hotels, called *paradores*, and its own inns, or *albergues*. The difference between a *parador* and an *albergue* is that you can stay as long as you like at the *paradores*, but only for three days at the *albergues*, the reason being that the *albergues* are all on main roads and are for the use of motorists and other travellers, while the *paradores* are generally in out-of-the-way places and are often ancient castles, medieval palaces or monasteries, which have been transformed into the most picturesque hotels in Europe. If the timid or the aged traveller wishes to see Spain in the greatest comfort, all he has to do is to write to the Department and arrange to progress from *parador* to *parador*.

Spain always has a surprise up her sleeve for you, and the surprise of the *albergue* is that without causing any trouble or sensation you can have luncheon at one o'clock! And the flashing, dark-eyed welcome of the *albergue* is worth going to Spain to experience, for the charming staff always manages to greet the dusty wanderer as if he were the young squire returning from foreign parts. In no time I was seated at a table covered with *entremeses*—little plates of olives, tunny fish, *langostinos*, and superb cured ham, with a jug of local Valdepeñas beside me, and in my hand a menu as long as your arm. I ordered an omelette of shrimps and mushrooms, and they strongly recommended the roast lamb.

An enormous coach drew up and the place was suddenly full of French, Americans and English. A young French monk with a woman who must have been his mother, for they were so alike, sat at the next table, and he visibly shuddered at the flesh-pots. He crumbled his bread unhappily and looked down at his plate, and I believe he was thinking it sinful to eat so much. His mother kept trying to tempt him to eat, but he countered her solicitude with little smiles and more bread-crumbling, and I thought it pretty certain that he would eventually confess the whole meal and demand penance. Who were they, I wondered. They could not be tourists, yet they had arrived with the tourists. I decided that he was a young French monk who was going to a Franciscan monastery in Spain, and his mother had seized the chance to take a holiday and go with him, much as a mother takes her boy to a preparatory school. The monk was certainly as nervous of his

223

mother in public as any schoolboy and disliked, as much as she was enjoying, the attention they caused. The tourists, who were having a grand time out in the garden at tables set under the acacias, were evidently just as puzzled by them as I was.

It was hard to leave the shade of the *albergue* for the blinding road and the dust, but I went on through Manzanares to Puerto Lapiche, where a rough road cuts across country to that immortal village of El Toboso, the home of Don Quixote's Dulcinea. This part of La Mancha is in the heart of what is known as 'the Don Quixote country', and indeed you cannot see a wineskin in a *venta*, or a windmill, or a fat man on an ass, or a country girl at a fountain, without remembering *Don Quixote*. And surely this should be enough. But it is not. Numerous people, who must have extraordinarily literal minds, want to see the actual inn in which Don Quixote kept his vigil, the particular village in which he fought the puppets, the one and only cave where he endured penance, and so on, evidently satisfying some deep spiritual craving which in earlier times was answered by pilgrimage. I have always thought of the 'Wordsworth country', the 'Shakespeare country', and the 'Doone country', as Protestant shrines which have replaced Canterbury and Walsingham; but it is odd, in a country where religious pilgrimage still continues, to find this secular one so popular and by no means only with heretical visitors.

For me Toboso is a worth-while shrine, for the first book I ever truly loved was a child's version of *Don Quixote*, by Judge Parry, with beautiful coloured illustrations by Walter Crane which I can see to this day in the greatest detail. I remember the startling black hairs on the Don's legs as he stood in his nightshirt fighting the wine-skins. Dulcinea was my first heroine and I took her as seriously as Don Quixote did; she was the exquisite princess whose existence justified all his adventures, and it was not until later, with the years of disillusion, that I realized sorrowfully that she was only a hefty country wench, the figment of his fancy.

The road continues to a junction called Alcázar de San Juan, an ancient town where the railway runs south to Granada and southeast to Murcia. It is a busy little place in which they make Castile soap. Soap and the small wax matches, sold in beautiful little boxes with heraldic labels on them, are two of the superlative products of Spain. In my opinion neither English soap nor English matches are as good.

The white road led ahead across the red land to villages that glittered upon the horizon. Churches huge as fortresses towered above the roof tiles. These villages were all much the same to look at; a huge sprawling Baroque church, its yellow plaster peeling, a bell swinging in a tower, a stork standing on an untidy nest; a plaza ringed with acacia trees; an ornate fountain where graceful brown girls lingered with jars poised on their hips, and a tangle of blinding streets. Sometimes the shops display a sample of their goods so that those who have not left the age of wisdom for that of literacy may know what to find inside. The ironmonger hangs a spade outside his shop, the draper may exhibit a pair of socks, but these medieval habits are fast vanishing. I looked everywhere in vain for that little brass cup with a nick out of the rim—Mambrino's helmet—which used to hang over the doors of barbers' shops. But it is still possible to see the barber using the helmet of Mambrino when he shaves a man. He fills it with soap and water and places it upon the chest of his customer so that the cut-away segment fits into his neck.

I came to a white town on a hill where windmills were dotted round about upon slight mounds; not the massive windmills of Holland, but neat little windmills that in a poor light a man might easily mistake for something else, particularly giants waving their arms menacingly. This was Campo de Criptana, the spot where Don Quixote charged the turning sails. Ford tells us that in the time of Cervantes the windmill was a recent importation into Spain—presumably from Flanders—so that Don Quixote had every reason to be dismayed by what to him and to many of his contemporaries was a strange and wonderful sight. A big Manchegan hay-cart with enormous wheels and open timberwork like the skeleton of a boat came creaking along, drawn by two mules and a pilot donkey. The old man who was driving said yes, the *compañero* was on the road to Toboso, and he pointed with his stick over the red plain; and the companion thanked him and went on.

A few miles further and I saw the white village of El Toboso slumbering on the red earth under the high sky. Not a soul was to be seen. The priest was not in the church and I could find no one to direct me to the *alcalde*. I heard a monotonous bee-like hum of young voices coming from the upper floor of a large building, and knew that the scholars of Toboso were still being taught in those rhythmic choruses which etch themselves upon the mind for ever. I thought I would go inside and find the village schoolmaster. A flight of stairs led up to the classrooms. While I was wondering upon which door to knock, I noticed, hanging in the corridor, a framed pictorial warning of the dangers of *El Alcoholismo*, which dated from the late nineteenth century. It told in pictures the lives of two men, one a teetotaller and the other a drinker. The teetotaller married a beautiful woman and had a huge and happy family. The girls were all well dressed, and when out of doors walked with their hands in little fur muffs and their feet in tiny laced-up boots. Little circular fur hats like sleeping cats sat on their hair, which cascaded over their shoulders. The boys were in sailor suits. The teetotaller's wife was always either bending affectionately over her husband as he read some good book, or else she walked rigidly beside him, fashionably dressed, the children in front, while passers-by lifted their hats and bowed respectfully. On the other side the drinker was seen, always with a mug or a glass in his hand, ragged, unshaven, surrounded by bottles and revolting companions, deserted by his flashy wife, his starving children weeping in a slum; and, finally, crime under a street lamp, and the police. The picture had a strange un-Spanish look about it; it was the sort of thing which must have been seen in Blackburn about 1890. And why it should hang in a village school in the most sober country in Europe is incomprehensible. The Spanish sense of human dignity rules out intoxication, neither is drink idealized and advertised as in Anglo-Saxon countries, nor is a drinker assumed to be a good fellow.

I knocked at a door, which was opened by a middle-aged man over whose shoulder I saw about thirty small children sitting on wooden benches, each one with a slate and a slate pencil. They did not giggle, laugh or nudge each other at this welcome interruption, but gave me one of those long, unblinking Spanish stares, gazing solemnly, almost in wonder, as if I might have been a wandering saint. This respectful reception of a stranger is one of the many beautiful characteristics of Spain. I explained my difficulty to the master, who called a small boy and told him to take me to the house of the mayor, though, he said, he thought the *alcalde* had gone away that morning with the priest to some distant place. The child led me across the plaza to a white house. The door was opened by a woman who said, alas, the *alcalde* was away, but would I please step inside. She opened a door on the right and I stepped into a room full of books. They stood on home-made shelves almost to the ceiling. This might have been the very room in which Don Quixote studied tales of chivalry. Glancing at the shelves, I saw that they contained copies of *Don Quixote* in every possible language, English, French, German, Italian, even Russian, Japanese and Hindustani. The woman returned with two men, while several others came in and shook hands with me.

I have learnt that upon such occasions it is a good idea to be as formal as possible. Until the formalities have been observed and a lot of resonant words enjoyed by all, levity or friendliness are out of place. That comes later. So putting on a solemn expression as if I were addressing the British Association, I told them as well as I could who I was, where I came from, what I was doing in Spain; that I was one of the most devoted readers of the great Spanish writer, Cervantes, and had had a great longing to see the famous village of El Toboso, whose name was known all over the world. One of the men replied, but I understood little of what he said, for he spoke too quickly and colloquially. I was, however, left with the impression that Toboso and everything in it was mine. After this we all shook hands, the public meeting was over, and we became jolly and human.

One of the men went searching along the shelves and placed in my hand the Nonesuch Press edition of *Don Quixote*. I opened it and read 'From Ramsay Macdonald, April 11, 1932'. He came back with another copy, a German edition given by Hindenburg in 1929. An Italian edition was signed by Mussolini. There was a copy from Mr. de Valera.

They told me that the library had been assembled by an ex-mayor of Toboso, Don Jaime Pantoja Morales, who was proud of his family's association with Don Quixote's Dulcinea, whose name in real life, it has been claimed, was Ana Zarco de Morales. About the year 1922 a brilliant idea struck His Worship. He founded a Cervantes Society and wrote to kings, presidents, and prime ministers all over the world, asking them to send a copy of *Don Quixote* to the library of the Society at Toboso. Who could resist such a letter from Dulcinea's home town? The result was that books arrived at Toboso from every part of the globe, a tribute to the enchantment cast by this village wherever men can read. I do not know whether modern commentators still believe, as apparently they did in Ford's time, that Dulcinea was drawn from life, and, if so, that her name was Ana Zarco de Morales; but nothing will shake the Tobosans from this theory, indeed they go much further and say that Cervantes was in love with her and so made Don Quixote her sweetheart. I thought that he must have been an odd lover to describe her as Sancho did to his master! Among the treasures of Toboso brought out for my inspection were two pretty skirts of faded brocade, one of them with hundreds of little slits for bows and ribbons, as worn in the time of Philip II. They are said to have belonged to Ana Zarco de Morales.

I was taken all round Toboso; into the church dedicated to St. James of Compostella, where a Roman St. James on horseback slays a prostrate infidel, and to a ruined building which was once an olive mill—I recognized the large jars sunk in the ground—and is said to be the house where Dulcinea once lived. The scene was a beautiful page or two of Cervantes; the old barn-like stone building, a pile of hay with hens picking over it, a country cart resting on its shafts, the group of good-humoured peasant faces, and big, brown hard-working hands pointing here and there.

We visited the wine shop and drank toasts to Dulcinea, to Don Quixote, and to Cervantes, in wine that tasted of the wine-skin and reminded me of the *retsinata* you get in Greece. By this time I was no longer the dignified *hidalgo* of early afternoon, I was the *compañero*; greater even than this, I was—a fellow *hombre*. And they all stood at the corner near the church and waved me goodbye.

I reached Madrid just as it was getting dark. The heat of the day, charged with petrol and oil, prowled about the streets like an assassin in the windless air, and the pavements were hot as the iron plates in the boiler-room of a ship.

## §9

In most hot countries the nights are comparatively cool and often a wind springs up which changes the air, but in Madrid, despite the high plain upon which it stands, the air in summer remains stagnant all night. The most bearable hours of the day I found to be from six in the morning until about nine o'clock. I liked to walk about Madrid at that time, though everything was closed except the newspaper kiosks; but the highly respectable old lady from whom I bought black market cigarettes was already on duty at her corner, openly displaying her contraband.

I visited a friend in his office at noon one day and found him working, his coat on, of course, while an electric fan blew cold air at him from a huge block of ice.

'But this is nothing,' he said when I mentioned the heat. 'Wait until the end of July.'

It was nevertheless sufficiently hot for those of my friends who could afford to do so to have sent their wives and families to little chalets near the Escorial, and even higher up in the Sierra, while they led bachelor lives in Madrid. Although I like heat and had brought tropical suits with me, I found that Madrid in July devitalized me. It was as much as I could do to walk for an hour round the Prado in the morning, then take a cold bath, have luncheon, and spend the afternoon in an airless bedroom. I wondered why Philip II had not built Madrid round the Escorial, or, if he were really looking for a grid-iron, the Escorial at Madrid. So with the siesta taking up all after-noon, I was obliged to keep the late hours of Spain, and I found myself just starting out to dine at the hour I usually go to bed.

I greatly increased my knowledge of Madrid's restaurants. There was one fitted with wooden settles, and whose walls were covered with bullfight posters, where the food was first-rate, and where sometimes I would see daring-looking men, whom I took to be *matadores*, dining with equally daring blondes who sometimes brought their lap-dogs with them. There was a Basque restaurant of superb quality which I visited only once, for when next I went there I found it had closed for the rest of the summer. They made the best *gazpacho* I had tasted and there was nothing they could learn about fish. I was disappointed by the well-known restaurant which has been cooking sucking-pigs since the seventeenth century and had this same feeling about others much patronized by tourists, where the rustic atmosphere was perhaps better than the food. There was an excellent Gallegan fish restaurant where I sat in an open courtyard and ate spider crab and drank white wine from the proprietor's vineyard in the north. Generally speaking I found the best food in the poorer-looking places. There was a splen-did little restaurant in a side street where they served steaks with a mushroom sauce, and another, decorated from floor to ceiling with scallop shells, where, once you had pushed your way through the crowd at the bar to a little room at the back, a perfect meal could be composed, and the wine was excellent. A good hot weather drink is *Sangría*, which is red wine and soda water, with ice and the peel of a lemon, and sometimes a small glass of cognac is added. Walking back at night after these late dinners it was strange to see the streets crowded with people. Midnight has no significance for Spaniards and Cinderella could mean nothing to them, for the ball would hardly have begun when the clock struck twelve. Sometimes I would come to little plazas —I remember particularly the Plaza de Santa Ana—where the entire surrounding population was sitting out in the open, the children play-ing as if it were day, the waiters running round in their white jackets, and people strolling round the square just thankful that the sun was absent. Even in Rome I have never felt the sight of fountains more welcome, and it was always delightful when the statue of Neptune and his sea horses, fenced with cool jets of green water, came into view in the Plaza de Cánovas.

On my way along the Medinaceli in the evenings I noticed a church with windows over the porch arranged so that anyone in the street could look along the length of the building and see a dramatic life-sized figure of Christ standing illuminated above the altar. In this land of the Blessed Virgin it was so unusual to see Christ in the place of honour above the altar that I went inside. I found that the figure, beautifully carved and coloured, answered the Spanish desire for intense realism. The Saviour was shown with bound hands, wearing the Crown of Thorns, and a magnificently embroidered robe of purple velvet. I think the hair, which fell to the shoulders on each side of the face, was real hair. One Friday evening I saw outside this church a queue of people which stretched all along the street, turned the corner and was lost in the darkness. When I returned two hours later the queue seemed just as long. It was composed of every type of Spaniard. I entered and saw that the church was almost empty save for the constant procession shuffling along the south aisle towards steps behind the altar. The people climbed the steps, passed in front of the figure, then descended on the other side and passed out along the north aisle. Each person, when he or she came to the statue, knelt down and appeared to kiss the feet.

I mentioned this to a Spanish friend, who said: 'That was the Jesús of the Medinaceli. Most of the young men and women you saw had gone to ask Jesús to give them a *novia* or a *novio*, for He is said to be particularly sympathetic to such requests.'

§ 10

One afternoon I walked past the royal palace and down the steep hill to the Manzanares to see the tomb of Goya. A big clean railway station now strikes the note of this district, but beyond it I detected a faint echo of the seventeenth century, for here the heavy coaches of that time used to lumber in the evening *paseo* beside the trickle of river. I came to a little church dedicated to St. Anthony, built in the form of a Greek cross. A caretaker unlocked the door and led the way to the altar, where the artist lies beneath a marble slab. A few feet away is the dome which he decorated so gaily with a scene that contains everything, colour, grace, beauty, charm, elegance; everything indeed except piety. How brilliantly he solved the problem of depicting the miracle of St. Anthony round a circular dome! He painted a balcony with an iron rail all the way round it, and he grouped his characters upon this so skilfully and so realistically that one feels, a false step and they would tumble down to the floor of the church. Needless to say, it is not the usual awe-struck crowd; it is a brilliant reflection of Goya's Madrid. The figures give one the impression that a camera obscura is reflecting a street of Madrid, with all its varied characters, upon the roof of the church. Somewhere in the background St. Anthony, an ordinary-looking Spanish monk, is bringing a man to life; but the gay court ladies, and others not usually to be found in a church fresco, are not particularly dumbfounded, nor are they driven to their knees in reverence. They are far more concerned about themselves; they might, as a matter of fact, be watching a minor street accident. I thought this was one of the most remarkable pictures Goya had painted.

Someone had placed a wreath on his grave, tied with the red and orange Spanish colours. He died in exile at Bordeaux, as so many distinguished Spaniards have done. When it was decided to bring his remains to Spain in 1888, his tomb was opened and a strange thing was discovered. It had been rifled and Goya's skull was missing. This mystery has never been solved, and is not made much easier by the report that a painting called 'Goya's Skull', by Dionisio Fierros, which has since vanished, was known in Spain during the nineteenth century.

# Chapter VIII

*To Segovia—an enchanted castle—St. John of the Cross—Avila of the Knights—the Mother of Carmel—Burgos and its cathedral—the women of Gil de Siloe—the royal tombs of Las Huelgas—the cathedral hen-coop of Santo Domingo—the fiesta of San Fermín at Pamplona— a visit to the Pass of Roncesvalles*

## § 1

THE smart electric train which runs from Madrid to Segovia was soon climbing into the foothills of the Sierra de Guadarrama, and for the first time for several days I enjoyed a breath of fresh air. The Escorial performed a stately ecclesiastical measure to the left, an architectural dance of the Seises, as the train twisted in its winding progress into the mountains. I saw the little villas, some with swimming pools, to which fortunate wives and families go in the heat of summer, and family groups were waiting on the platform at every station to welcome some pallid visitor from the metropolitan grill. What could be more extreme than this fire and ice of Castile? The great heat of July and August in Madrid is succeeded by winters so cold that the roads over the mountains are marked out with twelve-foot-high stone pillars like gateposts, to show the direction in a landscape obliterated by snow.

The train descended the reverse slopes and was soon speeding towards the hill town of Segovia.

I had been recommended to a new hotel, which I found in a narrow street, separated by a few yards of road from a Romanesque church that looked as old as the world. I was delighted with my bedroom, which was high up and with a glorious view across the roofs in the valley to a hill where Stations of the Cross mounted to what might have been Golgotha itself. The skyline was a curve of yellow wheat which the reapers were about to cut. In Andalusia the harvest had been carted for some time, and south of Madrid it was stacked in the fields, but here, only sixty miles to the north, they were just sharpening their sickles. Leaning out of the window, I could see the fine cathedral to my right and a stretch of the old wall running into the distance. Like most

medieval walls, it had semi-circular bastions protruding
intervals and many of these now formed the backs of houses.
of this succession of bays was extraordinarily like a terrace in
I wondered whether a window punched in an ancient tower
origin of the Georgian bow-window.

In the little church of San Martín opposite, I saw a figure of the
crucified Saviour, dressed in a kilt of purple. In Castile the crucified
Christ is never seen clothed only in a loincloth, and these kilts, which
are made of velvet and fringed with gold tassels, are detachable and
are changed from time to time with the liturgical year. Here also was
a wonderful example of an agonized dead Christ by Gregorio Her-
nández, a powerful and terrible work. The mouth was open in the last
agony, the eyes were glazed, and every wound poured blood.

Outside the church are flights of granite steps which lead to a
higher part of the town, and midway is a bronze statue of an heroic
young man in armour, who bears a certain resemblance to Joan of
Arc. His plinth simply bears the name 'Juan Bravo', and I suppose
Segovia believes that the whole world knows who he is. I must say
that in a country where the unsuccessful reformer is rarely commemorated, I thought this an interesting memorial.

Juan Bravo was one of the three chief leaders of the Comuneros,
who were members of the Comunidades, or municipal boroughs, of
Castile in the sixteenth century. Unlike modern people, who with
ox-like fortitude allow themselves to be bled white by the tax-gatherer,
the Comuneros blazed into revolt when young Charles I taxed his
Spanish subjects in order to bribe his way to the Imperial throne and
become Charles V, by which title he is better known.

As I looked round Segovia for the first time, my impressions were
all happy ones. I thought it one of the most restful places I had seen in
Spain and one of the most romantic. There are really two towns, an
upper and a lower. The upper town is grouped round the cathedral and
a splendid plaza, where Isabel was first proclaimed queen upon a platform in the open air. With a sword of state carried before her and the
banners of Castile and León about her, she walked to the cathedral,
where a *Te Deum* was sung. This was not in the present cathedral, but
in an earlier one which was later destroyed by the Comuneros. This
upper town of Segovia is quiet and restrained, and the atmosphere is
not unlike that of a cathedral close in England. It has not the vivid life
of the Plaza de Zocodover at Toledo, where the autobuses come snort-
ing up the hill; in Segovia the 'buses do not climb the hill, but deposit

their passengers in the lower town. There are several good cafés in the upper town, and at least one simple but admirable little tavern where the food is excellent and where the waiter always brought me a little gift with the bill, a china ashtray, a little brown jug, a small vase painted with flowers, and once a rather larger brown jug. There is a bookshop in the plaza with a window full of titles which were easily translated. I saw *Adventuras de la Pimpinela Escarlata*, by the Baroness Orczy, Louis Bromfield's *El Extraño Caso de la Señorita Annie Spragg*, Sidney Horler's *El Misterio de Balham*, and *Las Adventuras de Huckleberry Finn*. The publisher of Harlan Ware's *Veneno Implacable* noted *El alcoholismo y los gangsters, dos terrible plagas de Norteamérica*, which every Spaniard who has been to the venerable Wild West and gangster films shown in Spain knows to be true. I was glad to see that Walter Scott is read in a *famosas novelas* series.

The cathedral, whose doors creak even more agonizingly than most in Spain, is a beautiful church of warm, honey-coloured stone, with lovely cloisters. In the nave I saw a notice which read: 'Do not spit, piety and hygiene forbid it.' Spain is much addicted to this medieval vice, and is one of the last strongholds in the old world of the brass spittoon.

Segovia's lower town is grouped round an aqueduct which is one of the finest Roman remains in the world. The giant strides across the road and fascinates you every time you see it. Sometimes, with the sun behind, it is an enormous imperial silhouette, at others it is granite-grey and brown; and the autobuses, the taxi-cabs and the farm carts come in beneath its huge arches, while a few yards away a policeman in a white coat and helmet stands under a striped umbrella and directs traffic in and out of this superb piece of Roman engineering. It would be impressive in Rome, and to see it in what was once a small Roman provincial town is to think, as the medieval peasants did, that giants lived in those days. But it is no dead relic of the past. I was told that it still carries Segovia's water, but in a covered pipe.

The aqueduct is really the social centre of Segovia. There the 'buses arrive and start; there, I imagine, every story and rumour begins before it travels up the hill to the old city. The nightly *paseo* chatters and laughs its way down from the Plaza Mayor, through the narrow steep Calle de Juan Bravo, past the remarkable *Casa de los Picos*—the House of the Nails—which is decorated with projecting stones giving the effect of a nail-studded door, and ends in the tall shadow of the aqueduct. On a Sunday night, when the usual crowd with its small, neat dark girls is reinforced by many conscripts from a nearby barracks, all wearing khaki and white cotton gloves, the *paseo* has a truly metropolitan vivacity. The famous restaurant near the aqueduct, where you can eat regional food under festoons of garlic, in surroundings which look rather like an arts and crafts exhibition, is always full on Sundays, and the strangers go round reading the comments of statesmen, artists, poets, and even, I think I am right in saying, Franco, and certainly Primo de Rivera, with which the walls are covered. One day I ordered a soup called the Soup of Charles V, which seemed to be highly seasoned chicken broth into which an egg had been broken at the last moment, when the soup was boiling.

The speciality of Segovia is roast sucking-pig (I wondered how a pig ever manages to emerge from infancy in Castile), and delicious roast lamb fed on hillsides aromatic with wild sage. There are three zones of cooking in Spain and, as a Spanish saying puts it, *en el sur se fríe, en el centro se asa y en el norte se guisa*—in the south they fry, in the centre they roast, and in the north they stew. Segovia, of course, is in the heart of the roasting country, and I thought the cooking there of the highest quality. How dearly I should like to return to Spain and eat my way northward from Seville to Madrid, then to gnaw steadily through the Castiles and chew on to the Basque country, and so to pass, slowly and appreciatively, devouring like a caterpillar, through the Asturias into Galicia. *Through Spain with Knife and Fork!* Could there be a more appetizing title? Some gastronomic Borrow, or an epicurean Ford, could write a classic on this theme; for, in a world of dreary standardization and refrigeration, here is a country where each province is like a new restaurant, proud of its traditional food and drink; a country where men can give no higher praise to a town than the comment, 'they eat well there'.

One of the most beautiful moments in Segovia, indeed in Spain, is at sunset. Twilight is briefer than in England, but is not the sudden African swoop into darkness. Sometimes I saw the towers of the cathedral growing black against rose-red clouds that deepened to a fiery orange, and the whole plain, with its uplifted city on the hill, would fall into an important silence broken only by the sound of a church bell ringing out the last moments of another day. It is a time of intense emotion, the real moment of truth, when one feels that all the Saints of Spain, Isidore, Ildefonso, Eulalia, Teresa, Ignatius, St. John of the Cross, must be gathered together in some corner of heaven looking down upon the darkening land. Then all the colour passes from the sky and the stars are shining.

## § 2

The most notable sight in Segovia is the Alcázar, the castle of a fairy-tale, complete with thin candlestick towers capped with steep slate roofs like snuffers. It is built of whitish stone, which gives it an ethereal look, especially in the dusk, when it might be a drifting dream of chivalry or a chapter of Froissart that, having taken form and shape, has alighted upon this crag in Spain. Or—let me change the metaphor—it is a galleon called Tintagel sailing through the air, and all the Knights of the Round Table are within, polishing their armour while their squires groom the destriers, and the fair ladies, each one wearing a tall, pointed cap with a pendant veil, bend over their embroidery and slyly eye the knights. It is a lovely sight, a perfect picture-book castle.

The best view of this romantic building is from the valley, where you look up and see it riding against the sky, its walls and turrets fitting snugly into the outward thrust of rock; and if you have the energy to walk round the rock and up the steep road to the town, you will have another even more romantic view of it in a frame of slender poplar trees. It has now ceased to be prose; it is a song sung in Provençal by a jongleur who wears a pork-pie cap on his yellow head as he sits at a window tuning a lute and crossing a red over a green leg; and the song he sings is, of course, about love.

> *Anc sa bela bocha rizans*
> *non cuidei, baizan trais. . . .*

'I never thought her smiling mouth would betray me . . .', the old song that Vielart de Corbie used to sing in castles just like this, whose casements opened to precipices deep as human folly.

I enjoyed the Alcázar so much from the outside that I postponed a visit as long as possible, certain that it would be disappointing. But, oddly enough, it was not. I passed through a series of stone rooms whose windows give aerial views over the plain; some are beautifully decorated, and there is a charming little chapel and a screen of Córdoban leather from the late fifteenth century, stamped with parrots and parakeets from the Indies, which men were seeing for the first time. I am sure we exaggerate the discomfort of life in the Middle Ages, for, given plenty of tapestries and hot water, one could be as snug in the Alcázar as in any centrally heated flat in New York or London. I think tapestries were the solution to all the interior decoration problems of the Middle

236

Ages, and with a chest of it you could make a gaunt stone hall into a jewel casket in ten minutes.

The first thought of the amateur astronomer who visits the Alcázar is that here is the perfect place for a telescope, and it is delightful to be told that Castile's learned king, Alfonso X, did much of his mathematical, astronomical, legal and literary work in this castle. He was a contemporary of Henry III of England and of Roger Bacon, and he seems to have been the first noteworthy intellect in Spain, north of Córdoba. I was shown the window from which young Don Pedro, the son of Henry II of Trastamara, fell to his death in 1366, swiftly followed by his nurse, who avoided punishment by flinging herself after him. The prince's tomb can be seen in the cathedral, a curious little figure with long hair cut straight across the forehead, dressed like a medieval page, and lying with his hands on the hilt of a little sword. Isabel La Católica was living in the Alcázar when she was called upon to become Queen. It was here—perhaps in the large hall, or throne-room—that Philip II, aged forty-three and grey-haired before his time, mingled in disguise with his courtiers and caught his first glimpse of his fourth wife, his niece, Anne of Austria, whom he had wearily decided to marry for political and dynastic reasons. She made a good impression, by all accounts, wearing a dashing little Bohemian hat with a feather in it, and a riding-habit with a short cloak of crimson velvet. Philip's marriages well illustrate 'the triumph of hope over experience', in Dr. Johnson's words, but this time he was lucky, and the Hapsburg line tottered on in the person of Philip III.

The Alcázar also sheltered our Charles I as Prince of Wales, when he was on his way home to England after his visit to Madrid. It was here that he ate those 'trouts' of 'extraordinary greatness', taken no doubt from the Eresma and the Clamores, which tumble from rock to rock at the foot of the castle. The stranger will leave the Alcázar and walk down the hill to the cross-roads below the church of Vera Cruz, where he will look up at the castle, and think that while there may be larger and more impressive castles, there are none that so truly fulfil the requirements of the traditional castle in Spain, which is that it should look like a dream.

The little brown church of Vera Cruz, now no longer used, is, like the Temple Church in London, built on the model of the Rotunda of the Holy Sepulchre in Jerusalem, as it was seen by the Knights Templars. This is an impressive little building, and it reminds one that the Hospitallers and the Templars took a larger share than they are usually given credit for in the constant crusade of Spain. The little church may perhaps have been built by the Templars a few years after the battle of Las Navas de Tolosa, when the crusading orders had rallied round Alfonso VIII and covered themselves with glory. A peculiar two-storied structure stands in the centre of the church, and it may be symbolical of the Tomb of Christ. A flight of steps leads to the upper story where, it is said, aspirants to knighthood kept vigil over their arms, and in the morning descended to the lower part, where they were armed and received ₂e accolade.

Not far aw y there is a hot hillside, aromatic with the scent of wild sage, where ₐ thin tuft of water trickles down from the heights. Against the hill, indeed built into it in order to enclose a grotto, is the church of a Carmelite convent. As I stood looking through the bars of a great black and gold *reja* towards the high altar, where the Virgin is enthroned in baroque splendour, I could hardly believe that what I saw was not due to some trick of the light. Could the Virgin be holding a field-marshal's baton? It hardly seemed possible, yet it was so. A priest told me that during the Civil War General Varela conferred upon this Virgin the official title of Capitán-General of the Army. This reminded me of a similar story I had heard somewhere, but from the opposite camp, of the Virgin in a Socialist village who was made a member of the local trades union and issued with a membership card. Odd and even almost irreverent as it may sound to some, this is, of course, religion in daily life. It is what St. Teresa meant when she spoke of finding God among the pots and pans in the kitchen.

In another part of this church I came upon a small trap-door in the pavement and, as there was no one about, I ventured to lift it and found myself gazing into an empty tomb. I then noticed an inscription which said that the incorrupt body of St. John of the Cross had been deposited there until his beatification in 1675. I looked up and saw an enormous picture in brilliant colours depicting the apotheosis of St. John of the Cross and St. Teresa. Both saints are ascending to heaven through tremendous swirling clouds of glory, St. Teresa in a chariot drawn by blindfolded cupids and St. John of the Cross in a car drawn by crowned eagles. Her chariot represents the sun and his the moon, for he, of course, was a mystic of the school of night, who found light in darkness.

The body of St. John of the Cross was taken from the tomb and was placed in a large and ornate sepulchre nearby, which astonished me. It was such a tremendous tomb for such a tiny saint—he was only five feet, two inches in height—and such a pompous receptacle for a

238

little body whose owner, when alive, always considered it a great nuisance and hindrance and something to be punished. Of all Spaniards who ever lived, St. John of the Cross is the most appealing and the most ethereal. He drifts across the religious history of sixteenth century Spain like a spirit, indeed he scarcely seems anchored to the earth at all. He wrote love poems to God which are the most beautiful ever written by a saint. In his search for infused wisdom this great spiritual explorer was always wandering out at night to adore God in the darkness. It is impossible to think of him apart from St. Teresa who, meeting him first when he was a young man, saw his saintliness at a glance and drew him into the Carmelite reform.

The spiritual adventures of St. John of the Cross are well known to students of mysticism, but his mundane experiences are not perhaps familiar. It is odd to think of St. John of the Cross even fitting into mundane life at all. A number of stories about him were gathered from those who knew him when the Apostolic Process for his beatification was instituted, and these show him not in his uncomfortable cell, lost in rapture, but in everyday surroundings.

It is amusing to think of the five-foot-high saint ordering a couple of Spanish desperadoes to stop fighting. This happened, according to the testimony of Father Martín de la Asunción, when he and the Saint were journeying on mules not far from Granada. As they were passing an inn, two infuriated Andalusians rushed out with knives in their hands and began to attack each other. One was already bleeding. The Saint cried, 'In the name of Our Lord, Jesus Christ, I command you to stop fighting!' and threw his hat between them. To the amazement of bystanders, who had been trying to stop the fight for some time, the men looked at the little figure on the mule and obeyed. St. John then dismounted and is said to have effected such an unexpected reconciliation that the duellists not only embraced each other, but kissed each other's feet!

One day when the Saint was discussing divine matters with the Carmelite nuns at Granada, a sister quoted a verse from a book that had just been published. The Saint made her repeat the lines until he had them by heart. Then he went to his cell and wrote one of his most famous poems, which begins, in the translation by Roy Campbell:

> For all the beauty life has got
> I'll never throw myself away
> Save for one thing I know not what
> Which lucky chance may bring my way.

One dislikes to remember how this kindest and sweetest of all the saints was persecuted by the unreformed members of his own Order, and how they lashed the small body until it was a mass of wounds.

'I am happy, very happy,' he cried on his death-bed, 'for, without meriting it, I shall be in Heaven tonight.'

I knew that when my journey was over I should often remember those walks in the evening to the church of Vera Cruz, round the Alcázar hill, and up the steep road with a wooded gorge to the left, where the Clamores tinkles down to the Eresma. It was then that I felt as near to Spain as a stranger may feel. I was content just to be alone, to sit about and watch the pleasant pattern of life unfold around me, to ask no questions, and to live for the day, which, after all, is the secret of Spain.

§ 3

On an exceedingly hot afternoon a Spanish couple asked me to go with them to see the fountains play in the gardens of the palace at La Granja, seven miles from Segovia. It sounded a delightfully cool thing to do, and we arranged to meet at the aqueduct in the afternoon, where, after a little bargaining, we took a taxi-cab. We found ourselves in a queue of cars and buses crowded with holiday-makers, for the fountains are not often to be seen in action. The little village of La Granja was full of sightseers, and many thousands of them, as the car park proved, had come from as far off as Madrid.

We sat at a café under the trees near the palace railings, while my Segovian friend clapped his hands with firmness, as if summoning a slave—another Moorish relic, no doubt—and the overworked waiter came our way. My friend's wife was English, though no one would have suspected it. She had been born in Spain and had been to England once, during the first World War, to see relatives in the North. While we were drinking our coffee I became aware of a pleasant flutter in the air, as of hundreds of butterflies, and, glancing round, I saw that every woman was using a fan.

The palace was closed, and I could well imagine the succession of tapestried rooms, the clocks, the converging chandeliers, but it was interesting to walk round outside the enormous French conservatory which Philip V built to remind him of his beloved France. It is not in

240

the least like Versailles, as all the guide-books insist, but it has a certain lost French air and seems an eloquent relic of the change from Hapsburg to Bourbon. We examined the series of fountains, which begin close to the palace and extend upward in several directions among great trees. We came across Neptune and his sea-horses surfacing on a lake, while mythological groups and figures were poised on rocks, waiting for the magical moment when someone would turn a wheel and drench them in water.

At six o'clock everyone in La Granja had taken up vantage points in readiness for the great moment. The first fountain to play was to be the cascade that descends from the top of the gardens in a series of great steps and looks rather like a sublime tube staircase. The crowd was as enthusiastic as children, and among all the thousands of young people from near and far not one was wearing shorts, which would have been considered vulgar and indecorous away from a tennis court or a beach. After the usual Spanish delay there was a sudden gurgle of water, and the stone maidens were seen to be holding aloft a few uncertain pints, then everything died down. Suddenly the cascade was turned full on and water came rushing down in a silver river, while jets sprang up here and there, forming watery tents above the heads of gods and goddesses. No sooner had we admired it than it was turned off, and the crowd, who knew the procedure, suddenly took to its heels and ran, climbing up banks and through woods and gardens to get to the next group of fountains in time. What a contrast was this flamboyant and rather pointless display of water to the subtle little Arab fountains of the south, where the most modest jet quietly rising in a patio was more cooling, more beautiful than all the lavish machinery of eighteenth century cascade and jet. One felt sympathy with Philip V, who is reputed to have remarked, when he first saw these fountains playing, 'They cost me three million and have amused me for three minutes.' I suspect they would not have amused any of the caliphs even for that length of time.

§ 4

The autobus to Avila starts in the evening from a little garage near the aqueduct and, having reserved a place, I went there in good time, to forestall the person who always arrives first and is found firmly planted in one's seat. In these days of taxis there is something delightfully archaic in following the hotel boots down a narrow road, while he wheels one's bags on a little trolley. I passed the *Casa de los Picos*, and dropped in to bid farewell to the proprietor of the restaurant where I had eaten *cordero* and *cochinillo*, to say nothing of plump *perdiz*, then passed down to the aqueduct and the garage. The passengers were already assembling. There was a woman holding two apprehensive hens tied by the feet, a commercial traveller with several cases of samples, and countrymen returning to their villages.

The 'bus gave three or four backfires and began to move. We were soon mounting a steep hill and the passengers, stimulated by the noise of the antique engine and the sound of the worn-out gears, shouted to each other at the top of their voices, as Spaniards do, and were determined to make more noise than the 'bus. Lady Fanshawe noted in the seventeenth century that when the Spaniards travel, 'they are the most jolly persons in the world'; and that is as true today as it was then. There was a young man sitting near me with the profile of a parrot, who intoned nasal chants to himself in accompaniment to the engine, and when the old Rosinante backfired, took a corner on the wrong side (as every motorist does in Spain), or changed gear on a hill, his voice rose triumphantly, almost to *cante hondo*, in sympathy and perhaps in emulation. There was a village girl in her best frock, with waved hair, painted lips and finger-nails. In Ford's time I suppose she would have been wearing the beautiful scarlet and yellow of the district, with one of those intricate straw hats, plaited into hundreds of little ruches, which can still be bought in Segovia, and are worn over a gay scarf that is tied above the crown. But nothing can hold back fashion; it will penetrate the most remote hut on the most distant island. Some years ago a group of primitive bushmen and bushwomen were sent down from the Kalahari Desert to an exhibition in Cape Town, where I saw them. They were little parchment coloured people with stick-like legs and bulging bellies and the tallest was about the size of a child of ten. They talked together in a series of clicks. Among the withered, monkey-like women was one who was almost good-looking, and within a few hours of reaching civilization she had acquired, no one knew how, a lipstick, which, using a piece of glass as a mirror, she applied with all the assurance of a woman of fashion. Women are more conservative than men in everything that affects their comfort, but more adventurous in anything that concerns their appearance.

We travelled towards the setting sun, across a tableland that was mostly barren rock and scrub. There was a grand view of the Sierra de

Guadarrama to our left, and a vast melancholy seemed to descend from the setting sun and spread itself over the land as it does in Ireland. Fields of stubble and a few acres of corn would herald an approaching village; the white stone cottages would be standing in the shadow of a church; and the postmaster would be waiting at the 'bus stop. We would throw him a slender leather bag of mail and perhaps unload a couple of sacks or a wooden box. Departing passengers would be greeted by their assembled relatives as if they had returned from the Great Wall of China. Children would be passionately kissed. The village humorist would make a few remarks, which would be received with smiles in the 'bus, and off we would explode, scattering the hens, leaving the smell of wood smoke behind us, and carrying away a memory of women in black sewing at cottage doors. We pulled up at a humble little village where the girl with the painted lips and fingernails was met by father, mother, grandfather and grandmother, several other relations and innumerable *niños*. The 'bus stopped long enough for us to see this fashionable young woman enter a home that was already ancient when Don Quixote was wandering about the countryside. I suppose she would put away her war paint and emerge the next day as a simple country girl, to take her place at the fountain or give a hand on the threshing-floor. At another village two more fashionably dressed girls joined us, bound for Avila.

And now the sun had set and a rusty bar of red stretched across the cloudless sky. We passed threshing-floors where the *trillos* drawn by mules or oxen were slowly revolving in the twilight. The dark road was enlivened by the silhouettes of villages, unchanged and changeless. I was seeing the Spain of today, of Philip II, perhaps even of the Cid, and life was going on as it always has done; and watching over the community, its intermediary between this world and the mysteries beyond, was some oval-faced Virgin enthroned in a cloak of gold brocade above the candles.

Before we reached Avila a full moon sailed into the sky, and I could hardly believe that a month had passed since I had seen it shining upon the Gardens of the Generalife. It was now almost cold, for Avila is nearly four thousand feet above the sea and the highest city in Spain. Just as I was expecting the 'bus to gather itself for a race up the hill into the plaza, it swerved to the left and shot neatly into a garage. A number of young men who had been waiting for this moment each adopted a passenger and, shouldering his luggage, set off up the hill. Following my porter, I came at length to a tall embattled gateway,

. I could see towers and bastions running on into the moonlight
far as I could follow them. We passed through to dark streets
vith others, narrower and darker, leading from them, and I thought,
'Now I have done it! I have really passed through the door in the wall.
This is the Middle Ages about which I have so often read. I recognize it
perfectly. Shall I be able to get back?'

The young man took me to a rambling hotel, where I was told I
could have a room and a bath. Mounting four flights of stairs, I was
shown into a shabby room where an uneasy-looking bed stood with a
bath at its head, projecting into the room at right angles, as if the
plumber had just dumped it there. It was literally true. It was 'a room
and bath'! But I persuaded the boots to give me a less exotic room,
and from its window I looked across the little plaza to the west front
of Avila Cathedral, touched here and there by moonlight.

§ 5

Avila is the only completely walled medieval city in Europe. The
walls have eighty-six towers and the only way to get in or out of the
city is by one of the nine gates. When you look at Avila from the road
to Salamanca, which I think is the best of all the views, the town, a
narrow oblong in shape, is tilted slightly towards you. You can
see the mass of red-tiled roofs inside the walls, lying at various angles,
and the tallest building of all, the cathedral, is not in the centre of the
city, as you might expect, but forms an immense bastion in the eastern
angle of the wall. You notice too that quite an area in the western part
of Avila is waste and uninhabited, for the population within the walls
in the Middle Ages was greater than it is now. One day while I was
admiring this truly exquisite relic of the medieval world, a Spaniard on
his way to Salamanca stopped his car and joined me. 'Ah,' he said,
'but you must come back in the winter-time and see Avila in the snow.
Then she is most beautiful.'

I shall never forget my arrival by moonlight that first night. I soon
left the shabby hotel and was roaming about looking for somewhere to
dine. Near the cathedral was a plump little policeman wearing the
usual white helmet, and to him I went asking advice. He could not
have been more helpful or courteous, and he had such a friendly face
that when I thanked him and called him *señor*, I lifted my hat on the
impulse of the moment, before I turned away. To my utter astonish-
244

ment, not to be outdone in manners, and maybe considering a salute too officious, he lifted his white helmet several inches from his head as if it had been a bowler hat, at the same time bowing deeply. This put me in a good humour for days and I often smiled to remember it. The swift transition from the normal to the unexpected was the sort of thing that happened to Alice.

I found that the life of Avila deserts the old city in the evening and comes chattering out of the Gate of the Alcázar into the Plaza de Santa Teresa, where a statue of Avila's saint presides over the cafés and the excitement of the evening *paseo*. I went to the restaurant recommended by the policeman, but as it was only nine-thirty it was not really open. I was given dinner, nevertheless, in a deserted room set for about a hundred people. Veal is the speciality of Avila, also a little sweet cake made by the nuns and called *yemas* of Santa Teresa. The word *yema* means yolk and the centre of these cakes is too eggy for my taste; indeed they reminded me of some of the less successful Turkish sweet-meats, and though *yemas* have been converted in Avila, I have an idea that they were originally Islamic. After dinner I sat at one of the cafés with an *Anis Asturiana*, which I recommend to anyone who likes *ouzo*, *raki* or *absinthe*. The moonlight by this time was operatic. The walls with their white crenellation, and the great mass of the gate that leads into the plaza, stood washed in green light as if something dramatic were about to occur, and the succession of young Spaniards who passed through in their modern clothes seemed out of the period. It was difficult to realize that this was not a film set for *Hereward the Wake* or *Ivanhoe*, but a real wall that was contemporary with William the Conqueror. I walked to the end of the square and saw the battlements running on in the moonlight, bastion after bastion, as they followed the downhill lie of the land. On the left of the Gate of the Alcázar I saw a wide walk following the wall, and I continued along it for at least nine towers and one gate, the *Puerta del Grajal*, and decided to turn in at the next gate, which I did. I found myself in a little moonlit square with a church in one corner, which I was later to know as the church built on the site of St. Teresa's house; and I went on through the ancient streets, some of them lit by lanterns set high up on the old buildings.

As I approached the cathedral I noticed a faint light in the basement of an alley and, glancing in, I looked down into a cellar where an old man lay asleep on a pile of coal. A lantern near him threw its light upon black vaulting shrouded with grime and cobwebs, and the shadows held bulky objects and piles of sacks. It was a scene from a picaresque novel and the old man had obviously fallen asleep while waiting up for a highwayman!

Soon after midnight I was awakened by a great din below my window. Spaniards are utterly callous about making a noise at night, for they assume that everyone is still awake. Down below, in front of a dark house, stood a man and a woman calling and clapping their hands. Eventually an old man appeared with a bunch of keys and let them in. He was the *sereno*, or watchman, and, so early are the hours I keep, he was the first I had seen, although these men exist all over Spain.

I was up and out at seven o'clock in the morning, walking round the tawny walls of Avila. Here you can see how the old city has shrunk like an invalid in a suit that has become too large for him. In the Middle Ages, and before the Moriscoes were driven out of Spain, I imagine every inch of Avila was occupied; now there are large waste acres where grass-grown rubble is piled against the inside of the walls. How early the workmen start in Spain. The legend of Spanish laziness has surely been spread by those who have never seen the peasants harvesting by moonlight, or the carpenters at their benches, as they were in Avila that morning, at seven o'clock. I saw bakers loading circular loaves in horse panniers and I met the milkman on his rounds with mule or donkey, the milk in large dented metal cans. While I was admiring the cathedral and noting how the east end was built on a reinforcement of the wall, a sombre little procession emerged from the nearby gate. Five Civil Guards with slung rifles marched on either side of ten young men, who were handcuffed together. Beside the policemen, and tripping along to keep up with them, were two vivacious little blondes carrying small suitcases and chattering away brightly to the guards. It surprised me that Avila, apparently so sedate and ecclesiastical, should have scope for crime of any sort, particularly any associated with little blondes who were clearly not sisters of mercy.

I came to an open space where workmen were in the process of demolishing an old building. Most of it had vanished and their pick-axes were now attacking the stumps of vaults and cellars. It was the soil that attracted my notice. It was rank with age like the dust of Egypt. There were bits of red pottery in it and something that looked like pulverized bones. I was aware of a feeling of nausea for this burden of age, this living with the past, this tyranny of tradition, these bony

246

claws stretching out of the grave and interfering with the present. I took up a handful of this sour mixture of dead men and let it fall through my fingers. In England we take the past in our stride and if it interferes with us we kick it out of the way; but in Spain the past is an indestructible mummy and sometimes it seems more real than the present.

By this time the bells were ringing for Mass and I went to the cathedral. There were five old women in black, crouched together like devout ravens. This magnificent cathedral is the same age, almost to the year, as Durham. I was interested in two 'wild men' clothed in leaves, sculptured one on each side of the west door. I noticed them also inside the cathedral as supporters to the arms of the Valderrábanos family, and I came across them a third time as supporters on the shield of the Dávila House in Avila. These 'wild men' were popular figures everywhere in the Middle Ages. Sometimes knights are seen rescuing maidens from them; they were impersonated in masques and pageants by actors dressed in leaves; and in London they used to lead processions and clear the way by throwing fireworks into the crowd. They were often known as 'green men', and their memory is preserved in England by public-houses called *The Green Man*.

One afternoon in Avila I saw upon a plot of open ground, near one of the gates, the most rakish and most vagabond theatre that could be imagined. It was called the *Teatro Portátil*—the travelling theatre—and it was merely an immense square wooden screen fitted together and brought there on carts, which stood in the lee of the wall. It was made of plywood, and there were hundreds of parts which had to be screwed and nailed together. It was full of cracks and peepholes. The playbills announced that *El grandioso drama en tres actos* by Echegaray, entitled *Mancha que Limpia*, was to be performed, alas! on the night I should be away from Avila. There was a noise of hammering as the actors put the final touches to the theatre, and glancing inside I saw hundreds of little chairs facing a tiny stage erected on barrels where, against a gaudy backcloth showing a noble interior, stood a couch upon which a young man was stretched out fast asleep. I was sorely tempted to go inside. There were so many questions I should have liked to have asked him about life on the road. But it seemed a pity to wake him.

I often thought about those actors when I was living in comfortable hotels, and wondered into which of Agustín de Rojas' categories they came. They were clearly above the strolling players who were paid in kind, and must have ranked somewhere between the five men and a woman, who composed the *cambaleo*, and the seven men, two women and a boy, who made up the grander and more versatile *bojiganga*. To have known enough Spanish to have joined them for a week would, I thought, have been an irresistible adventure.

§ 6

St. Teresa once said, speaking of self-consciously holy persons, that 'they were saints in their own opinion, but, when I got to know them, they frightened me more than all the sinners I had ever known'. This, I think, is one of the most typical of her comments on life and people. Of all the saints in heaven, she is surely the most friendly, the most humorous, and the most understanding. As a woman she is related to all the capable and gallant women one has ever known, who go through life putting things in order; as a saint she travelled into regions where only another saint could follow her. That amazing self-revelation, her *Life*, and her other writings, almost persuade us that we too could become, if not saints, at least honourable travellers along that high and lonely road.

She is fascinating, also, as proof of the toughness and resiliency of the human body when powered by a strong spiritual force. To have seen her at the age of twenty-four, crawling about on her hands and knees, after a cataleptic seizure, during which she was nearly buried alive, would have been to deny the possibility that she could become the indomitable, middle-aged woman who rode all over Spain, sleeping in flea-bitten inns and on the boards of empty houses as she founded her reformed Carmelite convents.

She was born in Avila in 1515, of aristocratic parents, and her full name was Teresa de Cepida y Ahumada. She took the Carmelite habit at the age of twenty-one and received her first experience of visions and locutions twenty years later. She was forty-six when she began to reform the Carmelite rule; and for the next twenty years, until she died at the age of sixty-seven, she travelled all over the country, taking over empty houses and other buildings in which she established convents and monasteries where Carmelites could live a stricter and more contemplative life.

When one thinks of travellers in Spain the figure of Don Quixote comes immediately to mind, riding the roads, lance in hand, anxious to redress the wrongs of the world; and St. Teresa is easily a good second. She was to be seen sometimes on mule or donkey, accompanied by a few nuns and friars of the Reform, but more often in a springless, covered wagon drawn by mules and driven by shaggy muleteers. The Saint was interested in these rough characters and disciplined them as if they were Carmelites. Though the cavalcade might be moving in the heat of summer, and the travellers would be glad to drive away a herd of pigs from beneath a bridge and to shelter there in its shadow for a moment, or in the mud and floods of winter, the nuns were never allowed to forget their religious duties. A little bell was rung in the wagons at the time of the Divine Office, and upon hearing it all the muleteers had to maintain a strict silence. St. Teresa sometimes rewarded their silences with little gifts of dried fruit, if she had any to spare from her meagre store. She never had a penny and seems to have founded seventeen convents in twenty years on charm, faith and determination.

I like the famous story that once when St. Teresa was nearly drowned when crossing a flooded river at Burgos, she complained in a moment of exasperation to the Saviour. She heard Him reply, 'That is how I treat my friends,' and immediately retorted, 'Yes, and that is why Thou hast so few friends!'

When she grew old, and the journeys exhausted her, the nuns, seeing her so tired, sometimes sang her to sleep in a wretched lodging; and when the icy winds were blowing across the Castilian plains, would try to give her their own coverings to warm her, for she felt the cold acutely. Often she gave out sparks of vitality and was so full of amusing conversation that the nuns would follow her to her cell and beg her not to leave them. It is recorded that she had been known to take a tambourine and dance for them! She loved laughter and was full of charm. 'God deliver me from sullen saints,' she once said.

Of her mystical experiences it is not possible to write here, but readers of her books will know that she accepted the raptures of the spiritual life as something which any sufficiently devout, and devoted, person might achieve. It was typical of her that the strange phenomenon of levitation, which most of us experience only in dreams, dismayed and embarrassed her. She would hold on to anything in order not to be lifted off her feet. She considered levitation 'a most extraordinary thing, which would occasion much talk', and commanded her nuns never to mention the subject. When she felt she was losing weight and was about to be lifted into the air, she would throw herself on the ground and beg the nuns to hold her down. One Christmas Eve she fell downstairs and broke her left arm. The nuns believed that the Devil had pushed her, and asked her to tell them if this were so. She replied neither yes nor no, but remarked that he 'would do much worse things than that, if he were allowed to'. There was no one to set the arm, which eventually had to be broken again and re-set, a painful operation which, by the way, was suffered by another Spanish saint, Ignatius Loyola, whose leg was broken and re-set. Describing the agony of this experience in a letter, St. Teresa said, 'Still I was happy at experiencing some tiny part of what was endured by Our Lord.'

With such thoughts as these, I went to see the house just within the walls of Avila where the Mother of Carmel had been born. I found it transformed into an ugly church. It is extraordinary to see what piety can sometimes achieve in the way of bad taste. The room in which the Saint is said to have been born is now an ornate baroque chapel, and its chief object is a statue of her, wearing a gold crown, which I believe would have annoyed her considerably. In the sacristy I saw one of her fingers, covered with rings and enclosed in a crystal reliquary. I looked at it in horror, remembering how fastidious she was about her hands. I think the awful story of her exhumation and dismemberment in order to provide relics for the Church is one of the most shocking incidents of its kind in Spanish history.

Eighteen years before St. Teresa's birth, Spain was plunged into a sorrow so profound that the court, instead of wearing the white serge used at that time as mourning, wore sackcloth. This event was the death, at the age of twenty, of the heir to the throne, Prince John, the only son of Ferdinand and Isabel. The solemn funeral pomp came along the road from Salamanca, where the Prince had died, to Avila, where he was buried in the Dominican monastery of Santo Tomé, beyond the walls.

As I stood at his tomb and looked at his handsome face, carved so beautifully in white marble by a Florentine sculptor, I felt that something of his parents' grief still surrounded his lonely figure. They had driven the Moors from Spain, they had united the country, a New World had been revealed to them, and at the very moment of their triumphs their only son and heir was taken from them. Ferdinand was with his son when he died. Fearing the effect of the news on his wife, he sent off messenger after messenger to her, breaking it gradually and trying to prepare her to face the inevitable. When at last she knew, Isabel whispered, 'The Lord has given, the Lord has taken away.'

If this young man had lived and had carried on his line, S[pain's] history, incredible to think of, would have lacked the reign [of] Charles V and Philip II. The Prince was also the brother of Cathe[rine] of Aragon, and had he become King of Spain, perhaps Henry V[III] might not have found him easy to deal with when he wished to divorce her for Ana Bolena. History has many a question mark, and this tomb in Santo Tomé is one of them.

## § 7

I was on my way to Burgos, travelling to the north. I had retrieved my car from Madrid and now I was in a landscape of tall poplars and silver birches, with one of the splendid main roads of Spain stretching ahead. I stopped at Aranda de Duero to buy some petrol, and saw the river flowing westward to Portugal, brown as strong coffee. The high steppes of Madrid and La Mancha were far to the south and, thinking of them, I discovered in my mind a composite picture composed of Philip II in his Escorial; Don Quixote everywhere; El Greco's saints with the calves of ballet dancers, standing with outstretched arms and exquisite hands against apocalyptic skies; pale Philip IV sitting to Velázquez; Goya, Godoy and Napoleon; and in Toledo a clash of arms and a jostling crowd of Jews, Moors, knights and bishops. Incredibly far off now seemed that other more distant Spain where Arab jets rose and fell in fretwork patios, the Spain of cactus, orange and aloe; the Spain which stands with its back to Castile and its face to Africa.

This Spain of Old Castile was different too, not less bleak, but with its own particular kind of bleakness; less mystical maybe, but with the same long distances, where mud-coloured villages lay against the sky and vast churches stood upon the treeless land like ships at sea. Neither Roman nor Arab has left his mark as strongly here as in the south. At the very frontier of this northern land you feel that this is Iberia, this is Gothic Spain, and that, oddest of all, you are thinking no longer of Don Quixote. Instead there rides out of the plain a man who wears an iron crucifix beneath his coat of mail. He is a robber baron of a familiar type. He makes war on the next Christian castle as enthusiastically as he does upon the Infidel. At times he even intrigues with the Arabs to defeat an uncle or a son-in-law, or to share in some particularly tempting loot. There is no such thing as patriotism. There is yet no Spain or England or France, only this and the next castle, and, of course, Christianity, and the often charming Infidel. Yet no matter how often this robber baron sings Arab songs or tells Arab stories, he never forgets the crucifix next to his skin. It is always there to remind him that he belongs to the Church. Christianity is the strong rope that binds him, as the faith of Mahomet, with its deadly schisms, is the weakness of his enemy. Legend says that at one time the Christian power in Spain was reduced to a few guerrillas in a cave; but they resisted, and as time went on the kings of those fierce little kingdoms held their own. Other Christian princes came across the Pyrenees to help them, and Pope Alexander II preached a crusade in Spain a good twenty years before the time of Peter the Hermit. Old Castile is therefore the frontier of this resistance movement and it takes its name from the castles which still stand in ruin upon its hills. It is a Spain of confusing kinglets, of Sanchos and Alfonsos, and of ladies named Berengaria, Constance, and Urraca, that hideous name which once caused a French marriage embassy to turn aside for a Queen of France to a more euphonious Blanche. Above all it is the Spain of the Cid Campeador, Spain's Alfred the Great, Hereward the Wake and Robin Hood, all rolled into one tempestuous and wily knight, who still rides his charger Babieca through the spangled meadows of romance.

And now I saw the towers of Burgos Cathedral standing against a hill. There are no other towers quite like them. Mr. Sitwell compared them to the golden dried husks of bluebells, and a page later to the masts of medieval ships; and that, I think, is a true analogy. They look like the masts of old ships as drawn by monks, the cordage stretching down from the top-castles to the gunwales; and maybe the projecting cusps, which stand out like little flags, suggest that the ships are dressed for some happy occasion like the marriage of a princess.

No cities which are the result of the same historical influences could resemble each other less than the cities of Castile. Within a short journey Toledo, Avila, Segovia and Burgos enchant the traveller by their differences and their variety, and this individualism is of course a great part of the Spanish charm in cities as in men. Even allowing for the fact that industrialism has not standardized them, they are strangely and wonderfully different in appearance. Toledo, dark, secret and with an implied cloak-and-dagger violence; Avila like a saint kneeling on the rocks; Segovia, plumed and armed for the great wars; and now Burgos, as medieval as the others, and as Castilian, but with a frank, open, and I might say almost a Flemish air. It might be a Spanish relative of Bruges or Nuremberg. There is a Teutonic look about the cusped towers of the cathedral.

I thought that, having seen Toledo and its cathedral, no other church could impress me, but Burgos Cathedral took my breath away. It shoulders a hill, oddly, I think, for such a great and splendid building, and upon the summit of the hill once stood a mighty castle where many things happened, including the marriage of our Edward I to Eleanor of Castile. The river Arlanzon runs through the town between a high embankment, for no doubt it becomes temperamental in the winter. There is a plaza that took my eye at once as something lovely and unspoilt, a place of uncertain shape where old buildings are supported upon columns which form a covered arcade; and in the centre is a statue of that good but odd-looking Bourbon, Charles III, whose humorous face with its long nose gazes so quizzically from the walls of the Prado.

Burgos is not entirely wrapped up in the age of the Cid. They make cellophane here; there are cloth and thread factories; it is also, and always has been, a famous garrison town. An everyday sight in Burgos is a Spanish regiment on a route march. First comes the band, then the colonel and the adjutant, mounted, and a long line of tough-look-ing khaki-clad troops, each company headed by the company com-manders on horseback. All the officers wear swords and field boots. One day I saw a mountain battery marching along the dusty roads outside the town, the field guns slung on the backs of mules. And in the evening Burgos is filled with the best-behaved soldiery I have ever seen, each man wearing the inevitable white cotton gloves and not one trying to shirk a salute.

I do beg anyone who goes to Burgos to sit some afternoon at one of the cafés along the Paseo del Espolón Viejo, and watch the children and the old nurses. Even in the park of El Retiro in Madrid I did not see more beautifully dressed children or as many wonderful old nannies, each one a Rembrandt. On one side of the Paseo are shops and cafés, and on the other a well-planted park without railings, which runs parallel with the river. In the afternoon the children and the nurses compose a scene that reminded me of a long distant Kensington Gar-dens. At this hour Spanish children are always in party dress, the little girls in frilly muslin frocks, with satin sashes, and the little boys in white sailor suits. They play ball, bowl hoops, and the very small totter about and peep at each other from behind the trees. The little girls lure the little boys into trouble and the little boys get blamed for it. Sometimes a fat little *niña*, chasing a small *niño*, falls flat in the dust; and the spotted muslin is swiftly dusted by a pair of worn brown hands, while the little boy is scolded as if he were some infantile Don Juan. Later in the afternoon the officers of the garrison appear, sometimes with their wives, and I noticed many a stately Spanish don among them, tall and lean like an El Greco. Sometimes their air of gravity melts when they are greeted affectionately by *los niños*. Subaltern officers pull themselves up and make sure that every tunic button is right as they approach the colonel and his lady; and the scene, with its frills and its swords, spurs and field boots, the green trees and the old nurses, forms a picture of life as it was; and, as you narrow your eyes in the sunlight, it may be that it almost fades into a nineteenth century aquatint, or a scene, if one can imagine such a thing, from a Spanish Jane Austen.

The reaction of anyone accustomed only to the austerity of English Gothic would be to find Burgos Cathedral fussy and over-elaborate, for there is hardly a square yard that is not carved or in some way decorated. But as you begin to appreciate the architecture, this feeling passes, and you make discoveries which lead on to others. Incidentally, the Alhambra is also a fussy and over-decorated building, but it is the antithesis of Burgos. You see the Alhambra at one glance and there is little more; Burgos Cathedral you hardly know at all until you have been there five or six times. It is a wonderful example of a temple, a treasure chest, a museum and a library, designed for those who cannot read. That was its function in the Middle Ages, and its appeal to the eye is as great today as it was then.

In the *coro* is a recumbent effigy, made of copper hammered over wood, of a bishop who died in 1238, seven years before Henry III began to pull down old Westminster Abbey in London and build the present church. This is the figure of Maurice, Bishop of Burgos, an Englishman some believe, who came to Spain in 1219 with Beatrice of Swabia, when she married Ferdinand III, 'the Saint'. There are statues of Ferdinand and Beatrice on the left of the entrance to the cloisters, which are well worth looking at; he is a typical king of the period, and seems to be holding out a ring, or some gift, to the queen, who turns towards him, splendidly dressed in a fitted surcoat and a long cloak, and upon her head is a tall, brimless hat strapped beneath the chin, evidently the latest German fashion of the time.

Beatrice seems to have lived happily with Ferdinand and she bore him a large family. Her first son became Alfonso the Wise, whose astronomical tables and other studies I remembered when I visited the castle at Segovia. The German name, Frederick, and the Greek, Manuel, were introduced into Spain by Beatrice, who called two of her sons after her relatives. She died after a reign of sixteen years, and Ferdinand then married, as his second wife, the French Jeanne, who became the mother of Eleanor of Castile, the Queen of our Edward I. But by the time of Eleanor's marriage St. Ferdinand was dead, and lay buried in Seville, where, as I had seen, his remains are preserved in a silver casket.

The great architectural achievement of this reign was Burgos Cathedral, which was built under the supervision of Bishop Maurice, whose noble and serene face is one of the unfading memories of the great church. A few feet from him is a stone which covers the much-travelled remains of the Cid.

It is not possible to describe Burgos Cathedral; it would take years to know it properly and to understand even a portion of its contents. All one can do is to mention one or two things which catch the eye as one walks about amid so much casual magnificence. I met here for the first time the work of a German artist, Gil de Siloe, who could fashion alabaster and marble as if they were beeswax; a man who, it seemed to me, must have worked in an ecstasy of creation, making difficulties for himself just to prove that he could solve them. More attractive to me than his sculptured tombs were his wood carvings, which I thought the most beautiful I had seen in Spain. There are several *retablos* by him in the cathedral; my favourite is the *retablo* above the altar of St. Anne, in the Chapel of the Constable, where, on the pretext that he was creating a galaxy of female saints grouped about the figure of St. Anne, Gil de Siloe has really assembled a gallery of medieval women, all of the aristocracy, complete in the height of fifteenth century fashion. It is one of the most charming things in Spain, and seems to have such a foretaste of the Renaissance about it that I wondered how it had escaped the Inquisition. These women are certainly not saints, although Gil de Siloe must have told the models to assume saintly expressions. His masterpiece, the figure of St. Catherine in the monastery of Miraflores, about two miles out of Burgos, might stand as an emblem of the fashionable woman of all ages.

Who were these women, I wonder? If my surmise is correct, and they are all sculptured from life, they must have been notable women of the time, princesses perhaps and the wives and daughters of the great men of the period. I wonder if there is something more than a passing resemblance to Isabel La Católica in the beautiful little figure of a seated Magdalene in the reredos of St. Anne? Gil de Siloe was her contemporary and had designed the tomb of her parents.

The debt of Spain to France and Germany is immense. No matter how the cathedrals are elaborated, or how Spanish they look, their bones are mostly French, and the wooden *retablos* crowded with painted and gilt figures—and nowhere are there more of them—were Germany's contribution to the sacred art of the fifteenth century. The art of carving beautiful, lifelike wooden figures was centred at Nuremberg, where Gil de Siloe was born; and those who see his work at Burgos will agree that neither the better-known Veit Stoss and Peter Vischer, nor Adam Krafft, all fellow-countrymen of his, was his master. For something like two hundred years Burgos must have been a magnet to artists in Germany. The cathedral had grown up in the footsteps of Spain's German queen, and the German architect and craftsman were always welcome there. The towers of the cathedral and the lantern were the work of the German architect John of Cologne, who must have arrived at much the same time as Gil de Siloe, and perhaps it is these towers, so unlike anything else in Spain, which give Burgos, when you see it first, a faint Teutonic flavour.

Both these Germans settled down and spent their lives in Spain. They married and each had a son who grew up to be a famous artist—Diego de Siloe and Simón of Cologne. Mr. Sitwell puts forward the interesting theory that Gil and John may have been German Jews; if so, he says, 'we have the only considerable artists of Jewish origin to appear in Europe before the twentieth century, and with Gil de Siloe, it may be the greatest artist in the plastic arts that the Jewish race has produced'. It may therefore be significant that when Gil de Siloe designed the tomb of John II and Isabel of Portugal at Miraflores—the most splendid tomb in Spain, perhaps in Europe—he made the ground plan an eight-pointed star, which is, of course, the Star of David.

If these inspired carvings are the most beautiful objects in the cathedral, certainly the strangest is the miracle-working figure of the Saviour, known as the Christ of Burgos, which is shown dramatically floodlit in a chapel to itself. Against a dark background there hangs an emaciated, lifesize figure upon a cross, and, in accordance with the Castilian custom, it wears a full-length petticoat of red satin. The arms, and as much of the body as I could see, are anatomically perfect, and the figure wears a wig of real hair. The head and neck can move, the limbs are flexible, and in the old days the peasants believed that the nails and hair grew and had to be cut from time to time. A sacristan told me that the figure is made of buffalo hide and that it is soft and yielding to the touch. He had touched it and said that it felt like living flesh. He told me that during the Reformation the statue had been taken from the sea near Holland by a Spanish merchant. The body looks like polished wood, and even Ford believed that it was wood, one of the few instances when he was not infallible.

But in order to see the most popular object in the cathedral you have to go to the sacristy, where they show you, high up on the wall, resting on an iron bracket, the iron-bound chest of the Cid. This is the famous coffer which the Cid is said to have filled with sand when he was extremely hard up, and to have pledged as a chest full of gold to some unusually trusting Jews, and, as the books always take care to say, redeemed when he was in a position to do so. Burgos is of course the country of the Cid.

The *Poem of the Cid* was composed by an unknown minstrel within forty years of the hero's death, when old people were still alive who could remember the events described in it. It is a short poem of fewer than four thousand lines, but it glows with the true splendour of poetry; and even in translation its authentic rightness is such that one seems to be standing at the window of a castle, watching bright scenes inhabited not by the pompous heroes of legend but by ordinary men and women. This verbal Bayeux Tapestry is a living picture of the eleventh century, a true and tender picture of the habits and thoughts of men who lived in Spain at a time when William of Normandy was invading England.

It is the story of a warrior who is banished by his king and sets out, accompanied by his vassals, to make a new life for himself with his strong right arm. We meet the Cid as he is leaving home to go into exile. He weeps bitterly as he says goodbye to his wife and daughters; he looks round and sees his castle in disarray, his chests lying open and empty, the perches without their falcons. He rides into the streets of Burgos in the darkness. They are bleak and deserted. All the inhabitants are watching him from behind their shutters, with tears in their eyes, for they dare not risk the king's wrath by meeting one to whom the royal grace has been denied. 'What a good vassal was there,' cry the folk of Burgos, 'had he but a good lord!'; and they send out a little girl to tell him why they dare not open their doors to him. So the Cid rides out of Castile. It is all so simple and genuine, like a tale told by the fireside. There is no ranting or false heroics. Even when the Cid said goodbye to his family, he just felt 'as if a nail was torn from his flesh'. When he heard of a terrible injury to his daughters, he did not shout or bluster, but 'the tissues of his heart were torn', and 'he thought and considered for a long time'. He goes to meet his foes with a hundred knights at his back and—delightful touch—his long beard tied up so that no one could commit the insult of pulling it.

Popular fancy made of him the ideal Spaniard, the perfect *guerillero*, the incarnation of all the qualities the Spaniard best loves, bravery, temperance, dignity, magnanimity, fortitude, and, of course, Christian devotion. He was the first real crusader, though the First Crusade was not to be preached for another fifty years. He is also distinguished by 'the direct simplicity of the very great', in the words of Professor Trend, who adds the interesting thought, 'The nearest to him in our time has been General Smuts.'

That is the Cid of legend. Whether the real Cid was equally noble is questionable. His name was Ruy Díaz de Bivar, and his title, by which he was known to Christians and Arabs alike, comes from the Arabic *sídí*, my lord. He won his fame in a dark moment in the history of Christian Spain. The Spanish Arabs had been reinforced by fierce Berbers from Africa who swept over the country, striking terror into Christian hearts, with a new weapon, *los atambores*, the Moorish war drums. The Cid penetrated deep into enemy territory and turned Valencia into a Christian province, becoming a king in all but name. Even to this day Valencia is proud to call itself 'Valencia del Cid.' When he died at the age of fifty-six his widow, Zimena, tried to continue his rule, but the Berbers were too powerful. Under cover of a Christian army sent from Castile, she and all the Christian inhabitants of Valencia left the city and fled, taking with them the bones of the Cid. Romance says that his dead body was strapped into the saddle, and at the sight of it the Moors fled in terror.

But the Cid never died. His name has been upon the lips of his countrymen for over seven centuries. Mounted upon his steed Babieca, with his sword Colada in his hand, the Cid rides among the immortals, the defender of the Faith, the protector of the poor, the guardian of honour.

> *So, it is you, who have but to take the field*
> *And say 'Forward!' to sound through Spain,*
> *From Avis to Gibraltar, from Algarve to Cadafal,*
> *O Great Cid, the thrill of trumpets triumphant,*
> *And to draw hastening over your tents,*
> *Beating their wings, the swarm of singing victories.*

§ 8

I walked up the hill one morning before breakfast to see how much is left of the castle of Burgos. And, by the way, a word about Spanish breakfasts. As everywhere upon the Continent, the Spanish breakfast is a shameful affair. It is composed of fried batter rings called *churros*, which are sold by little boys in the early morning, in baskets covered with a cloth, and are quite pleasant at any other time than breakfast; so far as my observation goes, there is a coffee and a chocolate zone in Spain, the coffee lying to the south, but *churros* are eaten all over the country. They are considered unsuitable to give a foreigner in hotels, so the visitor is served with the usual deplorable French break-fast of coffee, a croissant, and a cocoon-shaped little roll, and a small saucer of jam, generally apricot. I have never seen a Spaniard eat a boiled egg. Moreover, there is no handy phrase for a boiled egg in the Spanish language. You have to ask for 'two eggs that have been passed through hot water for three minutes'; and these can always be ordered if you are firm about it. The Spanish waiter comes to respect you as an amiable eccentric if you make enough fuss about eggs, and ham and eggs, as I do; but fried eggs are comparatively easy to order, for after all they are the well-known eggs *flamenco* obtainable all over Spain. Rigid breakfast conservatives will, however, resent a little tampering with these by the introduction of unnecessary bits of pimento and olives; and it is sometimes difficult—for Spaniards can be led on by a phrase or a smile, but never driven—to make them give you two ordinary rashers of bacon or a slice of ham; and this in a country where the ham, bacon and pork are better than anywhere in Europe.

I have seen only one Spaniard eat a real breakfast. This was at Segovia. He was a small, elderly, well-dressed man, and he ate a large ham ome-lette and drank half a bottle of white wine at eight-thirty in the morning. He was a wonderful tribute to breakfast. His skin had not that recently exhumed look about it, he was healthy and pink, and as active as a grey-hound. Unlike most of his countrymen, he would not slink into bars and restaurants and eat shrimps all morning or stave off starvation with bits of cheese; he would, like all who eat breakfast, go straight through to luncheon. I mention this subject as a warning that the only words of Spanish absolutely essential to the breakfast-lover are *dos huevos pasados por agua caliente por tres minutos*. With that cumbersome yet magic phrase you may go through Spain with a high heart and two boiled eggs inside you.

The climb to the castle is a pleasant one, but when you reach the top there is nothing to be seen except a view over the surrounding country. The castle was blown up by the French and has been even more effectively destroyed in later troubles, so that there is nothing to indicate where so many mighty events occurred except a mass of weed-grown mounds and great slabs of stone half buried in the earth. A large flat area nearby was evidently a tilt-yard where tournaments were held.

To an Englishman the site is chiefly interesting as the place to which young Edward I, as a boy not yet king, was brought by his mother, Eleanor of Provence, in August, 1254, to be married to Eleanor of Castile. This was to turn out to be one of the few royal love affairs in English history. Charing Cross and all the other funeral griefs were in the distant future as the young Prince, aged fifteen, met his little bride, who was still about three years under the legal marriage age, which at that time was thirteen for a girl. Her father, St. Ferdinand, had been dead for two years and she was the child of his old age and his second marriage. Alfonso X, the Wise, who was now King of Castile, was her half-brother, his mother having been Beatrice of Swabia, St. Ferdinand's first wife. It is said that the young English Prince and the Queen of England were received with great pomp and rejoicing on the hilltop at Burgos, for the marriage contract was a political affair between Alfonso X and Henry III of England. Young Edward seems to have pleased Alfonso, and no doubt at fifteen he already showed promise of becoming one of the tallest and most formidable warriors of his time. After a great tournament held at Burgos, Alfonso knighted Edward, and the children were married at the neighbouring convent of Las Huelgas. When the marriage had been solemnized, the Queen of England took the young couple back across the Pyrenees and, like so many other child brides of the time, Eleanor returned to the schoolroom. Matthew Paris, who was living at this period, has left an account of the indignation caused in London by the money poured out on wedding festivities by Henry III, and by the luxury of the young Princess's quarters in London, which had been prepared by members of her Castilian entourage. The standard of comfort in Castile at that time, evidently derived from the Moors, was infinitely greater than anything known in England. Her rooms, grumbles the chronicler, 'were hung with palls of silk and tapestry, like a temple, and *even the floor was covered with arras*'. This was the first time that carpets had been seen in England. 'This excessive pride', says Matthew Paris, 'excited the laughter and derision of the people.'

But when Eleanor grew up and took her place in English life she became one of the best beloved of Plantagenet queens. Englishmen were only too ready to believe that in Palestine Edward's devoted wife had sucked the assassin's poison from his wound. She was his constant companion, and the birthplaces of eleven of her thirteen children speak eloquently of a wandering life of camps and castles—Windsor, Kenilworth, Acre, in Palestine (where she bore two children), Gascony, Windsor, Kennington, Windsor, Woodstock, Rhudlan, and Caernarvon, where she became the mother of Edward II. Her coronation with Edward I in Westminster Abbey was the first time a King and Queen of England had been crowned together.

When princesses married and departed into a foreign country it often happened that they never saw their native land again, but it is good to know that Eleanor returned to Spain when she was about thirty and stayed with her half-brother, Alfonso. She had just become the mother of a prince, whom she had named Alfonso after him, and that strangely Spanish-sounding prince remained the heir to the English throne for something like ten years, until his death in 1284. The whole of England shared Edward's sorrow when his faithful and beautiful Eleanor died before reaching the age of forty-eight; and stone crosses, of which Charing Cross is the last, marked the resting-places of her coffin on its journey to Westminster.

Having surveyed the scene of this happy romance, which was to lead the way for the Black Prince's excursions in Spain, and also to that of John of Gaunt, with its consequent contribution of a good dash of Plantagenet blood to the royal houses of Spain and Portugal, I descended the hill as the bells of Burgos were ringing and ordered my *dos huevos* to be passed through hot water.

## § 9

A short walk of about a mile and a half took me to the convent of Las Huelgas. I was prepared for this convent to be of interest to an English visitor, for it was founded by Eleanor of England, the daughter of Henry II and sister of Richard the Lionheart. She married Alfonso VIII in 1170, and both are buried here. I did not expect, however, to find that the convent contained a museum of relics, taken from their tombs and from other royal graves in 1942. It is the most remarkable museum of its kind in Europe.

Eleanor of England was only eight years old when her mother,

Eleanor of Aquitaine, handed her over to a Spanish embassy at Bordeaux in the year 1170. The child was taken into Spain, betrothed to the young King at Tarragona, and magnificently married to him at Burgos. He was then about twelve, and had inherited the throne in infancy, retaining it in a rough age by a mixture of good luck, the prudence of a few adherents, and the loyalty of the town of Avila, which had sworn to guard him until he was of age. To modern people the idea of these child marriages is preposterous, but in the Middle Ages marriage had nothing to do with love, in fact rather the reverse, and children were disposed of by their parents in return for financial and political benefits. The eight years old Queen of Spain presumably continued with her lessons; and the twelve years old King continued to be used as a figurehead by his nobles until the time came when the daughter of England and the son of Castile were old enough to become man and wife. Eleanor's marriage with Alfonso was as fortunate as the Castilian Eleanor's was to be in days to come with Edward I; indeed, with the notable exception of Henry and Catherine of Aragon, Anglo-Spanish matches seem to have been unusually happy.

Alfonso spent a busy life harrying the Moors. His greatest military triumph was the battle of Las Navas de Tolosa, which I mentioned when I came through the Pass of Despeñaperros, on my way up from Andalusia to Castile. Eleanor bore her husband thirteen children and had the rare distinction of becoming the grandmother of two saints. Her daughter, Blanche, married Louis VIII of France and became the mother of St. Louis; and another daughter, Berengaria, married Alfonso IX of León and became the mother of St. Ferdinand. All the records say that Eleanor was a lovely and worthy queen and a devoted wife. The troubadour Ramón Vidal has preserved a charming little glimpse of her at the court of Castile, carrying the lions of England upon the border of her gown.

> *And when the King had summoned to his court*
> *Many a knight, rich baron, and jongleur,*
> *And the company had assembled,*
> *Then came Queen Leonore*
> *Modestly clad in a mantle of rich stuff,*
> *Red, with a silver border wrought*
> *With golden lions.*
> *She bows to the King*
> *And near him takes her seat.*

King Alfonso died suddenly at the age of fifty-six, while on a journey, leaving Eleanor regent of his kingdom; but she was prostrated by her loss and followed him to the grave before the month was out, dying, so the chroniclers say, of grief. They were buried in the splendid convent of Las Huelgas, which they had founded some years previously.

When I arrived there, a clerk of works, who was waiting to show me round, asked if the building reminded me of an English church, which in some ways it did. It is surrounded by innumerable outbuildings and courtyards, and in former times must have been the most aristocratic convent in Christendom. I was taken first to a picturesque staircase which was lined from floor to ceiling with the armorial shields of abbesses; for it was exceptional for an abbess not to be of the blood royal, and only the most aristocratic ladies of Castile were admitted as nuns. The convent was once wealthy and the abbess, who ranked as a princess-palatine, had power of life and death over her dominions and appointed all her parish priests. Only as recently as 1936 has the public been admitted to all parts of the church, and the permission of the Pope had to be obtained before this was possible; until then under no circumstances were men allowed in the *coro de las Señoras*, where the royal tombs are to be seen. Las Huelgas is still a nunnery of the Cistercian Order and there are at the moment forty-three nuns. They are enclosed and are allowed outside the convent only in exceptional circumstances. They are also vowed to silence except for an hour a day.

I was taken into the church, which at first sight seemed almost the size of Westminster Abbey. It is a beautiful, austere church, and an iron grille separates the nave from the nuns' choir, where two rows of magnificently carved stalls face each other in front of the High Altar. There is a thirteenth century gilt pulpit, which can be moved round so that the preacher may direct his voice to the nuns or to the public part of the church. It was not easy to pay attention to the many exquisite objects the clerk showed me, for I had observed at the entrance to the choir what I had wanted to see as much as anything in Spain, the tomb of Eleanor of England and Alfonso VIII. They are buried in a double sarcophagus of stone, in shape like two long chests with low-pitched roofs, or lids. Every inch of the stone is carved and much of it is gilded, and the chests, or sarcophagi, stand on the backs of four small stone lions. Both tombs are covered with an arcaded design on the sides and roofs, divided into six divisions, in each one of which are carved the Royal Arms of Castile, a three-turreted castle. At the foot of Eleanor's coffin are the Royal Arms of England, three lions *passant guardant*, as borne first by her father, Henry II, who, it is said, added the third lion —the Lion of Aquitaine—in honour of his wife. I am no expert in heraldry, but I should think that this blazon of the Royal Arms, if not the earliest, is certainly the best preserved and the most beautifully carved in existence.

I was told that at the end of the Civil War it was proposed to open those of the royal tombs which had not been rifled in Napoleonic times, and eventually permission was obtained from the Government. When they were opened, the royal bodies were seen to be lying clothed in exquisite fabrics of Moorish manufacture and design, their heads resting upon small pillows which had retained their shapes and colours for seven centuries. Among the most interesting of the discoveries was that of the body of Queen Eleanor. Though not embalmed, her remains were well preserved; and she was lying covered with a great quantity of the finest muslin, pleated at the edges in a manner fashionable in the thirteenth century. There were three small pillows in her coffin, one of blue with gold stripes, another of tapestry, and the third of red with stripes of gold. Her headdress was a length of cloth twelve feet long, striped in red, gold and black; her sandals were of Arab design of the kind known as *Xervillas*.

Alfonso VIII was succeeded by his son, who became Henry I of Castile. This young man was named after his grandfather, Henry II of England. He succeeded to the throne in 1214, but reigned only three years and died, so history recorded, when a roof-tile hit him on the head, some say when he was playing pelota. When his coffin was opened his skull was seen to bear a hole about an inch and a half square, with the edges chipped by surgical instruments, which showed that doctors had attempted to perform an operation that looks as though it should have killed the young monarch if the tile had failed to do so.[1]

The most complete and spectacular discovery was that of the body

[1] The Spanish annals say that King Henry died six days after his accident, which does not agree with the opinion of a leading brain surgeon in London to whom I subsequently showed a photograph of the skull. This authority writes: 'This is a fascinating picture. There is no doubt at all but that the owner of that skull survived a very considerable time after the operation. . . . From the site of the craniotomy, I suspect that the superior longitudinal sinus may have been damaged. There must at the time of the accident have been available surgeons brought up in the traditions of the Salerno School.' These would, of course, have been found among the Jews and Arabs of Toledo.

of Ferdinand de la Cerda, the eldest son of Alfonso X, the Wise, whose death in 1275 brought about a civil war in which the King was hounded, harried and humiliated by his son Sancho. Ferdinand was seen to be lying completely clothed in garments of beautifully woven silk, covered all over with small shields bearing the arms of Castile quartered with those of León. His right hand rested upon the hilt of his sword, and he wore upon his head a tall, brimless cap upon which the lion rampant of León and the tower of Castile were embroidered against a background of small pearls. His clothes, a sleeved tunic and a pair of shorts, were worn beneath a surcoat which came to the knees, and all these garments were of silk embroidered with armorial shields. His sword belt was decorated with the arms of León and Castile and the three lions of England, which he bore, no doubt, in right of his grandmother, all beautifully sewn in pearls and in gold.

Having heard of these discoveries from an eye-witness, and having been shown photographs taken at the time, I was prepared for something wonderful when I was taken to a room in the convent which has been turned into a museum; but nothing I had imagined exceeded the reality. To anyone interested in the early history of Spain this museum at Las Huelgas is the most fascinating sight in the country. Here are not charters or buildings, but the actual garments worn by those distant kings and nobles, even to the little cushions which lay about their rooms seven hundred years ago and were placed with them in the tomb. The garments, the embroideries, the tapestries, the sword and the cap of Ferdinand de la Cerda, the pleated muslin from the tomb of Eleanor, as well as hundreds of fabrics, brilliantly coloured and in a perfect state of preservation, are shown in floodlit glass cases. In books about Spain one continually reads of the Arab luxuries and comforts adopted by the more Spartan Christian kingdoms of the north; and here you see how true this is, and how eagerly the princes and the great ladies of the time sought out the choicest silks and fabrics from the looms of the south. How extraordinary it is to see a piece of embroidery, worn by Queen Berengaria, in the form of a medallion which shows two Arab dancing girls surrounded by the Arabic slogan, 'There is no god but God'; and to see that princes who spent their lives waging war against the Infidel did not mind wearing shirts embroidered with the Arabic alphabet. The Byzantine influence is plain, and this work reminded me of the Coptic textiles found in Egypt, even to the Byzantine, or Coptic, fashion of decorating a woven garment with a richly decorated medallion. From the presence of animal designs, usually of birds, I wondered whether some of these fabrics had been woven by Christians under Arab direction, or whether the Arabs at times forgot their religious scruples in the interest of the export trade with the north. Many of the fabrics are, however, completely Arabic in detail, such as the cushion of Eleanor of Aragon, which is covered with intricate interlaced designs with a border of Arabic letters.

And what can be more fascinating than to see the history of Spain written in these garments? When Alfonso VIII died, he was King of Castile only and his arms consequently bore only the single castle of Castile. When his young son Henry was killed by the falling roof-tile, Castile passed to his sister Berengaria, who had been married to Alfonso IX of León. The marriage had been annulled by the Pope because of their close relationship, but not before Berengaria had had a son, Ferdinand, who was later to become St. Ferdinand, and this embarrassing problem was solved by making Ferdinand legitimate, although the annulment of his mother's marriage still held good—a curious legal subtlety! However, when Berengaria found herself Queen of Castile, she waived her claim in favour of her son, who then became Ferdinand III of Castile. This so infuriated his father that he flew to arms and cut Ferdinand out of the succession of the kingdom of León, leaving it to his two daughters by an earlier marriage. So the union of León with Castile might have been delayed indefinitely had not Ferdinand, upon his father's death, been clever enough to buy his succession to León from his half-sisters for nice fat dowries. So it was that León and Castile were united and remained so ever afterwards. Glancing at these garments, one can see how this strange piece of family history influenced the royal wardrobe. Immediately the two kingdoms were brought under one crown, the royal princes were dressed in clothes literally plastered with lions and castles, the emblems of the united kingdoms, and, incidentally, a most attractive design.

Hard as it was to leave so much of interest, I was lured away by the clerk of works to see the articulated statue of St. James. I remember reading some years ago of the strange custom of the kings of Castile of receiving knighthood not from another king, but from a statue with movable arms which, at an appropriate moment in the ceremony, lifted an arm holding a sword and lowered the point to the King's shoulder. Little did I think that I should ever see this statue, or even that it still existed.

We left the church and passed through a cloister which led to a small detached chapel. Above the altar, seated upon a chair, was a life-size

# An articulated statue

statue of a benevolent bearded man in painted wood. He had a magnificent head of hair parted in the centre, which fell on each side of his face to the shoulders. He was wearing one of the long, richly decorated garments, cut wide at the armholes, similar to those I had seen in the museum, and in his right hand he held an upright sword. The arms were uncovered so that I could see they had been cut through above the elbow and jointed like a doll's, which made the forearms movable. This was the statue which had given the accolade to St. Ferdinand and to many another King of Castile; and I wondered whether our own Edward I, who had watched over his armour at Las Huelgas, had also received knighthood from the patron saint, in the Castilian fashion.

At this point a message arrived from the lady abbess saying that she would like me to call upon her. As this, in Las Huelgas, was a royal command, we immediately left and walked to the courtyard which I had already seen, and ascended the staircase that was a mass of armorial shields. There was a touching symbolism about this. Here the abbesses of Las Huelgas hung the symbols of their blue blood and their worldly distinction at the threshold of the convent. They gave them up on the doorstep, at the last moment like true Spaniards, their final renunciation.

I had never before met an abbess and wondered whether she would be seated on a chair or a throne, whether she would be attended by nuns, or would be alone. I imagined that we should ascend several staircases in the old building until we came to the reception-room where the abbess was accustomed to hold such interviews. I was therefore surprised when the clerk of works unlocked a door and ushered me into a plain little hall, with an iron grill at one end like a cashier's desk in a country bank. Behind the bars stood a small, middle-aged Cistercian nun, who was wearing horn-rimmed glasses and was obviously waiting for us. I thought she was a nun who had been sent to take us to the abbess. The clerk bowed respectfully and introduced me, and I realized then that I was speaking to the Reverend Mother, Doña Rosario Díaz de la Guerra.

In the background was a bare little office with no carpet on the floor, a crucifix above a rolltop desk, and a calendar. The abbess might have been a Zurbarán which had stepped from its frame as she stood there, wearing the dress that is so familiar to anyone who has been to a Spanish art gallery. The clerk told her what we had been doing, and when the polite preliminaries were over I described my wanderings in Spain, and then we talked about the history of Las Huelgas. The

267

abbess knew it well and was familiar with the regal authority of her predecessors, one of whom, she told me, was such an autocrat that she wished to hear the confessions of her nuns! The temporal glories of her office had departed now, she said, and whispered, 'Thank God!' I asked if the vow of silence did not press rather heavily upon nuns, and added that the conversation of forty-three nuns who had been silent all day must be fairly brisk when the hour of talk arrived; and the abbess smiled and said, 'Well, after all, they're only women!' It was a remark which might have been made by St. Teresa.

§ 10

Every moment in Burgos was full of interest. One morning when I was passing a church I saw a regiment which had been attending Mass file out and form up on the road outside. The only fault which an English sergeant-major might have found with them were their boots; otherwise they were beautifully turned out and each man wore the white gloves which in Spanish military life are the symbol of rectitude. I went into the church as soon as they had marched off and saw two military motor-bicycles, in a state of almost celestial beauty and polish, standing on either side of the chancel steps. Whether a new issue of motor-cycles had been blessed by the priest I cannot say, but the entry of religion like this into ordinary life lends the commonest objects an aura of wonder.

One morning I went to see a Renaissance palace that was being restored and was to become the town museum. I found it in a narrow street occupied by similar palaces, but they had all been split up into tenements and the lower stories were mostly used for storing coal. I looked inside one or two and saw marble columns rising from piles of coke. Given the money, a whole street of Renaissance palaces could be restored in Burgos. The *Casa Miranda*, which was the house I had come to see, was one of the most beautiful palaces it has been my good fortune to visit in Spain. In a marble courtyard eighteen fluted Corinthian columns supported a richly decorated balcony from which rooms radiated. It gave me a good idea of the splendours concealed beneath tons of coal in this street.

I saw the richly decorated House of the Constable, where Columbus was received by Queen Isabel upon his second return from America, and where Philip I died, his body lying in state amid the candles while his poor demented wife clung to the bier and refused to admit his

268

death. And, as a contrast to these high scenes and memories, while I was walking along a street one day, I saw a coach go by with the name of the town of Stafford upon it; and I had an impression of a number of English faces gazing down upon the remarkable Spanishness of Spain.

It was with regret that after a farewell visit to the exquisite work of Gil de Siloe, I packed up and left Burgos for Pamplona, where the Feast of San Fermín was about to be celebrated. Everyone in Spain had told me that on no account should I miss the sight of the fighting bulls running through the streets of this city, as they do every year during this festival, and I therefore decided to hasten there. There are two roads from Burgos to Pamplona, one, the main road, and the other a secondary road which once formed part of the pilgrims' way to St. James of Compostela. This old route ran from France across the Pyrenees by the Pass of Roncesvalles, then down into Pamplona and so to Logroño, Burgos, Sahagún, León and westward to Compostela. That, I thought, would be the road I should take. It had been used by pilgrims from the Middle Ages and most of the towns were provided with hostels for their use, known as 'Frankish Quarters'. What a wonderful walking tour this old road to Compostela offers to those of sound limb and stout heart, who also have the energy to learn a little Spanish.

As I went on, the country changed to miles of scrub oak, heather and bracken, which I had not seen before in Spain. I seemed to smell France in the air, or possibly it was the Basque country. The peasants wore berets; the air was cool and pleasant; and it was indeed difficult to believe that in a few hours I could be back on the gridiron of Madrid. Having travelled about thirty miles, I paused in what seemed to me an attractive old town with a spectacular cathedral tucked away in a corner, a huge and venerable building of honey-coloured stone. This town was Santo Domingo de la Calzada—*calzada* means highroad. While I was walking round the cathedral, which is full of wonderful old paintings, ironwork and gilding, I heard a cock crow and thought that some bird must have strayed in. There was a second crow, this time almost over my head; and glancing up, I saw, to my astonishment, a white cock and a hen in what I can only call the most superb hen-coop on earth; a lovely little hen-temple from the Middle Ages, gilded and decorated with carving and pictures. In design it was like the doorway and porch of a medieval house, but in place of a bedroom window above the porch was an ironwork grille behind which the birds were visible. A small archway in the porch evidently led up by a concealed stairway to a door in the little house, so that the birds might be fed and watered. I stood looking up at them, remembering the peacock of Juno and the snake of Aesculapius, thinking that never in all my wanderings had I seen birds in a place of honour in a Christian church. While I was wondering why they were there, a woman entered the church with a broom and started to sweep, and this is the story she told me.

Long ago there lived near the town a holy hermit called Domingo, who was known as Domingo de la Calzada, because he straightened out the pilgrims' road in those parts, cut down trees and built a bridge so that men might more easily pass on their way to Santiago de Compostela. Among his improvements was a hostel in the town where pilgrims spent the night. The good hermit, his work over, retired to heaven, where in time he joined the company of the elect. After he had been dead many years, a good-looking young Frenchman with his father and mother arrived as pilgrims. The woman who managed the hostel fell passionately in love with the young man, but he, having set his heart on other things, was unresponsive. Her passion then turned to evil and as the young man and his parents were departing, she slipped a piece of silver into the young pilgrim's wallet, then ran to the *alcalde* and denounced him as a thief. He was caught and the piece of silver was found in his pack, and he was hanged on a gallows outside the town. The father and mother sorrowfully continued their journey to Santiago, where they confided their woe to St. James.

As they were returning home, they passed again through Santo Domingo de la Calzada and prayed beneath the gallows where the body of their son was still hanging. Suddenly they heard him say: 'I am not dead; God and his servant St. James have preserved me alive. Go therefore to the *alcalde* of the town and beg him come and let me down.' They hurried immediately to the mayor, who was just sitting down to supper with two roast chickens in front of him, one a cock and the other a hen. When the pilgrims had told their story, he laughed and said: 'You might as well say that these birds on the dish before me could get up and crow!' Whereupon they stood up and the cock crowed. The *alcalde*, amazed and startled, rushed to the gallows with his officers and cut down the young pilgrim, who continued on his way. And ever since the town of Santo Domingo has kept a white cock and a white hen in the cathedral in memory of the great miracle.

I asked how the two birds were selected for this honour and if they spent all their lives in the cathedral. The woman told me that when the peasants had reared a particularly fine bird of the purest white, they presented it to the church. There is a hen-run behind the verger's house where these birds are kept, and every fortnight a couple are placed in the church and at the end of that time replaced by another couple. They are kept in the church only from April to September, for at other times the building is too cold for them.

§ 11

Thinking of this story and of the tenacious character of Spain, I came in the course of twenty miles or so to the town of Nájera, whose name was familiar to me from the battle fought by Pedro the Cruel in 1367 against his illegitimate brother, Henry of Trastamara. Pedro had the Black Prince and an English army on his side, and Henry of Trastamara had Du Guesclin and a French army on his. Somewhere near at hand the English knights and bowmen had scattered the Frenchmen and had passed on into Spain, to die of heat and disease as they waited vainly for Pedro to pay their wages.

What a town is Nájera; small, dusty and antique, with little stone houses like fortresses, the river Najerillo running clear and sparkling from the mountains on its way to the Ebro, and a ruined castle upon a hill. Women were hanging out washing from balconies above carved coats-of-arms. I could see hay and coal stored in medieval vaults; sunlight sparkling upon stones as the river slid over them; and small boys with rolled-up trousers were standing in mid-stream with fishing-nets. It was one of those places I fell in love with at once.

A covered carrier's wagon was being unloaded in the yard of the little hotel by the banks of the river; there were mules tied to posts; and the scene had colour and the Gothic vigour that you notice northward from Avila. I found the dining-room upstairs next to the kitchen, where women were bending over steaming pots and pans; and the aroma of their efforts, deliciously laced with garlic, frisked merrily down the stairs and even invaded the street. I was given a table by a window facing the river, where I could watch the boys fishing. It was good to see a Spanish river which was not the colour of *café au lait*. A girl placed a bottle of red Logroño wine upon the table, and this was followed by bean soup, an omelette with bacon, roast chicken and salad, caramel custard and fruit; not a bad effort for a country inn. Most of the bread in Spain is good, but this of Nájera was particularly delicious. The carters came in, also a few shaggy-looking men who were evidently travellers, and lunched at surrounding tables. I liked

271

the place so much that had I not been hurrying on to Pamplona in time to see the bull-running in the morning, I should have gone no further, but would have stayed in that delightful little inn beside the river.

On leaving the dining-room I looked into the bedroom which I could have had, and made a note to return and occupy it some day. It was divided into two parts by curtains; in one half stood an impressive brass bed, and in the other antique chairs and a round table with a fine *brasero*, or brazier, which, when filled with red-hot pulverized olive stones in winter, would warm the air. The cosiest possession in a cold climate is surely the circular Spanish table fitted with a *brasero* and a curtain on rings, which can be tightly drawn so that no matter how the rest of the body freezes, the legs from knee to foot are in their private oven. I found afterwards that this inn had a long tradition of hospitality and had not changed its name since the time of Richard Ford.

While wandering round the town, fascinated by buildings which had come down in the world, I arrived at the gate of an old Benedictine monastery, Santa María la Real, which was drowsing in a somnolent atmosphere of departed grandeur. A monk eventually answered the bell and took me into a splendid church, large enough to be a cathedral, and down into a crypt where more than thirty of the remote kings and queens of Navarre, León and Castile are buried—Garcías, Sanchos and Blanches, just names from the confusion of early Spanish history. It was an awesome crypt. Two life-size stone halberdiers in armour guarded the foot of the stairway, as if to forbid entrance. Above them an early king and queen were sculptured upon their knees, with hands together in prayer, while round them and beyond were grouped stone coffins bearing recumbent effigies of men and women, a startling scene in the light of an unshaded electric globe. Here lay García and his wife Istaphania de Fox, Sancho of Navarre and Clara of Normandy, Sancho the Valiant and Beatrice, Sancho the Noble and Blanche, all monarchs of a distant day before Castile had become the leader of the Christian kingdoms. To an English eye it was as startling as if one had been taken into a vault to see the tombs of Saxon kings—Egberts and Ethelreds. The coffins were centuries older than the vault, which had been made to hold them when the church was rebuilt.

I was taken next to a cave transformed by masonry into a little subterranean chapel, where an extremely venerable statue of the Blessed Virgin is to be seen above the altar. It is a painted wooden figure unconcealed by vestments, and I could therefore form some idea of its antiquity. It is an early Gothic statue and belongs to a time when it was not considered irreverent in Spain to show the Virgin's feet. The legs from the knee to the ankle are outlined beneath the robe and the feet are covered with pointed slippers. The Virgin's left arm supports a Christ who might be a young Byzantine prince, and her right hand holds an orb which bears a curious conventionalized lily—that ancient symbol.

'When King García of Pamplona was out hunting one day in the year 1051,' said the monk, 'he saw a partridge fly into a thicket and rode after it. He cut the bushes down with his sword, but could see no sign of the bird. Then he noticed the entrance to a cave into which it must have gone. He dismounted and entered. There, to his amazement, he saw this statue of the Holy Virgin. A votive lamp was burning and a glazed vase of scented fresh white lilies was standing in front of it; and the partridge was nestling close to the feet of the Holy Virgin. This, my son, is the very cave, and the church of Santa María la Real was built over it.'

Here was another story similar to that of the discovery of St. Mary of Guadalupe; and is it not likely that these legends are true, and that such statues were hidden in caves to preserve them from Arab raiders, and were afterwards found by cowherds and by kings out hunting?

This interesting monastery took up so much of my time that I was obliged to give up the idea of looking for the battlefield where the Black Prince restored his unworthy ally to the throne. Speeding onward, I passed through Logroño, a picturesque town upon the banks of the Ebro, which is the centre of the best wine-growing district in Spain, and reached Pamplona in the late afternoon. I was surprised to find such a large and modern-looking city. I had expected something small and medieval which might recall the days of Richard the Lionheart, who, at a tournament here, first met Berengaria, daughter of Sancho of Navarre, whom he married. She was the only Queen of England who never set foot in England, but spent her unsatisfactory married life wandering about the Near East with her crusading husband. The site of Pamplona, set upon a fertile plain in the foothills of the Pyrenees, is magnificent, but what immediately interested me was the state of excitement into which the city had been plunged by the approaching Festival of San Fermín. The town had already given itself over to revelry. Everything was closed except cafés and bars. Bands of young men roamed the streets dressed in white, with red scarves, red sashes, and red laces in their rope-soled shoes. They were extremely

273

good-natured, and those who were not half drunk were pretending to be so; and they passed dancing through the streets, pausing only to drink from a tipped-up bottle or from one of those little leather wine-skins, a *bota*, which I soon gathered was the only object necessary for a pilgrim to this *fiesta*. Every English, French and American visitor in Spain seemed to be present, all the hotels were full, and there was nowhere to stay.

In my search for a room I was given two addresses by a distracted hall-porter, which led to an adventure that was more amusing in retrospect than at the time. The first address was a flat in a tall, dismal building in a dreary street. There was an automatic lift in the concrete hall which shakily ascended with me, then stopped between floors; and nothing would move it. The noise I made attracted several old women in black, who emerged from everywhere like black beetles, and while some spoke to me from above, others did so from below, telling me that the electrician had gone out and anyway the lift was really out of order! While they sent someone to find the electrician, I wondered whether he might have been one of those whom I had seen dancing with a *bota*, and if so, I thought it unlikely that he would be in a condition to release me. Fortunately he was, and after much hammering and shouting the lift rose to the next floor, where I leapt from it as hastily as if it had been on fire. It was hardly in a spirit of festival that I knocked at a door and was admitted to a dark little flat. The ancient dame who showed me a bedroom full of fumed oak said, with a pathetic mixture of firmness and apology, that I could have it for a sum in pesetas which amounted in sterling to £5 a night. It was a shocking demand, but I realized that the Feast of San Fermín was the only chance this poor old woman had during the year to make a few extra pesetas. I was half inclined to take the room, but looking over the flat and finding that beds had been put up everywhere, I visualized a night of the utmost discomfort and confusion and prudently withdrew.

The second address led to a magnificent old building in a high part of Pamplona, near the ramparts. I rang the bell and was shown by a nun into a dignified hall. While I was wondering what this building could be, my question was answered by the Mother Superior, who told me that I was in a convent. She said that in order to oblige a friend she had been willing to put up a female, and I must have been given the address by mistake! This was even more ridiculous than being locked in a lift, and with many apologies I departed.

I walked round Pamplona and saw that those streets through which the bulls were to be driven next morning, from the station to the bull-ring, were fenced with wooden barriers as a protection for the crowds and to keep the bulls to the road. Every balcony along the route had been booked up, and visitors were picking the best spots in the streets from which to see the sight of a few hundred young men running for their lives before the advancing animals. I bought some post-cards of former bull-runnings and thought the spectacle hardly worth watching. A man to whom I said this looked at me in amazement and dislike. His expression was that of a man a few centuries ago who had heard a particularly foul blasphemy and intended to go to the Inquisition. He told me that the young men were very brave and that every year someone was badly gored or killed, and he shrugged his shoulders and mentally abolished me as an outsider completely lacking in *españolismo*. I was glad to get out of Pamplona with its bands of dancing youths with their squeakers. I had expected a simple, rustic festival and had found the only touch of what looked like urban vulgarity in Spain.

Seventeen miles along the road to San Sebastián I came to a charming hamlet called Irurzun, where I saw a little country inn, dazzlingly white, and with the woodwork and shutters painted pillar-box red. Dozens of flower-pots painted in various colours were attached to the balconies and to ironwork. Alas! it was full up because of San Fermín, but there was a room at the grocer's shop almost opposite. So I found myself in a large room with two great beds in it, a washstand, floor-boards scrubbed white, and a number of holy pictures.

I walked over to the inn for dinner and shared a table with a delightful French family, a father, mother, and two exemplary small children with perfect manners. The man was delighted to talk English, which he had learnt from gramophone records with the idea of emigrating to Australia. But his scheme had foundered upon domestic affection. He was told that he would have to go out alone and that his wife and children could not follow until he had made a home for them; and this separation had seemed to him impossible. He told me that it was cheaper for him to take his car to Spain and motor round the country than to have a holiday in France. He was an *aficionado* and intended to rise at five in the morning and run into Pamplona to see the bulls. He did his best to persuade me to go with him, but by this time I had decided to read *Fiesta* instead and look at my post-cards.

I was awakened by the sound of bells. There were cracked cow-bells and small, clear goat-bells, and, glancing through the window, I saw a morning mist through which cows were being driven to pasture, and goats were being taken afield by boys grasping long sticks and holding little brass horns. I saw a boy lift a horn to his lips and blow a note, which was answered immediately by a billy-goat who came prancing out of a yard followed by several nannies and their kids, and together they moved off into the misty summer morning.

I dressed and went across to the inn for breakfast. A group of men in a yard opposite were plaiting the mane of a stallion which was evidently going to a horse-fair, and the breakfast-room in the inn was filled with herdsmen wearing berets and corduroy jackets, and grasping stout sticks. Before each man stood a steaming bowl of chocolate and a hunk of crusty bread. They broke the bread, dropping it into the chocolate, and ate it with a spoon. Some of the men drank a glass of *anís* and many took out tobacco pouches and rolled their own cigarettes. An insistent motor horn below suddenly emptied the room as the stocky, solemn Basques, grasping their sticks, went downstairs where two lorries filled with horses were waiting for them.

The chocolate was excellent, flavoured, I think, with cinnamon, and topped with whipped cream. All over Spain chocolate is good in cups or in packets, and this drink, which was brought to Spain by the conquistadores from the palace of Montezuma, has only recently given way to coffee in some parts of the country, while tea, as anyone knows who has tried to order it outside a tourist hotel, is still believed to be one of the nastier herbal medicines. Ford says that coffee was just 'creeping in' in his time, for it was, of course, unknown to the Arabs of Spain, and indeed was not adopted by the Arab world until after the expulsion of the Moors.

By this time the sun had come out and the mists had gone. Several little lock-up sheds took down their shutters and revealed hand-made agricultural implements, forks and hay forks made of wood, and sufficient besoms to fit out all the witches in the world. Much as I wanted to remain in this pleasant village, I felt that I should never dare to face my friends in Madrid unless I had seen something more of San Fermín. When I reached Pamplona, I found the city sobering up after the excitement of the bull-running and preparing to witness the solemn procession through the streets of the statue of the patron saint, San Fermín himself. I now had the impression of being in a medieval city. The church bells were ringing, men on hobby-horses, armed with bladders on sticks, were chasing any girls they could catch, and galloping after bands of excited children, who dodged away from them if they could, but not before they had received a smart blow on the side

276

*Court of the Lions, Alhambra, Granada*

*Printed in Great Britain*

*The Alcázar, Segovia, with the church of Vera Cruz in foreground*

*The articulated statue of St. James, Las Huelgas, Burgos*

*Fiesta de San Fermín, Pamplona*

*Four medieval women*
*from the Retablos of Gil de Siloe, Burgos*

*Girls in their first communion dresses*

of the head. Fashionably dressed women were beginning to assemble upon the balconies of public buildings, civic dignitaries in evening dress, and officers wearing orders and decorations, pressed through the crowds to their rendezvous. In a side street I came upon one of the lesser giants, a hook-nosed grandee dressed in a splendid suit of old brocade, his papier-mâché head a caricature, I am fairly sure, of the Duke of Wellington. All the *Cabezudos*, or 'Big-heads', and the *Gigantones*, had been taken from the cathedral and were parading the streets. I did not at first see the giants, but the *Cabezudos* were everywhere, much more horrifying than any giant because they were such life-like travesties of human beings. The men who wore these 'Big-heads' were dressed in eighteenth century clothes, and the huge masks were either completely expressionless or frozen in fearful grins. In a narrow street I encountered the eight giants of Pamplona, beautifully painted and dressed, solemnly tottering along in single file, turning stiffly this way and that, their gait slow and mincing, as the man inside the wicker framework took his ordinary man-sized steps. The giants represented Ferdinand and Isabel, four Moors, and two South American Indians. Ferdinand's face was brick red and his hair and beard were glossy black; his crown was gold, he wore a silver breastplate over a blue uniform, and, as he tottered onward, a silver gauntlet rested upon the hilt of a great sword. Isabel was in yellow and red, the Spanish colours, with a lace mantilla the size of a carpet upon her head. The Moors were fierce and wore turbans; one was a sultan, another a sultana, and two were warriors clothed from head to foot in white burnouses, while the Indians were ebony black with feathers in their hair. The crowds hailed these ancient figures with delight; the little boys ran round them admiringly, and those small ones who were seeing them for the first time were filled with wonder. How well the medievals knew how to impress an event upon the minds of those who could not read.

I took my place on the edge of the pavement and, as I waited for San Fermín, I read his obituary notice in a special supplement of the morning's *Arriba España*. This is hot news every July in Pamplona! The saint lived in the reign of the Emperor Decius (A.D. 201–51), in a Spain that was entirely Roman. He was the son of a distinguished senator of Pamplona—or *Pompeiopolis*, as it then was—and after his conversion he was sent as a missionary into Gaul. He became the first Bishop of Amiens, in which city he is still venerated, and where he was martyred, presumably during the Decian persecution.

I heard a band approaching and saw a procession come slowly into view which was to reveal the Spanish love of ceremony and formality, and also, I might add, the cult of dignity; for I never saw an occasion of this kind more free from those touches of humour or bathos which often attend them. First came the eight giants, led by Ferdinand and Isabel, in an unofficial procession of their own, surrounded by small boys beating drums. It was delightful to see these Spanish relatives of Gog and Magog tottering along in the sunlight, and I could sometimes catch sight of the face of the man inside the giant, peering through a gauze opening slightly below the level of the figure's waist. There was an interval before the procession proper began, and by this time the giants had turned into a narrow street and were to be seen stiffly turning now and again, as if to answer the greetings of those on the balconies, who were level with their heads.

Marching to the music of a band, there now appeared a troop of tall young men in the full-dress uniform of a cavalry regiment; Blücher boots, buckskin breeches, blue tunics with white belts, crossbelts and gold aiguillettes, and gold helmets from which rose emerald green plumes of cocks' feathers. The crowd, which had been laughing and joking while the giants went past, now became solemn—the medieval transition from comedy to solemnity. Behind these spectacular soldiers marched a troupe of young men wearing white costumes piped with red. They reminded me of superbly dressed Morris dancers. Their double-breasted jackets terminated at the waist, their breeches ended below the knees with scalloped edges, and each man carried a short stave bound in spirals of yellow and white cloth. A man in the crowd told me they were Basque dancers in their traditional dress; and this, with their resemblance to Morris dancers, reminded me that many believe the Morris is really the 'Moorish' dance and came to England from Spain, some say with John of Gaunt. The hobby-horses and the jesters with their bladders, the dancers with their sticks, which they click together during the dance, were features of the English May Day, and I can even dimly remember them myself when I was a child. But how long is it, I wonder, since anyone in England has heard a genuine Morris drum, I mean one beaten by a countryman and not a member of a folk-lore society?

The sunlight glittered upon the processional crosses of the cathedral and the parish churches, at least twelve of them, carried by cross-bearers in rose-coloured vestments; and as they passed, led by the cathedral sacristan in a red robe and wearing a white wig that fell to his shoulders,

I glanced along the road and saw the statue of the saint coming into view. San Fermín was seated upon a massive gold and silver throne, mounted upon a palanquin and carried by many men in white wigs, wearing red and blue livery. On each side of the saint, marching to a hymn tune played by a military band, were soldiers in khaki and steel helmets, grasping in white-gauntleted hands rifles with fixed bayonets. Provincial and municipal dignitaries walked in front of the palanquin, wearing white gloves and evening dress, and with them were military officers in uniform. As he drew near, the saint was a magnificent spectacle. He wore a jewelled mitre, a vestment encrusted with gold embroidery, and he held a crozier in his left hand, lifting two fingers of his right—two fingers beautifully made of silver—in benediction. The weight of the gold and silver throne could be guessed by the readiness with which the bewigged bearers, who bore the poles of the palanquin upon their shoulders, helped themselves along with the aid of staves. Immediately behind San Fermín came the Bishop and high ministers of the Church, then the solemn band, more soldiers, and finally, the remaining troop of gorgeous cavalrymen in gold helmets with which the procession had begun. And that is the way a Roman who died seventeen hundred years ago passes through the streets of Pamplona every July.

After a solemn Mass in the cathedral, the city gave itself over to gaiety. The same groups of men—never accompanied by women—dressed in white, with red scarves, came roaming through the streets, pausing to dance a few steps, their hands held above their heads as in a Highland fling, then they wandered happily and aimlessly along, enjoying the great *fiesta* of the year. I was told that nearly everyone was slightly drunk for a week, but there was never any fights or brawls.

While I was sitting outside a café, the young Frenchman from Irurzun came along and sat down. He was well pleased with his morning. The *encierro de los toros*, or the shutting-up of the bulls, had apparently realized all his expectations.

'I got a wonderful place near the bull-ring,' he said. 'Suddenly, I hear shouts! I hear women scream! Then the screams and shouts get nearer and I see men running—running for their lives—men without hats, in shirts and trousers, perhaps fifty, maybe a hundred; then just behind them come the bulls, six or possibly eight, big and black and galloping as fast as horses, sometimes twisting their horns right and left. It is terribly exciting! Sometimes, when a man knows the bulls are gaining on him, he falls flat on his face and lies still and the bulls go past; or he may do something that can be most perilous, he can step into a doorway and keep still; but there is a chance that a bull will stop and gore him! When the men fall down and the bulls gallop over them, all the women scream their heads off—you never heard such screams—and it is all very barbaric, very pagan. . . .'

'By the way, did you see the procession that has just gone past?'

'Yes, I saw it. Very Christian, very pagan! That is Spain! You have all Spain in this city. Christianity in the morning and paganism in the afternoon! It is going to be a marvellous bull-fight. Why don't you stay and see it? Ah, but I forget to tell you the most amusing thing of all. When the bulls were led away to the bull-pens, cows were let loose among the crowds. They had little rubber balls on their horns and they went charging about, knocking men down all over the ring. It was really a most extraordinary sight! These Spaniards dream bull-fighting. It is in their blood. You see small boys trying to play the cows with handkerchiefs, their shirts—anything—and if they make a good pass the crowd goes mad with delight. Generally they are knocked down, but they don't mind. Was anybody hurt? Yes, I think so. I saw a man being carried away on a stretcher. It was all tremendously exciting and you missed a wonderful sight. . . .'

So it goes on in Pamplona for a week. Half the Basque country is there with its *botas*. They tell me that at midnight on the last day, when the *fiesta* of San Fermín ends, men and boys walk through the streets carrying lighted candles. They sing a song which ends with the words, 'Poor San Fermín dies', and, as they sing these words, they lie down on the pavement or in the road, then rise again and continue singing.

§ 12

The road from Pamplona to Roncesvalles is twenty-eight miles of Switzerland; there are cow-bells and chalets, green meadows and wild roses, pine trees, and white tufts of water that come tumbling down perpendicular rockfaces through clumps of maidenhair fern. And the stolid Basques upon this road would as soon pay customs duty as click a pair of castanets. Indeed, I thought, a visit to Granada must be as great a change to the people of Navarre as Naples to an Aberdonian.

I climbed steadily from the valley of the Arga into mountains where there was often a drop on the side of the road that I did not care to look at. This great pass leads up to a plateau where there are farms and cornfields; then the pass begins again, to wind and twist into ever higher solitudes, and suddenly over the curve of a hill I saw enormous bare peaks, lonely and terrible. Somewhere ahead was Roncesvalles, one of the shining names of the earth, like Tintagel and Avalon.

The road went on, winding its way into the Pyrenees; sometimes I was facing north, sometimes south; and then I came to the last few villages on the Spanish side of the Pass, and eventually to the village of Roncesvalles. I had always imagined it would be in a terrifying cleft in the mountains, where an army could be destroyed, as Charlemagne's rearguard is said to have been, by boulders flung down by mountaineers. But there was nothing of the kind. It did not even look like one of the famous mountain passes of the world. The road turned abruptly into a small village where a few stone houses were grouped near a large and gloomy-looking monastery, and all round were fields and hills covered with fir trees. Although Roncesvalles is only about three thousand, five hundred feet high, less than half the height of the Great St. Bernard, it was bitterly cold and the air was charged with moisture. There was a little mountain inn near the monastery, which proved to be comfortable. The only other guests were a group of French botanists who were sorting their specimens on the tables in the little luncheon-room, and arguing excitedly about a small plant that looked to me like a shamrock. Steaming hot soup, an omelette, roast mutton and red wine cheered everyone, and, as we were eating, a motor-van in the last stage of exhaustion came up loaded with fruit and vegetables from the distant plains. One of the Frenchmen remarked that the Basques are the greatest, the most daring, and the most ingenious smugglers in the world, and he said that he knew some Basques who had smuggled a grand piano into Spain!

So this was Roncesvalles, the great road into Spain, the road taken by Charlemagne, the road of the pilgrims to Compostela, the way of armies, embassies, royal bridal processions and couriers since the beginning of history. Here Roland blew the enchanted horn Olivant, which he had won from the giant Jutmundus, to warn Charlemagne, who was ahead with the main body of the army, that the rearguard was in danger. At the third blast Olivant broke in two, but the sound was so tremendous that birds fell dead and the enemy were stricken with panic. Then Roland drew the great sword Durendal, which had once belonged to Hector and was taken, like Olivant, from the giant. In its hilt were preserved a thread from the cloak of the Blessed Virgin, a tooth of St. Peter, a hair from the head of St. Denis, and a drop of St. Basil's blood. But that day the saints were evidently looking the

281

other way, for Roland received his death wound and tried to break Durendal upon a rock so that it should not fall into the hands of the enemy. But the sword was unbreakable and, like Sir Bedivere with King Arthur's sword Excalibur, Roland cast it into water, where, so the song says, it will remain hidden for ever.

The monastery was wrapped in afternoon slumber. Even the workmen who were repairing the roof had deserted their ladders and departed. I wandered about and thought I had never seen a damper or a clammier spot. Moss was growing everywhere on the walls, and sometimes small ferns had taken root in dark and sunless corners; the stone in the ancient cloisters was flaking with the rain and the mountain mist. How great must be the love of God, I reflected, to content a man with this aquarium; or maybe the body, wracked with rheumatism and bent with sciatica, would incline itself naturally into a ladder for the soul. I came across the tomb of Sancho the Strong of Navarre, who fought at Las Navas de Tolosa, and lies buried with Clemencia, his wife. They have been lying here for seven hundred years. Their tombs were already old and of another age when the Black Prince came through the Pass with his English knights and his bowmen; and I fancied that perhaps he was taken to see them like any tourist.

I walked along the road and came to an ancient church which was full of stones and débris. I could just stand in the door and look inside and wonder when the last Mass was said there, and why the daily chain of faith with the House of the Upper Chamber had been broken, for the building looked sound enough outside. Untold thousands of pilgrims must have knelt here in the course of its history, but, like everything else in Roncesvalles, I suppose the mountain mists were eating it away. Roncesvalles can never have been more desolate than it is today. The last armies were Napoleon's; the last pilgrims were infinitely more remote. It was once one of the main roads on the map of faith and now it is just the last post-office in Spain. Well can I believe that in winter Roncesvalles would live up to the words of the minstrel, 'high are its hills, and its valleys dark, the rocks are black, and the country strange and fearful'; and I wondered if those who live there all the year round ever see shapes moving in the mist, or sometimes, when the wind is whistling up from France, hear the cry of 'Montjoie!' echoing from the wet rocks; for, like all places where great things have been done and great songs sung, it is a place in which those who can see ghosts should never feel lonely.

My own particular fancy in ghosts that afternoon was neither a gloomy nor a warlike one, but the lively Elizabeth of Valois, aged fifteen, who arrived at Roncesvalles in a snowstorm, on the first days of the New Year in 1560, to marry thirty-three years old Philip II of Spain. Mary of England had been dead for two years, and Philip had decided to assume for the third time what one writer has called 'the garb of matrimonial martyrdom'. There is a charming portrait of Elizabeth in the Prado which shows what a tall, good-looking girl she was. She wears a black dress, tight at the waist, a long, double string of pearls, slashed sleeves, and an insolent little hat tilted on the side of her head, with a red feather in it. A pleated ruff frames, from ear to ear, the face of a reflective page-boy. What the picture does not show, of course, is that she was clever and well educated—she used to correspond in neat verse with Mary, Queen of Scots, with whom she was brought up—neither does it show that all her life she was under the remote control of her able and scheming mother, Catharine de Medici, who had groomed her to be a cynical young queen. (I think, after all, that perhaps does show a little.)

One feels for these young girls taken from gay courts and condemned to a lifetime of gloomy etiquette, for once they had become Queens of Spain every step they took was laid down for them with mandarin-like precision. Elizabeth arrived at Roncesvalles half-frozen in the snow and sleet, and was taken into the monastery with her mountains of luggage, her ladies, and her band of proud and sensitive French nobles, who were ready to quarrel with the Spaniards on the slightest pretext, or on none at all. Their indignation was great because the Spanish envoys sent by Philip to take custody of the bride were waiting in a village five miles away. They were urged to come to Roncesvalles and save the young Queen the hardship of a handing-over ceremony in a snowdrift; but as Roncesvalles was not the appointed place, the grandees refused to move. High-flown and diplomatic language is devised for such predicaments, and much of this passed between the storm-bound Frenchmen at Roncesvalles and the storm-bound grandees five miles away. At last Elizabeth, becoming impatient, decided, to the horror and dismay of the Frenchmen, to go and meet the Spaniards; but at the last moment, just as she was setting out and had already sent the baggage train on ahead, the Spaniards, having relented, arrived at Roncesvalles to obey, as they said, the summons of their Queen. In great confusion, for the dresses, the furniture, and the rich tapestries were by this time winding their way down into Spain, a hurried reception was staged; and in the failing light of a winter's evening Cardinal Mendoza and the

A Stranger in Spain

Duke of Infantado, preceded by sixty Spanish grandees in state dress, filed into the hall of the monastery, where, beneath a cloth of state emblazoned with the lilies of France, young Elizabeth stood to receive them. The courtly ceremony was conducted by the light of torches; there was much unseemly jostling, and when the last speech had been made and the last hand kissed, the last chair, or stool, brought at the decreed moment, and the French nobles knelt to say farewell to the young Queen, the girl broke down and flung herself weeping into the arms of Anthony of Navarre.

She was led away by the grandees, and as her Spanish litter set off into the falling snow there was much noise of hautboys and trumpets and the beating of drums. The marriage was a success, and when Elizabeth died in eight years' time, aged twenty-three, she left behind a sorrowing Philip, who let the usual two years elapse before he donned the garb of matrimonial martyrdom for the fourth and last time.

# Chapter IX

*San Sebastián—Santillana del Mar and its palaces—the Picos de Europa—the Cave of Covadonga—Oviedo and a fair—the tomb of Sir John Moore—Santiago de Compostela and the shrine of St. James*

§ 1

A GENTLE rain was falling upon San Sebastián. It was the first rain I had seen in Spain and I liked it. The children had been called in from the superb sweep of sand, the sea looked grey and English, and the many cafés in this delightful holiday town were filled with those who had nothing to do but wait until the sun came out again.

My first impression was that San Sebastián must be the headquarters of Spanish Brummellism. I have never seen so many shops for men in a town of its size; I should think that they outnumber women's shops by about three to one. In this masculine Paris I came every ten yards to a window full of men's clothes and shoes. It may be that the men who spend their holidays in San Sebastián are, for some reason not readily apparent, filled with a passion for self-adornment; or that members of the Government, when they escape from Madrid, are consumed by a desire to look well, perhaps not only in the eyes of General Franco. And it may be that Frenchmen find it cheaper to buy their clothes across the frontier. I remembered that the Frenchman whom I had met at Irurzun had told me that hundreds of his countrymen arrive in Spain with empty suitcases and buy all the clothes they can afford.

I came across a fine example of a Spanish chemist's shop, a feature of Spain which I ought to have mentioned before. These shops have a gravity which is absent from the orgy of patent medicines called a chemist's shop in most other countries. The *farmacia* is a tribute to the artistic sense of the Spanish and also to their love of drama and mystery; for what could be more attractive than the huge carboys full of red, blue, green and yellow water, like some certain and delicious panacea, which decorate the windows and look wonderful at night when lit from behind; or what more dramatic than the beautiful glazed jars inscribed with such words as *Arsínico*, or more mysterious than the hundreds of little mahogany drawers, each one labelled with its appropriate hieroglyph? Your genuine old-fashioned chemist—but apothecary is the right word—obviously throws away all the show cards and advertisements about fatter babies and more beautiful skins, and while he keeps most of the mass-produced fads and fancies, he does so in the background, and his surroundings belong to a magic earlier than that of penicillin and the mycins. There is something about the place that strikes the most casual purchaser of a bottle of aspirin—just the faintest suspicion that someone in a back room might still be trying to discover the Philosopher's Stone.

Upon the slopes of a hill overlooking the old harbour I found an excellent aquarium, where I amused myself for an hour gazing at the fish and the people who were looking at the fish; but it is impossible in Spain to contemplate fish for long, especially the *crustacea*, without wondering what they would taste like. From live fish I passed to the *pescadería*, or fish-market, which was served by a fine collection of Rowlandson's better-looking fishwives and their apple-faced daughters, who seemed to be literally bursting with health. There were no sinuous Carmens here, but muscular women like those who went with Cortés to Mexico. There is something about fish which inspires all who handle it with life and cheerfulness, for I have never yet seen a gloomy fish-market. These Basque women behind their ramparts of lobsters and soles were a delightful glimpse of rude northern vitality; and if I had been able to understand the Basque vernacular I have no doubt I should have enjoyed the fish-market even more.

I came to a museum in the old town which was beautifully housed and arranged and was full of interesting things. There was the usual portrait of María Luisa by Goya—how he must have loathed her, or was she really like that?—and also many modern Spanish paintings; and, improbable sight in San Sebastián, the sword of Boabdil, the last Moorish King of Granada. There was also a collection of agricultural implements, ploughs, forks, spades, spinning-wheels, looms, and so forth, and a beautiful Mambrino's helmet in pewter. Suspended on a cord was the model of a *bruja*, or witch, riding a broomstick. In every detail, long nose, cone-shaped hat, spectacles, claw-like hands, she was just like an English witch, but there was one important difference; you ride an English broomstick handle first, but the Spanish ones are apparently flown bristles first. So if you should happen to see a figure cross the moon riding a broomstick the wrong way round, you will

286

know that it is a Spanish *bruja*, or *meiga*, as one of the custodians called her, which is the name for a witch in his part of Galicia.

Although it is well known that allies are not necessarily bound for ever in bonds of affection, you could travel all over Spain without realizing that British armies under the Duke of Wellington fought there during the Peninsular War, and did not rob the churches, break open the tombs, and carry away gold and silver. It was with surprise therefore that I came to a room entirely devoted to the Peninsular War, to engravings and aquatints which show British redcoats and Jack Tars fighting blue-coated French soldiers in Pyrenean ravines and hauling cannon up precipices. There was a picture of the Iron Duke in a blue coat, sitting his horse and surrounded by a prancing scarlet staff.

By the time I had seen all these things, the sun was shining. The Bay of San Sebastián was enchanting, a bay as fine as Weymouth Bay, curving on to the distant palace where the Kings of Spain used to spend their seaside holidays. As I have already noted, in hundreds of towns all over Spain there are streets where no traffic is allowed, generally the main shopping street or the most fashionable street; and in this civilized manner San Sebastián has abolished traffic from her splendid sea-front, so that the broad avenue, shaded by a tunnel of polled tamarisks, sweeps round in peace and in safety.

The sands were now covered with children and the sea was fringed with bathers. It was delightful to watch the children, who, though 'spoilt' in the English meaning of the term, were not sophisticated or bored with simple and inexpensive things. A sight which pleased me was a hot chestnut man who roasted his nuts in the boiler of a model locomotive, an antique descendant of the *Rocket*, with a high smoke-stack from which real smoke emerged. Men strolled about festooned with balloons; there were trolleys filled with aniseed balls, with sticks of liquorice, with sweets like beach pebbles, and little nets full of chocolate coins in gold foil, with imitation cigarettes, and the smallest of wrist watches. And now and again a little girl who might have been sketched by du Maurier would come up with a peseta and, with self-possession and the air of a grown-up woman, carefully select a balloon or a toffee-apple.

This simplicity which we associate with other times is, after all, a part of Spain's attraction. It goes much deeper than being old-fashioned or lacking foreign currency. It reveals a state of mind. The Renaissance, the Reformation, the French Revolution, the Industrial Revolution, and the Americanization of life, have not been the main influences in the history of Spain; and it is this older world that we sense and admire. Somehow the simple sweets and toys of San Sebastián are a part of it.

I abandoned myself to shameless gluttony in San Sebastián, and went from little restaurant to little restaurant in the old city as one might move from picture to picture in the Prado. The Basques are perhaps the greatest eaters in Spain and no one, even in France, knows better how to cook the finest and most varied fish in the world. The old city is full of small restaurants which offer their own specialities, and I thought the cooking the best I had come across. And this, I should add, was in one of the worst months of the year, for among the things out of season were oysters, clams, mussels, and *angulas a la bilbaína*, which is eel spawn fried in oil. I was also disappointed to learn that lampreys were out of season, a small eel eaten all over Spain and a dish I have longed to taste since a schoolboy, when I was filled with a macabre curiosity to eat the dish which is said to have killed Henry I.

Though these fish were unobtainable, there were trout, sea-trout and salmon, lobster, *langostinos*, soles, *chipirones*, or ink-fish, fresh sardines, roast tunny fish, and the great Basque dish, *bacalao a la bilbaína*, which is dried cod well soaked for twenty-four hours and cooked in oil with onions and other ingredients.

One of the peculiarities of Spain is the humble restaurant, or wine shop, which looks to the stranger like the hide-out of a robber gang, in whose dark interior, filled with wine barrels and bottles, he may dimly see garlic and every manner of sausage hanging from the ceiling, and wooden benches and trestle-tables scrubbed white. Sometimes an assassin walks to the door and gives the apprehensive stranger a charming smile. It is not unusual that the rougher the exterior the finer are the manners to be met with inside. I found in the old streets what at first seemed the sinister scene for a murder, but attracted by an announcement written in whitewash on the window that fresh grilled sardines were obtainable there, I went inside, and was incorporated with delightful courtesy into a happy domestic scene. The proprietor and his wife, surrounded by a great number of children, were eating in the aisles of a dim cathedral of casks, with two dogs and several cats in attendance; and when I asked for fresh sardines, a girl placed a hunk of bread and a jug of white wine on the trestle-table, and eventually sardines the size of sprats arrived. There were no knives or forks and the way to eat them was to pick them up by the head and tail and nibble them. I thought this gave a new meaning to the sardine.

# Basque food

A little more courage is required to try *chipironès in su tinta*, ink-fish cooked in its own ink. This comes to you looking rather as though someone has poured a bottle of Indian ink over a dish of black tripe; no doubt the taste for this could be acquired in time. Boiled codfish, one of the sadder memories of England, is elevated by the Basques to the utmost heights of epicureanism. Here is a noble way to cook it. Take cutlets of codfish and marinate them in a little olive oil, then partly fry them. Put each portion in its own individual small dish, in which it will eventually be served. Now prepare a sauce as follows: put two ounces of butter in a frying-pan and lightly fry in it some ham and mushrooms cut into small pieces, and, as they are frying, sprinkle over them about a dessertspoonful of flour to thicken the sauce. Add a little stock, some tomato, and white wine. Let this sauce simmer for two minutes and then pour it over the codfish. Put the dishes in the oven until the fish is cooked, and just before you serve it, piping hot, put a small ball of butter on each cod steak. I guarantee that if you make this dish properly, you will never return to parsley sauce.

I have no idea how many restaurants there are in San Sebastián, but there must be several in almost every street in the old city. I was told that the Basques take food so seriously that there are eating-clubs in the town whose members have the use of the kitchen, so that they may prepare their favourite dishes. In a town where men are not only gourmets but also cooks, one can see why the restaurants have to be always on their toes.

From Pamplona onward, I felt that I had left Spain behind and had crossed the frontier into a Scotland of musical comedy. What was San Fermín but a sunnier, less-spirituous hogmanay; and round San Sebastián the uncompromising, blue-eyed faces under blue or red berets, the tough-looking men and the bonny lassies, all reminded me of the north; and I thought that a difference as great as that which separates the Castilian and the Andalusian from each other divides both from the Basque. I remembered the lazy, fertile plains of Andalusia and the hills fat with olives, the high, bare ridges of Castile and the steppes of La Mancha, dry as a bone in summer; and now I saw this green, damp blend of sea and mountain, where rain falls in July and the crops, which had been cut and carted weeks since in the south, were only just ripening for the sickle.

There is, too, in the air of the Basque country the same consciousness of race that you sense when you cross the border into Scotland; and one had only to look at the faces round one to know that the Basques, like the Castilians, the Andalusians, and probably all the other types of Spaniards, are in their own estimation the one and only repository of the Truth and the centre of the world.

> *Here's tae us,*
> *Wha's like us?*
> *De'il the yin.*

I am sure there must be a Basque variant of this. Like the Scots, they are keen on money, hard-headed, and apparently uncomplicated. yet capable of spiritual fervour. St. Ignatius Loyola was a Basque; as was St. Francis Xavier.

I had the pleasant feeling in the Basque country, so unusual in Spain, that if I wrote anyone a letter I should quite likely get a reply.

§ 2

Rain from the Bay of Biscay flung an impenetrable sheet of greyness over the landscape as I passed through Bilbao and Santander. There was a ship in the docks at Santander, loading a cargo for South America. This was the port at which Charles V landed when he came from Flanders to take over the regency of Spain on behalf of his unfortunate mother, Joan the Mad; and here also another Charles, Prince of Wales, set sail for England after his flirtation in Madrid. In the hope of seeing what this bay looked like, I paused on some high land outside the town, but all I could see was a misty headland upon which stood a royal palace and in the far background the outline of the immense Cantabrian mountains.

The fifty miles of sea coast with Santander in the centre is, strange to say, Old Castile. It is Castile's only outlet to the sea, and the province elbows its way between the Basque region of Vizcaya on the east and the old kingdom of Asturias on the west; but why it is called *la montaña* I do not know, for it is no more mountainous than other parts of Castile farther to the south. The Castilians of *la montaña* have green fields and fat cows; they live in houses like chalets, with wooden balconies; they play *pelota* like the Basques, and sometimes even against the wall of the church. Here you will find many a wonderful little Romanesque church dedicated to a saint you have never heard of; how fascinating it would be to travel round this Cantabric rim of Spain, seeking out those massive little buildings which, like many Greek ikons, look more venerable than they are. In the north the Romano-Visigoth tradition of building continued well into the thirteenth century. This is a fine and noble district and, as a Spaniard said in describing it to me, 'very European', which made me smile at the time; but it is true, for it was here that European Christianity gathered itself for its long fight against Islam.

It was not until afternoon that the sun came out and by that time I was approaching Santillana del Mar, which is near the caves of Altamira, where the famous prehistoric paintings are to be seen. At the top of a steep hill I came into the strangest little town imaginable, a town of cows and coats-of-arms and solid little stone palaces standing in rows like the Street of the Knights in Rhodes. The inhabitants seemed to have vanished, giving the impression of a medieval town seen at a moment when the barons, the knights and the squires had ridden away to a tourney. This was Santillana del Mar, interesting to those who love to trace the haunts of fictional characters as the birthplace of Gil Blas.

On one side of the little plaza this very house, an old palace, had been transformed into one of the most romantic of hostels, the Parador Gil Blas; and there I was given a baronial bedroom with vaguely medieval light fittings and furniture, and a modern bathroom, all in green, which had everything except hot water.

From the balcony at the end of the hall outside my room I would look down to the small cobbled square surrounded by its ancient palaces, one with a fine medieval tower and a gateway like that of a cathedral, another black and white, with wooden balconies dripping with ivy geraniums; a stage superbly set for a drama, but there were no actors! I have never been in a place where life was more muted. This was the absoluteness of quiet which doctors sometimes order. The only life that ever drifted across the plaza was a dusty van bringing the mail and groceries, or a car full of tourists exclaiming in various languages, 'How wonderful!'; and every evening at milking-time a herd of black-and-white cows. They were the most aristocratically housed cows on earth, for many a byre bore above the gate the coat-of-arms of a noble family.

In his book on Antonio Pérez, Dr. Marañón says that the province of Santander has always been notorious for its exaggerated love of heraldry. Writing of Escobedo's village, Colindres, he says: 'There he had his mansion well studded over with coats-of-arms, as is the custom in that province where people are prone to go to puerile lengths in their vanity about heraldry.' How true that is of Santillana, for, if heraldry could ever be vulgar, one would say that the armorial bearings carved over almost every house, and some of the largest shields over the smallest houses, shout against each other like posters on a hoarding.

I could find no one who could tell me what life was like here when all the little palaces were occupied by their haughty owners. They were probably too proud to do any work or to farm, and I cannot imagine how they occupied themselves unless they sat in their palaces poring over their pedigrees. The same delightful inertia seems to have descended upon the present occupants of the palaces, though they at least have corn and maize to cut, and hay to make and cows to milk.

The finest thing in Santillana is the germ of its existence, a glorious Romanesque abbey, now the parish church, with an entrance door which we should describe as Norman, a magnificent arch which would be one of the marvels of any other country except Spain, where there are so many of them. The original church was built to house the bones of a virgin saint, Juliana, who is said to have been martyred in Bithynia in the fourth century, and the name Santillana is a corruption of the Latin, Sancta Juliana. Behind the church are old cloisters of squat, rounded arches, each capital covered with Gothic carvings which are finer than many of the better known Gothic remains in Spain. There is also an archaic stone Virgin and Child which is completely Roman in spirit. The Virgin does not hold the Child on her knee, as in most statues, but on her lap, gazing straight ahead, and He is shown as a young king about ten years of age.

In addition to the peasants and cows, I was told that the town has a population of absent noblemen who come at rare intervals and stay in their palaces, which are left in charge of faithful and devoted caretakers. You can see these women in the evening, sitting on chairs and benches at the palace gates, knitting or making lace. It is a strange experience to be shown over these beautifully furnished old buildings, clean and in perfect order, and some even with flowers on the grand piano as if the owner were expected home that night. I asked one woman when her master had last stayed there. She made a calculation and said that it must have been fifteen years ago. I visited three of these palaces and was impressed by the honesty and reliability of the caretakers. The furniture was polished and also the floors. Family photographs were dotted about, the owner's books were in their shelves, his pictures hanging on the walls, and even the gardens were looked after. It is gratifying to know that such honesty and loyalty are still left in the world; and it was easy to imagine the joy which would light up those faithful peasant faces if the duke or duchess suddenly arrived and they were told to get out the bed linen and air the sheets.

One of the most impressive houses I was shown belongs to the Archduchess Doña Margarita of Hapsburg-Lorraine and Bourbon. It was once the home of the abbot and the oldest parts of it go back to the thirteenth century, but it has been altered and adapted in later times and attractively modernized by the present owner. What a pathetic silence, a truly ghostly silence, lies over a house whose owner has been away for years; and how eerie the silence becomes when, entering a room, you see that everything has remained in its place just as it was when he or she said goodbye. The photograph of Franz Josef in uniform still stands in its regal frame upon the piano; King Alfonso XIII on the occasional table is still a fresh-faced but delicate young cadet in a white uniform; there are royal wedding groups; princesses holding infants in christening robes; laughing family groups in the dress of sixty years ago; and a sporting photograph of some now vanished royal personage, standing gaitered and with a feather in his hat, one foot proudly resting on a prostrate boar.

What an awful tyranny of the dead it is that allows a man to entail something which his descendants cannot dispose of, but must hand on to their successors, the assumption being that it is still as precious to others as it was to the dead man. I believe many of these old palaces were entailed in this way, which explains why some are still occasionally, and perhaps reluctantly, occupied.

§ 3

I set off for the caves of Altamira, which are only five miles away, to see the prehistoric rock paintings of bisons and boars and other animals, which are now reproduced in every other book about prehistoric art. The caves are in hilly, open country, and I was taken down into them by one of those peasant archaeologists whose enthusiasm is indescribable. He told me how the caves were discovered in 1868 by a certain Don Marcelino de Sautuola, who had a summer villa nearby, and was out shooting with a dog which had chased a fox into the caves. The Don, who was not an archaeologist, thought nothing of it and did not revisit the caves for seven years, when he took his young daughter María with him—and presumably some candles—for while they were exploring the caverns the little girl noticed the drawings on the roof and drew her father's attention to 'the bulls'. From that moment the caves became famous all over the world, and the learned travelled to Santillana to see this astonishing art gallery of fifteen thousand years ago.

We descended into a cold, dank cavern which was badly lighted by electricity. My guide cast a light on the roof and picked out large, coloured animals shining with damp. My first thought was how much better they looked in the books. They were considerably larger than I had expected and difficult to recognize, for they were painted on the uneven stone and were crossed in many directions by cracks and fissures. The artists had chipped the outline of the animal and then painted the picture with brown and red ochre and oxide of manganese. The cave had always been dark, so that the artist, or artists, must have worked by artificial light; stone lamps filled with fat are the accepted explanation. Many of the pictures I had to accept with the eye of faith, for the light was inadequate, but what struck me most about them was that authentic eye-witness touch which, incidentally, forgers have found so difficult to reproduce. The most extraordinary of all the drawings, I thought, was the wild boar which the artist had attempted to show in movement; he did this by drawing the animal with eight legs, painting the extra legs in a lighter tone and in a running pose. It was curious to see how the artist had tried to give a three dimensional effect to some of the animals by using a protruding stone. It was fantastic to stand in these caves and reflect that the paintings were made at a time when Great Britain was connected with the Continent by land, and when the south of Europe was still cold and full of wandering herds of reindeer and bison. Neither the reindeer nor the wild boar appear to have changed at all since those early times, but the horse has become a more impressive animal.

Forgery is one of those peculiar crimes, like impersonation, which is not a crime until you try to make money out of it. You can, for instance, paint a picture and call it a Vermeer; but no one will put you in prison until you have sold it as a Vermeer. Prehistoric antiquities have always attracted a type of forger who makes stone axes and flints and other objects, rarely with any financial intent, but for sheer love of his art; and more often than not, one imagines, for the pleasure of reading the nonsense written by archaeologists when the 'finds' are discovered. There was Edward Simpson, known as 'Flint Jack', in the nineteenth century, who was a pest to the learned in England; and

Switzerland also produced many whose labours of love must have contributed greatly to the caution of the archaeologist. Happily the Altamira caves have been so well vetted during the last century that one can examine them with confidence.

## § 4

About ten miles to the west of Santillana a beautiful salmon river, the Deva, flows down from the Cantabrian Alps and empties itself into the sea. This river is the boundary between Castile and Asturias, and I crossed it conscious that I was now entering that mountain stronghold where Christian Spain went into hiding long ago, to emerge and wage its long crusade against Islam.

The road ran uphill and there were fields on either side, and in the background were great mountains, their heads in the clouds. Sometimes the road with its banks and its briars looked oddly like a West Country lane. I would see men coming towards me, taking cows for a walk. A single cow is evidently a great possession here, and the owners seemed proud of the well-fed animals they led out to pasture. A donkey came along bearing panniers full of new bread, and on either side walked a girl with waved hair and a string of Majorcan pearls round her neck. The great-grandmothers of these maids wore the exquisite costumes described by early travellers in Spain; but the peasant girl today dresses up in antique splendour only for a festival, and the regional costumes are now treasured by dance and folk-lore societies, museums and poster artists.

The road became narrow and steep and entered a wild gorge through which one of the most beautiful trout rivers I have ever seen slid like glass over boulders, falling every fifty yards or so into deep, inky pools flecked with foam; and not a tree anywhere to catch a fisherman's fly! I came across two fortunate young men, their rods strapped to bicycles, who told me that the river is the Cares and is full of salmon as well as trout almost as large.

The road continued up through ten miles of wild Alpine scenery to a mountain village called Arenas de Cabrales. A mist now came creeping down and a thin drizzle of rain began to fall. I might have been in Wales. The village consisted of just a few shops and small stone houses, and a little inn called rather grandly the *Fonda de los Picos de Europa*. It was the hotel, general store, café and bar. When I told the *patrón* that I should like something to eat and drink, he suggested apple cider, cold smoked trout, and a cheese that is locally famous. He busied himself against a background of gumboots, suits of clothes, oilskins, groceries, sweets, tobacco, fox skins and otter pelts, and in a few moments he had placed the trout and cheese before me, with a pound of farm butter and some new bread. Taking a glass and holding a bottle of cider about two feet above it, he poured the cider so that it frothed and was given a head. I thought at first he was performing a trick and praised his dexterity, but this is the way cider is poured out all over Asturias. As soon as it goes flat, whatever remains in a glass is thrown away—the wine shops reek of stale cider and the floors are always damp with it—and the glass is then replenished from a height.

The smoked trout were delicate in flavour and the cheese, though it looked like Roquefort, tasted more like Stilton; but the cider was a little too sharp, or pert as they say in Devon, for my taste, and anyhow hardly the right drink for a cold day, with a mist edging down the mountain-side. When I told the *patrón* that I was on my way to *Nuestra Señora de Covadonga* his face changed, and from that moment he gave me the respectful attention due to one bound upon a holy mission.

His visitors were chiefly fishermen and mountain climbers, he told me, for this was the centre for those who wished to explore the mountains grouped about the local giant, the Naranjo de Bulnes, nearly eight thousand feet high, which was first climbed in 1904 and has not often been climbed since. The first *conquistador*—that was the word he used—was Don Pedro Pidal y Bernaldo de Quirós, Marquis de Villaviciosa, who reached the top on the fourth of August in that year, and, said the *patrón*, leaving the most dramatic part for the last, when he died his body was taken up into the clouds and buried on the mountain he had conquered.

The rain having ceased, I went on up the gorge. Before the road left the river I stopped the car and examined the dark, deep pools with a pair of field-glasses, in the hope of seeing some fish. Never have I seen better fishing-pools or a more beautiful place to fish; and I was evidently not alone in this thought, for suddenly there sprang into view a dark shape which slipped out of the river and rested for a moment on a boulder. He was a big, glistening otter—*nutria* is the Spanish word— and I could see every hair on him and his tense little cat face as he sat there a moment before he poured himself back into the pool in a snakelike undulation, making scarcely a ripple on the surface. I saw great mountains all round me and I could glimpse behind them, in the greyness of the sky, the mighty Picos de Europa, upon whose summit the snow lies all the year round. I left the gorge of the Cares and went on into higher solitudes where pine forests marched up the slopes of gorges and ravines; and there were more mountains and still more, and tilted against the sky I saw a distant line of white, which was several miles of summer snow.

Nothing I had seen in Spain impressed me more than this glimpse of the Asturias, an unconquerable land of mountaineers, the original school of guerrilla warfare. Pelayo's commandos, who hurled rocks down upon Moorish heads and trapped armies in ravines, were the ancestors of those Asturian miners who achieved a sinister glamour in the Civil War by their utter fearlessness and their casual familiarity with explosives. The *dinamitero* of those days, with a stick of dynamite in each hand, lighting the fuses from the stub of his cigarette, was the toughest of comrades. This is indeed a strange Arcady, with its dynamite and its apple cider, its memories of Pelayo and of Largo Caballero.

The Cave of Covadonga, now the shrine of the Virgin of Covadonga, who is said to have given the victory to Pelayo, lies at the head of a picturesque valley among ravines and pine woods. The wild country round about is now a national park where chamois and wild deer, wild cats, wolves, ospreys, vultures, and bears are to be found. The bears are harmless unless chased by dogs, when they can put up a ferocious fight. In the days when bears were not as rare as they are today, I believe the Asturians used to cure smoked bear hams which are said to have been delicious.

The approach to Covadonga could not have been more pagan; a mountain cave and a stream of water issuing from the rock. When I reached the top of the hill and came out upon a terrace levelled above a ravine, I saw four or five motor-coaches drawn up outside the basilica, which is dedicated to the Virgin of Covadonga—the Virgin of the Battles. I went to the church and found it full to the doors. It was a blaze of light and candles. I edged my way in sufficiently to see that the elaborate ceremony of High Mass in the presence of the bishop had just ended. Suddenly the doors were opened and the crowd burst out of the church and stood on the terrace, waiting for the bishop to appear. He came out, genially blessing right and left. Women ran up and lifted their children to him and he made the sign of the cross over their heads, smiled and walked on. There was not a tourist among them and they were mostly country folk in their Sunday clothes, old peasants with stout sticks in their hands, and women in black with little lace church veils over their hair.

Immediately the bishop had left, people rushed to the shops where medals of the Virgin of the Battles and other souvenirs of the shrine could be bought, and others hastened through a rock tunnel which led to the famous cave. Here upon a platform of rock above the cliff face, and framed by two overhanging shelves of rock, was an altar upon which a small jewelled and brocaded Virgin stood in the candlelight. The crowd pressed near to kneel and cross themselves. The devotion of some of the peasants, especially that of the old women, was beautiful to see. They approached the altar on their knees, and some even travelled the length of the long tunnel in this way, careless of the wet and the mud, and mounted the flight of steps still on their knees, refusing to be helped. And when they had hobbled up to the top step and saw before them the serene Virgin of the Battles standing up amid the candles, their old faces wore the expression which they will wear when they approach the gates of heaven. These simple old people possessed what this age lacks and needs, and I looked at them humbled and touched, rejoicing that such faith is still to be found in our sad and disillusioned world.

The cave in which Pelayo is believed to have hidden is near the altar. There are two ancient tombs in it, reputed to be those of Pelayo and his wife Gaudiosa; but who the warrior was no one is certain and legend has encrusted him as heavily as the Gothic crown he wore. It seems most likely that he was a Gothic chief who rallied the remnants of the Gothic army, and taught the wild mountaineers the old lesson of the Cilician Gates: that a few men on top with boulders can destroy an army below them. Legend says that three hundred Christians led by Pelayo slew something like a hundred and fifty thousand infidels, which is hardly possible; but it is history that Pelayo's successful action about 716, in the gorge at Covadonga, kept the Moors away from Asturias, which they never again tried to conquer. This victory was the beginning of the Reconquest and led to the birth of the first of the Christian kingdoms—the Kingdom of Asturias. Another tomb in the cave is that of Alfonso I of Asturias, who may have been a son-in-law of Pelayo and is said to have attacked the Moors in Galicia and to have taken the old Roman town of Lugo. There is no sight in Spain more stirring or more pleasing to the imagination than this cavern in which it may be said a nation was born.

On my way to Oviedo I passed through a little town called Cangas de Onis, where Pelayo is believed to have held his first court. The only notable object there today is a beautiful bridge which spans the river Sella in one great arc of stone. Then followed fifty miles of hill and valley, of apple orchards, of little stone towns where kneeling women were washing clothes in the river, of miners on bicycles, of Civil Guards, two by two, of cows walking beside their owners, of ox-carts, then the towers of a cathedral and Oviedo, the ancient capital of Asturias.

§ 5

The dish I would recommend to every visitor to Oviedo is *fabada*, which is the Asturian version of the *cocido*, or stew, to be found all over Spain and in as many varieties as there are regions. The principal ingredients of *fabada* are fat pork, haricot beans, highly seasoned sausage, and, of course, garlic. I thought it was one of the noblest of *cocidos*, a stew that Pelayo himself might have eaten after demolishing a few thousand infidels.

One wet Sunday afternoon I was eating this in a little restaurant at the back of a bar, marvelling at the amount of food which Spaniards can put away. At the next table sat a family of four who had consumed a great bowl of *fabada*, followed by trout and roast mutton, and finished off with basins of *fraises du bois*, each basin topped with about half a pound of whipped cream. A young man sitting near me leaned over and, with that excessive and adhesive friendliness which sets all English teeth on edge, said, 'You're British, I guess?' He was a puzzle to me. He looked Spanish, yet there was something foreign about him and he spoke with the strongest of American accents. He turned out to be a Puerto Rican who was studying medicine in Madrid. He seemed to be rather elderly for a medical student, and I asked why he had come all the way to Spain when he could have gone to the States.

'It's much cheaper over here,' he said. I forget how many fellow Puerto Ricans he told me were at Madrid University, but the number was considerable. Except for tourists and a man who was pointed out to me, I think in Seville, as a wealthy Mexican, he was the first living relic of Spain's old colonial empire I had met.

Oviedo on a wet Sunday afternoon was not looking its best. It is a large, well-planned commercial city, the centre of a big mining area, but there is little about it to remind the visitor of its tremendous past. When the Rev. Joseph Townsend visited the city in 1787 he seems to have been chiefly impressed by the amount of alms distributed by the Church, with the result, he said, that 'beggars, clothed in rags, and covered with vermin, swarm in every street'. He taxed his host, the bishop, with subsidizing idleness and asked if he did not think the Church's generosity did harm. 'Most undoubtedly,' was the reply, 'but it is the part of the magistrate to clear the streets of beggars: it is my duty to give alms to all that ask.' It is extraordinary to read Townsend's account of a city full of beggars, and one that obviously did not impress him with its riches, then to learn that, only twenty years after, Marshal Ney's troops sacked Oviedo *for three days*! One wonders what they found to sack in this place after the church plate had been looted.

I wandered round the gaunt cathedral of San Salvador, where I saw a delightful statue of St. Anthony the Great with his pig, which symbolized the material desires he conquered; and hung round him were little wax piglets offered by country people who had successfully prayed to the saint on behalf of their own pigs! This charming confusion of ideas pleased me for days.

I believed myself to be alone in the church until, mounting a flight of steps, I saw, as if painted by Rembrandt, an old woman in black sitting at a table. She was the guardian of one of Spain's most sacred treasures, the relics and jewels saved from the Moors in 711 and hidden in the Asturian mountains. I paid my money at the table and the old lady gave me a ticket. I walked to an illuminated grille behind which these remarkable objects are beautifully displayed.

The story is that when the Arabs invaded Spain the treasures were placed in a chest and smuggled out of Toledo. They were doubtless hidden in caves in the mountains and forgotten, for when the chest came to light three hundred years later no one knew what was in it. The legend is that some clerics who tried to find out were blinded by an extraordinary light; and it was not until Alfonso VI came to Oviedo with due ceremony, and after he and his knights had prayed and fasted for weeks, that the chest was opened on the third Sunday in Lent, in the year 1075. The astonished beholders saw a great collection of Gothic and Byzantine reliquaries containing objects which were recognized—it is not said how—as two fragments of the True Cross, drops of the Redeemer's Blood, shreds of His garments, crumbs from the Last Supper, relics of the Blessed Virgin, of the Twelve Apostles, and of saints whose Roman names proclaimed their antiquity. Alfonso ordered a chest of cedarwood, covered with embossed silver, to be made

300

to hold the most precious of the relics, and this chest is on view today. The side exhibited to the public shows the Saviour seated upon a throne enclosed in a frame held by four angels, while on each side, standing under a classical colonnade, are the Twelve Apostles; and running round this Christian chest is a Cufic inscription.

In the late afternoon someone told me that it was the feast day of St. Anthony of Padua and that a fête was being held a mile or so out of Oviedo. With visions of regional costumes and folk music, I hurried there to discover a scene that for dismalness could not have been equalled by an English church fête on a wet summer afternoon. A few hundred people were strolling about the sports field of a brewery, whose buildings could be seen in the background. A platform on barrels stood in the centre of the field, upon which the town band was playing modern dance music hideously relayed by loudspeakers. A few couples held each other clumsily and gyrated on the grass and many girls were dancing together. I observed an incident which could not have occurred in a less individualistic land. One of the bandsmen, recognizing his *novia* in the crowd, laid aside his cornet and descended to dance with her; having done so, he casually climbed back and resumed his performance. The conductor paid no attention to this desertion and indeed, I reflected, what could a conductor do in such a dilemma but stop the band and cause a scene?

There were coconut shies, skittles, and games of skill; old women sold roasted hazel-nuts, sweets, little cakes, and olives; there were trestle-tables stacked with soft drinks and lager beer; and every time rain began to fall there was a rush towards the belt of chestnut trees on the edge of the ground. Hearing the sound of an Asturian pipe, I saw two men approach, leading a heifer. One had a drum slung round his body which he beat with one hand, while he held the pipe to his lips with the other. His companion was selling raffle tickets at a peseta each. I bought one with pleasant thoughts of the international complications and the correspondence with the Ministry of Agriculture, and possibly the Treasury, if I happened to win the heifer and wished to take her home with me!

I came to the conclusion that industrialism had cast its sombre shadow over Oviedo, and also that these northern people are more phlegmatic than the southerners. It is inconceivable that any town in Andalusia could have put on such a lugubrious show.

I drove up the hill at the back of the city to see the two famous Gothic churches which are said to have been founded by Ramiro I in 858. They are small, solid buildings of great distinction and beauty, very weather-worn and eaten by lichen. They were built when Ethel-wulf was King in England and Alfred the Great was a small boy. I looked at them and thought of Spain and its Moors and England and its Vikings. While I was walking round them, I witnessed a most singular incident. A family party had spread out a rug on the grass near one of the churches and was having a picnic. There were seven women and two men. The men got up and walked round to the back of the church, where they began to abuse each other in the most violent terms. When one had exhausted his expletives, the other would begin. They would pretend to part, then suddenly swing round and become even more violent. Their dark eyes flashed, their hands were magnificent. The things an angry Spaniard can convey with his hands are incredible. They tore imaginary objects apart and flung them away; they lifted their closed fists and strangled handfuls of air; they crouched like fighting-cocks; they came close together with blazing eyes and hissed horrible words into each other's mouths. I have never seen two men reach such a stage of exasperation without coming to blows. The verbal lack of restraint and the physical restraint were remarkable to watch. The scene was made even stranger by the women, who were sitting just out of sight round the wall of the church, placidly gossiping and eating sandwiches.

§ 6

I was away from Oviedo early one morning and soon could have persuaded myself that I was travelling from Aberystwyth inland to Tregaron. There is, at times, a strange look of Wales about Asturias, then the resemblance fades away into hillsides covered with maize. A feature of the landscape are the little chalets with wooden balconies, lifted a few feet from the ground on stone mushrooms of the kind which support so many English barns. The walls of these chalets are pierced by slits and the slate roofs are often weighted down with stones. They seemed to me too small to be stores for wheat and I might have thought them dove-cotes if any birds had been perched on them. Having seen so many of these little buildings, all exactly the same, I stopped an old man and asked him what they were. He looked at me in courteous amazement. The ignorance of the foreigner is something to make the gods laugh!

'That is an *hórreo, señor,*' he replied.

'An *hórreo* is a *granero*?' I asked.

Yes, the *caballero* was perfectly right, but it is called an *hórreo* and it is used for storing maize. He explained to me how, when the corn-cobs had been cut, they were hung up to dry on the little wooden balconies, then they were packed away inside; and the *caballero* would notice that the *hórreos* stood on stone feet so that the *ratas* couldn't get at the maize. He added that batches of newly baked loaves were often stored in them until the next baking day. Big cheeses and fruit were also stored too. By this time we were becoming old friends and I was rapidly getting myself into the position when it would be impossible not to look inside an *hórreo* without offending the old man, so, thanking the *compañero* for his graciousness, for the clarity with which he had explained everything, and hoping that we might meet again, if not in this, in a better world, I shook hands with him and departed; and I thought that probably he then gave way to the mirth which he was too polite to show at the time.

I came to a village where whole families were out hay-making, and round them lay acres of maize not yet ripe enough for cutting. Now and again an ox-cart would lumber along squeaking an eclogue at every yard, the oxen swaying from side to side, wearing caps of sheepskin as if on their way to some Virgilian harvest. In one of these villages I noticed, as I was to notice all over Asturias, women wearing wooden sabots, or *zuecos*, raised two inches or so from the ground on little wooden knobs or feet.

One of the remarkable things about Spain is the change from one region to another. Suddenly the landscape alters. You become conscious that the geological formation is different, that the vegetation is no longer the same, and that the cottages look different; and nowhere is this more noticeable than upon the boundary between Asturias and Galicia. You become aware that you have left the high mountains behind and have entered a misty land of moors, low hills and bogs, where the white cottages take your mind to Ireland. As I travelled to the west on my way to Coruña I was reminded continually of Galway, and it was not only something in the greenness of the land, in the stone walls, in the wind-swept river estuaries, the little knolls and hills and the white stone cabins, but something also in the bearing and the glances of the people.

As in Asturias, the peasants of Galicia walked about the lanes and roads with their single cow, though here the cow was often accompanied by a sheep. Sometimes the cow was led by a man, sometimes by a woman, and the attendant sheep would come trotting along behind like Mary's little lamb. There were miles of maize and plenty of good grazing even beside the road. The barns of Galicia, the *hórreos*, were different from those of Asturias, and there was a point along the road where they ceased to be little chalets with wooden balconies and became oblong stone buildings pierced by many ventilation slits, each one surmounted by a cross. They looked like sepulchres, especially when you came across a group of four or five standing together inside a stone wall.

I came to a little village where a cattle fair was in progress. Peasants had tramped for miles with their horses, cows and pigs; and now they stood, a confused lowing, grunting and squealing mass of creatures, under the beautiful spear-headed leaves of great chestnut trees, while their owners leaned on their sticks and critically discussed the animals. I have so often seen the same scene in Ireland. Peasant women, their feet thrust into big wooden sabots, were holding the head-rope of a cow or a calf, and looking quite competent to drive the hardest of bargains. I sought in vain for that character seen always on market days in England, the prosperous farmer. The people at this fair all appeared to be smallholders, the one-cow men I had seen everywhere along the coast.

I saw many *zuecos* here, which, to the peasants of northern Spain, are what the gumboot is to the English farmer. They were beautifully made and I noticed that some peasants had specially large sizes, which they wore over their ordinary shoes like goloshes. I tried to buy a pair, but was told that they were made only to order. The maker of a *zueco* is not a shoemaker, who works in leather, but a wood-worker called a *zoqueiro*. But some makers evidently trespassed upon the cobblers' preserves for I saw many a *zueco* with leather sides, in fact a leather boot with a wooden sole.

I dipped down into a lovely river estuary. The tide was out and a fine stone bridge marched across a great expanse of wet sand.

I was looking forward to seeing Coruña, for no town in Spain has had more interesting associations with England. It was the port at which English pilgrims to St. James of Compostela disembarked after a voyage of four days from Plymouth or Bristol; Philip II embarked at Coruña for England to marry Mary Tudor; the Armada finally set sail from Coruña; and upon the ramparts Sir John Moore was buried 'darkly at dead of night'.

# Amazons of Spain

The town is built upon a narrow spit of land, in places only a few hundred yards wide, with a bay on each side of it. In winter it must be one of the wettest and windiest places on earth and the inhabitants try to protect themselves with glassed-in balconies. I was not prepared for such a large and lively little seaport, with tramcars, cinemas and smart hotels, and it looked particularly gay in the sunlight, with crowds filling the streets and sitting at cafés. Coruña had just recovered from its annual fête, an unusual one, in memory of a famous Amazon, María Pita, who, during Drake's reprisal for the Armada, fought side by side with her husband and slew the English standard-bearer and, turning the tide of battle, so they say, saved the old town. Spanish women have not only been political leaders—many still remember *La Pasionaria* during the Civil War—but they have often fought in battle and sometimes in men's clothes. There was the gallant María de Estrada—Mary of the Causeway—who, when Cortés was retreating from Mexico, was seen battling with sword and shield against the Aztecs; and there was Doña María de Gaucín, who left a nunnery to become a bull-fighter! It is recorded that when she had become a distinguished *torera* and had tasted fame, she suddenly gave it up and returned to the cloister; it is also said that the nuns were extremely proud of the fame her exploits cast upon their convent. Calderón was by no means extravagant when he made the heroine of his play, *Devoción de la Cruz*, a nun who left her convent to become a leader of bandits. I have sometimes suspected that Spanish women who would not hurt a fly could be persuaded to draw a sword and kill anyone who threatened anything they believed in; and the independence of women in Spain, who will call to you on a country road or laugh with you without the faintest trace of coquetry or the wish to make an impression as females, is something all strangers must notice. Infinitely more typical of Spanish women than the international picture of the *señorita* flirting behind a fan is the girl described by Blasco Ibáñez in his *Flor de Mayo*, who could meet 'audacious proposals with gestures of contempt, a pinch with a blow, and a stolen embrace with a superb kick which had more than once felled to the ground a big youth as strong and firm as the mast of his boat'. At any rate it seemed to me typically Spanish that a famous port like Coruña should once a year stop work and revere the memory of a woman who had slain Drake's standard-bearer.

I had luncheon in a small restaurant which was decorated from floor to ceiling with bull-ring posters. Ferocious animals of a size and pugnacity seen only on advertisements were charging in every direction, and still there was room for intimate photographs of famous *matadores*. There were groups showing a *cuadrilla* in costume ready to go into the ring, chins up, defiant and full of *españolismo*; and there were photographs of the moment of truth, and one when the moment had gone wrong and the *matador* had been impaled upon a horn; and another of the poor fellow lying in state covered with flowers and with candles burning round him. The *patrón*, who stood behind the counter and dished out the delicious *moules marinière*, looked like a retired *torero*, as I suppose he was. No doubt in Spain the 'little restaurant' figures in the dreams of the bull-fighter as the 'little pub' does in those of English boxers and other gladiators.

I went down to the bright and sparkling harbour and tried to imagine the sailing of the Armada. The general plan was that when the English fleet had been defeated, the Spanish ships were to cover the landing at Margate of a large Spanish army from the Netherlands. This was one of the worst kept secrets of the sixteenth century. For years soldiers had been discussing the plans in taverns all over Europe. Behind a smoke-screen of intrigue and bribery, and advised by a number of exiled English Catholics who had lost touch with the new Elizabethan spirit of England, Philip of Spain worked away at his desk in the Escorial like some overburdened civil servant who was in fear of losing his job. He arranged every little detail of the operation, and the preparations took years. The ships' biscuits rotted, the water supplies went bad, the ships' hulls became foul, and many a noble-looking galleon sprang a leak. Still Philip slaved away, poring over maps and plans, writing secret orders, interviewing ambassadors and spies, arranging for new supplies of biscuits, and even drawing up rules of conduct for the Spanish sailors which one writer has said would have befitted a convent school. They were not to swear or talk loosely, gamble or play cards. His general orders provided for the saying of prayers and Masses daily, and every one of the thirty thousand men in the Armada had to go to confession and receive absolution before the fleet sailed. Every man had to be made to realize that he was bound on a holy crusade against the enemies of God. In spite of this the Pope had been extremely difficult and had cannily refused to give a penny to the Armada until the Spanish army had established itself on English soil; even so he was apparently not willing for Philip to make himself King of England. If the Armada had been successful the candidate for Elizabeth's throne would have been Philip's daughter, Doña Clara

Eugenia, who would have based her claim to the throne upon her descent, through Philip, from John of Gaunt.

We are taught in school that everyone in Spain believed the Armada to be invincible, which is not so. Could we have been in Coruña in July, 1588, we might have heard the reluctant commander, the Duke of Medina Sidonia, talking in private about it. The poor man, who knew nothing of the sea or of great ventures and had confessed to the King that he was always seasick when out of sight of land, had been forced into command by the bureaucrat, who knew that the Duke had no initiative and would faithfully follow the orders drawn up in the Escorial. On the eve of sailing, the Duke wrote pathetically to Philip that

the fleet is now greatly inferior to the English; the crews are weakened by sickness, and numbers fall ill daily in consequence of bad food . . . The provisions are rotten, the water is stinking, and our stores will not last two months under the most favourable conditions. . . . Believe me, your Majesty, we are very weak; pray do not allow anyone to persuade you otherwise.

But Philip had worked out all the plans himself, and, above all, he believed that God was on his side. So on the 12th July, 1588, the people of Coruña crowded to the waterside to see the great ships with their gilded prows sail out to disaster, their long pennants flying in the wind and crucifixes upon the highest part of their bows. Far away in the Escorial the King knelt before the blessed sacrament, and all over Spain the church bells rang and a nation went down on its knees to beg God for victory.

One thing the great bureaucrat did not know, despite all his years of planning; that when the moment came the English Catholics, who had been represented to him as men longing to revolt, would draw their swords for England.

The old town lies upon a steep hill above the harbour, and narrow streets lead to the ramparts where Sir John Moore is buried. A marble urn lies in the shade of palm and beech trees and someone has tried to achieve a little English garden with daisies, fuchsias, geraniums and a privet hedge. There is a beautiful view from the ramparts over the waters which have seen so much coming and going. Children from the surrounding streets play round the grave of Sir John Moore, and nursemaids wheel perambulators into the little garden because it is shadier there than anywhere else in the old town. Sometimes an English tourist arrives, takes a photograph and audibly recites a few lines of the one poem of which every Englishman knows at least the opening lines. When Moore was being helped to his feet after the French cannon-ball had carried away his left shoulder, his sword became entangled in his legs and an A.D.C. began to unbuckle it. Moore stopped him. 'It is as well as it is,' he said. 'I had rather it should go out of the field with me.' His last words were to Captain Stanhope. 'Remember me to your sister.' This sister was Hester Stanhope and had Moore lived to marry her, as some believe, England would no doubt have lost one of her great eccentrics.

Before I left Coruña I went to the end of the headland to see the Roman lighthouse, known as the Tower of Hercules, which I thought one of the most interesting relics in Spain. It is more than three hundred feet high and is still used as a lighthouse. It is square, as the Pharos of Alexandria is believed to have been in its first stories, and the lower portion is Roman. During reconstruction years ago, the ramps were destroyed up which went pack animals loaded with wood for the beacon on the summit. I knocked and hammered at the door in the hope of seeing this building from the inside, but was unable to make anyone hear.

Forty miles away was Santiago de Compostela, a place I had always longed to see, the shrine of the patron saint of Spain, whose emblem was a scallop shell. Santiago is of course Santo Iago, or St. James, and some believe that Compostela is a corruption of *campus stellae*, a reference to the star which legend says shone above the tomb of the Apostle.

## § 7

I have often thought of the little scene I witnessed in the hotel at Santiago de Compostela within an hour of my arrival. Rain was falling with dull obstinacy and as I had no wish to go out in it, I wandered into the lounge of the hotel, which was empty. It was a large, bleak place and I was thinking how wonderful a cup of tea would be and that, alas! there was no substitute for it, when two old women entered and sat down. My first thought was that they had come in to sell something. They were peasants with baskets over their arms and they wore bunchy black skirts, ribbed woollen stockings which sagged at the ankles, and *alpargatas* black with rain. One had grey hair parted down the centre and both had skins seamed and brown like walnut shells. The hotel was built for tourists, bishops, priests, and ecclesiastical congresses, and these two old peasant women sitting bolt upright at

308

a little polished table gave a delightfully unusual touch to it. They sat placidly and patiently, their hands on their knees, never speaking a word.

In a few moments a smartly dressed middle-aged Spaniard, a man of the world and a successful one, entered the lounge and hurried towards the old women with outstretched arms. They rose to their feet with little cries of joy and the man embraced one and then the other, kissing them on their faces and on their hair. I looked on with interest and saw tears in the eyes of all three.

They edged their chairs nearer, and placing their heads together began to talk rapidly, and sometimes all three of them would talk at the same time. The man had a long story to tell, but first one and then the other old woman would put a hand on his knee and interrupt him, and he would turn to them in turn with some explanation. While he talked, they looked at him fascinated, watching his face and letting their eyes rove over it with that expression of wonder and worship which seems to come naturally to some of these old peasants.

Explanations over, the man put his hand in a breast pocket and produced two enormous wads of money. He gave one to each of the old women, who looked at the notes with the same bewildered expression, and held them as if they did not know what to do with them. There must have been several hundred pounds in each wad, and while the old women sat with their hands full of money the man went on talking, apparently brushing aside their thanks and answering the questions which they still put to him. I wondered where they would put all the money; surely not in their market baskets! At length the man rose and the old women lifted their black skirts and carefully stowed the notes away in the pockets of black petticoats. There were more kisses and hugs and they all walked out together.

It was a pleasing little scene and one charged with emotion. Was the man a son who had made good in America and had come home to shower riches upon the old folks? I could think of no better explanation. It was delightful to come across such a happy little meeting on a wet day in Santiago.

I went out in a mackintosh, impatient to see this famous city which shines so brightly in legend and in history, but in actuality appeared to me to be sadly like a medieval aquarium! It was not long before I was told that the annual rainfall is sixty-six inches. I reflected that a few hundred miles away the Castilians were gasping for breath, the Extremeños were watching the Guadiana trickle through perhaps two of the arches of the great bridge at Mérida, while Andalusia must be like a frying-pan. Thinking back over the ten days of almost incessant rain I had encountered westward from San Sebastián, I thought how wrong it is to call Spain a dry country; surely it is really one in which the rain is unfairly distributed.

Medieval Santiago began at the door of the hotel in a network of granite streets too narrow for traffic and lined with granite buildings of immense solidity, whose upper stories had been carried forward on round granite arches, thus forming arcades beneath which the inhabitants strolled dry-shod as if walking in endless cloisters. They reminded me of the Rows at Chester, but these colonnades at Santiago give the stranger the impression, according to his mood, that he is walking either in a vast cathedral or in some colossal wine cellar.

To the accompaniment of falling and gurgling water I strolled idly through the arcades, looking at the brightly lit shops and interested by the number of silversmiths which now, as in the Middle Ages, offer the pilgrim a selection of scallop shells, the sword of St. James, and St. James mounted on horseback with a drawn sword. It was once an offence, punished by excommunication, and forbidden by several papal bulls, to make and sell these objects outside the city; they were to be bought only by genuine pilgrims who had actually visited the shrine of St. James. I saw a silver statue of the saint on horseback and remembered that such a statue, if bought in Santiago, was once believed to cure ague and protect the owner from robbers. And how extraordinary it is to see that souvenirs similar to those taken home by pilgrims centuries ago are still made, but nowadays as cuff-links, tie-pins, and motor-car key chains. I bought a key chain with a pendant in the form of the sword of St. James, and another with a medallion of St. James on horseback, within a scallop shell, just the same designs which were popular seven and more centuries ago.

Santiago is a minute city, yet into this small space are crowded over forty churches, as well as convents and monasteries, hospitals, and a university; most of them old buildings any one of which would make the architectural reputation of an ordinary city. When I came to the cathedral I was filled with delight, even though it was raining and every statue, pinnacle and urn was dripping, and a sheet of grey was whipping across the west front. *El Obradoiro*, as this entrance is called, with its twin towers and the immense baroque gable between, rising in sophisticated ecstasy to a statue of St. James, seemed to me the most ornate building I had seen in Spain. I was in no mood to take my dripping garments inside, and so walked back under the massive colonnades.

The view from my bedroom window bore no relation at all to the medieval city I had just seen. I looked down upon a square where a great deal of the life of Santiago took place. Here beside some venerable looking petrol pumps was a 'bus station, where every now and then a coach would arrive with a fanfare of klaxons and another would depart with a salvo of backfires. There was the *Café Bar Galicia* near the station, and opposite stood the optimistic *Hotel Argentina*, with awnings, and chairs set out on the pavement. The crowds were converging upon a departing 'bus from every corner of the square, and the strangest bundles and parcels were roped to the top. Old peasants in their Sunday serge, girls in their best clothes—there seemed to be a vogue for cherry-red pullovers—priests and monks, women and children, all crowded round the entrance, for the Spaniard will not stand in a queue. I noticed how few gave way to the men of God, and that many priests let others go first and had to stand. I saw too for the first time the ability of Spanish women to carry heavy loads upon their heads. A neatly dressed girl came daintily along, remarkable only for the sewing-machine in its wooden case upon her head. No sooner had she lowered this to the ground than another young woman, dressed in a black frock and a white apron, appeared balancing upon her head in the most graceful manner a great chest as large as the Cid's; and when two strong men had lifted it to the ground, the girl smilingly thanked them and removed the little head-pad upon which she had balanced it.

At night I thought Santiago in its own stern granite way as romantic as Avila and Toledo. The light fell dramatically across the colonnades and shone on the wet pavements. I saw columns and arches in silhouette, touched with lamplight, and above them, towering into the night, a fantastic pinnacle encrusted with saints; and in some of the streets, silent as a church at midnight, the footfall of another night wanderer rang out almost ominously. If in Avila and Toledo one might expect to meet a knight in chain mail or armour, in Santiago it seemed one might surprise a band of Renaissance revellers, cloaked and masked, hurrying with a blazing cresset to some marble palace; or Romeo with a mandolin beneath his cloak hastening to serenade Juliet. Froude wrote somewhere that between us and the past lies a gulf that no pen can bridge, that our ancestors cannot come to us and that our imagination can but feebly penetrate to them. It is only, he said, in the aisles of a cathedral, as we gaze upon their silent figures sleeping on their tombs, that some faint conception floats before us of what these men were like when they were alive. Perhaps also we can hear an echo of those days in the sound of church bells, that peculiar creation of the medieval age, which falls upon the ear like the echo of a vanished world.

There are, however, times and places when those who have lived before seem almost to touch us on the shoulder, and midnight is the time and Santiago is one of the places. One can think of the credulity of the Middle Ages and their ignorance, but one can also think of the faith and the beauty of a world where at times earth and heaven seem almost to touch; and it is possible today to envy that age of faith, as in middle age we sometimes remember sadly the ecstasies and raptures of childhood. We know that among those who journeyed to Santiago were crooks and harlots, and cynical travellers who were just taking a holiday, but there were many good, sincere men and women, who laid at the feet of St. James 'faith's transcendent dower'.

I walked about Santiago until I came to a little park which I recognized as the Alameda. Here Borrow met a mortifying bore called Benedict Moll, who was looking for buried treasure. Then the last 'bus having exploded on its way, and believing that sleep might now be possible, I went up to bed in my room above the square. I thought that a long tradition of pilgrimage and discomfort had culminated in a bedside light that was out of order.

§ 8

The patron saint of Spain was James, the son of Zebedee, a member of the inner apostolic circle who, as we are told in *Acts*, was handed over to the Jews by Herod Agrippa and slain with a sword. It is possible to date this event by the subsequent death of Agrippa in A.D. 44. The Spanish legend is that for some years before his martyrdom St. James had preached the gospel in Spain, and after his death a band of faithful Spanish disciples took his remains by sea from Palestine back to Spain in a sarcophagus of marble. While passing the coast of Portugal the saint saved the life of a man who had been carried out to sea on a frightened horse, and man and horse emerged covered with scallop shells, which, it is said, ever after became the emblem of St. James. The remains of the saint were buried near the present Santiago and were lost and forgotten until the year 813, when angelic choirs and a bright star revealed them. Alfonso III of León built a little church over the tomb, which was later enlarged into a cathedral.

When the ferocious Moslem Vizier, al-Mansûr, carried his raids to the Atlantic coast in 997, the little town of Santiago had been in existence for nearly a century; and it is recorded that he burnt it to the ground and destroyed the church, but not the tomb of St. James. Early Christian scribes say that the terrible Moslem rode his horse into the church and tried to make it feed from the font, but the unfortunate animal 'burst asunder and died', which all animal lovers will agree was monstrously unfair. They say that the tomb of the apostle owed its preservation to an aged monk, who was praying there unmoved by the hideous commotion all round him. 'Who art thou and what does thou here?' asked al-Mansûr. 'I am a familiar of Sanct Yakob, and I am saying my prayers,' replied the old man. 'Pray on,' replied al-Mansûr, 'pray as much as you wish. No man shall molest you.' And he mounted a guard over the tomb to protect it, and the old monk, from his savage warriors.

Gibbon has noted the 'stupendous metamorphosis' which transformed a peaceful fisherman of the Sea of Galilee into a valorous knight who charged the Infidel at the head of Spanish chivalry; and it was indeed one of the most important events in the early history of Spain. That one of the chief Apostles should himself be taking a hand in driving the Infidel out of Spain, and cheering on the struggling little Christian kingdoms of the north, was in those days as important politically and strategically as the explosion of a new kind of hydrogen bomb today. The attention of Christian Europe was immediately attracted to a country slightly off the main road of Christendom; and the wise and clever monks of Cluny, who were the keepers of the Western conscience, soon saw that a European main road should be driven across Spain to Santiago, to be thronged with pilgrims from every country, who would form a living bridge with Europe. Henceforth Jerusalem, Rome and Santiago de Compostela, in that order, became the three most potent shrines in Christendom.

Of all the emblems which pilgrims brought home with them from Europe and the East, the cockle shell, or the scallop shell, of St. James, was by far the most common in England, so usual indeed that in later times people wrongly imagined it to be, as some still do, the emblem of pilgrimage in general. But to a man of the Middle Ages it meant only one thing, that the wearer had been to Santiago. No doubt Santiago became popular with English pilgrims because it was the most efficacious shrine within easy reach of England, and St. James had the reputation of being a quick and sympathetic worker who looked after his pilgrims well. The indulgences granted were almost as good as those from Rome and much cheaper. Ships reached Coruña from England in about four days, though sometimes it took longer. Those who wished to go the hard way for the good of their souls could, of course, always tramp across France and climb up through the Pyrenees to Roncesvalles and down along the 'French Road', as it was called, into Spain. But possibly one is wrong to think that the land journey was harder than the sea. At least there was pleasant company at the inns at night, food and wine on the way, and some of the pilgrims had their staves bored with holes so that they could play them like flutes, and so cheer themselves and their companions in the dark ravines and on bleak moorlands. Those who went by ship, so we learn from one who went that way in the reign of Henry VI, were often horribly seasick, were mocked and taunted by the sailors and a jest to the captain, and had to lie out on deck, often without straw. The summing up of these pilgrims was that

> *Men may leave all games*
> *That sail to Saint James.*

Still an enormous number did so, and to the truly devout this hardship was an essential part of the pilgrimage. A regular fleet of pilgrim ships left England for Coruña and their names and those of their masters, also their passenger accommodation, are known. The average carrying capacity of these ships was sixty, but the largest, the *Sancta Anna* of Bristol, owned by a man with the ominous name of Richard Stormy, could hold two hundred. In 1434 Henry VI granted permission for 2,433 pilgrims to go to Santiago and the regulations sound quite modern. They were forbidden to take gold out of the country or to reveal her secrets.

One of the most interesting pilgrims in this reign was William Wey, an original fellow of Eton College, who was always gadding about to various shrines. He went by sea to Santiago in March, 1456, in a ship called the *Mary White*, of Plymouth, and wrote an account of his journey, which has been preserved. He sailed in a convoy of several ships, one from Portsmouth, one from Bristol, another from Weymouth, and a fourth from Lymington. While he was waiting at Plymouth, he tells us that a man from Somerset came up to him and asked his advice. He said that, having made a vow to go to Santiago, he had got as far as Plymouth and began to feel so ill that he feared he might die. He told Wey he would much rather die with his family and asked whether he ought to return home or not. 'I advised him,' said Wey, 'that he should go to St. James, and that it would be better to die on the way than at home because of the indulgencies given to pilgrims to St. James.' The man, like most of those who ask advice, was displeased when it was given to him, because it did not fit in with his own opinion, and left immediately for home. Wey continued his voyage, and rather surprisingly heard the sequel to this story in Spain, when he saw the man in the Friars Church at Coruña. It appeared that having dragged himself painfully along the road to Somerset for some twenty miles, he staggered in great pain into an inn to spend the night, believing death to be near; but in the morning he had awakened completely cured of his pain and of the infirmity from which he had been suffering. He knew that this was the doing of St. James, and in gratitude he hurried back to Plymouth and resumed his pilgrimage.

When William Wey reached Santiago with the other English pilgrims, it was not surprising that on Trinity Sunday he should have found himself holding the poles of a canopy with three other Englishmen, who were named Austill, Gale and Palford; and on the way home he counted thirty-two English ships out of the eighty-four then in the harbour at Coruña. And among the English faces at Santiago we must not forget one that smiles merrily as she goes past, that indefatigable tourist, Chaucer's Wife of Bath, who, of course, had been 'to Galice at Saint Jame'.

Froissart, who describes in an admirable way the crisp, courteous and businesslike manner in which knightly affairs were usually managed in the Middle Ages, has an amusing account of John of Gaunt's invasion of Galicia; amusing because of the canny attitude of the unfortunate cities which, without armed garrisons, had to decide whether to close or open their gates to the foreigner who had suddenly appeared as their legitimate lord. The English army numbered fourteen hundred lances, thirteen hundred archers, numerous knights, and many ladies, including John of Gaunt's Spanish Duchess, Constance of Castile, the daughter of Pedro the Cruel. Her young daughter Catherine was there too, and also Philippa, the child of John of Gaunt by his first wife, Blanche of Lancaster. Having rested men and horses at Coruña for a month, the English marched on Santiago, which immediately closed its gates.

The marshal sent forward a herald to hear what the townsmen would say [writes Froissart]. The herald found at the barriers the captain of the guard, called Don Alfonso Sene, and said to him, 'A few paces hence is the marshal of my lord of Lancaster's army, who would wish to speak with you.' 'I am very agreeable to it; let him advance and I will parley with him.' The herald returned to the marshal with this answer.

The marshal left his army, with only twenty lances, and rode to the barriers, where he found the captain and some of the townsmen waiting. The marshal dismounted, with twelve others, among whom were the lord Basset and Sir William Farringdon, and addressed him as follows: 'Captain, and you men of St. Jago, the Duke and Duchess of Lancaster your queen (she being the eldest daughter of Don Pedro, your late king) send me to know how you mean to act: to open your gates and receive them as your legal sovereigns, as good subjects ought to do; or force me to assault your walls, and take your town by storm. But know, that if you suffer the place to be stormed, all within shall be put to the sword, that others may take warning.' The captain replied, 'We wish to follow the dictates of reason, and acquit ourselves loyally towards those to whom we owe obedience. We know well that the Duchess of Lancaster is daughter to Don Pedro of Castile; and if that king had reigned peaceably in Castile, she was heiress to his crown; but things are altered; for the whole kingdom turned to the obedience of his brother, King Henry, by the success of the battle of Monteil: we all swore fidelity to him; and he was acknowledged king as long as he lived: after his decease we all swore obedience to Don John, his son, who reigns at this moment. Tell us how those of Coruña acted; for it is impossible but that, during the month you lay before that place, some negotiations and treaties were concluded.' Sir Thomas Moreaux answered. 'You speak truly: we have had indeed negotiations with those of Coruña, otherwise we should not have marched hither, though that town is double the strength of yours. I will tell you what they have done: they have entered into a composition with us, by declaring they will act in the same manner as you do; but, if you force us to this assault, they will not follow that example. If Galicia surrender to my lord duke and his lady, they will surrender also; for which they have given us such pledges as are satisfactory.'

'Well,' replied the captain, 'we will agree to this: there are many large towns and cities in the realm: ride on, therefore, and leave us in peace; for we will act as they shall, and give you good security for our performing it.' 'Oh, this will never do,' said the marshal: 'such a treaty will by no means please the duke and duchess, for they are resolved to reside in this town, and keep their state as monarchs should in their own kingdoms. Answer me briefly what you mean to do: surrender, or have yourselves and town destroyed?' 'My lord,' said the captain, 'allow us a little time to consult together, and you shall be speedily answered.' 'I consent,' said the marshal.

The citizens then held a meeting and agreed to accept John of Gaunt and Constance as their king and queen, and soon the English army 'was advancing gaily in battle array towards the town of St. Jago', while another procession was seen coming from the town: 'clergy bearing relics, crosses and streamers, and crowds of men, women and children, and the principal inhabitants carrying the keys of the town which they presented on their knees with much seeming good will,' but, adds Froissart tartly, 'whether it was feigned or not, I cannot say.' There was much state and jollity and, we are told, strong drink 'of which the archers drank so much that they were for the greater part of their time in bed drunk; and very often by drinking too much new wine they had fevers, and in the morning such headaches as to prevent them from doing anything the remainder of the day; for it was now the vintage'.

Among the happier aspects of the Middle Ages was the pleasant belief that the sounds of war could be instantly silenced by the peal of royal wedding bells, and it was not long before Philippa, then the younger Catherine, were offered on the altar of politics. Like all women of the time, they had no choice at all in their husbands and were sold by their father as if they were horses, in return for hard cash and alliances. Philippa was fortunate, for John of Portugal was a handsome young man in his twenties, who looked every inch a king in the clothes he always wore, of white lined with crimson, with the green cross of St. George over his heart. At a great conference between the young King and John of Gaunt this marriage, eventually so fortunate for Portugal, was arranged, and Froissart tells how John of Gaunt broke the news to his wife when he returned to Santiago.

'Well, and what was done in regard to the marriage?' asked the duchess. 'I have given him one of my daughters.' 'Which?' asked the duchess. 'I offered him the choice of Catherine and Philippa; for which he thanked me much, and has fixed on Philippa.' 'He is in the right,' said the duchess, 'for my daughter Catherine is too young for him.'

The marriage of young Catherine of Lancaster took place later. She was married to the eight years old heir to Castile, who became Henry III. With this marriage John of Gaunt and Constance renounced their claim to Castile. John of Gaunt's first reaction, when the Castilian envoys arrived and proposed the marriage, was, 'I must have my expenses reimbursed, for I would have you know that my expedition to Castile has cost England and me upwards of five hundred thousand francs. I should like, therefore, to hear what you say of repayment.' No bank manager could have put it more bluntly! The final outcome of the deal was that the Duke and Duchess of Lancaster handed over their daughter and, of course, peace between England and Castile, in return for a yearly income of fifty thousand francs, for which several unfortunate Spanish towns were taxed; and in addition the Duchess received for her household expenses the sum of sixteen thousand francs. It was also stipulated that the young couple were to have Galicia settled upon them and, in imitation of the title of Prince and Princess of Wales, be given the title of Prince and Princess of the Asturias. The contracts were drawn up and solemnly signed, and so ended John of Gaunt's expedition into Spain.

Such royal contacts with Santiago naturally increased the number of English pilgrims to the shrine of St. James. Until recent times the memory of the great pilgrimage was unwittingly perpetuated by London children, who built in the streets little shrines decorated with oyster and cockle shells. I well remember seeing them in London round about St. James's Day, and I recollect the shrill cry, 'Please remember the grotto', with which passers-by were invited to contribute a penny. These displays were, of course, a memory of the street shrines of pre-Reformation England, which were decked out with scallop shells at that time of year to remind those who were unable to go to Spain to pay their devotions to St. James.

## §9

I was surprised to find that a man I had met only once in Madrid had taken the trouble to write to a friend in Santiago, asking him to look me up. If I had suggested this, probably nothing would have happened. It seems to me that Spaniards often act from impulse, just as they have the feminine capacity for arguing, not with reason, but emotionally, giving one the helpless feeling that comes over a man who is trying to argue with an angry woman. The man who was waiting for me in the hotel turned out to be an agreeable companion. We walked out together into a Santiago I had not yet seen. The sun was shining! How wonderful the old town looked with the light touching the dark colonnades and warming the tawny towers and the honey-coloured walls.

'You Galicians remind me of the Irish,' I said.

'Why not?' he replied. 'We are Celts, like the Irish.'

I asked him to tell me a Galician ghost story, and he spoke of the *Santa Compaña*—the Holy Company. He said that when you are travelling at night in Galicia, you may in certain marshy places see flickering lights which dart here and there over the mournful landscape. You must now be very careful. It may be that you will find an invisible presence trying to place a lighted candle in your hand, and should you open your hand and accept it, you are lost. You have joined the Holy Company of souls condemned to wander about Purgatory with lighted candles until they can thrust their candle into the hand of some unsuspecting stranger. So it can happen that you may simply disappear from life and spend an eternity trying to get rid of your candle, haunting the moorlands and the waste places where the ghostly lights flicker, until at last you can lure some human being into the Holy Company and escape yourself!

'Yes,' I said, 'that would pass in Galway.'

He added that in Galicia the plight of those in Purgatory was always present in the mind, and that the peasants believed these souls became visible in the dark winter as a long procession of people with flames at their feet and lights upon their heads. You could always tell when the *Santa Compaña* had passed by the strong smell of candlegrease and burnt olive oil.

'Although I am not in any way superstitious,' he said, 'when I have wanted to be awakened at an unusual hour and have no alarm clock with me, I have often prayed for a soul whose expiation was near its end—for one, let us say, who needed just one Paternoster to release him—and I have never found it to fail. I have always been awakened when I wanted to be, and, as I say, I am the least superstitious of men.'

He agreed, however, that most of the peasants were deeply superstitious and firm believers in magic.

'One night some years ago,' he told me, 'I was travelling towards the Puebla del Caramiñal in my car. It was late in August and the moon was full. There is a stone bridge before you get there, and I noticed some people standing about and thought there must have been an accident, for, as I approached, they held up their hands and stopped me. They were four young girls and they had with them a boy tightly bound with cords and handkerchiefs which they begged me to untie. I was very puzzled and asked why. They said the boy was dumb, and it was believed if four girls took him to the bridge when the moon was full, and bound him, and asked the first stranger who passed to untie him, he would regain his speech. Of course I did what they asked.

When I made inquiries, I found that this was an old superstition in those parts and that the girls must be virgins.'

By this time we were standing in front of the superb west front of the cathedral, where Don Iñigo drew my attention to the great bell towers; in one the bells could be seen against the sky, but the other was closed and contained the wooden gong or clapper, the *carraca*, which was used in Holy Week when all the bells were stilled.

'It is a strange sound,' he said, 'and when the French heard it they took to their heels, thinking it was the noise of approaching peasants in their wooden *zuecos!*'

We walked round the cathedral, where I saw a row of silversmiths' workshops and forges in which silver scallop shells and other objects were being cast or beaten out with hammers; and again I thought that in Spain, where everyone thinks constantly of death, nothing ever seems to expire. These forges have probably been in the same place since the eleventh century, or maybe earlier. I bought a beautiful little scallop shell which, had it been discovered in a medieval grave, would have gone straight into a museum.

I thought the interior of the cathedral the greatest surprise in Santiago. I had fully expected to enter a tremendous piece of baroquerie, but instead six hundred years fell away at the door and I entered a magnificent Romanesque cathedral which might have been a relative of Durham. Like most Spanish churches it was dark and gloomy, and the round, headed arches rose towards a roof some seventy feet above the nave; and this was the very church upon which the eyes of our ancestors rested when they made the pilgrimage to 'Galice'. Masses were being said at side chapels, where a few kneeling figures were silhouetted against the light of candles, and there was no sound but the murmur of the priest at the altar and the sudden ring of a sanctus bell. The transepts were immense, and my friend pointed out the machinery and the chains in the roof used in working the giant censer, *el botafumeiro*, which upon feast days is swung from transept to transept. Before us, in the *capilla mayor*, and above the high altar, we saw the silver-covered statue of St. James, seated upon a throne, with a pilgrim's staff in his hand.

A stairway behind the altar led up to the statue and descended on the opposite side. I mounted these steps and found myself behind the statue, gazing down the nave of the church; and it was a curious feeling to stand there, with my hands upon the silver cape of St. James and to see the scallop shell at his back, worn thin and smooth by the kisses of countless pilgrims. Beneath the high altar is a lighted crypt in which you can see the silver casket which is said to hold the bones of the Apostle.

In one of the transepts we found a fine statue of the saint on horseback, looking like St. George, but instead of a dragon he was slaying a Moor. 'When Franco came here with his Moroccan troops,' said my friend dryly, 'we thought it only polite to cover up this statue of our patron saint!'

We went to the sacristy to see the six-foot-high *botafumeiro*, which is an extraordinary object. It is used only on great feast days and in Holy Year, which is held whenever St. James's Day, July 25th, falls on a Sunday. The censer is then carried to the crossing of the transepts and attached to the chains which hang from the roof; then quite a large charcoal fire is lighted inside it, and incense added. It takes seven men to swing and control it once it is in motion. With every pull on the chains it rises higher and higher, swinging from the north to the south transept and back again, the charcoal glowing and clouds of incense puffing from it whenever it pauses in mid-air before it begins its return flight. Eventually it is slowed down, until the moment arrives when the seven men fling themselves on it and bring it to rest.

'It comes whistling through the air like a bomb!' said my friend. 'You should see the way the people run and make a path for it!'

There have been accidents when *el botafumeiro* has got out of control and has crashed out into the plaza outside, but I believe no one has ever been killed by it. This happened when Catherine of Aragon visited Santiago on her way to Coruña, where she embarked for England. It was a bad omen.

My companion had an amusing habit, whenever we talked about anything legendary, of raising his shoulders until his neck disappeared, and of holding out his hands, with the palms upward, in an almost oriental gesture, expressing helpless resignation. 'I do not know,' he would say, 'but it is the tradition.' He never turned anything down, but said it was a picturesque story, or a legend, or a parable. It was not the first time I had met this point of view in Spain, and I wondered whether tradition was taking the place of faith. It was difficult to discuss such questions. When discussing religious matters with Spaniards I often felt that the shade of the Inquisition was hovering above us.

We paid a visit to the great beauty of the cathedral, the *pórtico de la Gloria*, which a certain Master Matthew finished in the year 1188, after twenty years of work. G. E. Street called it 'one of the great glories of Christian art'; and I stood amazed by the genius

321

of the sculptor who populated these arches with something like a hundred and thirty figures of angels, apostles and saints, grouped by the hand of a master and carved with a devotion which later ages could only try to imitate. My friend took me round to the back of the door, where he pointed out a humble kneeling figure which, he said, tradition claims as that of Master Matthew himself. The great Henry II was King of England when Matthew began his work. This was the same year, by the way, that a little girl, the Princess Eleanor of England, came to Spain to marry Alfonso VIII, and she must have seen this great work when it had just been started. When Master Matthew laid aside his chisel the whole of Christendom had gone into mourning for the loss of the Latin Kingdom of Jerusalem; and Richard the Lion Heart, brother of the young Queen of Spain, was arming for the crusade.

# Chapter X

*The road of Sir John Moore's retreat—the beauties of León—Valladolid
—the English College—Golden Salamanca—a Congress of Poets—
Barcelona—dancing the Sardana—the Black Virgin of Montserrat*

§ 1

A FAIR proportion of Santiago's annual rain must have fallen while
I was there, but the day of my departure was brilliantly fine and
almost warm. Don Iñigo came to see me off, and gave me a letter to a
friend of his in Valladolid whose Christian name could not have been
more Christian. It was Jesús.

The road led into green and hilly country where tall, kingly men
strode beside ox-carts with long sticks in their hands. The green
maize shone in the fields after the recent rain, a strange, foreign-looking
crop that took the mind back to Cortés and Pizarro, who had no idea
that the true wealth of the Americas was not gold, but the potato and
maize, tobacco and cocoa. In the exchange of vegetation America did
very well, receiving wheat and other cereals she had never known
before. The story of the first American wheat is a pleasant one. It is
that Pizarro's sister-in-law, a keen gardener named Inés Muñez, was
one day winnowing a barrel of rice that had come from Spain. Noticing
a few grains of wheat which had fallen in by mistake, she picked them
out and planted them in flower-pots with as much solicitude as though
she were planting shoots of mignonette or basil; and in time the wheat
harvests of Peru could be traced to the flower-pots of Inés Muñez.
This is as pretty a story as that of the Sultan who planted out pomegranate seeds which became the parents of all the pomegranates in
Spain.

My road now led out of Galicia back into Castile. How many different Spains I had seen; a Spain like Switzerland, a Spain like Ireland,
a Spain like Africa; and of them all I thought Galician Spain the most
remarkable and possibly the most comprehensible. The transient visitor
is much at the mercy of chance encounters and is always liable to draw
wrong conclusions from them; therefore it may have been just luck
that threw in my way Gallegos who were prompt and businesslike and

323

left upon me an impression of alertness and liveliness. I had the feeling that this north-western corner of Spain was still on the main routes of the world. Like Ireland, Galicia has a long tradition of overseas emigration. Just as you are never surprised to see a photograph of the Statue of Liberty in a cabin in Connemara, so you would not be surprised to see a picture of Mexico City or Buenos Aires in any little cottage in Galicia. It is often assumed that the Celt emigrates because he is poor and his homeland is stony and bleak, but there is more in it than that; the Celt is born with restless feet and a poetic longing for something over the horizon. There is a melancholy about Galicia, too—*morriña* they call it—just as there is in Ireland, which either roots a man to the soil in a kind of hopeless spell or else drives him off to the other end of the world. But with all this other-worldliness the Gallego is an astute person and is often a shrewd politician. Franco is a Gallego, and one often hears people say of him, 'He's a canny Gallego—the only one who got the better of Hitler!' It is a fact that after arguing with Franco for nine hours, Hitler said to Mussolini: 'Rather than go through that again, I would prefer to have three or four teeth taken out.' One also hears people ask, 'What will Franco do now?', and the reply is invariably, 'Nothing. He's a Gallego!'

There was something about the mist and the rain of Galicia, the white cottages, the little Gothic churches, the people, gay and full of *morriña* by turns, that appealed to me enormously and touched my heart as Andalusia, warm and romantic though it is, could never do.

I crossed the most beautiful river I had seen in Spain, the Miño, as wide and clear and splendid as the Wye, and, climbing a steep hill, I saw the capital of Galicia, Lugo, standing behind a Roman wall. Is there a finer one in the world? It is a mile and a quarter long and nearly forty feet high. Parts of it are twenty feet thick, and though it has been polled, that is to say the tops of the eighty-five semi-circular bastions have been pulled down to the general level of the wall, this does not detract from its impressive majesty; indeed I thought it as fine a sight as Avila.

I found a restaurant where they gave me the Galician soup, *caldo*, and an omelette full of shrimps and mushrooms. At a table in the corner sat a family with a fat little *niño* of about eight who had never been corrected. His individuality was intact and it was in great form that afternoon. He was pushing his food about with a fork and spoon, begging for food from his parents' plates, which they obediently gave him, and attracting the attention of people at neighbouring tables. A young couple at the next table were enchanted by the child and, spotting them instantly as the perfect stage for his exhibitionism, he began to make overtures to them, and at last, struggling down from his chair, went across to their table, to the amusement of his parents and the delight of the strangers, who fed him with ice cream. Are young Spaniards never spanked? I wondered.

I walked to the cathedral to see Our Lady of the Large Eyes— *Nuestra Señora de los Ojos Grandes*—of which I had heard so much from devout Spaniards. The church, a large and beautiful one, has the rare distinction of having the Host always *manifestado*, or exposed, upon the high altar, with two priests in perpetual vigil. As the high altar is always occupied by the Sacrament, the problem of enshrining the famous Virgin of the Large Eyes was solved by building a circular lady chapel behind the *capilla mayor*. As I approached this dark end of the church, I saw that two of the oldest and frailest women imaginable were encircling the altar upon their knees. They were dressed in black, their faces were hidden by the black church veils they wore, and they clasped their old parchment hands and hobbled round one behind the other. They would disappear behind the altar and come into view again, muttering their prayers. Sometimes one would stop in front of the Virgin for several minutes and gaze up towards the statue, delaying the other, who would wait patiently, then both would hobble round again. They had evidently vowed to encircle the Virgin so many times on their knees, and one old woman, who finished first, rose and went away, giving me a glimpse of a worn face transfigured by faith.

The Virgin of the Large Eyes stands above the altar, gently illuminated in a grotto formed by hundreds of tumbling, frisking baroque cupids. She is a tall, standing figure of painted wood and different from any I had seen in Spain. She wears a long gown that descends to her feet and a cape almost as long falls from her shoulders. Her head-veil, worn under a huge gilt crown, does not, as usual in Spanish Virgins, conceal the line of her cheeks and her neck. Two coils of hair lie on each side of her face, she wears large ear-rings and a necklace, and her face has a rigid, fixed expression as her eyes seem to follow you wherever you go.

When I left the cathedral and was walking towards the Roman wall, which is just a few paces away from the west door, I paused to look at a wonderful collection of household pottery of the kind so often seen spread upon a Spanish pavement; and the old woman who came forward in the hope of selling me a casserole or a *jarro* was one of the two who had been hobbling round the shrine of the Virgin.

The journey I now took from Lugo to León I shall always remember as the most beautiful but the most exhausting I made in Spain; and I would never do it again, or advise anyone else to do it, between late afternoon and nightfall. As the crow flies, it was only about a hundred and twenty miles, but it was a mountain journey over tremendous gradients, made more hair-raising by the Spanish habit of cutting corners at sixty miles an hour. I never knew what kind of an opponent I might meet at a bend in the road, or what desperate *suerte* I might be obliged to make in order to avoid him. Fortunately there were few cars once I left the immediate neighbourhood of Lugo, but there were many *bravos camiones* and some extremely *bravos* autobuses on the down gradient, so that I could never relax for a moment. Also there was a great deal of *obras públicas* going on at all the critical corners, with steam rollers and red flags and gangs of navvies who had never heard of a pneumatic drill and were manfully attacking the sides of mountains with picks and spades.

But what a heavenly afternoon it was! I had been actually chilly in Santiago and now with every mile a little more summer seemed to come into the air. The glorious river, the Miño, flowed in the valley at my right hand, reminding me more than ever of the Wye. Cows stood in the lush green meadows and sometimes I caught sight of a fortunate fisherman. The fields were divided by low walls of slate and stone as in Cumberland and parts of Ireland, and the grey stone cottages were roofed with stone beautifully weathered and tinted with moss and lichen. On every side I saw acres of kale and maize. There were foxgloves beside the road and blackberry bushes. Here, it seemed, the legend of poster Spain had finally expired.

Then I left the lovely valley of the Miño and mounted into a lonely wilderness which was the southern end of the great Cordillera Cantábrica, whose northern heights I had skirted on my way to Covadonga. I went up into mountain gorges and then down again, and I thought this one of the loneliest roads I had seen in Spain. I came across miles of heather and oddly shaped patches of cultivated land tilted so steeply against the sides of the mountains that I wondered how they could ever have been ploughed; they could certainly be reaped only with a sickle.

In this awful solitude my thoughts turned to an unhappy chapter in the history of the British army, the retreat of Sir John Moore to Coruña; for this was the appalling road taken by his armies while rain fell in torrents and snow lay on some of the higher parts. I passed through Puerto de Piedrafita, the boundary between Galicia and León, at the summit of the *sierra*, where the retreating army abandoned £25,000, which was rolled down the mountain-side in barrels. This road in December, in wind, rain and snow, with the French cavalry occasionally catching up on groups of stragglers and slashing right and left with their sabres, must have been terrible. Discipline seems to have cracked. The British soldiers thought their Spanish allies had let them down; stragglers pillaged the wine vaults in villages and towns as they passed through; the Spanish drivers deserted the transport mules and the ox-carts, and, as the animals did not understand English words of command, stores had to be left on the road. At Nogales, which I passed high up in the mountains, the bodies of two soldiers and a Spanish woman, who had drunk themselves to death, were seen lying frozen stiff in the snow. To travel this road even on a summer's day is to wonder how Sir John Moore's army ever got to Coruña at all, and the landscape explains why Napoleon's more numerous armies did not surround it or cut it off. Though some stragglers fell by the wayside, or rather by the wayside taverns, the French did not capture one British standard or gun, and the rearguards held them off all the time and even inflicted damage on their cavalry. Moore was greatly loved by the men whom he commanded, and the Highlanders who carried him dying in a blanket at Coruña did so with tears streaming down their faces. I think that if only Moore had had a great love affair he might have occupied a much higher place in the affections of a nation with whom, as Philip Guedella wisely noted, 'one sound, romantic defeat goes twice as far as three vulgar victories'.

I came down to the beautiful little village of Vega de Valcarel, with great walnut trees everywhere, herds of goats, and another fine river. What a place to stay and fish and learn Spanish! Then up once more into the mountains, the road turning and twisting and hardly straight for more than twenty yards at a stretch, and at length Ponferrada in the light of the sunset, with a noble castle of the Knights Templars rising above its cobbled streets.

Here was another change of scenery as dramatic as any in Spain. Here were vines and poplars, and a great plain whose soil was brick red. Coal-miners passed riding bicycles. Then came a stretch of bleak moorland. Although it was now nearly dark, the peasants were still at work in the hayfields and the loaded ox-carts trundled slowly along on their way to villages. It was dark when I came into Astorga, where

I stopped to drink a *café con leche* and found afterwards I should have ordered chocolate, which is a speciality here. It was a queer little moorland town, with an arcaded plaza and an old town hall whose clock is struck by two mechnical figures, a Maragato and a Maragata, wearing the baggy trousers and the silver trinkets which Ford noted over a century ago, but now seen no longer. These mysterious people still exist, but no one knows their origin, though some believe they are descended from the Berbers.

It was now dark and I began to repent my resolve to get to León that night, for the road led over a gaunt and fearful moor that I felt rather than saw. I came into a dark village where the headlights picked out young people solemnly engaged in their evening *paseo*, the girls in groups of threes and fours, the boys together, just as if they were in a city. It is unusual for a Spanish village to have no lights and I wondered whether the electricity had failed. Then I dipped down towards the lights of Veguellina and crossed a bridge over the Orbigo. This was the scene of a ridiculous exploit in 1434, known as the *paso honroso*, when a Don Quixote in real life, wearing an iron chain round his neck, a token of his enslavement to his loved one, held the bridge with nine companions and challenged to mortal combat every passing knight who refused to agree that the enslaved knight's lady was the most beautiful in the world. It is odd to think that such a piece of chivalric archaism, though common in the thirteenth century, could take place only eighty-five years before the discovery of America. But it is odder still that this knight errant should have been taken seriously, with the result, we are told, that during the thirty days he and his friends held the bridge no fewer than seven hundred and twenty-seven contests took place, in the course of which one knight was killed and several were wounded. Thus the ways of the thirteenth century lingered on in Spain into the fifteenth; indeed as recently as the seventeenth century a Sevillian don challenged to combat any gentleman who doubted the Immaculate Conception.

At last I saw the lights of León, and it was only when I was signing those hotel papers which must eventually light the fires of police stations all over Spain, that I knew how tired I was. One of the blessings of the preposterous hours kept in Spain is that when you arrive at eleven o'clock, no reluctant waiter tells you that, although the kitchen staff have 'gone off', he might possibly be able to get you a cheese sandwich; on the contrary, you find the dining-room in full swing and the waiter shows you to a table with a bow and a smile.

I was too tired to sleep. When eventually I did lose consciousness my dreams were of Sir John Moore and his stragglers, of Suero de Quiñones holding the bridge at Veguellina, and of two old women in black hobbling round on their knees. I awoke shortly after five and looked out of the window. León was actually silent and asleep. The big café in the plaza was closed but still illuminated, and the 'chairs had been taken inside and packed upside down on the tables. I looked to the left, where I saw an unforgettable sight. The towers of León Cathedral rose against the night sky, a sky just beginning to pale slightly, and above them shone Venus, Jupiter, and one of the giants, I think Aldebaran, all close together, burning like three great lamps in the dawn.

§ 2

The story goes that God once summoned the patron saints of Europe before Him and offered to grant whatever virtues they asked for their respective countries. St. James asked that Spaniards should possess greater wit and beauty than any other nation on earth and this was granted. But, so great was St. James's love for Spain, that he could not resist trying to get a little more, and he added, 'and the best government on earth'. This angered the Almighty, who sprang from His throne and said: 'No! Spain shall never have any government at all!'

Nevertheless Spain can boast more capital cities than any other country in Europe—Oviedo, León, Burgos, Toledo, Seville and Valladolid have all at various times been the seat of court and government. This gives to Spanish history a feeling of movement and an atmosphere of campaigning, as of army headquarters moving on during an advance, which is more or less what happened. León's regal splendour occurred early in history, when the Christian kingdoms felt bold enough to descend from the mountains and move a little to the south. Alas! the terrible al-Mansûr, who destroyed Santiago, made León a ruin and his muezzins gave the call to the prayer from a minaret of corpses. But with the vitality of a Roman legionary camp—León's name is a memory of *Legio Septima*—the old town rose from its ashes and bravely became a capital again. That was in 1001, about the time that, in England, Ethelred the Unready was planning his massacre of the Danes.

Except for a few buildings, I thought the city uninteresting and formless. As with Oviedo, its grandeur is in a past too remote to have left many visible traces, and, unlike Burgos, it does not immediately impress itself upon the eye and the mind. Five minutes' walk from the hotel took me to the cathedral, where I admired the richly carved west doors and a version of the Last Trump which must have worried many a medieval rustic. Angels and devils are seen busily engaged among the tombs, sorting out the good from the bad. The good stand on the left, nicely dressed and obviously well pleased with themselves, and a boy plays tunes on a portable organ. The unredeemed, stark naked, are being hauled out of their tombs by fiends who give them a fireman's lift or toss them to voracious devils who, unable to wait, devour them head first. A delightful touch is the central figure, a young and kingly person who, gracefully, as if there could be no doubt about it, has strolled over to join the saved, but an angel has stopped him and, with the smiling and deferential air of an usher at a wedding, is clearly saying: 'The other side, sir, if you please.'

I passed through the west door—into France! This cathedral of León is one of the surprises of Spain. I was in a conservatory of medieval stained glass, whose architects had used as little stone as possible, with the object of using as much glass. The effect, after the dark cathedrals of Spain, is bewildering. Everywhere there are immense windows and one stands amazed by the richness and beauty of the colour. All the wonderful tints of genuine old church glass are here, the cobalt blues, the copper greens, the manganese purples, the yellows, and the lovely ruby reds and red-browns. I was enchanted by this blaze of glory. I wondered how it happened that León had decided to build a cathedral so unlike anything else in Spain, a church that instead of keeping out the light, as most Spanish churches do, actually invites it. How the architects, who had been brought up in the tradition of St. Denis, of Chartres and Rheims, must have longed for the moment when they could see the effect of the strong Spanish sunlight on the glass. The sun was shining when I was there, showering this mosaic of colour all over the church. You could hold out your hand and see your fingers stained purple and yellow and red. It is the gayest church in Spain and, in its own way, the most beautiful. It is as if music is playing all the time. There are wonderful things in this cathedral, ancient tombs, sculpture and so forth, but I had eyes only for this exquisite coloured glass.

I thought, as I have done so often in Spain, that one of the chief functions of a medieval church was to instruct the illiterate and to give them pictures which they could understand, to show them the story of the Gospels, and the legends of the saints, which were the novels of the medieval world. What more glorious picture-book could there be than this church, whose illustrations are illuminated by God's own light?

On the way out I studied again the Last Judgement and noticed that the wicked were also being boiled as well as being eaten alive. Villon was thinking of a scene like this when he put into the mouth of his mother that touching little poem which begins, 'Femme je suis pourette et encienne'.

> *A woman old and poor am I,*
> *Who knows nothing, I could never read,*
> *I see in my parish church*
> *Paradise painted, where are harps and lutes,*
> *And a hell where the damned are boiled.*
> *The one frightens me, the other brings joy and mirth.*

I saw many other things in León. There is a stretch of Roman wall striding on into the distance as boldly as at Lugo. I saw the crypt of St. Isidore, covered with Byzantine frescoes, where the early kings and queens of León sleep in anonymous tombs, for the Napoleonic French had been there. And upon the high altar in the same church I saw a silver urn that held the bones of the great and wise St. Isidore of Seville, which were exhumed with the permission of the Moslem king al-Mu'tamid, who, after delivering a respectful speech of farewell, despatched them to the Christian north.

The road to Valladolid stretched in sunlight across the khaki plain. Gone now were the green hills of Galicia, the crystal streams tumbling from the mountains, the dark, deep rivers. Here the heat dominated the waterless landscape. Rivers trickled among boulders beneath impressive bridges. On the rim of the sky the villages, dust-coloured like the plain, stood clear and sharp in their own shadows.

## § 3

Don Jésus, to whom I had an introduction, turned out to be one of those fantastically occupied Spaniards with a dozen jobs, yet ready to drop them all at a moment's notice as if time were of no account. All afternoon we had wandered round Valladolid, which I thought a fascinating but rather shapeless city, fascinating for what it had been rather than for what it is. We had seen the building where Ferdinand and Isabel were married, where Philip II was born, the museum of polychrome sculpture, and the massive, unfinished cathedral in whose sacristy I discovered two old London clocks, one made by David Samuel of Goodmans Fields and the other by 'Higgs y Diego Evans' of Sweeting's Alley. Now it was nine o'clock and almost dinner-time. The streets were thronged. The air was almost as hot and breathless as that of Madrid. Two coloured fountains lifted their jets into the night, and as we strolled slowly with the *paseo* we lifted our hats gravely every two or three yards to the friends of Don Jésus.

We settled in the corner of a little Basque restaurant. My friend was a great admirer of Valladolid, which he considered ought to have been the capital of Spain. There was no city to touch it. Holy Week in Seville! Pooh; it was nothing. It was a mockery organized for tourists. If you really wanted to see Holy Week, you must come to Valladolid. There you would see something indeed! The *pasos* were the finest in Spain. You would see the Scourging of Christ by Gregorio Fernández, the Elevation of the Cross by Francisco de Rincón, the Crucifixion by Francisco de la Maza, and the famous Virgin of the Anguish, with five daggers in her heart, by Juan de Juni; and as these came slowly along in the darkness, lit only by a thousand candles, then, *señor*, you have seen Holy Week!

He brought out his pocket-book and produced a photograph of a *paso* surrounded by the hooded members of a confraternity. He pointed to one little figure in a line of identical inquisitors, all wearing the same white robes and black pointed hoods, and said proudly:

'This is myself.'

His *cofradía* was one of the most exclusive in the city, he explained. Boys were entered for it in infancy much as we enter children for public schools. I looked at the little man with new interest, thinking how strange that for a week every year he turned himself into a sinister medieval figure which even his family would be unable to recognize. He told me he had fought for the Nationalists and had been captured by the Reds in Madrid and flung into prison. His captors threw dice for the lives of prisoners and called them out without warning to face a firing-squad. The fearful things he had seen in Madrid! He would tell me over the coffee in order not to spoil my appetite. Is anything more terrible than civil war? he asked. He had had a brother, to whom he was devoted, on the Republican side. He had been shot by the Nationalists. His brother-in-law had also been a Republican and was now in France. 'Perhaps when the King comes back there will be an armistice for political exiles,' he said. 'Who can say? Let us hope so.'

After dinner he told me about the horrors. I had heard the same things about the other side. A stranger cannot judge such things.

'You wish a king to return?'

'It is the great hope of my country.'

I wondered whether the Spaniards at the next table would have agreed. We parted at the corner of a street and he went off into the darkness and the impenetrable mystery of his private life. My way back to the hotel lay through the Plaza Mayor, which, though it was not yet midnight, was practically deserted. I glanced round it with interest, for it was here that Philip II inaugurated his reign by attending a great *auto-de-fe*, the famous occasion when he is said to have replied to a poor wretch who appealed to him as he was led past to the stake, 'If my son were a heretic like you, I would gladly carry the wood to burn him.'

There is a tendency today to minimize the horror of the Inquisition, which I think strange in a generation that remembers the Gestapo and fought to prevent the spread of such tyranny. The methods of modern dictatorships, consciously or unconsciously, owe much to those of the Holy Office: the spies, the secret informers, the careless, fatal word, the unsuspecting victim, the sudden swoop of the Inquisition, often at dead of night, the ransacking of rooms, the disappearance of the accused and, if he proved obdurate, his torture and the persecution of his family. All this we have seen again in our own day. Even if we judge the Inquisition against its historical background and admit that its tortures were the normal methods in use at the time, it must still appear one of the most monstrous rackets in history. Its immense wealth was derived from the confiscated property of its victims. It had no other source of income. It would have gone bankrupt without prisoners, and the more people it condemned the richer it became. Every time its officers arrested a man, they were accompanied by a notary who made an inventory of the prisoner's possessions, thus enormous estates often passed into the keeping of the Holy Office. The Inquisition had a keen sense of business and did not scorn money which it ought to have regarded as tainted. As its ears were always open and always ready to believe the worst, it gave obvious opportunities for the envious, the malicious and the ignorant to pull down and ruin those whom they hated or could not understand.

There is a popular belief that the Inquisition was a Spanish institution, which is not so. All medieval countries had such courts. It will be remembered that, with English approval, French inquisitors burnt Joan of Arc as a witch. Spain revived the Inquisition after the fall of

Granada, when it had become more or less moribund in other countries, with the object of punishing heretical Christians who had lived for centuries under the Moslems, and of detecting the nominal Christianity of Jews and Moors, some of whom after baptism, it was said, went home and had a bath to wash off the holy water. Then the rise of Protestantism provided more fuel for the fires.

It is not true, as many imagine, that Philip II, and other kings, sat gloating while heretics were burnt to death, for no one was ever burnt at an *auto-de-fe*. The awful ceremony was merely a parade of persons who had been tried and who were then publicly either 'reconciled' to the Church or 'relaxed' into the hands of the civil authorities for execution. There was a great deal of hypocrisy in this. With a show of compassion the Inquisition handed over the condemned to the civil authorities, bidding them deal with them 'kindly and with mercy', though everyone was aware that the legal penalty for heresy was death at the stake. The spectators knew that the victims would be marched away to the *quemadero*, or burning-place, outside the city gates, where faggots had been ready for some time, and a huge crowd would be waiting to see them die. 'Here indeed a terrible and gloating sadism was displayed by the public,' writes V. S. Pritchett, 'sanctified by the Church and approved by the rulers. The Spaniards have strong stomachs.'

An *auto-de-fe*, or an act of faith, must have been a fearsome spectacle, carried out with all the pomp and drama of the Church to impress spectators and to deter any who may have had dangerous thoughts. These ceremonies were of two kinds, the *auto particular*, which was held in a church, and the *auto público*, a costly pageant that sometimes did not take place for years. For weeks beforehand carpenters transformed the main square of a city into a huge theatre. If the king were to be present, a royal box was arranged on a balcony, with others for the court. The centre of the square was occupied by a tribune, with pulpits flanked on each side by grandstands covered with tapestry and rich hangings. At six o'clock in the morning all the church bells would begin to toll and the audience would assemble. Some who had received an invitation from the Inquisition no doubt wondered whether it was a compliment or a warning! No one in his senses would have dared to refuse to be present.

As the king and the court took their places and the grandstands filled with officers of the Inquisition, with bishops and abbots and with representatives of every activity in the realm, the wretched prisoners were called from their cells and dungeons and dressed for the ceremony. To each one was given a hideous yellow shift of coarse material called a *sanbenito*, round each neck was tied an end of rope, and upon each head was placed a cardboard fool's-cap on which insects and reptiles were painted. The prisoners were lined up and into each hand was thrust a green candle, and off they were marched, with a hooded familiar on each side of them, those spies and general handymen of the Inquisition, drawn from every class, whose presence infiltrated into every nook and corner of Spanish life. Those prisoners who were obdurate were also accompanied by confessors who called upon them to repent. Those who were what was termed 'persistent' were often gagged with wooden wedges to prevent them from shouting defiance or heresy. Last of all came the ghastly effigies of those who had cheated the Inquisition by flight, and boxes of bones, the remains of those who had cheated it by death. Both effigies and bones would be burnt at the *quemadero*.

The procession entered the square to the solemn singing of the *Miserere*, to the swinging of censers and the glint of crosses; then came the great green banner of the Inquisition and the file of grotesque figures in their cardboard hats and yellow shifts. The proceedings sometimes lasted from six in the morning until the afternoon. After the religious ceremony and a sermon, each prisoner's case was read out while he knelt humbly in his humiliating shift and hat. It often happened that a man or woman who had disappeared into the dungeons years before, strong and able-bodied, limped forward or had to be assisted, for torture, especially that of the pulley, often dislocated the joints, while the *aselli*, or water-torture, had other effects. At the end of these interminable proceedings the 'reconciled' were led back to the cells to perform their penances, while the 'relaxed' were handed over to the officers of the law and, mounted on donkeys, were led away through shouting and derisive crowds to the place of burning. By that time, no doubt, those who had been making their act of faith since six o'clock were longing only to get away and have something to eat and, if possible, to forget the spectacle they had seen. Few indeed could have wished to follow the grotesque procession to the *quemadero* and witness the final horrors, when those who repented at the last moment were strangled before their bodies were cast into the fire.

As I walked back that night, I wondered whether the Inquisition is responsible for the lack of intellectual curiosity one sometimes senses in Spanish life, for the absence of bookshops and a belief, perhaps held by some Spaniards, that dogma is more important than morality and that the formalities of the Church are all that is needful for the Christian life.

§ 4

Years ago I once gathered material for a novel, which I never wrote, about that exciting period in English history, in the time of Elizabeth, when exiled English Catholics on the Continent were planning the restoration of the Catholic faith in their native land. The old Catholic families constructed 'priest holes' in their houses, behind panelling and in chimneys, in cellars and lofts, to hide the Jesuits who crossed the Channel in disguise to bring them the sacraments of the Church. A curious character at the time was a little man with a limp known as 'Little John', who was in great demand as a designer of 'priest holes'. His real name was Nicholas Owen. He had been a builder before he became a Jesuit lay-brother and was therefore able to impart a professional solidity which was absent from the usual run of hiding-places. Indeed, it happened so often that those caught with a priest in the house persuaded the wretched man to climb the bacon hooks into a vast chimney that priest-hunters, as a matter of routine, lit a fire before they began their search. 'Little John', who was eventually starved out of one of his own hiding-places in Worcestershire, died under torture in the Tower of London rather than give his associates away.

It was a tremendously exciting period, as melodramatic as our own. The priests who entered England in disguise were mostly trained in the English Colleges at Douai, in France, at Rome, or at Valladolid. They were prepared for their dangerous missions rather as during the late war we trained the young men who were dropped one dark night by parachute into occupied territory. If caught, the sixteenth century priest met the same fate as the intelligence officer of the twentieth.

Remembering these things, I was interested to find that the English College in Valladolid still exists, and still trains English priests. It was founded in 1589 by that remarkable character Father Robert Parsons, S.J., who had the energy of ten men and not only wrote an incredible number of books and pamphlets, but also left a mass of documents which have never been seriously examined.

When I rang the bell of the English College, I was asked to wait in a hall that might have been in England, perhaps a corridor in Stonyhurst or in the Birmingham Oratory. I was struck by the Englishness of everything, the way the chairs were standing against the wall, the linoleum, the pictures. I had the feeling that, had the time been more appropriate, I might have been offered (wonderful thought in Spain) a cup of tea and given one of those capacious, creaking basket-work arm-chairs which were the rage at Oxford long ago. While I was enjoying the Englishness of this place, and looking for the pictures of the Colosseum and of Cardinal Newman which I was sure were there, my eye was caught by something that, odd as it may seem, I had not noticed before in Spain. It was a large framed photograph of the Pope.

I reflected that, though I had travelled many hundreds of miles all over Spain and had entered many shops where religious objects are sold, and also vestries and monasteries, this was the first picture of His Holiness I had noticed, and I thought that many a stranger unfamiliar with the Spanishness of the Church in Spain might go on his way believing that Spain owed no obedience at all to the Holy See. This, of course, is not so, for Spain, as everyone knows, is among the most dutiful daughters of the Church; yet she has evidently no desire to gaze upon the features of the Pontiff. And, now that I thought of it, no Spanish priest, monk or devout layman, though they had talked at great length of Spanish shrines, had ever mentioned Rome.

Monsignor Henson, the rector, took me all over the interesting old building, for so loug a home for those who had left England. Upstairs we entered a fine library founded in the sixteenth century, which the rector has catalogued, and he has also rendered a great service to the history of English Catholicism by publishing the registers of the College. Taking down the register for the year 1677, he opened it at a place where a leaf had been torn out. It appears that during the reign of Charles II the unspeakable Titus Oates, pretending to be a Catholic, wormed his way into the College with the object of spying upon the young men who were then in residence. He was eventually expelled, according to the register, 'ob pessimos mores', a phrase which in this instance meant unnatural vice, and the scoundrel's parting gesture was to tear a page from the book containing names which he thought would be of use to him.

In the beautiful little chapel I noticed a graceful painted statue of Our Lady above the altar, and I asked the reason why part of her face was missing and why the figure bore other signs of damage. I was told that she is known as the *Vulnerada*—the Wounded One. She was picked up in the streets of Cádiz in 1596, after Drake and Raleigh had plundered the city for sixteen days and reduced the cathedral and other churches to ashes. As I listened to this story, memories of schooldays came to me, the stuffy classroom, the uncomfortable desks, the smell of rubber and the stains of red ink, but all forgotten in the glorious story of the singeing of the King of Spain's beard. It did not seem quite so wonderful in the presence of the *Vulnerada*.

The gallery of the chapel is enclosed by curious red lattice-work screens like those seen in eastern churches, or in the boxes of theatres to which Moslem potentates take the ladies of their harems. I was told that this screen was put up long ago to hide the faces of the seminarists from people like Titus Oates.

I felt all my old interest in this period of history returning as I talked to Monsignor Henson in the rooms where the Jesuits had been trained for their 'drop' into enemy territory, and where tumultuous schemers like Father Parsons had arrived to whisper behind closed doors. The benevolent smile of Monsignor Henson has banished most of these ghosts, but there are still a few dark corridors and corners!

The English Mission failed for a number of reasons, and the most interesting perhaps was the change in the mind of England between the accession of Elizabeth and her later years. Parsons and his associates were out of date. They were thinking of the England of Mary Tudor, in which they had been brought up, and they had no conception of, or refused to believe in, an England where Catholics would defend their country against a Catholic invader, especially a Spanish one. It may be that Philip II's famous hesitations and delays were not entirely due to a cautious temperament, but were based on a sounder knowledge of what was really going on in Elizabeth's England than that possessed by his exiled advisers.

A few hundred yards away is a Scottish link with the old faith: the Scots College founded in 1627 by Sir William Sempill, or Semple, and still a training ground for Scottish priests. I was shown portraits of the founder and his Spanish wife, Doña María de Ledesma. Sempill was one of those Scots soldiers of fortune who were scattered all over Europe three centuries ago, the forerunners of the Scots engineers and business men now found in every part of the globe. In youth he had been attached to the court of Mary Stuart, and he died at a great age in the reign of Charles I, having spent a busy life in the wars and plots of the period.

In 1941 the old chapel of the Scots College was transformed into a Spanish-American shrine known as the National Sanctuary of the Great Promise. This refers to the vision of a young Jesuit, Father

Hoyos, in 1753, when it is said Christ appeared to him and said, 'I will reign in Spain more than in any other part of the world.' In those days, of course, Spain included most of South America.

Two of the Virgins in this church have a unique history, and a very different one from the ancient images which were found in caves and hiding-places. They came flying through the air to Spain, one in an air-liner from South America, the other from the Philippine Islands. The South American Virgin of Guadalupe is a picture enshrined in a chapel built for her by all the ex-Spanish possessions in America—the names of twenty-one republics are inscribed on its walls—and the Virgin of the Philippines came in great state in an aeroplane, accompanied by the Bishop of the Philippine Islands. Her chapel is decorated with a Pacific landscape of palm trees and blue seas.

The Church of the Great Promise is an impressive monument to the modern policy of *Hispanidad*, or the cultural and spiritual linking together of all the Spanish-speaking peoples of the world.

On the way to Salamanca I saw the town of Tordesillas standing up above the river Duero, and I remembered poor Joan the Mad, who died there after nearly half a century of confinement.

§ 5

While I was unpacking in Salamanca, I heard the noise of fireworks in the street outside and concluded that small boys were having fun. I had been given one of the best rooms in the hotel, immediately above the porch, with a fine view of the streets leading into the famous Plaza Mayor. One is always delighted to be shown up to such a room in daylight, with its commanding prospect of everything happening round about. It is only at night you discover the catch as you lie sleeplessly listening to the explosions of motor-bicycles, the grinding of gears, and the piercing shouts of those saying good-night at two o'clock in the morning.

I had arrived at the moment when one of those rust-red, almost African sunsets was fading to darkness, and I was hurrying to change my dusty clothes to go out and see the famous square which is said to be the finest in Spain. Again I heard the fireworks and this time also a band, a sound that always sends me to a window. It was now almost dark, a hot, still night without a breath of air. Looking out, I saw a most beautiful sight. Crossing the street opposite, which led into the

Plaza Mayor, were people solemnly singing a hymn, and each one was holding a lighted candle. I could not see where they were coming from or where they were going to; they just crossed the street ahead like people marching across a stage. Then I noticed that they were all women and that nearly every woman had with her a little girl wearing her white first communion dress. There were hundreds of these diminutive bridal figures holding candles, the light shining up on little dark, solemn faces. There seemed to be no end to this procession, and every now and then a parish priest, for the marchers were grouped in their parishes, with banners and crosses, would drop out of the line of march and beat time, to encourage the treble voices to rise higher in praise of *Nuestra Señora del Carmen*—Our Lady of Mount Carmel—whose feast day it was.

I hurried down into the Plaza Mayor and saw this marvel of Europe slowly ringed with pin-points of fire. The hundreds of little white figures continued to advance. The flames of their candles rose without a flicker into the windless night. At one moment the lighted candles were half-way round the square, then round three sides of it, and at last the square was completely encircled, and the first marchers were on their way out. It was an unexpectedly lovely sight; the children's faces, the young voices, the thousands of moving lights, and the noble and beautiful eighteenth century background of tall, arcaded houses. Then, at the moment when the square was completely ringed with light, an illuminated statue of Our Lady of Mount Carmel, seated and wearing a blue robe, was drawn in upon a carriage. The large silver crown upon her head shook as the statue vibrated with every revolution of the wheels. There was now a movement in the square as all those who had been seated at café tables rose to their feet, and many people knelt as the carriage approached.

I followed the procession out of the Plaza Mayor and into the dark streets of Salamanca. Sometimes I walked beside the statue of the Madonna, who seemed to nod and smile in the candlelight as she trembled over the roadway. Sometimes I went ahead to see again some little face that had attracted my attention. It was the simple annual procession held in many Catholic countries, but here it was conducted with that beautiful Spanish sense of style that I love to see. The little girls, who had been allowed to wear their first communion dresses again, carried themselves, even the smallest, like proud little queens, and among them one caught sight of a small brother dressed as a little admiral.

One thought leads to another, and my mind went back to Mount Carmel, upon its headland near Haifa, to the monastery, so like a fortress with its thick walls and its barred windows, to the life of the monks, with whom I once stayed for some time, and to the grotto and the splendid shrine of Our Lady of the Scapular. I remembered, what I had long forgotten, how one day I went off with four Carmelites in an old Ford car to take the post to a nunnery buried in the mountains. We wheezed up and down the appalling roads, the torn celluloid sidescreens flapping in the wind, and came at last to a white convent standing among pine trees. I remember thinking how interesting it was to see the meeting of the monks and the nuns; how the monks sat bolt upright on kitchen chairs and made jokes, and how even the poorest joke was welcomed by the nuns, who bustled about, pressing us to eat little cakes, and giving us saucers of rose-petal jam, beaming at us all the time and asking hundreds of questions. . . .

Now the car of Our Lady of Carmel was halted at the top of a steep hill, and as I looked up from the bottom of the road I saw a winding snake of fire coming slowly down, twisting on to the Church of the Carmelites, which was a blaze of light and full of people waiting to welcome the Virgin after her journey. Both the west doors were open and she was skilfully carried in, the top of her silver crown almost touching the arch, and borne through the candlelight to the high altar.

I thought I could not have had a more beautiful introduction to Salamanca.

## § 6

This beautiful golden city is one of the glories of Spain. I am not sure that it is not the finest of its glories. Here the stranger thinks again for the hundredth time that the Spaniards were the greatest architects and builders since the Romans. There is not a building of any age in Salamanca that is not worth looking at. The Plaza Mayor is the eighteenth century descendant of the seventeenth century Plaza Mayor in Madrid, but it has not come down in the world, like its predecessor. I cannot think of a more beautiful and graceful memorial of the eighteenth century in Europe; it is the eighteenth century, not in a toga, as at Bath, but in a satin coat, with a snuff-box of Bolivian silver in its hand.

In the freshness of the morning I walked across the Roman bridge to the place opposite Salamanca where women are always on their knees, honouring the god of cleanliness as they wash clothes in the river Tormes. The sun was rising over the lovely city, touching the pinnacles of the two cathedrals, which stand side by side, and falling into the old streets where the University, the churches, the monasteries, the convents, and the palaces stand in Parthenon-coloured stone. The rain of centuries had not obliterated from these golden walls the handiwork of students in the Middle Ages, who, when they had taken their degrees, also took a ladder and inscribed their names in red ochre upon the walls of their lodgings.

Then I walked back into Salamanca and went to the early markets to watch the unloading of fish lorries from the coast. I went to early Mass at the little twelfth century church of St. Martín, which has a Gothic group above the door showing the saint sharing his cloak with the beggar. On the way back to the hotel for breakfast I came across an old stone-cutter in a side-street, sitting across a block of yellow stone with a chisel and a mallet in his hands. He was repairing one of the old buildings, and as I watched I wondered how much inherited skill directed his chiselling. Noticing that I was interested, the old man dismounted from the stone and in five minutes gave me the secret of the Plateresque and Churrigueresque decoration one sees in that part of Spain. How often I have paused before a gateway or a façade carved with a thousand fancies, such as the *Escuelas Mayores* at Salamanca and the *Colegio de San Gregorio* in Valladolid, wondering how an artist was able to embroider stone so intricately. The answer is simple—water! The old man showed me a block of dry stone as hard as steel, and the same kind of stone soaked in water, which could be cut as easily as cheese.

An hour or two later, while walking round the Plaza Mayor, whose cafés seemed to be unusually full for that time of day, I heard my name called, and saw an aristocratic form rise from a group of men and come towards me with signs of pleasure. I found myself greeted by one of El Greco's noblemen; it was Don Mariano, a friend from Madrid.

'My dear fellow,' he cried, 'This is splendid! You have arrived at just the right moment. Had I only known where you were, I would have sent you an invitation and asked you to be here. We are holding the annual Poets' Congress. Come and meet some of them!'

A Poets' Congress! What a strange thought was this! Most of the poets I have known have been solitary men, lacking in the community spirit. I could not think of one who could have been persuaded to attend a congress, least of all a congress of other poets! Spanish poets are evidently more companionable. As Don Mariano led me towards the poets, I thought that there was just a touch of light opera about it; a chorus of poets in Salamanca, itself a poem inscribed in golden stone against the Castilian sky. I was introduced to a number of young men and a few middle-aged ones, and as they all appeared cheerful and well-to-do I reflected that they must have other sources of income. They had come from many parts of Spain. One, the distinguished Italian poet, Signor Ungaretti, had come from Italy; the well-known Catalan poet, Carles Riba, had come from Barcelona; and hardly had we resumed our seats than the secretary of the Congress ran up waving a telegram from Roy Campbell, saying that he was on the way. Everyone cheered.

'Do tell me what this is all about, Mariano,' I asked.

'The Poets' Congress at Segovia last year was such a success,' he replied, 'that we decided to have another. The idea behind it is semi-political.'

Here he looked wise and diplomatic.

'We have brought the Castilian and the Catalan groups together,' he whispered with an air of triumph. 'And I may tell you, it's working wonderfully well. They're getting along famously.'

'But why shouldn't they?' I asked.

He looked at me in pity.

'Well, Catalonia and Castile!' he said. 'The distrust is due to a lack of personal contacts on both sides. But the Congress is doing wonders. They are getting on marvellously together.'

Regional Spain! How did Ferdinand and Isabel ever unite it? I looked at the poets, thinking of them not as Spaniards but as Gallegos, Basques, Castilians, Catalans and Andalusians, as obviously they thought of themselves. But there was no doubt that they were getting on well; they were all shouting at the tops of their voices. Castilian, like its ancestor Latin, is a wonderful language for shouting and oratory. One young man opened a brief-case and drew out the page proofs of an intellectual quarterly.

'And the *señorita*?' I whispered. 'Is she also . . . ?'

Mariano whispered back that she was a *poetisa*.

The secretary then arrived to say that we would all be late for the reception at the palace. We must hurry. He was having a terrible time rounding up a coterie of young poets who had stayed up all night talking. and were now apparently scattered over Salamanca trying to chase away their hangovers. Some now appeared, feverish and bright-eyed, apparently ready to write an ode to anything.

We trooped across the square, pausing to talk in little groups, for few Spaniards can talk and walk at the same time, and came at last to a steep street that led to the splendid palace which Archbishop Fonseca built about the year 1500. A flight of steps led to a grand Renaissance hall parallel with the street, where waiters in evening dress were standing behind a loaded buffet. Here we were greeted by the Mayor of Salamanca and the Chancellor of the University, and passed in to a crowd of professors and councillors with their wives. There were speeches, flashlight photographs, and a cocktail party that might have been in London or New York. I became wedged in a corner with a vivid little woman who was convinced that I was an Italian poet, and I thought it less trouble to let her believe this; indeed I think it a good rule never to contradict anybody at a cocktail party.

Even above the conversation of a hundred Spanish poets I heard the sound of a drum and a pipe from the courtyard below. Edging my way through the crowd, I glanced over the gallery into the court-yard, where I saw the enchanting spectacle of fourteen dancers, eight women and six men, wearing the splendid traditional costume of Salamanca. The women wore black dresses encrusted as thickly as an *espada's* jacket with embroidered flowers, carnations and roses that stood out a quarter of an inch from the background like real flowers. Some had pink, some blue, and some red panels let into the front of their skirts, and when they executed a twirl scarlet petticoats flashed into view. They all wore mantillas of white lace, and round their necks were collars of big gold beads the size of chick-peas, while enormous necklaces of these same beads fell in loops almost to their waists. The men wore short, waist-length jackets of black velvet and almost skin-tight trousers, terminating in black leggings that buttoned down over the shoes like those of a bishop. They wore black silk sashes and black hats with wide brims and little cone-shaped crowns. The leader of the troupe was a wonderful old man with a paunch, who still looked splendid in his dress and was, they told me, a village tailor and a famous dancer. He held a drum and a pipe and one of the younger men held a maypole.

When the poets were all grouped on the balconies, or seated on the palace steps, the dancers took up their positions in the centre of the courtyard. They first performed a square dance, men and women facing each other, and instead of castanets they clashed *tapaderas*, which are small cymbals with handles. As they danced, the old man stood apart beating the drum and playing upon the pipe. Then, handing these instruments to another, he suddenly leapt with surprising agility into the centre, while one of the prettiest girls faced him. They danced the story of a man whose advances are scornfully rejected by the woman; he then loses his temper, to her amusement, and finally, becoming persuasive, approaches her with a gift, whereupon she becomes charming, languishes, and surrenders. The old man was amazing. He leapt about like an ancient cockerel, his chest out, stamping in fury, his black legs working like pistons, and when the dance was over we gave him a volley of applause. The maypole was produced and the dance performed just as we know it in England. The dancers twisted in and out, men and women, each dancer holding a yellow or a red ribbon until the pole was neatly bound with them.

While this delightful scene was in progress, two American women with cameras, who had been gazing through the iron gates into the patio, entered and asked me in Spanish whether they might take a photograph. I referred them in English to the secretary and they thanked me and complimented me on my accent.

## § 7

There was a poor and rather out-of-the-way parish called Santo Tomás, a saint who was, I discovered, no other than Thomas à Becket. The little Romanesque parish church with its rounded, Byzantine-looking windows might have been one of the solid, golden-coloured churches of Syria. It was built in 1179, which was nine years after Becket's murder in Canterbury Cathedral, and five years after Henry II had gone there barefoot and in penitential sackcloth. I like to think that Henry's daughter, Eleanor, who was Queen of Castile at the time, had perhaps built the church to please her father and help to ease his soul.

Then one afternoon Don Mariano and I went off to discover the house where Wellington stayed in Salamanca, and after some difficulty found it in an unfrequented part of the town, Number 3, Plaza de San Boal. It is an old house with a wooden gallery running round a courtyard, and it looked as though nothing had been changed since the time of the Peninsular War. The courtyard, we fancied, looked as if it remembered the arrival of heated young hussars and dragoons with despatches, the clatter of swords on stone steps and the ring of

345

spurs; and I suggested that some of the poets might like to go there and write an overdue tribute to the man who drove Napoleon out of Spain.

The House of the Shells was, for me, one of the most memorable sights in Salamanca. The walls of this old palace are covered with scallop shells beautifully carved in stone and arranged in thirteen symmetrical rows, one above the other, completely covering the façade, and carved in such bold relief that each shell casts a long shadow. This house of innumerable sundials is a triumphant solution of the problem of breaking a blank wall with shadow, a difficulty which faces anyone who builds in a sunny country.

Then, among many other things, there was the wonderful old lecture room of Luis de León in the University, which has been kept as it was four hundred years ago. You sit on the hard wooden benches and are told the famous story of Luis de León's return after five years in the prisons of the Inquisition. His lecture hall was crowded. Everyone was wondering what he would say. Glancing round an audience he had not seen for five years, he began: 'Dicebamus hesterna die . . .', 'We were saying yesterday . . .'

Now I was back again in the heat of Madrid. It was, if possible, even hotter than I last remembered it. Nothing quenched my thirst. I drank *horchata de chufas*, tried *helados*, and ordered *granizada*, but still the thirst remained. The crowds sat about in the breathless air until the small hours, *flamenco* blared from fifth-floor tenement windows, and not a breath of air arrived from the Sierra during the night.

While I waited a day or two for an air passage to Barcelona, I did something I had been thinking of for many a week; I went to see the Escorial again and to stay at the hotel there. The memory of this grey palace had haunted me. It lay at the back of my mind. The more I thought about it, the surer I became that it is one of the greatest things in Spain. It was a different Escorial I now saw in the early morning light, in the heat of afternoon, and under the stars, with people walking about in front of it, laughing and chattering in their nightly *paseo*. It was no longer repellent, no longer cruel or haughty; and I thought it perhaps the finest expression in Spain of the Castilian spirit.

§ 8

I flew to Barcelona seated next to a fair-haired young man who might have been taught English by Maurice Chevalier. He was fluent, irrepressible and pathetically young. He irritated me by treating me much as a male nurse with financial expectations might have handled some venerable invalid tottering on the edge of the grave. But when I had made it clear that I could carry my own luggage, that I liked to sit in a draught, and that I was capable of getting anything I wanted, he calmed down and became quite a pleasant boy. He was a Swiss medical student and his age was eighteen. Some three years previously his parents had taken him for a holiday in Spain which had made such an impression upon him that his one thought was to return. His father, however, opposed this and refused to give him a penny. The boy then determined to make sufficient money in his holidays, and for more than two years had been working in his spare time. He had sold ice-cream in the streets; he had worked in hotel kitchens; he had been a spare-time postman at Christmas; he had been a car-park attendant, and had done all sorts of odd jobs, and at last had scraped together enough money. He was now staying with Spanish friends and this was a considerable saving. He travelled third-class on the railways, and the flight to Barcelona was his only extravagance.

The unexpectedness of humanity is one of its greatest attractions. I would never have believed that this frail youngster had this drive in him, and I said that his father must be proud of him.

'My father!' he cried. 'Why, he will not even speak to me.'

I asked what attracted him to Spain.

'Oh, everything. The people and the way they live, the country itself, the old towns, the churches, the bull-fights. It is, for me, a new world. It is so different from Switzerland.'

'Are you a Catholic?' I asked.

'No.'

'Is there perhaps a *señorita*?' I suggested.

'Indeed no, nothing like that!' he said.

'Do you think Spain a romantic country?'

'On the contrary, it is cold and matter-of-fact and realistic. That is what I like.'

This told me that Spain had made a true convert. I should like to have seen more of this strange young man, but the aeroplane swooped down upon Barcelona and I stepped out into one of the most fascinating of all the Spains. There was the usual long drive from the airport into the city, then a taxi to an hotel at the top of the *Ramblas*. Here I was given a room with a balcony above this attractive street. I stood looking down upon a sight that became delightfully familiar; the broad promenade with its plane trees, the seats, the newspaper kiosks, the shoe-blacks, the perpetually moving crowds. There was a strange fountain opposite that looked like an iron lamp standard, from which all day long young men filled water-pots and jars as if at a village well. And among the many people beneath my window I noticed one, an elderly shoe-black, who felt in his pocket and brought out a handful of breadcrumbs, and stood there covered with pigeons which fluttered to him from every direction. On each side of the broad promenade was a narrow, one-way street along which small, noisy tramcars came jangling like angry little juggernauts, while taxis swooped up as if the drivers had been offered a fortune to reach their destinations in record time.

My first impression was that the people of Barcelona walk twice as fast as any other Spaniards. Madrid saunters idly, even at midday; Barcelona walks fast as if it were going somewhere.

## §9

It was surprising to discover a perfectly preserved medieval city buried away in the middle of Barcelona. No one had told me of this. Barcelona's industrial growth during the past century has been so remarkable that it is her modernity that is always emphasized. Nevertheless, there it is, tucked away just off the *Ramblas*; a medieval city complete with its cathedral, palaces, winding streets, and even a rather assertive drainage, almost as if in the middle of London there still existed the city that Chaucer knew. I can only explain this extraordinary survival on the assumption that Barcelona found it impossible to demolish the massive black stones of which this old city is composed. The network of fortress-like slums in the middle of old Barcelona cannot be imagined. Some of the streets are mere slits in a canyon of stone, a crack in which a crooked lamp leans outward on an iron bracket and two venerable walls of stone, on which the sun never shines, face each other with their grim windows and balconies. There are many streets in this old city that are crying out for Georges Simenon. Everything is ready for him: the black entrance to an alley, a figure disappearing round a corner, the sound of a gramophone wheezing out an ancient melody, a woman standing against a lighted window in a tenement, and a few drinkers carousing in a cellar.

This was not the medieval Spain I had seen. It bore no resemblance to Avila and Segovia and the knightly cities of Castile, still less had it

348

any relationship with baroque Spain, where the domed brown bell-towers soak up the sun and the curly, restless façades culminate in a cargo of saints and urns, all as crisp and brown as newly baked biscuits. This was something dark and rather sinister, much as one imagines Paris must have been in the Middle Ages.

The cathedral of the old city stands at the top of a wide flight of steps. It is the darkest and most mysterious cathedral in Spain. You stand for a moment unable to see anything; then you notice candles burning in a side chapel and a coloured window high up in the great walls. The first chapel on the right glows with light, and people are always kneeling in prayer before the miracle-working Christ of Lepanto. This large crucifix, almost life-sized, is said to have been fixed to the mainmast of Don John's flagship. The figure is oddly twisted to one side and you will be told that during the battle it bent itself to avoid a shot.

You go on into the darkness and come to the choir, the little church within a church. It is locked and you peer into the darkness, aware of half-seen carving, gilding and painting. If the verger is handy, and if you have an electric torch, you may go inside and flash your light along the stalls of the Knights of the Golden Fleece until you come to the Royal Arms of England and the stall reserved for Henry VIII. These blazons were painted for the Chapter of the Order held in 1518 by young Charles I of Spain, who was not yet Charles V of Germany; indeed the news that he had been elected Emperor came to him that year when he was in Barcelona. Henry VIII did not attend the Chapter, but he and Charles met later in England, when the twenty years old Emperor was treated very much as the callow and inexperienced nephew by Uncle Henry and Aunt Catherine, neither of them guessing what a cold and brilliant mind lay concealed in that unprepossessing young Hapsburg.

When you leave the *coro* you may notice a peculiar object hanging under the organ. Yes, it is the head of a dark and bearded Moor in a turban. It may be a memory of the terrible al-Mansûr. I do not know. They say that until recently, upon certain feast days, the mouth was made to vomit sweetmeats for the children. It is odd that the Moors should be commemorated in a city that knew less of them than any other part of Spain. While the rest of Spain fought the Moslems for eight hundred years, Barcelona was occupied by them for only eighty-eight years—from 713 until 801, when the Franks drove them out. This in itself makes Barcelona, and Catalonia, different from the rest of Spain. Barcelona could afford to turn her back on occupied Spain and look across the Mediterranean to Alexandria, to Genoa, Pisa, Venice and Constantinople, her true companions. Burgos was a more alien city to Barcelona than any of the great sea-ports of the Mediterranean, and she stood prosperously with her back to Spain for centuries. The differences which still separate Catalonia from Castile date from these far off times.

I walked into the magnificent cloisters, where geese have been kept for centuries. These fat birds, as white as snow against the ancient stone, swim in little ponds arranged in an angle of the cloister, or waddle slowly, turning a reflective eye upon those who venture to offer scraps of bread to them. I would as soon offer a canon of Barcelona a pea-nut as try to feed these sanctified birds with crusts! They call them the 'Capitoline geese', and no one could tell me why, or explain the origin of this custom. Perhaps their remote predecessors were Roman geese who lived on the same spot when the full name of Barcelona was Colonia Faventia Julia Augusta Pia Barcino. There is a little goose house, or goose canonry, where the birds sleep, and duckboards lead down towards the water. Pigeons and squirrels which live in an adjacent palm tree help to get rid of the superfluous bread.

Another interesting sight in the cloister is a new Virgin, Our Lady of Light, the patron saint of electricians. While I was watching them put the finishing touches to this shrine, one of the guides who haunt such places came up and spoke to me in excellent English. He was a gaunt, middle-aged man with an ingratiating manner which he wore like a badly pinned on mask that was ready to fall off at any moment. I was so curious to find out what lay behind this that I took him on for an hour. It was not long before the mask came off.

The man was violently anti-Franco, anti-clerical, anti-everything. He took a delight in showing me churches which had been burned out during the Civil War. He strode contemptuously past the holy water stoups and deliberately refrained from making any gesture of respect, even to the Sacrament. He told me that the geese had been placed in the cloisters because the clergy could not attract children to church!

'Do you know why the churches are so dark here?' he asked. 'It is because the priests have a monopoly of the candle trade.'

He thought Franco the ruin of Spain. Among Franco's uncountable sins was the suppression of newspapers written in the Catalan language. Nothing would ever be right until Franco went! I asked if a king would improve matters. He spat angrily in the gutter. His bitterness was such that I began to wonder if he were a member of some subversive group. He was an unpleasant man and I was only too thankful to pay him off and see the last of him.

The Roman level of Barcelona is about thirty feet below the modern streets. When excavations were made under the medieval buildings a few years ago, someone had the brilliant idea of preserving the discoveries *in situ*, supporting the buildings above with concrete walls, and so making it possible to go down and walk about the Roman streets. This I thought was one of the strangest experiences in Barcelona. You go down a flight of steps and find yourself in what looks like half an acre of rather tidy bomb damage, lit by electricity. Wooden duckboards lead over the uneven ground and the path takes you along lanes used by the Roman inhabitants and past several buildings, with a glimpse of some efficient-looking drain pipes on the way. To descend into this tomb of time, and to walk where men walked so long ago, was more stirring to the imagination than a score of show-cases in a museum.

As you emerge into the modern world again, you stand in the Plaza del Rey—the King's Square—which is enclosed by tall and solemn medieval buildings of dark stone. In one corner a beautiful flight of steps rises to the gate of an impressive hall, which was the hall of the old palace of the Counts of Barcelona. I could recall at least two extraordinary scenes that took place there. In 1479, when the body of John II of Aragon, the father of Ferdinand the Catholic, lay in state, the courtiers entered the hall on horseback and rode round the catafalque weeping, and crying, dragging their standards along the ground and even throwing themselves out of the saddle in exaggerated grief. Fourteen years later, in April, 1493, Ferdinand and Isabel and all their court assembled in the hall to hear from the lips of Columbus the story of the discovery of the New World. It has been said by Salvador de Madariaga that Columbus, had he lived today, would have made a superb Minister of Propaganda. His arrival in Barcelona was as spectacular as his departure from Spain the year before had been modest. He marched from Seville like a circus, with six so-called 'Indians' in his train—the first natives of the American Continent to set foot in Europe—with gold, with parrots, and with trees and strange fruits from the West Indies. And it is said that this exotic procession, which drew wondering eyes wherever it was seen, mounted the steps in the corner of the Plaza del Rey and entered the hall of the old palace.

What a moment this was in the life of Columbus! For years he had haunted the court, neglected and laughed at by many as a vain babbler; now he had come back with proof that the New World existed, or rather (as he believed to his dying day) that he had found the back door to China and Japan. And he also believed that he had discovered gold in enormous quantities, which was not so. Not a hint did he ever possess of the gold of the Aztecs and the Incas that was waiting to be looted by Cortés and Pizarro. As he entered the hall, Ferdinand and Isabel astonished the court by rising as he kissed their hands. Then, to the amazement and resentment of the court, they called for that mark of royal favour granted only to those of royal blood, or to the greatest in the land. They called for a stool so that Columbus might sit. Even Columbus must have thought this as remarkable as the discovery of a New World. It was indeed a new world for him, the world he had always dreamt of, the world of fame, wealth and nobility. When he had finished his story, the singers of the Queen's Chapel sang the *Te Deum*; and that evening, by royal orders, the whole court accompanied Columbus to his lodgings. Further proof of his greatness was forthcoming when he was asked to dinner by Cardinal Mendoza and, for the first time in his life, his food was tasted for poison. Such is the measure and penalty of fame!

§ 10

Although the discoverers of the New World were almost to a man from Extremadura, and Seville was the port that chiefly profited by the discovery, Barcelona has erected a tremendous column to Columbus, only a few feet lower than Nelson's Column, though it looks much higher.

At the summit of the column is a huge golden globe on which a colossal statue of Columbus stands, pointing out to sea. A little mahogany lift takes you up inside the column to a gallery below the globe, which, like all such places, fills you with an intense feeling of insecurity. Indeed it seems that at any moment the column might slowly tilt and measure its length upon the earth. I stepped out into a brisk wind and found—such bizarre moments do sometimes occur in travel—that I shared the top of the Columbus Monument with a Japanese.

The view on both sides is superb. You see Barcelona stretching away to the hills where Tibidabo stands, the black spire and the queer-looking towers of the cathedral rising in the centre of the old town. Immediately below is one of the most curious antiquities in Barcelona, which looks like a group of enormously long goods yards, side by side. It is a group of ancient shipyards and dry docks, where the fleets of Barcelona were built and careened from the fourteenth century until the eighteenth. It has been admirably restored and cleaned up and is now a naval museum which illustrates the great story of Spain's prowess upon the seas. There are halls full of ships' figure-heads, models of every kind, pictures, charts and naval relics. I was interested in the coffers painted by Spanish seamen in the days of sail, when presumably they had plenty of time to cover these chests with highly original oil paintings; and nearly all, curiously enough, were of one theme, the old, old sea story of the peril of unstopping one's ears to the song of the sirens! Some of them might have been painted by St. Anthony.

Upon the opposite side of the column you look down upon the water-front, and to a scale model, moored next to a training-ship, of the *Santa María*, the flagship of Columbus. This delightful little caravel, which is dwarfed by everything around it, was built to exact specifications for a Spanish exhibition in the nineteen-twenties. She is obviously seaworthy, for she has been afloat ever since. For a few pesetas visitors can go aboard and look round, and, as they do so, wonder how anyone could have crossed the Atlantic in such a cockle-shell—she is only one hundred and twenty-eight feet long, twenty-five feet wide, and of about one hundred tons burden. But the really remarkable thing is that the men who took this pretty little ship across the Atlantic did so in spite of the fear that they might fall off the edge of the world, or become involved in some fearful cataclysm. It is almost impossible for us to imagine the fears of the lower deck, and it is amusing to read in his *Diary* how Columbus faked his log, putting down less than the distance covered every day, in order not to alarm the crew by the length of the voyage.

Another beautiful scale model of the *Santa María* was made in Spain for the Chicago Exhibition of 1893, and this little ship was actually taken across the Atlantic under sail by a Spanish crew, following the same course as that taken by Columbus on his first voyage. The time taken was thirty-six days (Columbus took seventy), and the maximum speed was six and a half knots. The vessel is said to have pitched horribly. The original *Santa María* never returned to Spain. At midnight on Christmas Day in 1492, while Columbus and his companions were asleep, the steersman, strictly against orders, handed the helm to a boy, and the ship was carried away by strong currents and went ashore off the island of Haiti. Columbus built a fort with her timbers.

The lift came up with a few soldiers and *señoritas*, and the Japanese and I descended to earth.

I took a seat on the *Ramblas* and watched the Catalan crowds, fascinated by their outward difference from other Spaniards. The women have not the superb carriage of the Madrid women; they do not walk as if they are carrying an invisible water-jar on their heads, but as if they were late for an appointment. They dress their children differently, more as modern French children are dressed. The Barcelonese are fond of pets. You can buy a marmoset, if you want one, or a tortoise, a kitten, or goldfish, in stalls under the plane trees. They love flowers. The stalls in the *Rambla de las Flores* gorgeously reflect the changing seasons, and beneath the white, red and blue parasols, where the impressionist, Ramón Casas, found a favourite model who became his wife, the market women stand ready to sell you an armful of roses. One of the sad things about London in our time is that we have allowed the flower 'girls' to be driven from Piccadilly Circus under some squalid by-law, and my heart warms to the Catalans who so proudly give a stretch of their most famous street to flowers. I imagine if some wretched clerk tried to abolish these stalls, the Catalans would kick him round the town as we should have kicked those who stamped that little touch of beauty out of London.

Do these flowers, dogs, tortoises, goldfish and children mean that Catalonian home life is different from that in other parts of Spain, less secret and oriental maybe, more as we know it north of the Pyrenees? What can a stranger know of such things? He can only speculate. But it would not be surprising to be told that all this coming and going through the centuries between the Mediterranean world and Paris has made the people of Barcelona the most cosmopolitan of Spaniards.

It is a wonderful experience to sit and watch the faces in a city that was trading with Tyre and Sidon at a time when the tides of the Thames were lapping against a deserted Ludgate Hill. All Spanish crowds give one the impression of a mixed ancestry and here it is no different. One imagines that there must be a streak of Phoenician and Carthaginian in these active, keen, quick people. There are moments in Barcelona when one could believe oneself in Marseilles, except that the city itself is infinitely more attractive; indeed I think it the most pleasing modern industrial city I have seen.

It is not necessary to speak Catalan or Castilian, or to have been here for a long time, to sense the vitality of Catalonia. It is a fundamental vitality that no disasters have been able to extinguish. The capture of Constantinople, and the turning of the Mediterranean into a Moslem sea, must have been a terrible blow, but Barcelona survived it. The discovery of America, the centralization of everything Spanish in Madrid, must also have been blows, and there were others; yet she has survived them all. She has always been the home of enterprise and adventure. What could have been more extraordinary than that band of Catalans in the early fourteenth century, who for six years challenged the Byzantine Empire, camped out at Gallipoli, and ended by fortifying the Acropolis?

Among my happiest memories of Spain will be Barcelona and the *Ramblas* on a summer evening. A little way down, near the flower stalls, was one of those beautiful Spanish markets where fish and fruit rivalled each other in colour. I never became tired of walking round, perhaps buying a bag of peaches or pears, delighted by the easy good manners of the market people and their sense of beauty—of the beauty of common things, as I said of a similar market in Madrid. Here it was impossible to say which were more brilliant in colour or more beautiful, the fish or the fruit which faced each other across the aisles. The market occupied the centre of a square, which it completely concealed. But if you went round to the back, you would see hidden away a dignified group of houses built over a century ago by Francisco Daniel Molina, who was so enchanted by Regent's Park and Nash's Piccadilly that, in imitation, he built this little Regency square in Barcelona.

As it grows dark the foreigners in Barcelona may be seen lingering near the kiosks in the *Ramblas*, waiting for the airborne newspapers to arrive. The foreign population must be varied, for you can buy English, American, French, German, Italian, Swiss and other newspapers. The first time I asked for *The Times*, the man in charge of the kiosk looked puzzled and shook his head. He had never heard of it. When I pointed to a copy in a rack, his face broke into a radiant smile. Ah, '*El Teemis!*' After that I knew what to ask for, and never had any trouble.

§ 11

St. George is the patron saint of England, Portugal, Aragon, and, in Greece, of lunatics. I know Greek churches in the Levant where madmen are still chained at night in the belief that St. George will heal them during their sleep. The saint known to the Aragonese and Catalans is the familiar slayer of dragons. He appeared early in the history of Aragon, cheering on the Christian armies against the Infidel, as

St. James cheered on the armies of Castile. The most splendid building in Barcelona is full of his statues. He is seen killing huge and furious dragons, and dragons of lesser breeds; in one instance, on foot in full armour, and in solid silver, he thrusts his lance into a nice little dragon hardly bigger than a terrier. This glorious building is the Palace of the *Diputación Provincial*, where the district council meets in medieval splendour.

Noble stairs lead up to a Gothic colonnade and a sort of medieval roof garden where orange trees are growing in small squares of grass inset in the paving. And here is the most delightful St. George of all. He is small and he rides on top of a fountain. The dragon, which lies beneath his horse, rears up his head and from his open mouth shoots a thin jet of water which curves upward and breaks against the saint's leg.

This Spanish Doge's Palace gives some idea of the splendour and wealth of medieval Barcelona. There is a solid and sumptuous Victorian comfort about the rooms in this palace, also perhaps just a little too much opulence. The council chamber is a heavy jewel-box with a lid of gilded and panelled wood, and the sides are pale, beautiful Flemish tapestry. There is a throne at one end, flanked by two rows of heavy seats like choir stalls. There is also a superb hall and a beautiful church; but it is difficult to contemplate sheer magnificence for long, and I was glad to go out into the sunlight and the orange trees and watch the dragon shoot water at St. George.

One Sunday evening I was returning from the dock district, where I had gone to find a little restaurant which had been recommended to me for its superlative *zarzuela* of shell-fish. The word *zarzuela* means an operetta or a variety act, and a *zarzuela de mariscos* is a dish composed of all the shell-fish in season, fried and served in a good sauce. It varies greatly from place to place and, naturally, from month to month. It must reach the peak of perfection about November.

While walking back up the *Ramblas*, I thought I would go into the cathedral for a few moments, and turning off into the maze of ancient side-streets I approached the Plaza de San Jaime. I heard a band playing a cheerful tune, and was surprised to see the Plaza filled with solemn, dancing people. There must have been a thousand, perhaps more. They were dancing hand in hand in circles, a man and a woman alternately, and some of the rings were large, some small. At first sight the scene reminded me of something Hans Andersen might have written, or of the queer dancing mania that affected whole towns in the Middle Ages; but as I watched more closely, there was nothing abnormal about it, nothing of enchantment or madness. These were ordinary citizens of Barcelona in their Sunday clothes, who had come to dance to the inspiring music of the band that was mounted on a platform at the corner of the square. This was the famous Sardana, the most popular of all Catalonian dances.

The best dancers, and those who had evidently set the whole thing going, were groups of young men and women whose expertness and footwork suggested that they belonged to some folklore society, and this proved to be so. But as every Catalonian is familiar with this dance, it was not long before others joined in. Numbers of people who just happened to be passing soon found themselves dancing. The dancers were increased either by newcomers joining already existing circles or by forming a ring of their own. I saw a mother and her son, a boy of about fourteen, start dancing hand in hand. In a few moments they were joined by two more people, and so on until their ring contained at least twenty. It was amusing to see a woman put her handbag down on the pavement in the centre of a ring, place her gloves on top of it, and join the dance. The one unbreakable rule is that the sexes must be separated, a woman must have a man dancing on each side of her.

The dance is simple and graceful and, like most things in Spanish life, formal and with strict rules. It reminded me of a Greek dance I saw years ago on the island of Thasos, when lines of girls with hands on each other's shoulders danced to the right and then to the left, just as they do in the Sardana.

A sudden strike in the music denotes the end of a dance and the groups relax and wait for the next tune. There are hundreds of different tunes and new ones are composed every day. I would advise anyone who visits Barcelona to buy a gramophone record of *Angelina*, *Cobla Emporium*, *Al Quines Noies*, *La Font de l'Albera*, or *La noir alegre que no sap plorar*, all of which are beautiful Sardana tunes. The music has a strong touch of the rustic pipe and woodwind.

When the band considers that the dancers have rested long enough a warning note is sounded on the *flabiol*, and the dance begins again. The dancers face the centre of the ring with joined hands, then, as the music strikes up, they dance the short steps, called *curts*, sideways and back, then the long steps, called *llargs*; and with the *curts* the hands are held low, while with the *llargs* they are lifted to shoulder level. With the last note the dancers suddenly push forward their arms towards the centre of the ring, clasping hands in a gesture of thanks and friendship.

A charming feature of the Sardana is that every stranger is encouraged by smiles and nods to join in. I saw a young American couple do so to the delight of the dancers. Anyone who has seen the Sardana danced will agree that the dignity and the pleasure with which thousands of people dance it in Barcelona every Sunday are among the delightful memories of Spain. Like so many things in Spain, this dance just seems to happen. You may make inquiries about it and no one knows anything; then, by chance as I did, you come across it in full swing.

I carried away with me an unforgettable picture of dignity and grace against a noble background of palaces, of merry music through which a rustic pipe gambolled like a young faun, and of an old lamplighter who passed among the rings of dancers, shouldering a long pole and turning on the lights.

My cell in the monastery of Montserrat was small, white and neat. It contained only a soldierly bed, a washstand, a chair and a little table. In a room on the other side of the passage a young honeymoon couple lived in a wonderful transport of love. They went about hand in hand, they called to each other anxiously, like birds, if temporarily separated, and they leant out of the window with entwined arms. It was very Spanish that they should have brought this love to the Virgin of Montserrat, the 'Rose of April, the Dark One of the Mountain'.

The monastery lies about thirty miles from Barcelona, high in a cleft of a wild and improbable landscape. The mountains have been formed by long centuries of erosion; the soft rock formations have disappeared, leaving the hard rocks standing in weird, isolated cones and pinnacles, like a landscape that might have fallen from the moon. Such eerie places, that bear no relationship to their surroundings, but seem to lead a separate existence, have always had an attraction for the recluse. The highest pinnacles of Montserrat are scattered with the caves of hermits who lived there long ago. The medieval German legends placed the castle of the Holy Grail there, and these were the legends which inspired Wagner when he composed *Parsifal*.

To Spain the mountains of Montserrat have been sacred for about eleven centuries as the shrine of the Black Virgin, who is the patron saint of Catalonia. The Benedictine monastery, in which her image is kept, stands upon a ledge about three thousand feet above the sea and is surrounded on all sides by the saw-toothed pinnacles of Montserrat— Mons Serratus—which tower for another thousand feet. When you arrive at the monastery, it seems quite a large place; but if you look up at it from the distant plain you find it with difficulty and see it, if you see it at all, as small as a swallow's nest, plastered precariously in the corner of an immense cliff.

But there is really quite a large village grouped round the Basilica of the Black Virgin. It has its own post-office, an hotel, and shops where you can buy food, films and candles. Scattered about at peculiar angles, owing to the strange lie of the land, are guest-houses which can shelter two thousand pilgrims. You can stay there for three days without question, and longer with the permission of the abbot, and when you depart you are expected to leave whatever you can afford; but no one would ask you to pay anything.

Every pilgrim brings his own problems from the world below to such a shrine. Some may be seen upon their knees in the church, others you will meet strolling along the mountain paths, perhaps examining their consciences; but those who seem to me to give such a happy air to Montserrat are the young honeymooners who have come to ask the Virgin's blessing on their union. You see them after Mass in the morning, going off together singing and laughing as if there were no such things as sorrow or responsibility in the world; and you wish that such a state of happiness could be prolonged for a lifetime.

The Black Virgin is dark with age and the candle-smoke of centuries. Like so many ikons and statues, she is said to have been the work of St. Luke, and one wonders once again how he is supposed to have had the time to have written the *Acts* and also to have been a sculptor as well as a doctor. It may be just another way of saying that she is ancient. It is a pity that piety sometimes leads to reckless inaccuracy, asi t does in the otherwise excellent little guide-book sold in the monastery. Here it is stated that 'the Virgin of Montserrat has no similarity to any other image'; but this is not so. She is typical of the Gothic Virgins of Spain and is very similar to *Santa María la Real* in Nájera. Her story is also the same as that of many famous Spanish statues; she was concealed by the monks when the Arabs invaded Spain, and long after her hiding-place had been forgotten, it was revealed by miraculous sights and sounds.

Throughout the Middle Ages every public and private crisis in the history of Aragon and Catalonia was brought to the shrine of the Virgin. At a difficult moment in his life, Pedro III of Aragon, dressed as an ordinary pilgrim, sat at the feet of the Virgin all night long; Pedro IV came to beg the Virgin's support for his invasion of Majorca and borrowed one of her rings to take with him; the good Queen

Violante, wife of John I, climbed the mountain barefoot—one wonders how she endured it—and fell exhausted before the shrine. When Castile and Aragon were united, the Virgin of Montserrat became revered by the whole of Spain. Charles V was one of her notable devotees. He visited her at least nine times and was there when the news was brought to him of the conquest of Mexico. As he lay dying, Charles held in his hand a candle from the Virgin's shrine, and so did his son, Philip II. Upon his squalid death-bed in Flanders, Don John of Austria asked to be buried at Montserrat if he could not lie near his father in the Escorial.

But the most notable of all the pilgrims was a man of thirty, who limped up the mountain one March day in the year 1522. He was richly dressed, a nobleman with a sword at his side and a dagger in his belt. He was a soldier whose leg had been shattered during the siege of Pamplona. His first thought, as he lay helpless, was how poor a figure he would now cut in the eyes of his mistresses. Twice he ordered the surgeons to operate on his leg, once to break it and re-set the bone, and again to cut out a piece of bone that protruded, agonies which he suffered without an anaesthetic or a groan. As he waited for the bone to heal, he began to read the lives of the saints and a profound spiritual struggle took place within him; at one moment he longed for his old life and at another he wished to devote himself to God. Finally, as he says in his Life, the memory of his mistresses was replaced by a vision of the Blessed Virgin. As soon as he could do so, he saddled his mule and rode towards Montserrat. On the way he fell in with a Moor and the conversation turned on the Immaculate Conception. The Moor made fun of the doctrine and the soldier decided that it was his duty as a Christian knight to slay him. However, he decided to leave this decision to fate. When they came to cross-roads he allowed his mule to choose the way. If it took the same road as the Moor, the Moor must die; if not, then it had been decreed otherwise. His mule took the other path and the Moor rode on unharmed.

When the soldier reached Montserrat and had made his devotions to the Virgin, he placed his sword and dagger on the altar and watched them all night, as knights did of old, vowing himself for ever as a soldier of Christ. It was the end of his old life. He gave away all his fine clothes, and, dressed in a shabby garment of rough stuff, limped down the long road to the town of Manresa, which you can see slumbering in a heat haze far off on the plain. There he lived in a cell and began to punish and discipline his body. He starved himself; he scourged himself; he humiliated himself and begged in the streets. His austerities are painful to contemplate. Twice he nearly died. Such was the beginning of the new life of St. Ignatius of Loyola, the founder of the Society of Jesus.

The fame of Montserrat is great, but great also have been its many disasters. During the Napoleonic Wars the French sacked the monastery and took away the accumulated splendours of centuries; during the Carlist War it was suppressed; and during the Civil War it suffered damage. But you would never guess this. No one ever mentions it at Montserrat. The monks have always returned with courage and industry and have made good the damage and healed the scars.

During the time I was there, I walked about the mountains and sometimes never spoke to a soul all day. They leave one beautifully alone at Montserrat. I was grateful for having seen something of Spain and for having learnt many things I did not know. I thought a lot about the dignity of Spain. It is a dignity founded upon a sense of the mystery of life and on the belief that man is made in the image of God. What is precious and noble about Spain is something that has been saved from an earlier world. 'I feel that my soul is medieval,' said Miguel de Unamuno, 'and that the soul of my country is medieval: I feel that it has passed perforce through the Renaissance, the Reformation, the Revolution, learning from them, but never letting its soul be touched; and Spanish Quixotism is nothing but the despairing struggle of the Middle Ages against the Renaissance.'

The most beautiful moment at Montserrat is the time of vespers. The shrine of the Virgin, blazing with light above the high altar, sheds its radiance into the dark church. The choristers of a school of music, that has been in existence since the Middle Ages, file into the sanctuary, their arms inside their surplices to prevent fidgeting. The altar is lit up and bunches of pink gladioli stand between the candlesticks. The choir sings that most beautiful of all Catholic prayers, the *Salve Regina*. As I hear it, I remember that it was the custom in olden days for all sailors of Spain at sea to gather at sunset and sing this prayer. Columbus has told us how the *Salve Regina* was sung each evening on the voyage to America. It was just after the singing of this prayer, as the sun had set and the lanterns were being lighted in the little ships, that Columbus spoke to the crew and told them of God's favour in giving them signs of approaching land—they had picked up sticks and a piece of wood in the sea—and bade them keep good watch that night.

As the *Salve Regina* ends, the choir begins softly and sweetly to sing the *Virolai*, with which each day ends. It is a Catalan hymn written by

361

a monk of Montserrat in honour of the Virgin. The young voices rise clear in the quiet church.

> *Rosa d'abril, Morena de la serra,*
> *de Montserrat estel;*
> *illuminau la catalana terra,*
> *guiau-nos cap al cel.* . . .[1]

Outside it is dark upon the plain, but the high peaks of the mountains are still pink. Slowly the light fades; the first star burns. I go out into the dusk, thinking that there are some places where hatred, the monstrous evil of our time, has no place.

---

[1] Rose of April, Dark One of the Mountain,
　Star of Montserrat;
　Shed light over Catalonia,
　lead us up to heaven.

# Index

# Index

# Index

# Index

Monasteries and Convents (cont'd):
  Jerez, 192–3
  La Rábida, 185, 186, 187–9
  Montserrat, 358–62
  Nájera, 272
  Roncesvalles, 281, 282
  Santiponce, 196–8
  Segovia, 238
  Zafra, 152–3
Monteros de Espinosa, 12–13
Montezuma, 130, 131, 132–7
Montserrat, monastery of, 358–62
Moore, Sir John, 304, 307–8, 326–7
Moors, the, 66, 88, 90, 192, 204–5, 222, 258, 298, 349
  architecture, 164, 191, 201–3, 213–14
  costume, 25
  craftsmen, 63
  damascening, art of, 98
  horsemanship, 14, 60, 141
  influence in Seville, 158
  See also Arabs, the
Morales, Ana Zarco de (Dulcinea), 227–8
Morales, Don Jaime Pantoja, 227
Morena, Sierra, 153–4, 221–2
Moslems, see under Arabs and Moors
Mozarabes, the, 106, 108
  Mozarabic Mass in Toledo Cathedral, 107–8
Muñez, Inés, 323
Murat, Joachim, 75, 76
Murray, John, 110
Mûsâ, 192

Nájera, 271–3, 359
  battle of, 165
  monastery, 272–3
Najerillo, river, 271
Napoleon Bonaparte, 73, 74, 75, 76, 327
Naranjo de Bulnes, mountain, 296
Narváez, 136, 137
Navalmoral de la Mata, 115
Navarre, kings of, 272–3
Navas de Tolosa, Las, battle of, 222, 238, 262
Nelson, Horatio, 182
Nevada, Sierra, 209
Ney, Marshal, 300
Niebla, 190–2
Niña, ship of Columbus, 189
Nogales, 327

Oates, Titus, 337
O'Brien, Kate, 40
Odiel, river, 187
Olivares, Count, 22, 23
Olive-growing, 207, 208–9, 221
Olmedo, Father, 130, 133, 134, 136
Omayyad dynasty, 102–3, 202
Orbigo, river, 328
Oropesa, 115
Osorio, Doña Urraca, 196
Oviedo, 299–302
  Cathedral, 300–1
  churches, 301–2
Owen, Nicholas, 336

Padilla, María de, mistress of Pedro the Cruel, 162
Palaces:
  Aranjuez, 78–80
  Barcelona, 351, 356
  Burgos, 262, 268
  Córdoba, es-Zahrâ, 203
  El Escorial, 32–51, 77, 229, 232, 346
  El Pardo, 31
  Granada, the Alhambra, 210, 212–15, 254
  La Granja, 240–1
  Madrid, Royal Palace, 9–16
  Mérida, 149–50
  Pastrana, 62
  Salamanca, 344, 346
  Santillana del Mar, 291–3
  Segovia, Alcázar, 236–7
  Seville, 159
    Alcázar, 163–6
  Trujillo, 141, 142
  Zafra, 151–2
Palos, 187, 188, 189, 190
Pamplona, 273–80
  Feast of San Fermín, 269, 273–80
  road to, 269
Pardo, El, 31
Paris, Matthew, 260
Parsons, Father Robert, S.J., 336, 338
Pastrana, 60, 61–2, 70
  church, 63–7
  palace, 62
  tapestries, 63–6
Patagonians, the, 140
Pedro III of Aragon, 359
Pedro IV of Aragon, 359
Pedro, Don, son of Henry II, 237

369

# Index